Psychometrics in **Coaching**

Using Psychological and Psychometric Tools for Development

Edited by
Jonathan Passmore

**KOGAN
PAGE**

London and Philadelphia

Publisher's note

Every possible effort has been made to ensure that the information contained in this book is accurate at the time of going to press, and the publishers and authors cannot accept responsibility for any errors or omissions, however caused. No responsibility for loss or damage occasioned to any person acting, or refraining from action, as a result of the material in this publication can be accepted by the editor, the publisher or the author.

First published in Great Britain and the United States in 2008 by Kogan Page Limited

120 Pentonville Road
London N1 9JN
United Kingdom

525 South 4th Street, #241
Philadelphia PA 19147
USA

www.kogan-page.co.uk

ISBN 978 0 7494 5080 9

British Library Cataloguing-in-Publication Data

A CIP record for this book is available from the British Library.

Library of Congress Cataloging-in-Publication Data

Passmore, Jonathan.
  Psychometrics in coaching : using psychological and psychometric tools for development / Jonathan Passmore.
      p. cm.
  Includes index.
  ISBN 978-0-7494-5080-9
1. Psychometrics. 2. Personal coaching. I. Title.
  BF39.P27 2008
  658.3'124019--dc22

2007042292

Typeset by Saxon Graphics Ltd, Derby
Printed and bound in India by Replika Press Pvt Ltd

Contents

Part II   Individual instruments and their use

About the contributors

THE EDITOR

Jonathan Passmore

Jonathan is one of the UK's leading executive coaches. He is a chartered occupational psychologist, a fellow of the Chartered Institute of Personnel and Development and an accredited Association for Coaching coach and coaching supervisor. Jonathan works as a coach and supervisor and teaches at the University of East London. Jonathan is the author of eight books and numerous articles on organizational change, coaching and leadership. Jonathan is a regular conference speaker. He can be contacted at jonathancpassmore@yahoo.co.uk.

ABOUT THE CONTRIBUTORS

Dr Elizabeth Allworth

Elizabeth is a director of Allworth Juniper Pty Ltd, a private organizational psychology practice based in Sydney Australia. She has a PhD from Macquarie University (Sydney) and a Master of Psychology (Applied) from the University of New South Wales. Her consulting experience is primarily in the area of psychological assessment in selection and career development. Elizabeth also teaches psychological assessment in the Coaching Psychology Unit at the University of Sydney. She has published chapters and articles on assessment and career development in Australian and international professional journals and edited volumes. Elizabeth has also presented her research at professional psychology conferences in Australia, the United States and Europe.

Professor Beverly Alimo-Metcalfe

Beverly is professor emeritus of leadership studies, University of Leeds, and professor of leadership at the School of Management, University of Bradford. She has over 20 years experience in leadership research and consultancy. Her passion for translating research into practical workplace applications lies behind the creation of a University of Leeds spin-out company, Real World Group in 2001. She is a member of several national advisory bodies.

Richard Barrett

Richard Barrett is an internationally recognized speaker, author and consultant on values-based leadership. He works with CEOs and senior executives in North and South America, Europe, Australia and Asia to develop values-driven organizational cultures that strengthen financial performance, build cultural capital and support sustainable development. He is the creator of the internationally recognized Cultural Transformation Tools (CTT) which have been used to support more than 700 organizations in 42 countries in their transformational journeys. Richard is the author of several books including *Liberating the Corporate Soul* (1998), *Building a Values-Driven Organization* (2006) and *Full-Spectrum Leadership* (2008). Richard is a Fellow of the World Business Academy, and Former Values Coordinator at the World Bank. Richard can be contacted via: www.valuescentre.com.

Professor Dave Bartram

Dave is research director of the SHL Group plc. He is a chartered occupational psychologist, fellow of the British Psychological Society (BPS), and received the award for Distinguished Contribution to Professional Psychology from the BPS in 2004. He is past president and a Council member of the International Test Commission (ITC), chair of the British Psychological Society's Steering Committee on Test Standards, chair of the European Federation of Psychologists Association's (EFPA) Standing Committee on Tests and Testing, and president of the International Association of Applied Psychology's Division 2 (Measurement and Assessment). He is the author of several hundred scientific journal articles, papers in conference proceedings, books and book chapters in a range of areas relating to occupational assessment, especially in relation to computer-based testing. He can be contacted at dave.bartram@ shlgroup.com.

Richard Brady

Richard Brady is a chartered occupational psychologist with eighteen years experience in psychometrics. Richard is Managing Director of Mentis (www.mentis-consulting.com), the UK distributor of Hogen.

Eugene Burke

Eugene is SHL's director of science & innovation. At SHL, he has held posts in product development as well as heading up assessment consultancy and delivering coaching and development programmes for major companies. Prior to SHL, Eugene served as a military psychologist and worked extensively with the emergency services. He is a past chair of the British Psychological Society's Steering Committee on Test Standards and of the Division of Occupational Psychology, and has published articles and book chapters as well as books on a variety of subjects including training and development, applied psychometrics, and the selection and development of personnel for high-risk roles. Eugene can be contacted via eugene.burke@shlgroup.com.

Sally Carr

Sally is an independent consultant who specializes in leadership development and executive coaching. She has extensive experience of using the MBTI in these applications, and of training other professionals in these areas. Prior to going independent, Sally was a principal consultant within OPP.

Dr David R Caruso

David is a founder of EI Skills Group, and a research affiliate in the Department of Psychology at Yale University. He provides leader development, executive coaching and emotional intelligence training to clients around the world. He is a co-author of the Mayer, Salovey, Caruso Emotional Intelligence Test and *The Emotionally Intelligent Manager*. He has dozens of scientific publications to his credit. After receiving his PhD in psychology, he held positions in market research, strategic planning, and product line management with P&L responsibility. Website: www.eiskills.com.

Roy Childs

Roy Childs is the Founder and Managing Director of Team Focus, an Associate Fellow of the British Psychological Society (BPS) and a Chartered Occupational Psychologist. He has been working in organizations at senior levels for more than 20 years and the main thrust of his work involves developing capability and building relationships – usually in a leadership context. He has helped select board members for blue chip companies and works both as a coach and facilitator. He combines a developmental approach with the rigour of strong numerate and psychometric approaches to understanding people. Author of tests such as the Type Dynamics Indicator and the Decision Analysis Test, he has worked with some of the best known authors of personality questionnaires including Ray Cattell (16PF) and Will Schutz (FIRO). He was asked to serve as a member of the BPS's Standing Committee on Test Standards as well as serving on the committee for the BPS's Division of Occupational Psychology and as a Level B verifier.

Dr Peter Clough

Peter is head of Psychology at the University of Hull. He is a chartered occupational and chartered sport psychologist, researching in performance enhancement in stressful environments.

Bernard Cooke

Bernard is a principal consultant with OPP and uses the MBTI extensively in executive coaching and working with teams. He also runs training programmes for coaches in the use of psychological methods and psychometrics in coaching. Prior to becoming a psychologist he worked in management and organizational development for a range of organizations.

Keith Earle

Keith is a chartered psychologist and a founder member of the BPS Division of Sport and Exercise Psychology. He is a lecturer in the department of Sport, Health and Exercise Psychology at the University of Hull and is a co-author of the MTQ48.

Dr James M Fico

James is a consulting psychologist in independent practice, providing selection, promotion and manager development services to a wide variety of industries. Organizations he serves include 39 police and fire departments. He is also the lead examining psychologist for the Federal Flight Deck Officer program, which arms selected commercial airline pilots in the United States. He has conducted test validation studies that include police officers, firefighters, police and fire managers, SWAT team members and leaders, and hostage negotiators. James can be contacted via www.alphacourage.com.

Dr Alexander Fradera

Alexander has been interested in facilitating learning and developing potential since teaching at University College London. More recently, he has turned his attention from higher learning to the workplace. He has a PhD on the psychology of remembering and making sense of the past. His publications include a series of how-to articles on memory and emotion for the popular book *Mind Hacks*, peer-reviewed articles in *Learning and Memory*, *Memory*, and *Neuropsychologia*, and a forthcoming chapter in the *New Encyclopedia of Neuroscience*. He currently works at SHL and can be contacted at Alexander.Fradera@SHLgroup.com or via his website, http://understandingpeople.wordpress.com.

Leanne Harris

Leanne is a lead consultant in OPP and has been a practitioner, trainer and author on using type for over 15 years. Her particular focus is on using the MBTI to enhance self-development through the coaching process. She has developed approaches and training as well as presented internationally on applying type dynamics and development in coaching.

Professor Robert Hogan

Robert is fellow of the American Psychological Association and president of Hogan Assessment Systems. He was McFarlin Professor and chair of the Department of Psychology at the University of Tulsa for 14 years. Prior to that, he was professor of psychology and social relations at the Johns Hopkins University. Robert has received a number of research and teaching awards, and is the editor of the *Handbook of Personality Psychology*, as well as authoring more than 300 journal articles, chapters and books. He is the author of the Hogan Personality Inventory.

Thomas J Hurley

Tom Hurley serves as a senior advisor and executive coach for leaders seeking innovative approaches to key strategic issues and whole systems change. He can be reached at thomas@tjhassociates.com.

Quentin Jones

Quentin is Human Synergistics' Australian director. His role spans leading the Human Synergistics' Australian business, training accredited coaches and facilitators, and consulting to create individual and organizational transformation. His 10 years of effort to transform Australian organizations culminated last year with the publication of *In Great Company*, a two-year research project with Professor Dexter Dunphy reporting the keys to cultural transformation.

Quentin can be contacted at: quentin@human-synergistics.com.au.

Dr Carol Kauffman

Carol Kauffman, PhD PCC is an Assistant Clinical Professor at Harvard Medical School where she teaches Positive Psychology and Coaching. She is also Co-Editor in Chief of the new academic and professional journal, *Coaching: An International Journal of Theory, Research and Practice*. She is Chief Supervisor at Meyler Campbell Ltd, a business coaching programme based in London. Dr Kauffman maintains an active UK, Europe and US executive coaching and coaching supervision practice. She also speaks regularly on coaching and positive psychology in keynotes, master classes and for the media. For more information and to submit to the journal please contact Carol by e-mail on Carol@CoachingPsych.com.

Betsy Kendall

Betsy is a co-founder of OPP, the European distributor of the MBTI instrument. Betsy was centrally involved in designing qualification training for MBTI in Europe and now heads OPP's Consulting and Learning teams. She has extensive experience in consulting and training related to the MBTI instrument. Website: www.opp.eu.com.

Dr Rainer Kurz

Rainer is a seasoned assessment expert with 20 years of test development experience. At SHL he specialized in on-screen tests and expert system development, created the WoW model and initiated the development of the Great Eight competencies. Since joining Saville Consulting he has led the development of the Aptitude Assessment range and the Work Evaluation inventories, and contributed to the development of Saville Consulting Wave. Rainer can be contacted through the company website www.savilleconsulting.com.

Dick McCann

Dick is an author and co-developer of Team Management Systems. He is currently director of research for Team Management Systems, CEO of Team Management Systems Asia-Pacific and a director of the UK-based organization TMS Development International Ltd. His background is in science, engineering, finance and organizational behaviour. Earlier in his career he spent five years with BP Chemicals in London before moving to Sydney University as a senior research fellow. Holding a PhD in engineering, he is the author and co-author of many leading books and articles on teamwork and workplace behaviour. Full details about TMS, and how coaches can become accredited in the TMS instruments, are available at www.tms.com.au (Australia & Pacific), www.tmsdi.com for EMEA and www.tms-americas.com for the Americas.

Rab MacIver

Rab is a commercial, client-focused psychologist with strong technical development skills and a proven track record in formulating and implementing effective recruitment and development solutions. At SHL he investigated the reliability and validity of personality and competency questionnaires and managed multidisciplinary teams responsible for the redevelopment of questionnaires, most notably the OPQ32. He later went on to establish a Scottish Office for SHL before embarking on a freelance career. Rab led the development of Saville Consulting Wave and manages the Wave product range. You can contact Rab through the company website, www.savilleconsulting.com.

Dr Almuth McDowall

Almuth is a lecturer in psychology at Surrey University, and closely associated with the Psychometrics Centre at Cambridge Assessment as an associate senior consultant. She acts as a consultant to private and public organizations and favours a coaching approach in all her work. Almuth's areas of expertise are employee development, the research and practice of psychometrics, juggling work and non-work and effective feedback at work and in education. Her recent research on age and gender bias in the allocation of development opportunities, including coaching, to employees was featured widely in the national press and radio. She can be contacted at a.mcdowall@surrey.ac.uk.

Helen Marsh

Helen is a Chartered Occupational Psychologist specializing in talent management and leadership development at SHL. Her work involves psychometric assessment and feedback, coaching and the facilitation of behavioural change workshops, delivered for a range of clients across both public and private sectors. Helen is a member of the BPS Special Group in Coaching Psychology, holds a diploma in performance coaching and is co-author of a chapter on international assessment and development in *Business Psychology in Practice*, published by the Association of Business Psychologists. Helen aspires to continue professional development as a performance coach, and to work alongside others in promoting the role of psychology in coaching. Email: Helen.Marsh@SHLgroup.com.

Dr Kenneth M Nowack

Kenneth is a licensed psychologist, president and chief research officer of Envisia Learning. He received his PhD in counseling psychology from the University of California, Los Angeles where he is a guest lecturer at the UCLA Anderson School of Management. Email: ken@envisialearning.com. StressScan: http://www.envisiatools.com/products/Stress-Inventory/Stress-Scan/index. asp.

Peter Pritchett

Peter works for the Real World Group on transformational leadership. He can be contacted via the Real World website: www.realworld-group.com.

Professor Peter Salovey

Peter is the Chris Argyris Professor of Psychology, and was appointed dean of Yale College in 2004. He served previously as dean of the Graduate School at Yale University and chair of the Department of Psychology. Salovey received an AB in Psychology from Stanford University and was awarded a PhD in psychology from Yale University. He joined the Yale faculty in 1986 and has been a full professor since 1995. Salovey has published more than 300 articles and chapters, and he has authored, co-authored or edited 13 books. Website: www.yale.edu/psychology/ FacInfo/Salovey.html.

Professor Peter Saville

Peter joined the National Foundation for Educational Research in 1970, rising quickly to the position of chief psychologist at the Test Division. He left in 1977 to co-found Saville & Holdsworth (now SHL Group) where he led the development of Occupational Testing and Occupational Personality Questionnaire tools. He was the first ever industrial psychologist to receive the BPS Award for Distinguished Contributions to Professional Psychology. Peter founded Saville Consulting in 2004 to create a new generation of assessment tools for the world of work. Peter can be contacted at peter.saville@savilleconsulting.com.

David Sharpley

David Sharpley is a Chartered Occupational Psychologist and Associate Fellow of the British Psychological Society. He has extensive experience relating to leadership development and team effectiveness, and builds on the latest research relating to behaviour at work. David is a director of Pario HR Solutions Ltd, whose services include online 360 degree feedback and employee engagement surveys – designed to create insight and enhance motivation and performance.

Jordan Silberman

Jordan began his career as a piano major at the Eastman School of Music, and has performed throughout the United States. Since changing course in 2002, he has earned a master's in positive psychology, published articles on healthcare communication, psychology, bioethics and proteomics, chaired a symposium in Hong Kong, and completed two marathons. He works full-time in palliative care at a Philadelphia hospital, and part-time in positive psychology with a Harvard professor. Contact: jsilberm@sas.upenn.edu.

Jeff Staggs

Jeff Staggs is President of Business Coaching International. He has been a professional coach for 19 years and coaches executives and teams internationally. Jeff is a founding member of the International Coaching Federation and serves on their Credentialing Committee. He also trains and supervises coaches in the USA. Jeff can be contacted at jeff@bcicoaching.com.

Doug Strycharczyk

Doug possesses more than 30 years experience in a variety of line, HR and consultancy roles with a number of businesses in the private and public sectors. He is the managing director of AQR and can be contacted at: http://www.aqr.org.uk/.

Foreword

Coaching has come of age. Through the concerted efforts of professional bodies such as the Association for Coaching, the bar has been raised and coaches are expected to demonstrate competence and knowledge in coaching theory and practice if they wish to progress professionally. However, being qualified and experienced is no longer sufficient, as ongoing continuing professional development (CPD) is considered important to maintain high standards.

In recent years, when coaches are being interviewed for work in organizations, the purchasers of coaching are now less concerned about marketing hyperbole such as 'My coaching is fantastic', but ask critical questions about how the coach's approach will help their staff and where the evidence is for its effectiveness. This is even more evident when human resources professionals employ coaches who intend using psychometrics tools within their workplace coaching.

Although psychometric testing may be seen as a relatively new concept, it may be surprising that researchers such as Spearman (1904) were debating how to objectively measure aspects of human function a century ago. Yet the use of psychometric tools has only really become established over the past four decades in the fields of psychology, education, human resources and more recently, coaching.

It is important for coaches and other practitioners to understand the underpinning psychology that informs the psychometric tests they use within the coaching setting so that their clients can benefit from the right tool being used to enhance the coaching conversation. This can provide a route to discuss the client's behaviour and preferences. If used by the coach appropriately, the feedback can help the client gain increased self-awareness and insight. This can be the catalyst that leads to self-development.

The inappropriate use of psychometric tests can occur if a coach lacks sufficient training or knowledge in their use and their application to coaching. Fortunately, the large majority of test suppliers expect practitioners wishing to use or purchase their tools for application in occupational settings to provide evidence of competence. This can be demonstrated by coaches having gained the British Psychological Society Occupational Level A and Level B Certificates or by successfully completing relevant training (BPS, 2006).

This book provides an excellent overview to some of the key tests that can be used within coaching. For a coach new to using psychometric testing it also explains basic but important concepts such as 'validity' and 'reliability'. For more experienced practitioners this book is useful as continuing professional development (CPD). In essence, this book highlights that there is an art and science to the successful use of tests. How the coach provides the feedback is the art, and the in-depth research and psychological theories underpinning the psychometric test are the science. All are essential.

Professor Stephen Palmer PhD
Director of the Coaching Psychology Unit, City University, London, UK
Honorary President of the Association for Coaching

References

British Psychological Society (2006) *Psychological Testing: A user's guide*, BPS Psychological Testing Centre, Leicester

Spearman, C E (1904) General Intelligence, objectively determined and measured, *American Journal of Psychology*, **15**, pp 201–93

Preface

I am delighted to launch *Psychometrics in Coaching*. This book follows the success of the first book *Excellence in Coaching*, which has proven that having a number of approaches in one book, by key industry experts, is a formula that serves the industry well.

Furthermore, I would like to thank not only Jonathan Passmore, but also the numerous contributors who have donated their time and energies to the Association for Coaching, all without pay, as a token of giving something back to this dynamic and emerging profession.

We do hope you enjoy the book, which we feel truly reflects both the spirit of the Association for Coaching and the diversity we embrace. Through its more academic bias, our intention is to provide a number of instruments and theories to apply in practice, as the role of psychometrics in coaching continues to grow.

Katherine Tulpa, Chair and Co-founder
Association for Coaching

Acknowledgements

As editor, I would like to express my thanks to the many people who have contributed to this book or made it possible. To the Kogan Page team particularly Charlotte, Helen and Jo for their support in developing the proposal and in getting the book out at events and conferences. To the contributors for their energy and dedication in coping with repeated requests for rewrites from me, in a desire to ensure we created a consistent look and feel with some 30 different authors both within chapters and across the book. To Iris and Katharine who have lost me for periods while I have been writing, editing, negotiating and generally not being there for them during the 18 months it has taken to bring this book about, and for their continual encouragement to keep moving this forward. To colleagues at OPM who were so encouraging about *Excellence in Coaching* and supportive about the idea of a second book, and particularly to Hannah Roscoe for her contributions including Figure 0.1 in the Introduction, and my colleagues in our coaching training team; Lesley Campbell, Ian Roberts, Elaine Clough and David Love. To Almuth McDowall for her contributions to the Glossary section, and to the Association for Coaching, particularly Katherine Tulpa and Alex Szabo, for their commitment to the project and their contributions.

This book is dedicated to Iris Passmore; whose love, hope, inspiration and support has made all things possible.

Jonathan Passmore

Introduction

Jonathan Passmore

After the successful publication of *Excellence in Coaching*, it became obvious that there was a strong demand for a series of coaching books which brought together leading writers in their field. In this series we wanted to offer evidence-based and practically focused writing that helps coaches to develop their coaching practice.

For those who were at the launch of *Excellence in Coaching* in 2006, a coach asked 'Will there be another book to follow this?' A similar question was asked in a review of the volume, suggesting that there was a demand for an annual book on current themes and topics in coaching. We share this view and this book was planned before *Excellence in Coaching* had been launched.

The exact focus of the book, however, did create much debate. We have been determined to ensure that we do not repeat what is already on the market but instead try to offer something new. We felt that while a growing number of books were focusing on the psychology of coaching, a more practical approach may be to focus on an element within this: psychometrics and psychological models.

There is a growing demand from coachees and growing interest from coaches in using psychometric questionnaires in coaching, whether that is OPQ, Wave or MBTI. However, personal experience suggests that there is a wide range in the competence of those using these instruments and often a narrow selection of questionnaires being used. A surprising number of coaches do not know about the reliability or validity of the questionnaires they are using, or do not know about the theory or research evidence which underpins it. Yet questionnaires can provide a useful entry into a coaching conversation. These conversations can be enhanced when coaches have a fuller understand of the different tools available and a more detailed understanding of the tool which they are using.

Psychometrics can help coaches to reflect on their own behaviours, preferences and styles, and by so doing deepen their self-awareness and thus provide an opportunity for coaches to change or develop their styles. Psychometrics can also offer useful insights for coachees, alongside other benefits (Figure 0.1), most often as part of a wider development conversation. The reports provide feedback or insights that, when combined with discussion, can provide a useful way of thinking about current ways of being and planning new ways of being. Our aim in producing this title was twofold: first to contribute to improving coaching practice in psychometrics in general and in their favoured tools in particular, and second to widen coaches' understanding of the diverse range of instruments which are available.

The book is divided into two parts. The first consists of two chapters that set the scene about using psychometrics and also providing feedback; the second – and the majority of the book – is given over to individual instruments and how the coaching practitioner may make use of these. We asked authors to take a practical focus to chapters. Each chapter is broken into four main sections:

▌ theory and research behind the questionnaire;
▌ overview of the questionnaire;
▌ using the questionnaire to deepen self-awareness with the coach;
▌ using the questionnaire as a tool with coachees.

We hope this structure makes the process of reading or accessing the information in the book easier for the reader, providing a common structure and style throughout. We also hoped that the book would be of value to a wider group of readers who use psychometrics for development in organizations, to students interested in personnel development, coaching and psychology, and to those interested in human behaviour.

As in any guide, it is left to the author or editor to select which items to include and which to exclude. I chose some of the more popular tools in the UK, United States and wider English-speaking world. There are many others that could have been included, but given space, time and contributors'

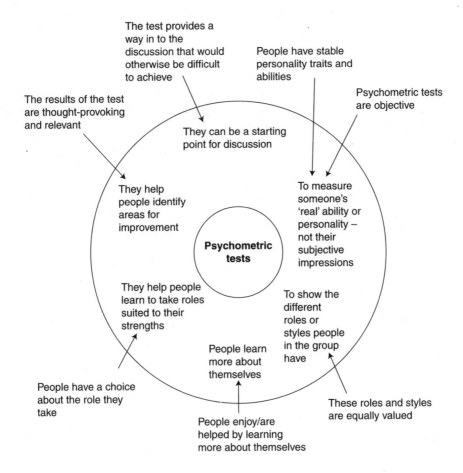

Figure 0.1 The potential of psychometrics at work

availability it was not possible to do so. The psychometrics that we have included were not selected because these are 'the best' or because I or the Association for Coaching (AC) recommend that coaches use these specific tools. In fact there are some psychometrics that I use that we did not feature in the book, simply because there was not space within the word limits we agreed with our publishers, Kogan Page. However, in Chapter 20 I have tried to provide an overview of a wider selection of questionnaires. This includes a short summary about the instrument, with the key dimensions and some background to the questionnaire, plus details of the publishers. Again this is not an exhaustive list. The very nature of such questionnaires makes this an impossible task; we have simply tried our best to include the ones most widely available.

As with *Excellence in Coaching* each of the contributors have given their time and writing efforts for free, as part of their commitment to developing the coaching profession, and all of the royalties from the book go to the AC. For my part I would like to thank the contributors for their efforts and energies in bringing this book to publication and achieving this within around six months from outline draft to finished manuscript. I apologise to each of them for the constant requests for redrafts, corrections and revisions to fit the layout, or to expand one section and reduce another. Our plan was to try to create some consistency in each chapter as well as a readable guide on complex topics.

This book we hope will provide readers with an enjoyable, stimulating read and will help you further your coaching practice.

References

Passmore, J (2006) *Excellence in Coaching*, Kogan Page, London
Passmore, J (forthcoming) *Diversity in coaching*, Kogan Page, London

Part 1

Psychometrics and feedback

1

Using psychometrics and psychological tools in coaching

Dr Elizabeth Allworth and Jonathan Passmore

INTRODUCTION

Coaches have an expanding range of psychological assessment tools from which they can draw to assist coachees build the self-awareness that is necessary to identify new career and life goals, and to enhance their performance at work. The burgeoning psychological testing industry has produced a myriad of measures enabling coaches to support coachees to better understand their behaviour, their preferences and their capabilities as they relate to work and life. Personality tests, aptitude tests and question-naires assessing values, interests, leadership and motivational needs represent some of the kinds of tests currently available on the market inter-nationally. Many of these psychological tests have made a positive contri-bution to coaching and have been rigorously tested to ensure their reliability and validity (terms we shall explore later). There is, however, considerable variability in the level of research undertaken and the reliability and validity of these tools.

The aim of this chapter is to provide the background information that will help coaches to choose technically sound tests that are appropriate for the situation in which they intend to use them. First, we present the various kinds of tests that are available to coaches, what they measure and their role in the coaching context. Second, we describe the psychometric properties of tests and the standards that are required for test reliability and validity. Third, profiling and criterion-oriented approaches to assessment are compared, highlighting the need for coaches to broaden their perspective beyond the skills, knowledge and personal attributes of the coachee by also taking account of the demands and the rewards of the environment in which the coachee lives. Fourth, the benefits of psychological testing for the coach and the coachee are explored, and in the last part of the chapter, ethical guidelines and best practice in psychological testing are presented.

PSYCHOLOGICAL TESTS

A psychological test is a standardized measure of one or a number of psychological attributes. The attributes of an individual that are most commonly of interest in the coaching context include personality (attributes such as conscientiousness, interpersonal confidence, sociability), career interests (for example, preference for working with people or engaging in artistic activities), values (such as altruism or protection of the environment), motivational needs (that is, what drives the person such as money, status, autonomy), and cognitive ability (for example, numerical or verbal problem-solving abilities). Here, we briefly describe the kinds of tests that measure each of these attributes.

Personality questionnaires

There is an abundance of personality questionnaires on the market, each measuring a broad or narrow domain of individual behaviour and personal preferences. Here, we look at four kinds of personality measures that may be used in work-related coaching: multidimensional measures, measures of the Big Five personality factors, measures of personality type and competency-based tools.

Multidimensional measures of personality assess a wide range of personality attributes or traits such as achievement drive, sociability, self-control, flexibility or empathy, to name just a few. The results of personality testing should provide comparisons of an individual's personality attributes with those of others from a 'norm' group, such as others in the general population or other managers. The validity of multidimensional personality measures as predictors of performance is enhanced when the test is carefully chosen to measure the attributes that coachees require, or will require, on the job or in their personal life. As an example, if interpersonal confidence and achievement drive are required in a role, the personality test should be able to measure these same constructs or attributes in the person as closely as possible.

Multidimensional measures of personality are particularly helpful in the coaching relationship to build the coachees' awareness of their preferred styles of thinking and behaving across situations. This kind of assessment can help to explain why some people are well suited to some kinds of work environments or situations while others are not. It can also help to explain why some situations or tasks are more stressful than others.

Measures of the five-factor model of personality are based on the accepted premise that all personality attributes are represented in five core, broadband attributes, commonly referred to as the 'Big Five' (Goldberg, 1990). The five factors are: Conscientiousness, Extroversion, Agreeableness, Openness to Experience, and Neuroticism (Emotional Stability). The five factors are defined in Table 1.1.

Although there is considerable research showing the generalizable validity of some of the five factors, a measure of these factors alone may be too parsimonious to be practical in the coaching context. In selecting an appropriate measure based on the five-factor theory, those that provide

Table 1.1   The five-factor model of personality

Big Five factor	Description
Conscientiousness	careful, reliable, hard-working, well-organized, punctual, disciplined, ambitious
Extroversion	sociable, fun-loving, affectionate, friendly, talkative, warm
Agreeableness	courteous, selfless, sympathetic, trusting, generous, acquiescent, lenient, forgiving, flexible
Openness to experience	original, imaginative, creative, broad interests, curious, daring, liberal, independent, prefers variety
Neuroticism (emotional stability)	worrying, emotional, high-strung, temperamental, insecure, self-pitying, vulnerable (emotional stability: calm, at ease, relaxed, even-tempered, secure, hardy)

Source: McCrae and Costa (1987).

facet scales or subscales can offer finer definition to the broader five factors, and as such, can enable more detailed information and finer definition of the coachee's personality. Examples of facet scales or subscales of Extroversion include being friendly, sociable or assertive. It is possible that an individual may be friendly and sociable without being assertive, or vice versa. Understanding these facets can be more informative for the coachee than simply knowing their result on the broader trait of Extroversion.

Measures of personality type provide a categorization of the individual into a personality typology that defines a specific set of behavioural tendencies, reflecting broad differences in attitudes and orientation. While multidimensional measures of personality are used to profile individuals across a range of individual attributes, measures of personality type profile people according to a cluster of attributes that represent their preferences. These kinds of personality measures are very popular with coaches as they often provide a more succinct description of the individual across a manageable number of dimensions.

In addition to the kinds of personality tests discussed above, coaches may draw from a range of special purpose tests that are designed to measure specific aspects of behaviour such as leadership style, team orientation, sales orientation and emotional intelligence. Examples include MSCEIT, which measures emotional intelligence, MTQ48, which assesses mental toughness, and TLQ, which measures leadership competence. These kinds of measures of personal attributes can have value in specific contexts. For instance, a measure of leadership style could be relevant for those coachees who want to better understand their preferred way of leading and managing others. On the other hand, a measure of team orientation can offer insights into the way in which a coachee prefers to contribute in the work environment.

Vocational interests

The assessment of vocational interests can be useful in the coaching context by providing insights into the fields of employment and the range of occupations that are attractive to the individual. Career interest assessments ask people what they enjoy doing, not just at work but also in other domains of their lives such as school, university and leisure.

Generally speaking, vocational interest theories categorize jobs and careers into those that involve working with people, those that involve working with data and those that involve working with things (Fine, 1955). Occupational preferences are also closely linked to personality style (Holland, 1997). To illustrate, while artists often describe themselves as creative, expressive and independent, accountants tend to describe themselves as stable, organized and dependable. By comparing an individual across a broad range of occupations and vocational fields, interest inventories are particularly useful with those coachees who are considering a career change. They can enable insights into occupational areas that may not necessarily have been previously considered by the coachee.

Motivational needs and values questionnaires

The assessment of motivational needs and values is possibly the least defined aspect of the assessment, particularly in view of the multitude of motivational theories upon which motivational assessment tools are based. Most questionnaires and tools that assess motivational needs and values focus on one or a combination of four areas: sources of motivation, how the person likes to be rewarded, the kind of management style that brings out the best in the person, and the kind of work environment that the person prefers.

The assessment of motivational needs and values may be of benefit to coachees who are dissatisfied with their current role or work environment and who want to be clear about the kinds of environments and reinforcers that are particularly important to them. They can also be useful with coachees who are weighing up some alternative job options. In this instance, the coachees can evaluate each option in terms of the extent to which their needs and values are likely to be satisfied, thereby helping their decision making around employment options.

COGNITIVE ABILITY TESTS

Cognitive ability tests assess aspects of intellectual functioning such as numerical, verbal and conceptual problem-solving abilities. In the work-related coaching context, cognitive ability testing offers the potential to determine the extent to which an individual's performance on the job is related to their learning, problem-solving and decision-making capabilities. The cause of coachees' underperformance or lack of confidence in a management or professional role, for example, may be explained by difficulties they are experiencing in managing the more complex conceptual problem-solving aspects of their role. Alternatively, cognitive ability testing can provide an indication of people's potential to progress to a more senior position and to quickly acquire the specific knowledge and skill that will be needed in order to perform effectively.

Cognitive ability tests are perhaps the least utilized form of assessment in the coaching context. While cognitive ability tests are among the best predictors of overall job performance (Hunter and Hunter, 1984; Schmidt and Hunter, 1998) cognitive functioning is less amenable to change than other individual attributes such as motivational needs or the behavioural manifestations of personality. There may, therefore, be greater risks associated with the use of these kinds of tests, as coachees may feel powerless in addressing and improving performance in areas in which their performance is not as strong as those of their peers.

THE PSYCHOMETRIC PROPERTIES OF A PSYCHOLOGICAL TEST

It is the standardized administration and scoring of a psychological test that differentiates it from other kinds of assessments that coaches may use with coachees, such as structured interviews, behavioural observations, checklists or questionnaires. A good psychological test is one that meets three criteria. First, it must be an accurate measure of the attribute of interest. Second, it should help the test user differentiate between those individuals who have more of the attribute of interest and those who have less of the attribute. Third, it needs to be a good predictor of an outcome of interest such as job performance or success in training.

A well-constructed, valid and reliable psychological test is one that has been subjected to a comprehensive and scientifically rigorous process of development. Readers are referred to *Standards for Educational and Psychological Testing* (American Educational Research Association, American Psychological Association and National Council on Measurement in Education, 2004) or Hinkin (1995) for information on test development. As best practice, publishers will make available to accredited users the test's technical manual, which outlines the extent to which it reliably assesses the attributes of interest (referred to as reliability) and the normative data against which test takers can be compared. Some test developers will also show how the test compares with other tests that purport to measure the same attribute or set of attributes (referred to as construct validity) and how effectively the test predicts an outcome of interest (referred to as criterion-related validity). See Table 1.2 for a summary of definitions of reliability and validity.

Reliability

No psychological measure is absolutely perfect. There is always an unavoidable margin of error in the measurement of psychological attributes. The aim of the test developer is to maximize the reliability of the test so that, regardless of when the test is administered, the results are consistent across

Table 1.2 Definitions of the psychometric properties of tests

Psychometric property	Definition
Reliability	The stability and consistency of test results
Test–retest reliability	The stability of test results over repeated administrations of the test
Internal consistency	The extent to which test items that measure the same attribute are related with each other
Construct validity	The extent to which a measure accurately assesses the attribute it intends to assess
Convergent validity	The extent to which test scores are related to scores on alternative tests or measures of the same attribute
Discriminant validity	The extent to which test scores are unrelated to scores on alternative tests or measures of different attributes
Criterion-related validity	The relationship between test scores and a measure of an independent outcome, eg job performance, job satisfaction, tenure
Predictive validity	The correlation between a test score and an outcome measure that is gathered at a later point in time
Concurrent validity	The correlation between a test score and an outcome measure that is collected at the same point in time
Norm group and normative data	The sample of the population that participated in the development and validation of the test and whose test results provide the average distribution of scores against which future test takers can be compared

time (test–retest reliability). In addition, the questions used to measure a particular personal attribute should be consistently and predictably related to each other (internal consistency). Reliability is expressed as a correlation coefficient. The more reliable the test, the closer the correlation coefficient will be to 1.0. Murphy and Davidshofer (1998) suggest that reliability values over 0.80 are good while those less than 0.70 have limited applicability and should be interpreted cautiously.

Test–retest reliability refers to the stability of test results over time. That is, the results of a test administered today should be similar to those for the same person tomorrow, next week or at some later date, assuming no actual change in the attribute is expected as a result of some other influence such as normal growth and development, training, aging, illness or disability. Test–retest reliability is calculated by correlating the results obtained from the test when it is first administered with the results obtained on the test when it is administered on a later occasion.

Internal consistency refers to the extent to which test items are related to each other and, by inference, measure the same personal attribute. To illustrate, assume a measure of Extroversion comprises 10 questions, each tapping some aspect of this particular attribute such as sociability, social self-confidence or assertiveness. If the measure of Extroversion has adequate internal consistency, all 10 items will be correlated. That is, people who score high on some of the items that measure Extroversion are likely to score high on the other items and vice versa.

There are a number of possible sources of variability in test scores including a) those related to the test taker at the time of testing, such as fatigue, concentration or poor motivation; b) those related to the test administrator, such as giving inconsistent or incomplete instructions to test takers; or c) an inadequate testing environment, such as one that is noisy or poorly lit.

Construct validity

Construct validity refers to the extent to which a measure accurately assesses the attributes it purports to assess. In testing construct validity, two questions are asked: to what extent are scores on the test related to scores on tests that measure the same attribute (convergent validity) and to what extent are scores on the test unrelated to scores on tests that measure different attributes (discriminant validity)? That is, a test with adequate construct validity will show higher correlations with alternative measures of the same attribute or constructs than it does with measures of different constructs (Campbell and Fiske, 1959; Thompson and Daniel, 1996). Take, for example, a test of assertiveness. If the test has adequate construct validity it should show higher correlations with other measures of assertiveness than with measures of other, conceptually unrelated attributes such as attention to detail or achievement drive.

Criterion-related validity

For a test to be useful in career coaching, it needs not only to be a reliable and valid measure of the constructs or attributes of interest, but also to bear some relationship with a criterion or outcome of interest. The relationship between scores on a psychological test and an outcome is referred to as criterion-related validity. In the coaching context, the outcome or criterion might be greater job or life satisfaction, career advancement, or improved well-being. Criterion-related validity varies according to the correlation between people's scores on a test and their scores on the outcome measure. When the outcome data is gathered at a later point in time, the correlation between test score and outcome measure is referred to as the test's predictive validity. Concurrent validity refers to the correlation between test and outcome measures that are collected at the same point in time.

Criterion-related validity is expressed as a correlation coefficient that shows the strength and direction (positive or negative) of the relationship between scores on the test and the criterion. Correlation coefficients for criterion-related validity that are greater than 0.35 are considered very beneficial; those from 0.20 to 0.35 are likely to be useful; while those less than 0.11 are unlikely to be useful (Murphy and Davidshofer, 1998).

Normative data

One of the attributes of a psychometric test that differentiates it from other forms of assessment is the ability of the test user to compare an individual's results with those of others in a relevant sample or norm group. The norm group is that sample of people who participated in the development and validation of the test and whose test results provide the average distribution of scores against which future test takers can be compared. The norm or comparison group may be as general as working adults or as specific as engineering graduates from a particular country.

All well-developed tests offer normative data and clearly state the demographics of the norm group. The norm group needs to be of an adequate size for the test user to be confident that it is sufficiently stable. The ideal sample size will depend on a number of different factors including the number of items in the test, the sampling method used (random or representative) the size of the population from which a sample can be drawn, and the method of test development. Test users should, as a rule of thumb, be very cautious of norm groups below 100 participants and ideally look for sample sizes in the hundreds.

APPROACHES TO PSYCHOLOGICAL TESTING IN COACHING

A psychological test can be used in two ways, namely, to measure an individual attribute or set of attributes in a person (a profiling approach) or to predict a certain outcome (a criterion-oriented approach). The two approaches are applied in different contexts, depending on the referral question.

Profiling approach

In a profiling approach to psychological testing, the emphasis is on building awareness and understanding of the coachee's attributes such as that person's abilities, interests and personality style compared with those of a relevant norm group. Here, the referral question may be 'How do the coachee's leadership skills compare with those of other managers?' or 'What kinds of occupations interest the coachee?'

Psychological testing can provide insights into a number of areas. First, a profiling approach to psychological testing can provide insights into the coachee's relative strengths and areas for development. For example, testing may show that the coachee has better developed numerical than verbal abilities, and prefers creative work activities to those that are routine and procedural. Here, attributes are compared within the person, highlighting the individual's relative capabilities, preferences, personality attributes or motivational needs.

Second, a profiling approach can provide insights into how an individual's personal attributes compare with those of others in a particular reference or norm group. For example, the testing may show that the coachee is more numerate, outgoing and energetic than most other managers, but less organized and task-focused. These between-person differences may be expressed in ranges (above average, average or below average) or as standardized scores (such as a percentile ranking that shows the proportion of the population that scores higher or lower).

The profiling approach can be valuable in clarifying people's development needs, and future personal and career goals, or simply understanding why they think and behave in the way they do. The profiling approach is most commonly applied with those clients who are looking for a new direction or to resolve a particular issue that is impacting on their life or career.

CRITERION-ORIENTED APPROACH

Many coaches, particularly those engaged in work-related coaching commissioned by the coachee's employer, are required to consider not only the individual coachee's profile but also the job and organizational context. These kinds of referrals may be for the purpose of assessing people's potential for career progression, their fit with their current role, or their development needs in the context of the capabilities required in their current or future roles. In these instances, there is a criterion against which an individual's assessment profile is compared. The criterion typically relates to actual or potential performance on particular aspects of a job, potential for training or job satisfaction.

Person–job and person–organization fit are fundamental to the criterion-oriented approach. That is, the coach is not only interested in profiling the coachee, but is also concerned to understand how the coachee's profile relates or fits with a particular context. Coaches taking a criterion-related approach should build the skills of analysing jobs in terms of the demands they make on the incumbent's knowledge, skills and attributes (KSA) and ensure that they gather data relevant to the coachee's current or future jobs. Such data may be gathered through job descriptions, job-analysis interviews with those who know the job, or structured job-analysis questionnaires. Readers are referred to Brough and Smith (2003) for a useful overview of job analysis techniques.

If job performance is the criterion of interest in the coaching relationship, those tests that best predict job performance, or aspects of it, should be selected. In order to select the appropriate tests, however, coaches need to be able to define the performance domain. There are some well-established models that coaches can draw on to guide their analysis of this. Campbell (1990), for example, identified the various dimensions of performance, including job-specific task performance, non-job-specific task performance, demonstrating effort, written and oral communication, maintaining personal discipline, supervision/leadership, and management/administration. Borman and Motowidlo (1993) subsequently narrowed the performance domain down to two dimensions: task performance (the core technical activities of the job) and contextual performance (helpful, constructive and cooperative behaviours that management values). More recently, researchers have expanded models of the performance domain to take account of the adaptive performance requirements of the changing work environment (Allworth and Hesketh, 1999; Pulakos *et al*, 2000; Griffin and Hesketh, 2003). Further references to job performance models can be found in Viswesvaran and Ones (2000).

When taking a criterion-oriented approach to assessment, coaches must also rely on a model of person-job or person-environment fit. For example, the Minnesota Theory of Work Adjustment (TWA: Dawis and Lofquist, 1984) describes people and work environments in terms of the demands that they impose on each other and what each can offer, or supply to, the other. On the one hand, the work environment requires that certain tasks be performed and the individual brings skills to perform the tasks. In exchange, the individual requires the work environment to reward and satisfy his or her needs, interests and values. Both individuals and organizations adjust to meet each other's requirements. The outcome of work adjustment is tenure, which results when the individual is satisfied with the rewards of the role and the organization finds that person's performance satisfactory.

BENEFITS OF PSYCHOLOGICAL TESTING FOR THE COACH AND THE COACHEE

There are many reasons why assessment can be useful in the coaching relationship. Not only can the results of the assessment provide a valid, reliable and efficient profile of an individual that can help the coach gain insight into the coachee's capabilities and preferences, it also provides some indicators of the coachee's potential. In this section, we explore some of the benefits that both the coach and coachee can derive from psychological testing.

Valid prediction of job performance and other work-related outcomes

Assessment can add value in the coaching relationship through the capacity for some measures to predict performance in work and training. For example, there is consistently strong evidence of the validity of cognitive ability tests as predictors of job performance (Hunter and Hunter, 1984; Schmidt and Hunter, 1998) occupational level attained (Schmidt and Hunter, 2004) and career success (Judge et al, 1999). Although a better predictor of performance in more complex roles than in lower-level, more routine roles (Ackerman, 1992; Hunter and Hunter, 1984), cognitive ability is nevertheless predictive across all jobs and settings.

The Big Five personality factors of Conscientiousness and Neuroticism have also been shown to predict performance across most jobs (Barrick and Mount, 1991; Barrick, Mount and Judge, 2001). Although the relationships are not as strong, Openness to Experience (being curious, inquisitive) seems to predict success in training, while Agreeableness (getting on with people) and Extroversion predict performance in roles where these attributes are required, such as team environments, sales and management.

In general, personality tests can effectively predict job performance if the attributes they measure are required on the job (Robertson and Kinder, 1993). For example, the ability to persuade is more likely to predict performance in sales and management than in clerical or accounting roles, where attention to detail may be more important. Conceptually relevant personality factors can also predict leadership (Judge *et al*, 2002) and teamwork (Morgeson, Reider and Campion, 2005). Dudley *et al* (2006) provide evidence of the ability of facets of Conscientiousness (dependability or achievement) to provide higher levels of validity in predicting job performance in specific occupations.

Although the selection research indicates that values, needs and vocational interest assessments are not necessarily good predictors of job performance (Schmidt and Hunter, 1998), these are useful tools to assist individuals in the process of job or occupational change to explore alternative career options. Hansen (1994) reports numerous studies that have shown 60–75 per cent accuracy in predicting occupational choice.

Raised awareness of individual style, preferences and capabilities

Normative data enables coachees to gain insights into their relative strengths and preferences (or areas for development) and examine them in relation to others in a relevant comparison group. The skill of the coach, however, is required to ensure that the results of the assessment are given meaning in the context of the coachees' lives. For example, it may or may not be relevant to people's satisfaction, performance or lives to know that they are less outgoing, less ambitious and less interested in artistic activities than many of their peers. It is the impact that knowledge has on those individuals' lives, in a positive or negative way, which gives it relevance and makes it important in development and career planning.

Open up new avenues for exploration

Some aspects of the assessment can help the coachee explore possibilities that might not otherwise have been considered. Mastie (1994) points out that psychological testing in the context of career assessment is used to empower the coachee. The information gathered from the assessment is used to inform their exploration of possible options. In considering career possibilities, coachees may be limited by their own experience and the level of exposure that they may have had to alternative career options.

A platform for feedback, goal-setting and planning for change

Psychological testing provides coaches with a valid basis for feedback, counselling and development planning. Psychological tests should not be seen as an alternative to other forms of assessment that can contribute to the coaching relationship, such as interviewing, behavioural observations, or information from managers and employers. However, the results of psychological testing can be used for planning the coaching approach and for development or career planning on the part of the coachee. The results of psychological tests can also highlight strengths from which the coachee may leverage change, and areas for development that may be points of focus for change.

Monitoring and evaluation

Herr (1994) suggests that assessment in the coaching or career counselling context can also have the benefit of monitoring an individual's progress and the effectiveness of career interventions. For example, the coachees may use psychological testing to track their progress by re-evaluating opportunities, and reassessing their skills, interests and motivational needs or values. The coach may use psychological testing to evaluate and ensure the accountability of the coaching programmes.

ETHICAL GUIDELINES AND BEST PRACTICE IN TESTING

Finding a good test that has been well developed and shows the technical capabilities that are required to justify and support its use is just one part of the challenge for test users. Just as important is the need to use the test in an appropriate and ethical manner. Test users should be familiar with issues of privacy and their duties of care as they relate to the jurisdiction in which they work. Coaches who are not covered by a code of practice should refer to the International Test Commission's (ITC) *Guidelines for Test Use* (2000) which provides a framework from which specific local testing standards can be developed. In this section we examine some of the principles that underlie ethical and best practice use of psychological tests. A summary checklist is provided in Table 1.3.

Testing should be evidence-based

Users of psychological tests need to be able to differentiate those tests that have been developed through a programme of rigorous, scientific research from those that are based on a loose conceptualization of the attributes

Table 1.3   Checklist for ethical and best-practice psychological testing

▮ Define the purpose of the assessment, for example:

- to explore future career options;
- to explain low job satisfaction, stress or poor performance;
- to identify development needs for a target job.

▮ Determine the kinds of tests that will best address the purpose of the assessment:

- personality profiling to raise awareness of preferred ways of behaving;
- vocational interest assessment to explore career and occupational preferences;
- motivation assessment to identify factors that drive the coachee's performance;
- values assessment to determine the kind of environment that best suits the coachee;
- cognitive ability testing to determine potential for advancement or training.

▮ Select the best test for your purpose:

- ensure each test is based on a well researched model or theory;
- check the reliability and validity;
- ensure it offers norms that fit the coachee's demographics and that the sample size is adequate.

▮ Select only those tests that you are competent and trained to administer and interpret.

▮ Gather relevant collateral information (such as job descriptions, competency data, coachee's resumé) to better understand the context in which the assessment is being conducted.

▮ Consider who will receive feedback and a report of the assessment and gain informed consent from the coachee.

▮ Ensure the coachee understands the purpose of the assessment and how the results will be used.

▮ Make adequate arrangements to ensure standardized administration.

▮ Take account of any factors that may impact on the coachee's ability to complete the assessment, eg disability, illness, language.

▮ Be aware of your ethical and professional responsibilities, and the rights and responsibilities of coachees who undertake psychological assessment.

measured with inadequate research backing. Ideally, tests should be linked to plausible theory, and if not, they should at least be able to demonstrate an empirical or statistical relationship with an outcome of interest: that is, they should be evidence-based.

Tests should be selected carefully to address the referral question

The test user needs to be clear about what he or she wants to find out about the individual and, as such, will be guided by the referral question. If the referral question is 'What kind of career will best suit me, the coachee?' the tests used should be able to provide results that will help the coachee answer this question by profiling his or her needs, interests, values or abilities. A different set of tests may be relevant if the referral question is 'What are my development needs if I am to achieve my current career goals?' Here, the coach needs to have a good understanding of the coachee's career goals and ambitions, and tailor the assessment to assess the coachee's capabilities against these.

Only tests with adequate psychometric properties should be used

All good tests should have an accompanying manual that documents their technical properties and outlines the method of test development. Although test developers are justified in protecting their intellectual property, they need also to be transparent in providing details of the method of test construction, the reliability and validity of test scales, the demographics of the normative samples, and guidelines for administration and interpretation. Care needs to be taken by the test user to ensure that the claims made about test results can be justified on the basis of the psychometric properties that are known.

Test users should be competent to administer and interpret tests

Most publishers and owners of psychological tests require users to be accredited in the administration and interpretation of their tools. For some tests, this accreditation may be automatic by virtue of the test user's professional qualifications such as in psychology or education. Test users who do not have a professional background in psychometrics or psychology should be aware of the boundaries of their competence and ensure that they undertake the relevant training and development that will enable them to use tests in an appropriate and professional manner. Tests should be administered under standardized conditions and the results should be interpreted and reported accurately.

Test users should respect the privacy of the test taker

Before conducting a psychological assessment, the test user should advise the test taker of his or her rights and responsibilities, the purpose and nature of the testing, and the limits of confidentiality. Informed consent should be gained. The test user should avoid causing harm or distress through the testing process and should be aware of the fairness of testing for those coachees whose gender, cultural background, language, education, ethnic origin, physical capabilities or age differ from those for whom the test was developed.

SUMMARY

Good psychological tests used appropriately can be useful tools for coaches to support their clients in building awareness through self-exploration and understanding. In assuming a test-user role, coaches need therefore to be very aware of the theoretical and psychometric background to testing, and use comprehensive models to guide their choice of tests. In a world in which test users are confronted with a plethora of tests of varying reliability, validity and value in the coaching context, coaches should ensure that they are adequately trained, informed and knowledgeable about the limitations and capabilities of the tests they use. Test users should also be aware of the ethical issues that impact on the use of tests in coaching and ensure that they apply only the highest standards of test usage. As the legal and ethical requirements of test users and the rights of test takers can vary across countries, test users have a responsibility to ensure that they operate in accordance with those that are relevant to their jurisdiction. While the inappropriate and unskilled application of psychological testing can have damaging effects on individuals, where they are used wisely, ethically and with the required knowledge and accreditation, the benefits to coaches and coachees can be substantial.

References

Ackerman, PL (1992) Predicting individual differences in complex skill acquisition: dynamics of ability determinants, *Journal of Applied Psychology*, **77**, pp 598–614

Allworth, E and Hesketh, B (1999) Construct oriented biodata and the prediction of adaptive performance, *International Journal of Selection and Assessment*, **7**, pp 97–111

American Educational Research Association, American Psychological Association and National Council on Measurement in Education (2004) *Standards for*

Educational and Psychological Testing, American Educational Research Association, Washington

Barrick, MR and Mount, MK (1991) The Big Five personality dimensions and job performance: a meta-analysis, *Personnel Psychology*, **44**, pp 1–26

Barrick, MR, Mount, MK and Judge, TA (2001) Personality and performance at the beginning of the new millennium: what do we know and where do we go next? *International Journal of Selection and Assessment*, **9**, pp 9–13

Borman, WC and Motowidlo, SJ (1993) Expanding the criterion domain to include elements of contextual performance, in *Personnel Selection in Organizations*, ed N Schmitt and WC Borman, Jossey-Bass, San Francisco

Brough, P and Smith, M (2003) Job analysis, in *Organizational Psychology in Australia and New Zealand*, ed M O'Driscoll, P Taylor and T Kalliath, pp 11–30, Oxford University Press, Melbourne

Campbell, DT and Fiske, DW (1959) Convergent and discriminant validation by the multitrait-multimethod matrix, *Psychological Bulletin*, **56**, pp 81–105

Campbell, JP (1990) Modelling the performance prediction problem in industrial and organizational psychology, in Handbook of Industrial Psychology, 2nd edn, Vol 1, ed MD Dunnette and LM Hough, Consulting Psychologists Press, Palo Alto

Dawis, RV and Lofquist, LH (1984) *Psychological Theory of Work Adjustment: An Individual Differences Model and its Application*, University of Minnesota Press, Minneapolis

Dudley, NM, Orvis, KA, Lebiecki, JE and Cortina, JM (2006) A meta-analytic investigation of conscientiousness in the prediction of job performance: examining the intercorrelations and the incremental validity of narrow traits, *Journal of Applied Psychology*, **91**, pp 40–57

Fine, SA (1955) A structure of worker functions, *Personnel and Guidance Journal*, **34**, pp 66–73

Goldberg, LR (1990) An alternative 'description of personality': a big-five factor structure, *Journal of Personality and Social Psychology*, **59**, pp 1216–29

Griffin, B and Hesketh, B (2003) Adaptable behaviours for successful work and career adjustment, *Australian Journal of Psychology*, **55**, pp 65–73

Hansen, JC (1994) The measurement of vocational interests, in *Personnel Selection and Classification*, ed MG Rumsey, CB Walker and JH Harris, Lawrence Erlbaum Associates, Hillsdale, NJ

Herr, EL (1994) The counselor's role in career assessment, in *A Counselor's Guide to Career Assessment Instruments*, ed JT Kapes, MM Mastie and EA Whitfield, National Career Development Association, Alexandria VA

Hinkin, TR (1995) A review of scale development practices in the study of organizations, *Journal of Management*, **21**, pp 967–88

Holland, JL (1997) *Making Vocational Choices: A Theory of Vocational Personalities and Work Environments*, 3rd edn, Psychological Assessment Resources, Odessa, FL

Hunter, JE, and Hunter, RF (1984) Validity and utility of alternative predictors of job performance, *Psychological Bulletin*, **96**, pp 72–98

International Test Commission (2000) *International Guidelines for Test Use*, Retrieved 30 January 2007 from http.//www.intestcom,org

Judge, TA, Bono, JE, Ilies, R and Gerhardt, MW (2002) Personality and leadership: a qualitative and quantitative review, *Journal of Applied Psychology*, **87**, pp 765–80

Judge, TA, Higgins, CA, Thoresen, CJ and Barrick, MR (1999) The Big Five personality traits: general mental ability, and career success across the life span, *Personnel Psychology*, **52**, pp 621–52

Mastie, MM (1994) Using assessment instruments in career counseling: career assessment as compass, credential, process and empowerment, in *A Counselor's Guide to Career Assessment Instruments*, National Career Development Association, ed J T Kapes, M M Mastie and E A Whitfield, Alexandria VA

McCrae, RR and Costa, PT (1987) Validation of the five-factor model of personality across instruments and observers, *Journal of Personality and Social Psychology*, **52**, pp 81–90

Morgeson, FP, Reider, MH and Campion, MA (2005) Selecting individuals in team settings: the importance of social skills, personality characteristics, and teamwork knowledge, *Personnel Psychology*, **58**, pp 583–611

Murphy, KR and Davidshofer, CO (1998) *Psychological Testing, Principles and Applications*, 4th edn, Prentice Hall, Upper Saddle River, NJ

Pulakos, ED, Arad, S, Donovan, MA and Plamondon, KE (2000) Adaptability in the workplace: development of a taxonomy of adaptive performance, *Journal of Applied Psychology*, **85**, pp 299–323

Robertson, IT and Kinder, A (1993) Personality and job competencies: the criterion-related validity of some personality variables, *Journal of Occupational and Organizational Psychology*, **66**, pp 225–44

Schmidt, FL and Hunter, JE (1998) The validity and utility of selection methods in personnel psychology: practical and theoretical implications of 85 years of research findings, *Psychological Bulletin*, **124**, pp 262–74

Schmidt, FL and Hunter, JE (2004) General mental ability in the world of work: occupational attainment and job performance, *Journal of Personality and Social Psychology*, **86**, pp 162–73

Thompson, B and Daniel, LG (1996) Factor analytic evidence for the construct validity: a historical overview and some guidelines, *Educational and Psychological Measurement*, **56**, pp 197–208

Viswesvaran, C and Ones, DS (2000) Perspectives on models of job performance, *International Journal of Selection and Assessment*, **8**, pp 216–26

2

Using feedback in coaching

Dr Almuth McDowall

INTRODUCTION

'That's great feedback' is perhaps one of the most abused and misunderstood catchphrases. While feedback is omnipresent, we may actually not understand it and only be interested in good news.

Psychology researchers have long been concerned with what feedback is, how it works and what the results are. This has produced many studies which are equivocal about the value of feedback. This chapter considers the parties and processes involved in the communication of feedback in our section on the core principles underlying feedback:

■ Who is involved in feedback processes?
■ When and under what circumstances do we give feedback?
■ What is the 'feedback message'?
■ What factors affect how feedback is received?

Next we review the research evidence including a separate section on 360-degree feedback. This will lead us to a practical discussion of the implications of existing research for coaches, critically appraising a prevalent feedback model. Finally, we provide guidelines for best practice.

The approach taken in this chapter will encourage and enable practitioners to develop their own feedback models, and optimize these for their own, as well as their coachees' and clients' benefit. In general, we have focused this chapter on the world of work and related feedback activities, but refer to other contexts where appropriate.

THE PRINCIPLES OF FEEDBACK

The assumption that giving feedback to someone else changes how they behave underlies a whole variety of fundamental organizational and educational as well as interpersonal processes. Feedback is also an integral part of the coaching relationship. We utilize feedback both consciously and formally (as with the use of 360-degree feedback tools) and in an informal and unstructured manner through the ongoing dialogue with our coachees and clients. We may also deal with feedback from other sources during our involvement, such as performance appraisals.

Feedback derives from communications theory and refers to a process where a 'sender' sends a 'message', a piece of information, to a 'recipient'. In order for feedback to happen and a message to be relayed, the following assumptions need to be met:

▌ The sender initiates a communication process.
▌ There is a message that needs to be communicated.
▌ This message is understood and discussed by sender and recipient.

In coaching, most feedback activities are likely to happen in person, although coaches may also use written or electronic documentation such as 360-degree feedback reports to feed into any sessions. Figure 2.1 outlines this process in overview, and also serves as a visual outline of this chapter.

It is important that coaches understand various sources of feedback, and how these differ. The sources affect the feedback message, in terms of whether this is shared only between coach and coachee (and thus confidential), but affect also other factors such as the 'sign' (is feedback positive or negative). The feedback recipient is usually the coachee, whose reactions to feedback are likely to be subjective, depending on the coachee's levels of confidence, self-esteem and so on.

The feedback sender

The feedback sender initiates the sending of the feedback message, either by agreement with the recipient or unprompted. In a work context this will

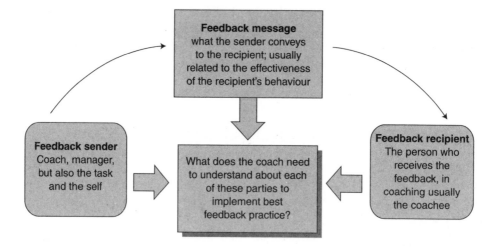

Figure 2.1 The feedback process

usually be a coach, manager or co-worker. Several researchers have considered sources of feedback even more broadly, as we also get implicit feedback information from performing any tasks. If we are struggling to do something, feedback from the task is that 'this is difficult', leading to feelings of frustration, or even anger. Whereas if we do something that comes easily to us, the message might be 'this is easy', leading to feelings of satisfaction or pleasure.

It is more commonplace for feedback to come not just from one but from multiple sources. Examples for this are 'bottom up' feedback, where managers get feedback from their staff, or 'peer feedback'. The latter refers to feedback from people on an equal level, which is increasingly popular both in work and educational settings. Getting feedback from several sources adds an extra layer of complexity, as the various feedback senders may all be saying entirely different things, or they may be expressing a similar core message in different ways.

There are a variety of reasons why messages sent by different senders may have different impacts. Credible people are likely to have greater effect. (See Kluger and DeNisi, 1996, for a full discussion.) Other influential factors are to do with the environment and the context and cannot necessarily be controlled by the sender, such as status and seniority. To illustrate, research typically finds that those who are perceived to be in a position of authority are listened and adhered to. (Examples here are the famous Milgram experiments (1963) and Zimbardo's observations of participants who took the roles of prisoners and guards (Haney, Banks and Zimbardo, 1973).)

However, the senders have control over other more proximal and potentially more impactful aspects of feedback, such as their own interpersonal styles, although sadly research has much less to say on these. In work or executive coaching, the feedback sender is first and foremost the coach, who may draw on other sources of feedback such as the manager, co-workers or even customers.

The feedback message

The message is the information that the sender relays to the recipient (ie, the content of the feedback). In the context of work, this is usually information about the effectiveness of someone's work behaviour (Bastos and Fletcher, 1995), but could also refer to other sources of information such as a psychometric profile. In an educational context, the message typically contains 'formative feedback', such as tutors' guidance during personal or group tutorials, or 'summative feedback', such as exam or coursework marks. In the coaching relationship, the message is any information that is given by the coach to the coachee. This may or may not be shared with other parties such as the commissioning client, and hence varies in terms of formality and structure. An example for highly structured feedback in coaching practice is the use of a 360-degree feedback profile; which is discussed in depth below.

A feedback message could equally be informal and unstructured, such as a comment in passing during a coaching session, or a quick catch up by the coffee machine between manager and subordinate.

The feedback recipient

The recipients are individuals who are receiving any feedback messages. Some people will take feedback on board but others will not. This depends on many issues and in particular the characteristics of the recipients, including their capabilities, how much they believe in these, what kind of goals they have and their self-esteem. Situational factors such as mood swings, distraction through interruptions such as emails or mobile phones, or even nutritional habits have not yet been researched enough at work but have been recognized in other fields. Hydration has long been recognized by sports coaches (eg Douglas *et al*, 2000). Nutrition in relation to educational performance has come under the spotlight in the UK, and the government is making increased efforts to promote the link between healthy eating and effective learning (eg Sorhaindo and Feinstein, for DfES, 2006).

In the coaching relationship, the feedback recipient is first and foremost the coachee. However, any feedback may also be shared with the commissioning client. This is important, as the feedback message may need to be tailored for different recipients.

Aims and purposes of feedback

Essentially then, feedback is the relaying of information from one party to another. However, real life applications are diverse and linked to different aims and purposes that we briefly outline here. In the workplace, staff are appraised in many organizations on past performance by line or HR managers; this usually includes a development review to devise training plans or other activities.

Thus, appraisals have a dual purpose, which does not always make for a 'happy marriage': to assess what has or has not been done in line with what is agreed and expected, and to develop and motivate staff for the future (Fletcher, 2001). Research and anecdotal evidence suggest that appraisals are a source of discontent for managers and staff alike and may not achieve their aims at all. Evidence from the United States suggests that the mere evaluation of employees leads to decline in various outcomes such as trust, morale and communication (Coens and Jenkins, 2000), and the UK has historically not fared much better (Bevan and Thompson, 1991). Managers' perceived incompetence to conduct appraisals seems to be a key factor (eg, Crail, 2006).

Recognizing these shortfalls, large organizations have increasingly implemented processes that involve feedback from several sources, such as peer feedback, upward feedback and full 360-degree feedback. While these arguably provide a more rounded assessment, there are other limitations. Implementation can be costly and time consuming (particularly if processes are developed from scratch), making multi-source feedback suitable only for organizations where a large budget for staff development is available and there are prospects of returns.

Psychometrics in organizations, and in particular personality measures, are also a widespread application involving feedback. The rationale behind their use is that detailed discussion of one's natural preferences with an expert feedback giver will enable employees to gain greater insight into their respective strengths and weaknesses. This in turn will allow focused adjustments to workplace behaviour and enable personal, as well as professional, growth.

At the most negative end of the spectrum, feedback is used for disciplinary matters, for instance when formal warnings are given to employees and justified, or when underperformance is discussed in appraisals. Here, the expectation is that such a formal discussion of shortcomings or inappropriate behaviours will prevent future occurrences.

In summary then, the general agenda for feedback is wide, ranging from the simple conveying of information to purposeful and planned uses for employee development and review of work-based performance (or indeed other forms, for instance in education) to the discussion of malfunction or underperformance.

How does all of this relate to the use of feedback in coaching practice? Coaches may be called in to help employees work on development needs that were initially diagnosed in appraisal discussions, and may then use the feeding back of psychometric profiles to facilitate greater awareness of strengths and weaknesses. Multi-source input can be valuable for coaches, particularly when they need concrete information about work-related behaviours, or when coachees are likely to resist other sources of input.

Of course, feedback processes also take place informally throughout the entire coaching process, as coaches and coachees are likely to continually discuss and review any agreed goals and milestones. We will return to the practical elements of coaching practice at the end of this chapter, once we have reviewed the research evidence on feedback processes.

FEEDBACK THEORY AND EVIDENCE

As outlined above, the basic assumption for any activity relying on feedback is that it changes people's behaviour for the better. The jury is still out, however, whether this holds true in real-life contexts. This part of our chapter draws together the key research evidence which we first summarize in Table 2.1 in order to facilitate our readers' understanding.

Over 10 years ago two authors reviewed an exhaustive set of studies and concluded that there is a link between feedback and performance; however, although in most of the studies performance improved, performance actually declined in a third of the observations (Kluger and DeNisi, 1996).

The authors then scrutinized their data further to investigate what could account for the overall relatively weak effect, and the fact that feedback can either improve or make worse what went on before, to develop a model for future research and practice. As outlined above, there are many factors that influence feedback processes in different ways, such as the actual content, where feedback comes from, at what time it is received and how the recipient reacts. One of the main conclusions of the authors was that we often confuse desirability with usefulness. In other words, most of us seem to want feedback, but whether we act on it is another matter. Research has subsequently tried to disentangle why some react to it and others do not, in particular studies on multi-source feedback which we review below (eg Bailey and Fletcher, 2002; Maurer, Mitchell and Barbeite, 2002).

Table 2.1 Outline of feedback research

Research topic	Key messages
Link between feedback and performance	Not consistent; performance can go up as well as down following feedback (Kluger and DeNisi, 1996).
The feedback sender	This could be a number of sources: one individual, several individuals, a task, or the self. **Not all feedback sources have the same impact**; for instance it is important that the source is credible (eg Bastos and Fletcher, 1995).
The feedback message	**People like receiving and giving praise** (eg Anseel and Lievens, 2006), but are less comfortable with criticism; however, we can't conclude that praise will always have a positive impact, and criticism a negative impact. The message has more impact if it is linked to goals.
The feedback recipient	**People interpret feedback subjectively**, in their own frame of reference (Ilgen, Fisher and Taylor, 1979); any behaviour change following feedback depends on individuals' characteristics such as their self-esteem (Shrauger and Rosenberg, 1970) and their belief in their capabilities (Renn and Fedor, 2001). People need to be motivated to learn from feedback, otherwise behaviours are unlikely to change.

Early research on feedback interventions emphasized the content of the feedback, and in particular the 'sign', in other words whether we praise or criticize others. People remember positive feedback better (Snyder and Cowles, 1979) and it also increases motivation (Deci, 1972). Negative feedback, on the other hand, is linked not only to negative outcomes such as reduced commitment to the organization (Pearce and Porter, 1986) but also to positive outcomes in the context of staff appraisals (Fletcher and Williams, 1996). Therefore, we cannot simply infer that all people will react more positively to praise; we need to take into account that different people may have different reactions. However, there is evidence that people are motivated to see themselves as positively as possible (Anseel and Lievens, 2006).

Individuals who believe that it is important to continuously improve performance ('need for achievement') do better if they have a lot of feedback (Steers, 1975). Self-esteem is also important, as individuals with high self-esteem have a more positive self-image, regardless of what feedback they receive (Shrauger and Rosenberg, 1970), they will raise their game more after positive feedback, and experience less failure following negative feedback than those who have less self-esteem.

There is also a link between what the feedback says and where it comes from. A practical study surveying employees of a manufacturing company demonstrated that negative feedback from supervisors and others was related to poor performance, whereas positive feedback was associated with higher performance (Becker and Klimoski, 1989). Feedback from peers did not have any impact. This is consistent with more recent findings that peer feedback has little impact within a 360-degree feedback process (Bailey and Fletcher, 2002). Nevertheless, peer feedback has taken hold firmly, not only in organizations but also in educational settings, where pupils and students are increasingly asked to evaluate, and potentially coach, others.

Feedback is interpreted subjectively (Ilgen, Fisher and Taylor, 1979), as the same feedback message might mean completely different things to different people, and have a different result every time. Goal-setting theory may help to explain these observations. It holds that feedback itself is merely data, which only has an impact if individuals are motivated to direct their attention to goals. The setting of specific as well as difficult goals leads to the best improvements in performance (Locke and Latham, 1990) as these are understood easily and offer a motivational incentive. The implications are that feedback should be explained clearly and relate to future-orientated targets to ensure that it is relevant to individuals and achieves lasting impact – it should not matter as much whether the message is positive or negative. In addition, it is important that individuals believe that they can actually change things: 'self-efficacy' (which pertains to the 'can do' aspect of performance) is associated with the achievement of feedback-related goals (Renn and Fedor, 2001).

To sum up at this point, it is important that one of the key purposes of feedback is to strengthen people's motivation to change as otherwise there will be no lasting impact.

360-degree feedback

Perhaps the most comprehensive recent evidence on feedback stems from studies on multi-source-multi-rater (MSMR) or 360-degree feedback. This entails the planned comparison of ratings from various sources, such as the supervisor, subordinates, peers and also occasionally internal and external customers, on agreed work-based performance dimensions and interpersonal aspects. Tools for 360-degree feedback can either be bought 'off the shelf' (akin to a psychometric test) or developed as a bespoke tool that is usually based on the organization's competency-based framework. Reports are almost always generated from a PC or web-based system, and may contain graphs that show the ratings from different sources on different dimensions, and also structured narratives or free-flowing comments.

A self-assessment is usually the basis for 360-degree feedback, using the same format as feedback from other sources. The purpose of the actual feedback session (which should be conducted by a trained professional) is to explore any gaps between self- and other-assessments and to learn from these. This should promote greater learning through the discrepancy of feedback from different sources (Fletcher and Baldry, 1999). Many claims have been made about the effectiveness of 360-degree feedback, but at the very least it should meet the following conditions:

▮ The 360-degree feedback provides a comprehensive and valid measure of workplace behaviour.
▮ Learning through feedback from different resources will prompt people to change, and engage in relevant follow-up development activities.
▮ Feedback from each source will provide valuable information in its own right.

We shall address whether or not these conditions are always met in reality. To start, using 360-degree feedback systems is not a simple solution to problems associated with traditional one-to-one assessments. Feedback from several sources may be just as biased, particularly if decisions such as promotions or pay rises hang on the outcomes (Fletcher and Baldry, 1999). The measures also need to be scrutinized and tested just like any other psychometric tool (Fletcher, Baldry and Cunningham-Snell, 1998), otherwise we cannot be confident that the results will hold up across time or across employees, and they may in fact not even measure what the organization had intended to measure.

Nevertheless, 360-degree feedback has offered the unique opportunity for comparing the effects of feedback from different sources against how people rate themselves. The evidence suggests that individuals who are self-aware, by being able to see their own strengths and weaknesses in the same way that other people see them, perform better than those who lack this insight (eg Bass and Yammarino, 1991; Yammarino and Atwater, 1993). So the idea is to raise or corroborate people's level of self-awareness through multi-source feedback, but we refer back to our earlier observation that these sources may not have equal impact. Feedback from the boss generally has the greatest impact (Bailey and Fletcher, 2002; Gregura, Ford and Brutus, 2003), whereas peer ratings may be of limited use as they seem to vary a lot over time (Bailey and Fletcher, 2002).

Will 360-degree feedback achieve lasting impact? An early study (Hazucha, Hezlett and Schneider, 1993) found that self-awareness increased following participation in 360-degree feedback, and that this in turn was related to career progress. Those who perceived more support from their supervisors put more effort into their development and engaged in more development activities. Not only is such support crucial, but also follow up, in terms of subsequent evaluation and personal development plans (PDP) and other tools that enable employees to transfer any learning to the workplace (Wimer and Nowack, 1998).

The link between 360-degree feedback and follow-up activities tends to be small (Maurer, Mitchell and Barbeite, 2002). A thorough review also found the link between feedback, whether from traditional appraisals or multisources, and performance improvements to be negligible (Smither, London and Reilly, 2005). One potential explanation for this seeming lack of effectiveness could be that, as explained above, people react differently to feedback. A positive self-belief seems to be crucial, in that people actually need to believe that it is within their power to change (Maurer, Mitchell and Barbeite, 2002; Atwater and Brett, 2005). In addition, it is also important that people react positively to the feedback process (Atwater and Brett, 2005) as a negative attitude makes people reluctant to change their behaviour effectively. Thus, it is important that 360-degree processes are communicated well and buy-in is sought from those involved. Where this is done, managers value the thoroughness of 360-degree feedback compared with other approaches (Mabey, 2001), and particularly appreciate graphical and numerical information (Atwater and Brett, 2006).

Feedback effectiveness improves if processes are followed up and supported by executive coaching, as performance evaluations improve, more and more concrete goals are set and adhered to (Smither *et al*, 2005). This holds true not only in organizations but also in education (Marsh and Roche, 1997), indicating that coaching is helpful for embedding behaviour change that results from feedback, but also more generally furthers a supportive environment at work.

One issue that is generally problematic both in 360-degree feedback and in appraisal is who is best placed to rate others. Line or senior managers may have little idea of what an individual actually does on a day-to-day basis. One study found individuals' self-assessments to be the best predictors of behaviour change (Bailey and Austin, 2006), which implies that we should give as much attention to self-evaluations, as to ratings from other sources.

How to get the most out of feedback in coaching

In essence, we cannot rely on feedback itself to prompt behaviour change. It certainly matters who gives feedback. Multiple sources provide extra information that we can utilize to good effect if this is offset against an effective self-assessment; however, we need to check whether these assessments are accurate. Chances are that the most credible source has the greatest impact. This is important to note for work-based coaches, who need to ensure a) buy-in from client and coachee to ensure that feedback leads to concrete action, and b) a supportive environment that allows transfer of learning back into the workplace.

Reactions to feedback vary depending on the sign, and more importantly on how much people believe they can change, on their underlying capability, how useful they think the feedback process is, and whether there is a real interest in learning (see Kluger and Nir, 2006, for a full discussion). Where does this leave the coach? It is perhaps unrealistic to try to assess all these potential differences before we convey feedback. However, we do need to develop an awareness that these factors matter, so that we can investigate further, particularly when a feedback process does not produce desired outcomes.

Regardless of these differences, feedback always needs to be clear and linked to personal goals to be effective in the long term. A wealth of studies reports that goal setting is effective, if goals are specific and realistic (eg, Locke and Latham, 1990). Table 2.2 illustrates how goals and the level of generalization in feedback interlink.

Table 2.2 Goals and feedback in coaching

Feedback in coaching	*Goals set within the coaching process*	
	Specific	*General*
Specific	Feedback is easily understood by the coachee and results in future learning	Subsequent evaluation of any goals is difficult
General	Feedback is interpreted within the recipient's 'frame of reference' and unlikely to result in behaviour change	Feedback is difficult to interpret and apply for the coachee

Source: after Ilgen, Fisher and Taylor (1979).

Here are some examples of how this may manifest in coaching practice.

- ▮ 'Your colleagues seem to think you are not doing well, so you need to improve' is feedback that is too general. Neither coachee nor the client is likely to gain any benefit.
- ▮ 'The evidence from your 360-report shows that one area that we can work on is your effective contribution to team meetings' is specific feedback, but lacks a future-orientated goal.
- ▮ 'You need to improve until we meet next time' is not a helpful goal; whereas a targeted and concrete action plan is likely to result in effective behaviour changes.

Note that while coaches may already be practising effective feedback, it is less likely that managers in organizations are. Thus, it may often be helpful to revisit the content of any feedback that the coachee has received from others, pull out the key messages and link them to future planning as outlined above.

The goals set should be benchmarked and followed up by the coach to ensure that learning is transferred to other situations. It is vital that these goals are negotiated in agreement, and not superimposed on the coachee. Otherwise, people may not have the motivation to follow these through. We should also remind ourselves that by and large people tend to prefer positive news. Negative feedback, particularly if it comes out of the blue, can have detrimental consequences if not given sensitively.

It is also important that the coach holds the belief that coachees can actually change. Coaches or managers who hold the views that some personal attributes are fixed are less likely to help others change (Heslin, Vandewalle and Latham, 2005). As coaches, we need to shape our own practice to reflect this. We can also train managers to shape their own beliefs and thus help them to adapt a more conducive 'coaching style'.

People in general do not like giving critical feedback (Tesser and Rosen, 1975; Bond and Anderson, 1987). This has two implications for our practice as coaches. First, we need to be comfortable ourselves with conveying critical information to others. Second, we need to be aware that coachees may not be aware of any potential counterproductive behaviour, due to managers' reluctance to criticize.

What we seem to be missing at the moment is a simple but effective model for giving feedback. One prevalent model is the 'sandwich'. This holds that we should give people some good news first, then convey criticism, and finally conclude on a positive note. In practice, however, this is not always workable or desirable. To start with, there are situations when we are only working with negative information; for instance results from a 360-degree process may entail altogether low ratings and critical comments. Also, the sandwich can seem contrived in practice as many employees are now familiar with it, and know when 'it's time for bad news'. Lastly, the sandwich does not engage the recipient of the feedback in the process. As discussed above, self-assessments are an important aspect of the feedback process, and we should incorporate these whenever we can.

Psychological research offers us guidance for best feedback practice. All of us have the tendency to attribute success to factors that relate to ourselves and are under our control. Failure, however, we tend to attribute to causes which are external to us and out of our control (Jones and Nisbett, 1972). Plus, we have a tendency to view ourselves more positively than others do; however, such positive illusions are actually good for our motivation and esteem (Taylor *et al*, 2003). Thus, we need to be very careful that we back up any criticism with concrete examples, and also take care to direct these at specific behaviours, and not at the person. To illustrate, a statement such as 'You don't seem to listen to others in team meetings, as xyz and zyx both report in their feedback that you continuously interrupt them,' is more conducive to improvement than 'You have a disruptive attitude'.

Note that one area that appears to have been largely neglected by academic research is the style of the feedback giver. Feedback processes rely on good interpersonal communication and rapport, and all feedback givers will bring their personal approach to the process. However, we know that most of us are not comfortable with criticism. Some of us may compensate for this by being very soft in the feedback interview, and thus avoiding the core issue. Others may come straight out with the criticism, and appear particularly cruel. It is important that we recognize our own feedback style, and learn mechanisms for adapting this. Regular feedback on our own feedback approach is therefore essential through coaching supervision, peer feedback from colleagues and our own reflective practice.

In addition, there is a danger that we jump to conclusions too quickly, before getting the full picture (Argyris, 1982), when we try to understand feedback messages. Different interpretations of the same set of data are always possible, and we need to ensure that our interpretation is the most appropriate and realistic. Imagine, for instance, that you would have to convey the following piece of information (a narrative comment from a 360-degree tool that focuses on interpersonal behaviour) to a coachee: 'You have a lot to contribute to our team meetings as your forward style ensures that you get your points across.' There are several potential explanations. It is possible that this individual is actually being constructive by making sure that important information is considered in the meetings, which otherwise may take too long or lack focus. It is equally possible that this individual is too forward in his or her communication style and talks in meetings at others' expense – thus interfering with an effective process. Further evidence is clearly needed here, and the coach would need to elicit several pieces of information, perhaps contrasted against a coachee self-evaluation, to get the full picture.

Lastly, we need to address what kind of pieces of information we use in our feedback processes, and how we structure the process around these.

A whole range of psychometric tools are addressed elsewhere in this volume. Personality questionnaires are increasingly favoured by many coaches, as the discussion of any profiles is purported to provide individuals with greater awareness of their personal preferences or 'type'. It is important, however, that coaches do not rely too heavily on the profiles themselves, but remain conscious that their value rests with the actual feedback discussion. This in turn should be conducted with a clear understanding of individual differences as well as the purpose and style of the coaching relationship.

The research evidence on 360-degree feedback tools is cautiously optimistic. Our review above shows that discrepant feedback from various sources can provide a valuable source of information to coach and coachee alike. This can be particularly useful if feedback recipients have blind areas (see Summerfield, 2003), or are resistant to change. Not all 360-tools are equal, as not all of them have undergone the same rigorous validation process as psychometric tests (Fletcher, Baldry and Cunningham-Snell, 1998). If we bring such information into the coaching process, we must make ourselves knowledgeable about the properties of the tool and corroborate whether the information provided is actually reliable and valid. In addition, 360-degree feedback tools tend to be rooted in workplace competencies, and it is important that the coach understands, and potentially even challenges, these if feeding back such information to coachees. Many competency models use relatively vague descriptors such as 'business acumen' or 'results orientation'. It is important to translate these into concrete workplace behaviours with coachees, and get them to provide real life examples. This is particularly important when feedback is critical.

There is also a difference with regard to who has sought the 360-degree feedback. It may be that we ourselves have chosen in our role as coaches to solicit such feedback with agreement from the client and the coachee, in which instance we have control over some of the feedback process, such as observing confidentiality. But it is equally possible that feedback already exists when the coaching relationship is formed. In this instance, we need to be vigilant to ensure that the information is actually useful and conducive and has been handled in a sensitive manner. Once more, particular attention has to be given to the administration of the feedback when the content is negative, as coachees may be particularly defensive in this instance (Antonioni, 1996).

SUMMARY

The overall message from the research available is that we cannot say 'one size fits all' as there is no generic model of feedback that is suitable for each and every individual and situation; however, we summarize the key principles for effective and ineffective feedback for coaches in Table 2.3.

We need to be aware that results from feedback vary between different people and situations, and also depend on whether we praise or criticize people. Thus, we need to take a flexible approach and adapt how we give feedback to the specific context. There are some key rules that are important for our practice when giving feedback as we need to be a) credible, b) objective, and c) good communicators. We should ensure that we practise and nurture these skills through regular training, personal development and reviewing our own feedback style.

Table 2.3   Feedback effectiveness for coaches

Effective feedback	Ineffective feedback
▌ The complexity of feedback is understood by the coach, eg that individuals will react differently.	▌ There is no common frame of reference – what was this all about?
▌ There is effective communication and interpersonal rapport between coach and coachee.	▌ No goals, or insufficiently specified goals, have been agreed.
▌ The coach is seen as credible.	▌ The coach lacks credibility.
▌ The coachee is in a receptive state, and has the motivation and ability to do something as a result of the feedback.	▌ The coachee lacks self-esteem and belief that he or she has the power to change.
▌ The feedback message contains clear evidence of behaviours.	▌ There is little support in the environment and from the client.
▌ Feedback is given at the right time, in the right place.	▌ The coach shies away from offering criticical feedback.
▌ The coach believes that the coachee can change.	▌ The feedback message is threatening and personal.
▌ The coach is able to adapt his/her feedback style in an appropriate manner.	▌ Feedback is negative and out of the blue.

The feedback message needs to be clear and appropriate, and we need to recognize that few individuals react positively to criticism. Thus, we need to ensure that we corroborate any feedback information given to us (such as existing appraisal information, 360-degree feedback profiles) and agree the accuracy with the coachee. Any criticisms should be directed at behaviours, and not at the person.

We need to always bear in mind that reactions to feedback vary; for instance some coachees will respond well to 360-degree feedback, even to quite harsh criticism, whereas for others this may be demotivating and upsetting. We need to address such reactions effectively within the actual coaching relationship, but also ensure that appropriate follow up and support is available back in the workplace, in order to ensure effective transfer of learning. If people are not motivated to change, even the best feedback will have little effect, so we need to facilitate this motivation in our coachees.

Most of all, we need to remain aware that good feedback should result in effective learning, and that includes our own development as coaches and therefore feedback givers.

References and further reading

Anseel, F and Lievens, F (2006) Certainty as a moderator of feedback reactions? A test of the strength of the self-verification motive, *Journal of Occupational Psychology*, **79**, pp 533–51

Antonioni, D (1996) Designing an effective 360-degree appraisal process, *Organizational Dynamics*, **2**, pp 24–38

Argyris, C (1982) *Reasoning, Learning, and Action*, Jossey-Bass, San Francisco

Atwater, L and Brett, JF (2005) Antecedents and consequences of reactions to developmental 360-feedback, *Journal of Vocational Behaviour*, **66**, pp 532–48

Atwater, L and Brett, JF (2006) Feedback format : does it influence manager's reactions to feedback? *Journal of Occupational and Organizational Psychology*, **79**, pp 517–32

Bailey, C and Austin, M (2006) 360 degree feedback and developmental outcomes: the role of feedback characteristics, self-efficacy and importance of feedback dimensions to focal managers' current role, *International Journal of Selection and Assessment*, **14**, pp 51–66

Bailey, C and Fletcher, C (2002) The impact of multiple source feedback on management development: findings from a longitudinal study, *Journal of Organizational Behavior*, **23**(7), pp 853–67

Balcazar, FB and Hopkins, L (1985) A critical, objective review of performance feedback, *Journal of Organizational Behaviour Management*, **7**, pp 65–89

Bass, BM and Yammarino, FJ (1991) Congruence of self and others' leadership ratings on naval officers for understanding successful performance, *Journal of Applied Psychology*, **40**, pp 437–54

Bastos, M and Fletcher, C (1995) Exploring the individual's perception of sources and credibility of feedback in the work environment, *International Journal of Selection and Assessment*, **3** (1), pp 29–39

Becker, TE and Klimoski, RJ (1989) A field study of the relationship between the organizational feedback environment and performance, *Personnel Psychology*, 42, pp 343–58

Bevan, S and Thompson, M (1991) *Performance Management in the UK: An analysis of the issues*, Institute of Personnel Management, London

Bond, C and Anderson, E (1987) The reluctance to transmit bad news: private discomfort or public display? *Journal of Experimental Social Psychology*, **73** (2), pp 199–207

Cannon, MD and Witherspoon, R (2005) Actionable feedback: unlocking the power of learning and performance improvement, *Academy of Management Executive*, **19**, pp 120–34

Casa, DJ, Armstrong, LE, Hillman, SK, Montain, SJ, Reiff, RV, Roberts, WL and Stone, JA (2000) National athletic trainers' association position statement: fluid replacement for athletes, *Journal of Athletic Training*, **35**(2), pp 212–24

Coens, T and Jenkins, M (2000) *Abolishing Performance Appraisals: Why they backfire and what to do instead*, Berrett-Koehler, San Francisco

Crail, M (2006) Line managers fail in performance evaluation, *Personnel Today*, 5 September [Online] http://wwwpersonneltodaycom/Articles/2006/09/05/37071/line-managers-fail-in-performance-evaluationhtml (accessed 17 April 2007)

Deci, EL (1972) Intrinsic motivation, extrinsic reinforcement and inequity, *Journal of Personality and Social Psychology*, **22**, pp 111–20

Douglas, JC, Armstrong, LE, Hillman, SK, Montain, SJ, Reiff, R. Rich, BSE, Roberts, WO and Stone, JA (2000) National Athletic Trainers' Association Position Statement: Fluid Replacement for Athletes, *Journal of Athletic Training*, **35** (2), pp 212–24

Fletcher, C (2001) *Appraisal: Routes to improved performance*, CIPD, London

Fletcher, C and Williams, R (1996) Performance management, job satisfaction and organizational commitment, *British Journal of Management*, **7**, pp 169–79

Fletcher, C and Baldry, C (1999) *Multi-Source Feedback Systems: A research perspective*, International Review of Industrial and Organizational Psychology, Wiley, Chichester

Fletcher, C, Baldry, C and Cunningham-Snell, N (1998) The psychometric properties of 360-degree feedback: an empirical study and a cautionary tale, *International Journal of Selection and Assessment*, **6**, pp 19–33

Gregura, GJ, Ford, JM and Brutus, S (2003) Manager attention to multisource feedback, *Journal of Management Development*, **22**, pp 345–61

Haney, C, Banks, WC and Zimbardo, PG (1973) A study of prisoners and guards in a simulated prison, *Naval Research Review*, **30**, pp 4–17

Hazucha, JF, Hezlett, SA and Schneider, RJ (1993) The impact of 360-degree feedback on management skills development, *Human Resource Management Journal*, **32**, pp 325–51

Heslin, PA, Vandewalle, D and Latham, GP (2005) Keen to help? Managers' implicit person theories and their subsequent employee coaching, *Personnel Psychology*, **59**, pp 871–902

Ilgen, DR, Fisher, CD and Taylor, MS (1979) Consequences of individual feedback on behaviour in organizations, *Journal of Applied Psychology*, **64**, pp 349–71

Jones, E and Nisbett, R (1972) The actor and the observer: divergent perceptions of the causes of behavior, in *Attribution: Perceiving the Causes Of Behaviour*, ed E Jones, D Kanouse, H Kellye, S Nisbett, S Valins and B Weiner, General Learning Press, Morristown, NJ

Kluger, A and DeNisi, A (1996) The effects of feedback interventions on performance: historical review, a meta-analysis and a preliminary feedback intervention theory, *Psychological Bulletin*, **119**, pp 254–84

Kluger, A and Nir, D (2006) Feedforward first – feedback later, keynote address presented at the International Congress of Applied Psychology, Athens, July 2006 [Online] http://plutohujiacil/ mskluger/klugerfiles/Publicationshtm (accessed 26 November 2006)

Locke, EA and Latham, G (1990) A *Theory of Goal Setting and Task Performance*, Prentice Hall, Englewood Cliffs, NJ

London, M and Smither, JW (1995) Can multi-source feedback change perceptions of goal accomplishment, self-evaluations, and performance-related outcomes? Theory-based applications and directions for research, *Personnel Psychology*, **48**, pp 803–39

Mabey, C (2001) Closing the circle: participant views of a 360-degree feedback programme, *Human Resource Management Journal*, **11**(1), pp 41–53

Marsh, HW and Roche, LA (1997) Making students' evaluations of teaching effectiveness effective: the critical issues of validity, bias, and utility, *American Psychologist*, **52**(11), pp 1187–97

Maurer, TJ, Mitchell, DRD and Barbeite, FG (2002) Predictors of attitudes toward a 360-degree feedback system and involvement in post-feedback management development activity, *Journal of Occupational and Organizational Psychology*, **75**(1), pp 87–107

Milgram, S (1963) Behavioural study of obedience, *Journal of Abnormal and Social Psychology*, **67**(4), pp 371–72

Pearce, JL and Porter, LW (1986) Employee Responses to formal appraisal feedback, *Journal of Applied Psychology*, **71**, pp 211–18

Renn, RW and Fedor, DB (2001) Development and field test of a feedback seeking, self-efficacy, and goal setting model of work performance, *Journal of Management*, **27**(5), pp 563–83

Shrauger, JS and Rosenberg, SE (1970) Self-esteem and the effects of success and failure feedback on performance, *Journal of Personality and Social Psychology*, **38**, pp 404–17

Smither, W, London, M and Reilly, RR (2005) Does performance improve following multisource feedback? A theoretical model, meta-analysis, and review of empirical findings, *Personnel Psychology*, **58**, pp 33–52

Snyder, CR and Cowles, C (1979) Impact of positive and negative feedback based on personality and intellectual assessment, *Journal of Consulting and Clinical Psychology*, **47**(1), pp 207–09

Sorhaindo, A and Feinstein, L (2006) *What is the Relationship between Child Nutrition and School Outcomes?* Brief Series Report published by Department for Education and Skills (DfES), No RCB03–06

Steers, RM (1975) Task-goal attributes, n-achievement, and supervisory performance, *Organizational Behaviour and Human Performance*, **13**, pp 392–403

Summerfield, J (2003) Giving high-value feedback: a guide for trainers [Online] wwwworkingone-to-onepartnershipcom (accessed 29 March 2007)

Taylor, SE, Lerner, JS, Sherman, DK, Sage, RM and McDowell, NK (2003) Portrait of the self-enhancer: well adjusted and well liked or maladjusted and friendless, *Journal of Personality and Social Psychology*, **84**, pp 165–76

Tesser, A and Rosen, S (1975) The reluctance to transmit bad news, in *Advances in experimental social psychology*, Vol 8, ed L Berkowitz, Academic Press, New York

Wimer, S and Nowack, KM (1998), 13 common mistakes using 360-degree feedback, *Training and Development*, **5**, pp 69–80

Yammarino, F and Atwater, L (1993) Understanding self-perception accuracy: implications for human resource management, *Human Resource Management*, **32**, pp 231–47

ACKNOWLEDGEMENT

I would like to thank my colleagues Lynne Purvis, Adrian Banks and Kiriaki Riga for their helpful comments.

Part 2

Individual instruments and their use

3

Coaching with MBTI

Sally Carr, Bernard Cooke, Leanne Harris and Betsy
Kendall

INTRODUCTION

Of the many psychometric tools used by executive coaches, the
Myers–Briggs Type Indicator® questionnaire (MBTI®) is one of the most
popular. It is based on a model that describes personality in positive, non-
threatening terms, enabling coachees to appreciate their strengths while
recognizing the value of personality types different from their own. It
therefore underlines the benefits of diversity and the potential to use differences constructively.

It is a versatile coaching tool, and can help address issues such as communication and influencing, problem solving, team development,
leader–follower interactions and career development. In addition, the
model has powerful theoretical underpinnings that enable exploration of
the complexities of mid-life issues and out-of-character reactions to stress.

In this chapter, we outline the core assumptions of type theory and
explain the practicalities of using the MBTI. We then show how the model
can be used in coaching on two levels: first, for coaches to understand themselves better and to enhance their own effectiveness, and second, to help

coachees make sense of their patterns of behaviour and meet their coaching objectives.

BASIC ASSUMPTIONS OF TYPE THEORY

The MBTI instrument is based on C G Jung's theory of psychological type, as interpreted by Katharine Briggs, and particularly by her daughter, Isabel Briggs Myers. Jung (1923) described three pairs of opposite psychological elements: the 'attitudes' of Extroversion and Introversion, and two pairs of 'functions' – the functions of perception, which he called Sensation and Intuition; and the functions of judgement, which he called Thinking and Feeling. Jung suggested that each of us has an innate predisposition for one of each of these pairs to become more developed in consciousness. The opposite element of each pair is less conscious and less under control of the ego.

Myers' term for this predisposition was 'preference': an in-born tendency to use one side of each of the opposites more naturally and with a greater sense of control. We can also use and develop skills associated with the other side, but it is likely to take more effort than using or developing skills in the preferred side. A useful summary is: 'We have both, we use both, we prefer one.'

Myers included four pairs of opposites within the MBTI framework: the three explicitly described by Jung, and a fourth that she believed was implicit within his writings – the orientations of Judging and Perceiving. These four dimensions have been extensively described in many publications, such as *Introduction to Type* (Myers and Kirby, 2000) and *LIFETypes* (Hirsh and Kummerow, 1989), and will be covered here only very briefly.

Summary of preferences

▌ Extroversion/Introversion (E/I) These are concerned with how we are energized. When we are in the extroverted attitude, our focus is on the outer world of people, things and action. When we are in the introverted attitude, our attention is on the inner world of private reflection.

▌ Sensing/Intuition (S/N – the second letter, 'N' is used for intuition, since 'I' has already been used to designate Introversion) These are concerned with how we take in information. When we are using sensing, we are attending to the specifics of reality as experienced through the five senses. When we are using intuition, we are attending to the patterns and possibilities suggested by the big picture.

▌ Thinking/Feeling (T/F) These are concerned with how we evaluate information and reach decisions. When we are using thinking, we are using non-personal logic to evaluate and decide. When we are using feeling, we are using personal values to evaluate and decide.

▌ Judging/Perceiving (J/P) These are concerned with how we approach the outer world. When we are using judging, we are approaching the world with an emphasis on decisions and closure. When we are using perceiving, we are approaching the world with an emphasis on openness to respond to ideas or events as they arise.

In each case, we are likely to use both sides every day; our preference is our 'default mode' – the one which comes more naturally, which tends to be more energizing, and which we do not have to work so hard to develop.

Type theory suggests that, all else being equal, we will tend to operate according to our preferences and to show the characteristics that are typical of our type. In practice, the environment – present and past – offers a host of demands, to which people adapt their behaviour. Type theory assumes that these demands do not change a person's type, but that they may well affect behaviour. For example, those preferring Perceiving are typically spontaneous and like to go with the flow, but may make extra efforts to be organized and planful if working in an environment that emphasizes plans and structure. Individuals are the best judges of their own type, as others can only go on behaviour – they do not know what is going on inside.

Two common misconceptions about the MBTI framework

MBTI theory is sometimes criticized by those who claim that, first, the theory pigeonholes you and limits you, and second, the theory ignores the impact of environment and learning on personality. Both of these criticisms stem from misconceptions.

First, people may assume that because the MBTI instrument comes out with one of 16 overall types, it assumes there are only 16 types of people. In fact there are many aspects of personality that are outside type theory, such as intelligence, neuroticism and self-confidence, giving ample scope for individual differences within the same MBTI type. The concept of preference is not limiting, as it allows for development of both preferred and non-preferred sides, and assumes that people develop and change in the way they express their type over a lifetime, as explained below.

Second, because type theory suggests that the preferences are inborn, some people assume that it denies that environment or learning have any influence. The discussion above will have made clear that, on the contrary, the theory assumes that environment and learning play a strong part in shaping the way that type is expressed.

Two underused areas of MBTI theory

Many MBTI practitioners confine themselves to working with clients at the level of individual preference pairs. While this has some value, experience shows that incorporating the following two advanced aspects of type theory will greatly enhance any application of type: first, the dynamic interaction between the elements of an individual's type (type dynamics); and second, the development of type over an individual's lifetime.

Type dynamics explains why a person's whole type is greater than the sum of the parts. It creates an integrated and more nuanced picture by putting the functions (S, N, T and F) into a hierarchy and by showing how some functions are typically used in relation to the outer world (extroverted) while others are typically used in relation to the inner world (introverted). Understanding this aspect of type often leads to major insights concerning clients' experiences and the perceptions they create. For example, the dynamics of type helped an INTJ coachee understand why colleagues primarily commented on how logical and decisive he was ('auxiliary extroverted Thinking'), although he felt more motivated by exploration of ideas and their connections in his inner world ('dominant introverted Intuition').

Type development concerns the shift in balance between conscious and unconscious processes over the course of a lifetime, and the way in which this affects people's expression of type at different stages. This aspect of type theory becomes particularly important when working with mature people who may be experiencing mid-life issues – a situation that often occurs in coaching.

We cannot give a full explanation of these complex areas in this chapter. They are well described in many publications, such as *Introduction to Type: Dynamics and development* (Myers and Kirby, 2000). The section later in this chapter headed 'The role of type development' gives examples of the usefulness of these ideas in coaching.

Summary of core assumptions of type theory

▌ It is concerned with preferences, which are not absolutes.
▌ Everybody uses both sides of each preference.
▌ Using and developing non-preferred sides requires more effort.
▌ Environment affects development and expression of preferences.
▌ Preferences are of equal intrinsic value.
▌ People are the best judge of their own type.

▌ The whole type is greater than the sum of the individual preferences.
▌ Expression of type changes and develops over a lifetime.

THE MBTI QUESTIONNAIRE

It is possible to work with the ideas of type without using any formal psychometric assessment, by remaining at the level of concepts and self-assessment. Usually, though, it is helpful to use a standardized instrument as a starting point for clients' self-understanding. The best-researched and validated instrument for working with type is the MBTI instrument. It is, in fact, the world's most frequently used personality assessment for personal development. The first form of the questionnaire was published in 1962 and it has been regularly updated since that time. It is now available in over 20 languages. As with many instruments, coaches who wish to use the MBTI questionnaire must be qualified to do so.

Taking the MBTI assessment involves two key elements. First, the individual completes the 88-item questionnaire, either online or on paper. This generally takes between 20 and 30 minutes. Scoring is a quick and easy process, either online or by hand.

Second, the MBTI practitioner works with the individual to help verify which of the 16 types fits him or her best. Usually, people are asked to make an initial self-assessment of their type on the basis of a description of the preferences, before seeing their reported type. This process reflects Myers' insistence that the MBTI instrument be seen as an aid to people's self-understanding rather than as a definitive test. The 'best-fit type' is the type settled on as right for the person, in the light of his or her self-assessment and reported type. In the majority of cases, this 'best-fit' is the same as reported type, but in a substantial minority there is a difference of one or more letters. Establishing the individual's best-fit type can take time, but is crucial if the model is to be meaningful and useful. If coachees say they have already 'done' the MBTI, it is wise to revisit the model, in order to check their understanding of the concepts and to make sure that they have had adequate opportunity to decide on their best-fit type.

The type verification process can be an integral part of coaching, providing a vehicle for greater understanding on the part of both coach and coachee. Coachees often have powerful experiences during the verification process. For some (particularly those whose type is different from most of those they work with) it is the first time their natural approach has been validated and supported. When coachees settle on their best-fit type, they often feel energized and connected to a source of intrinsic motivation.

MBTI AND COACHES

Building rapport and establishing purpose

A coach who understands and values the coachee's perspective naturally tends to build greater trust and rapport with the coachee (see Bayne, 2005, for further discussion on this). The MBTI framework is invaluable in supporting coaches here because it describes all types in constructive and non-evaluative ways. Any suggestion that the coach judges the client's views as 'wrong' will be counterproductive in a relationship where the emphasis is on facilitating a learning process for the client. At the same time, it is vital that the coach is authentic in his or her expression. This is particularly true if the coach uses techniques involving 'use of self' within the coaching process – for example, telling coachees about a reaction he or she experiences, within the session, to something the coachee says or does.

Coaches who are aware of their MBTI preferences and how these might be expressed in their coaching style are in a better position to minimize the risks of unhelpful conflict with clients of a different type, or unhelpful collusion with clients with similar preferences to themselves. Before looking at these issues more closely, we might ask whether there are MBTI types that are more common among executive coaches.

In a study by Passmore *et al* (2006), the most frequently occurring type in a sample of coaches was ENFP (19 per cent). This finding mirrors data from OPP Ltd that the most frequently occurring type attending courses to qualify to use the MBTI questionnaire is also ENFP. The Intuitive and Feeling preferences are also frequently found in professionals working in the areas of counselling. These findings are very different from the distribution of MBTI types found in the UK population in general (see below).

Table 3.1 MBTI type distribution of coaches (n=228)

ISTJ	ISFJ	INFJ	INTJ
0.9%	0.9%	7%	11%
ISTP	ISFP	INFP	INTP
1.3%	0.9%	11.4%	9.2%
ESTP	ESFP	ENFP	ENTP
0.4%	1.8%	18.9%	9.6%
ESTJ	ESFJ	ENFJ	ENTJ
5.7%	3.9%	9.2%	7.9%

Reproduced with permission from Passmore *et al* (2006).

Table 3.2 MBTI type distribution of UK population (n=1634)

ISTJ 13.7%	ISFJ 12.7%	INFJ 1.7%	INTJ 1.4%
ISTP 6.4%	ISFP 6.1%	INFP 3.2%	INTP 2.4%
ESTP 5.8%	ESFP 8.7%	ENFP 3.2%	ENTP 2.8%
ESTJ 10.4%	ESFJ 12.6%	ENFJ 2.8%	ENTJ 2.9%

The type distribution among coaches is also very different from distributions typically found in populations of managers and executives. In these populations, the four TJ types – ISTJ, ESTJ, INTJ and ENTJ – are found to predominate. This suggests that executive coaches will often find themselves working with clients with different preferences from their own, and should be aware of the challenges and benefits this presents.

Of course, not all coaches have preferences for N and F, and all 16 types are represented in the coaching profession. To some extent, the techniques favoured by coaches reflect their preferences. For example, Bayne (2004) found that those with a preference for Feeling tended to choose a counselling model for coaching, while those with a preference for Thinking were more likely to use a cognitive model.

The preferences of the coach are likely to influence how he or she sees the purpose of the work. For example, ESTJ or ENTJ coaches (who typically approach the world through the Thinking process, seeking order through logic) may emphasize their role in challenging clients to find solutions to issues, in order to meet organizational demands. By contrast, ENFJ or ESFJ coaches (who typically approach the world through the Feeling process, seeking harmony with their values) may be more concerned with supporting individuals to ensure that their personal development needs are met, with less emphasis on organizational requirements.

Coaching styles and techniques

Coaches with different type preferences are likely to differ in the type of information they gather, and the way they develop actions with the client. For example, a Sensing-preference coach may like to gather data that is tangible and to develop practical actions, while an Intuitive-preference coach may work more at the level of concept and metaphor, exploring possibilities at a more abstract level. Both approaches have their merits, but either will be less effective if used as the only available style. Effective coaches constantly review client needs, asking themselves whether these are being met by their current approach or whether they may need to 'flex' to a different style. Coachees of different types will have different learning styles and will be engaged by different techniques in the coaching process (Hirsh and Kise, 2000).

Table 3.3   Coaching styles related to dominant type preference

ESTJ/ENTJ (Extroverted Thinking)

Focus

∎ Sees coaching as an interesting challenge and an opportunity to affect business and individual effectiveness.

Style and approach

∎ Enjoys the problem-solving aspects of coaching.
∎ Tends to be assertive in expressing judgements.
∎ Likes to use challenge and debate.

ISTP/INTP (Introverted Thinking)

Focus

∎ Sees coaching as an opportunity for interesting problem solving.

Style and approach

∎ Analytical and incisive approach.
∎ Is comfortable with silence. Uses pauses to encourage clients to think or say more.
∎ Can appear critical and aloof.

ESFJ/ENFJ (Extroverted Feeling)

Focus

∎ Sees coaching as an opportunity to facilitate others in getting what they need and want.

Style and approach

∎ Warm and caring; will 'go the extra mile' for the client.
∎ Works from a basis of explicit, shared values.
∎ Can find it hard to remain detached; clients can become friends.

ISFP/INFP (Introverted Feeling)

Focus

∎ Sees coaching as an opportunity to create space and support for clients to live in accordance with their values.

Style and approach

∎ Wants to remain authentic and human during all interactions.
∎ Approach can seem unconventional to those with a preference for logical analysis.
∎ Tends to use own emotions as a barometer of the state of the client.

ENFP/ENTP (Extroverted Intuition)

Focus

▌ Sees coaching as an opportunity to explore and create new ideas and possibilities.

Style and approach

▌ Emergent, flexible and adaptable style.
▌ May be perceived as leaping around and going off at tangents.
▌ Optimistic and positive about possibilities for the future.

ESTP/ESFP (Extroverted Sensing)

Focus

▌ Sees coaching as an opportunity to have a tangible effect on the lives of others.

Style and approach

▌ Charming, fun-loving and energetic.
▌ Pragmatic focus on what will work in the here-and-now.
▌ Realistic and down to earth.

INFJ/INTJ (Introverted Intuition)

Focus

▌ Sees coaching as an opportunity to understand and make things meaningful.

Style and approach

▌ Reflective, serious and insightful.
▌ Can act as long range visionaries.
▌ Attributes symbolism to events.

ISTJ/ISFJ (Introverted Sensing)

Focus

▌ Sees coaching as an opportunity to use his/her accumulated experience to be of practical help to others.

Style and approach

▌ Reliable and steady.
▌ Uses tried-and-trusted approaches.
▌ Methodical and thorough.

Knowledge of a client's type will help the coach to choose a style most suited to that client. For example, Introverted clients may need more time before they will talk about what is really important to them and may value reading and time for reflection between sessions; an Extrovert would probably value plenty of time to talk things through in sessions and enjoy getting quickly into action and trying out new ways of doing things.

A Sensing client is likely to want to focus initially on the details of the current reality and history of his or her situation (often referred to as the problem frame) before being encouraged to consider future options (moving to an outcome frame). Many coaching approaches (eg the GROW model) suggest starting with the outcome frame or focusing on future goals before looking at the reality of current situation; this may need to be adapted to fit with the preferences of a Sensing type. An Intuitive client, by contrast, is likely to be enthused by the future focus as well as enjoying approaches using imagination and metaphor; such clients would need support and encouragement to examine the reality of their situation in more detail, and to plan concrete steps toward their future dreams.

Thinking clients typically want to understand the coaching process and techniques, and may come across as challenging as they seek to establish why the coach is following a particular path; they often enjoy cognitive-behavioural approaches while being less comfortable with exploring and revealing their feelings. Feeling clients are likely to be more concerned with the impact of change on their relationships and to value a warmer and more empathic approach from the coach. Judging clients value a structured and goal-oriented approach, and may need to be encouraged to spend more time exploring options before closing on a particular decision. Perceiving types prefer a more open-ended and spontaneous style, and may need to be encouraged to make choices for action rather than holding all options open.

Coaches need to provide a balance of challenge and support in working with coachees. This is tricky, as in judging what is appropriate the coach is always aiming at a moving target. At times, the client may need to be challenged or even confronted quite firmly; for some (although by no means all) Feeling-preference coaches this may feel insensitive. Conversely, a more supportive approach may be needed – this may be less comfortable for some Thinking-preference coaches. By understanding their own areas of comfort, coaches can make more conscious adaptations to the evolving interactions with clients.

Supervision is an important – many would say vital – ingredient in safe and effective coaching, as it provides an opportunity for coaches to look at their own needs and responses, and to guard against responding more to these than to those of the coachee. Finding the appropriate balance of challenge and support would be an obvious topic for such sessions. For example, one Feeling coach berated himself after one session for having had 'too cosy a chat' with a client who had the same preferences as himself. During supervision, he recognized that although this could have represented some form of collusion, it had served a useful role in establishing rapport. This gave him a sound base, from which he now needed to 'flex' to a more challenging style. Conversely, a Thinking coach worried that she had been 'too confrontational' with a Feeling-preference client. In supervision, she agreed that she needed to check how the coachee had felt following this session and to demonstrate concern for his well-being. At the same time, she realized that she might well have facilitated a useful stretch in him, by encouraging him to look at issues through an alternative and less-used lens.

Coach/coachee combinations

People sometimes ask whether some coach-client combinations of MBTI type are more successful than others. When there is type similarity, it can be easier for the coach to 'tune in' to the client. On the other hand, a coach who differs from the client may offer more in the way of fresh perspectives. Evidence is limited, but suggests, if anything, that coaching tends to be seen as more effective when there are differences (see, for example, Scoular and Linley, 2006).

It would be a mistake to over-interpret such findings as suggesting that a coach could not be effective with a client of similar type – this would ignore the host of other factors affecting the success of such relationships. It does, however, suggest that when coach and client are of similar type, the coach needs to ensure that they do not overlook areas that tend to be blind spots for them both. A valuable tool here is a model of problem solving which encourages systematic use of each of the four functions (S, N, T and F), as well as appropriate use of the attitudes/orientations (E/I and J/P). Versions of this model are found in various places, including the back of *Introduction to Type*.

MBTI AND COACHEES

Validating the coachee's natural style

One of the most important benefits of understanding type is that it enables coachees to make more conscious choices about the degree to which they adapt their natural style to the demands of the workplace. Coachees work within roles and organizational cultures that carry expectations about how they will behave. Typical business and managerial cultures tend to favour, in particular, the expression of Extroversion, Thinking and Judging. While these demands are not usually conscious or explicit, people soon pick up messages as to the kinds of behaviours that are expected and seen as 'right'.

Without a type perspective it might be assumed, by both coach and coachee, that a coachee who differs from the majority should just conform to the expectations of the culture. However, coachees are unlikely to achieve their best if they suppress their natural style, especially if they do this unconsciously, in response to the unspoken message that their natural approach is wrong. Often, their very difference is the area where they can make the greatest potential contribution. Learning about type often helps clients to feel good about themselves and their natural style, encouraging them to capitalize on their natural strengths, while recognizing that they may choose to make adaptations in order to be accepted and to influence others effectively.

For example, a coachee with a preference for Introversion was criticized by colleagues for not saying much at meetings. If the coach had simply encouraged him to speak up more, it is unlikely that he would ever have made his best contributions. Instead, the coach helped him to recognize the conditions that enabled him to formulate and express his ideas. The coachee then asked for simple changes to the way the meetings were run – such as having time in advance to consider agenda items, some quiet thinking time within the meeting itself, and turn-taking in offering responses. These changes allowed him greatly to increase his contribution, and it is also likely that the whole team benefited, as everybody tends to give better-quality responses when they use some balance of the Extroverted and Introverted attitudes.

Similarly, a Feeling-preference coachee received feedback that she was seen as 'too emotional' about issues. During coaching, she recognized how much the organization needed her willingness to speak up for values – but also that she needed to modify the style in which she expressed herself, to avoid being labelled and having her views dismissed. The MBTI framework helped her understand why she so often saw things differently from her peers, and why they seemed to ignore factors that seemed glaringly obvious to her. This helped her to feel less alienated and frustrated, which in turn made it easier for her to express her views firmly and confidently, without the edge of exasperation that had tended to turn off her colleagues.

Using the MBTI to raise coachee awareness of self and other

In the sections above, we have discussed examples of coachees finding ways to use their natural strengths within the demands of the culture. For coachees whose preferences match the prevailing culture, the issue tends to be a little different. Because expression of their preferences is reinforced by the culture, they may overuse their strengths and become one-sided. For such coachees, the type perspective offers insights into other ways of operating in the world that are equally important and valuable.

For example, a coachee with ESTJ preferences had always fitted in well with the no-nonsense, business-like atmosphere of his organization. His style had worked well for him early in his career in terms of achieving results, so he saw it as a winning formula. However, as he moved on he needed to work more through others. He received feedback that people found him abrupt and unapproachable, and that this turned them off. Table 3.4 shows coaching suggestions typically relevant for people of his type. The MBTI framework helped him to recognize the intrinsic value of paying attention to people's feelings, and he found that this had the additional benefit of helping him achieve tasks through people.

In many situations it is important to make at least some use of both preferred and non-preferred sides, for example in influencing and persuading others (Brock, 1994). In most cases, coachees will not know the specific MBTI types of their co-workers, but they can use the model to expand the range of influence tactics they employ. Similarly, in problem solving it is most effective not only to consider the reality and facts of a situation (Sensing) but also to envision future outcomes and possibilities (Intuition), to weigh up logically the pros and cons of a decision (Thinking), as well as to be aware of and consider impact on others (Feeling). Understanding type will help people to be aware of the strengths they offer in any situation as well as where their blind spots may be.

Table 3.4 Coaching suggestions for ESTJs

If you have this development need:	Try this suggested development practice:
Becoming so goal-focused that the impact of actions on others is overlooked.	Remember, people get things done and often work harder if their needs are considered in your plans. Acknowledge and reward contributions of others.
Being too rigid in your expectations of others, forgetting niceties.	Practise allowing some give and take. Start in small ways and work to increase openness and attentiveness to others.
Not making exceptions where others would.	Explore why others would make an exception, then determine whether the standard should be changed.
Exhibiting 'You can't argue with my success' syndrome.	Clarify whether you could have been even more successful by being less forceful. Are other areas of your life as successful?
Deciding before collecting all the necessary information.	Learn and use techniques of problem definition, brainstorming, and idea generating before rushing to act.

Overcoming these blind spots will often involve getting help from others. On learning about type, many coachees initially assume that they need to master everything and to develop equal competence in all areas. However, the task of the coach is more to encourage an attitude of openness to the opposite perspectives. Instead of trying to master non-preferred sides, it is helpful to encourage coachees to be curious – to ask questions relating to the non-preferred sides and listen openly to the responses (again, for examples of such questions, see the problem-solving model at the back of *Introduction to Type*). A useful strategy in coaching is to invite coachees to consider the people with whom they work, and to identify those who may offer complementary skills and perspectives to their own.

If the coachee makes a conscious effort to use the skills and preferences of others, this has benefits both for task and team. It is highly motivating for other team members to work with someone who is keen to use their skills and to understand their point of view – especially if that someone is the boss. Frequently, those co-workers who turn out to be of the most value to coachees are people they have previously found difficult or dismissed. For some coachees, the coach's support is crucial in helping them deal with the discomfort of accepting that they may have misjudged someone, or that they do not have all the answers.

For example, a coachee with a Sensing preference had a difficult relationship with a colleague, whom he regarded as a 'head in the clouds' type. The MBTI framework helped him to see this person as a potential resource, offering balance to his own practical, realistic approach. Nevertheless, he felt uncomfortable about appealing to this man for help. Through discussion and role play, he realized that he had an emotional resistance that stemmed from a fear of appearing weak. Once this was made conscious, he was able to overcome the resistance and the relationship became much more productive.

The role of type development

As has been mentioned earlier, type is not a static model of personality differences, but rather views preferences in the context of a dynamic system that develops over time. The confidence and effectiveness with which an individual develops his or her preferences depends on the degree to which the environment has supported expression of those preferences. In addition, the emphasis of type development changes over time. Early on (childhood, teenage and early adult years), it is important to specialize in those areas that come naturally, in order to develop them most effectively – to play to one's strengths. With increasing maturity, it becomes more important to develop flexibility and balance in the use of both sides of the preferences. For a fuller outline of type development, see Myers and Kirby (2000).

This means that people of the same type may come to coaching with very different needs and goals due to their life experience and stage of type development. Having an understanding of such type developmental issues can be very helpful in ascertaining what the client most needs from the coaching. We have already seen that for people whose environment has not encouraged expression of their preferences, coaching can have an important role in helping them 'come home' and work comfortably in their natural style. We have also seen that coachees whose environment has supported their natural types may become one-sided and need to develop balance.

With increasing maturity (40s onwards), a further scenario arises which calls for more balance in the individual. This is the stage that Jung termed 'mid-life'. Now it is not the outer world demanding flexibility, but the intrinsic dynamic of the personality, calling for internal balance. At this point the specialization stage diminishes and there comes a stage of integration (see Myers and Kirby, 2000). The development of the innate preferences starts to run out of energy and there is a pull back to those parts of the individual that have been less developed and remain more unconscious. An analogy might be the stretching of an elastic band; the more it is stretched in one direction, the greater the pull back in the opposite direction.

Coachees at this stage may experience loss of meaning and direction in relation to their current lifestyle and they may wish to explore changes of career direction. They may experience the pull of unfamiliar ways of being, which may feel uncomfortable and threatening as they oppose their more usual identity. This can be a confusing time, and type can be very effective in helping clients to understand what they are experiencing as well as finding ways to integrate new ways of being without losing the original strengths of specialization. For a very useful discussion of coaching issues with mid-life clients, see Fitzgerald (2002).

SUMMARY

As emphasized throughout this chapter, the MBTI framework is a tool for personal development and growth, both for coaches and coachees. We can use its insights to recognize the areas that come easily and the areas where we need to work harder – without taking these as limitations. As a framework for raising self-awareness, it can enable us to make more conscious choices about the way we approach our work. We can also use the framework to be gentle with ourselves and others, remembering that 'we can use type to understand and forgive ourselves, although not as an excuse'.

References

Bayne, RS (2004) *Psychological Types at work: An MBTI perspective*, Thomson, London

Bayne, RS (2005) *Ideas and Evidence: Critical Reflections on MBTI theory and practice*, CAPT, Gainesville, FL

Brock, SA (1994) *Using Type in Selling: Building customer relationships with the Myers–Briggs Type Indicator*, Consulting Psychologists Press, Palo Alto

Fitzgerald, C (2002) Understanding and supporting development of executives at midlife, in *Executive Coaching: Practices and Perspectives*, pp89–117 ed C Fitzgerald and JG Berger, Davies-Black, Palo Alto

Hirsh, S and Kise, A (2000) *Introduction to Type and Coaching: A dynamic guide for individual development*, Consulting Psychologists Press, Palo Alto

Hirsh, S and Kummerow, J (1989) *LIFETypes*, Warner Books, New York

Jung, CG (1923) *Psychological Types*, Kegan Paul, London

Myers, IB and Kirby, LK (2000) *Introduction to Type: Dynamics and development*, Consulting Psychologists Press, Palo Alto

Myers, IB, Kirby, LK and Myers, KD (2000) *Introduction to Type: A guide to understanding your results on the Myers–Briggs Type Indicator*, 6th edn, European English Edition, Oxford Psychologists Press, Oxford

Myers, IB, McCaulley, MH, Quenk, NL and Hammer, AL (1998) *MBTI Manual: A guide to the development and use of the Myers–Briggs Type Indicator*, 3rd edn

Passmore, J, Rawle-Cope, M, Gibbes, C and Holloway, M (2006) MBTI types and executive coaching, *The Coaching Psychologist*, **2**(3), pp 6–10

Scoular, A and Linley, A (2006) Coaching, goal setting and personality type: what matters? *The Coaching Psychologist*, **2**(1), pp 9–12

®MBTI, Myers–Briggs Type Indicator and Introduction to Type are registered trademarks of the Myers–Briggs Type Indicator Trust.

4

Coaching with teams

Team Management Systems (TMS)

Dick McCann

INTRODUCTION

Effective coaching is an intensive and transformational learning process. To deliver on learner needs, coaches are required to generate deep levels of coachee insight, awareness and understanding. Additionally, they must help create a sustainable way forward for their coachees and organizational clients. To excel at this, the coach must master a variety of skills.

In this chapter we will look at how coaches can improve their skills by integrating a variety of instruments developed by Team Management Systems (TMS) into a coaching process for individuals and teams.[1] The basis for this framework is the Workplace Behaviour Pyramid, which gives personal feedback on three measures of workplace behaviour: preferences, risk and values. This information provides an 'in-depth' answer to the question 'Who am I?' – a fundamental starting point for personal and team development. This can be measured against the question 'What is expected of me?' to develop a personal learning action plan that charts the way forward for the coachee.

COACHING COMPETENCIES

Coaching models and associated competency frameworks abound. As an example of the type of skills considered critical, the International Coach Federation (www.coachfederation.org) provides a reasonably straight-forward set of 11 'core coaching competencies', clustered into four groups.

∎ The first cluster of competencies addresses 'Setting the Foundation'. This includes two competencies, Meeting Ethical Guidelines and Professional Standard, and Establishing the Coaching Agreement.
∎ The second cluster focuses on 'co-creating the relationship', and includes both establishing trust and intimacy with the coachee, and coaching presence.
∎ The next cluster is concerned with 'communicating effectively', covering the three competencies of active listening, powerful questioning and direct communication.
∎ The final cluster is geared towards 'facilitating learning and results', containing four skills of creating awareness, designing actions, planning and goal setting, and managing progress and accountability.

Team Management Systems (TMS) can be incorporated within all four clusters. The self-awareness generated through the TMS Profiles is critical for both coach and coachee throughout the entire process. For example, in terms of establishing intimacy and trust with the coachee, coaches need to understand and respect the learning style and approach of the coachee, as well as the impact their own approach has on the coaching relationship.

However, it is within the last cluster, 'facilitating learning and results' that the application of TMS is most evident. Typically, it is in this area that TMS is applied as a coaching tool, providing the frameworks, the language and the data to enable meaningful and focused discussion geared towards 'awareness creation' and 'action planning'. By offering a clear and practical frame of reference, coach and coachee can work together to analyse and evaluate the current reality and determine how best to proceed to a new future.

TMS also has a role to play in the third set of competencies, 'communicating effectively', where the TMS tools can chart the best way to develop the necessary rapport between coach and coachee, as well as developing improved communications between the coachee and his or her team.

Three personal TMS feedback profiles form the basis of both leadership coaching and team coaching. The tools highlight many of the interrelated factors affecting workplace behaviour and impacting personal effectiveness. They help coachees establish an honest understanding of who they are by providing a language for personal, team and organizational development.

A particular benefit of TMS within a professional coaching context is the explicit link back to work processes. While maintaining psychometric rigour, all models were developed so that the terminology was self-explanatory and readily understood by those without a psychology background. This makes it much easier to deliver effectively in the coaching competency clusters.

THE WORKPLACE BEHAVIOUR PYRAMID

Perhaps the greatest challenge facing leaders and their teams is to understand why people behave the way they do. The TMS framework addresses this using the Workplace Behaviour Pyramid (Figure 4.1) which defines three levels of workplace behaviour – preference, risk and values. The three associated personal TMS feedback profiles form the basis of both leadership coaching and team coaching. The tools highlight many of the interrelated factors affecting workplace behaviour and personal effectiveness. They help coachees establish an honest understanding of who they are by providing a language for personal, team and organizational development.

Figure 4.1　The Workplace Behaviour Pyramid

Values

At the base of the pyramid are values. These are fundamental concepts or beliefs that people use to guide their behaviour in the workplace. Values will drive our decision making and cause us to summon up energy to preserve what we believe in. They go beyond specific situations and determine how we view people, behaviour and events. Often, major sources of conflict and disillusionment are due to mismatched values. Whereas we are often willing to work on tasks that we dislike, we are much less likely to compromise when our values are under threat.

Values are difficult to observe in others, as they are inner concepts often buried in the human psyche and not readily accessible by the conscious mind. When these values are violated, then the conscious mind takes over and appropriate behaviour occurs to preserve and defend this attack.

Workplace values can be measured by the Window on Work Values (McCann, 2002a). This is a model that groups values into clusters of eight 'value types', which are depicted as window panes, rather like those in the rose windows of many European cathedrals (see Figure 4.2). The model has good structural validity, meaning that value types close to one another in the window are related, whereas those on opposite sides of the window are unrelated.

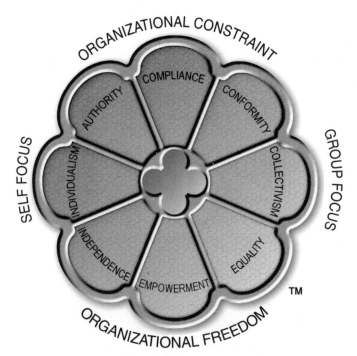

Figure 4.2 Window on Work Values

Risk

The middle layer of the Workplace Behaviour Pyramid addresses the way people approach risk. The behaviours associated with this operate at the middle level of the human psyche. They are not so fundamental as values, as they can be influenced to some extent by the work environment and the attitudes of colleagues.

All through our life we are faced with opportunities and obstacles; they crop up in every project we undertake no matter how much forward planning is undertaken. What determines people's risk profiles is the different emphasis they place on either 'seeing the opportunities' or 'seeing the obstacles'. Some people treat obstacles as an opportunity to take a new direction, while others use them as an excuse to give up. Some people treat obstacles as stumbling blocks but for others they are stepping-stones to the future.

People's approach to risk is calculated from five sub-scales: Optimism, Moving Towards Goals (MTG) Energy, Multi-pathways, Faultfinding and Time Focus. These are represented by the risk-orientation model in Figure 4.3. These scales load to produce an opportunities score and an obstacles score. The ratio is called the QO2® (McCann, 2002a).

Figure 4.3 The risk-orientation model

Preferences

Preferences are dimensions of individual differences in tendencies to show consistent patterns of relationships, thoughts, feelings and actions. They determine the conditions we set up to allow our mental and psychic processes to flow freely. They guide our behaviour, but if we have to work outside them at various times then we can usually cope. Preferences are just another name for what we like doing. Often our preferences at work are different from our preferences outside work, leading to the distinguishing labels of work preferences and non-work preferences.

Preferences are usually transparent and are often the first thing we notice in others – 'He's rather quiet, isn't he?' or 'She never stops talking.' Some people prefer to think things through on their own while others need to talk out loud to clarify their ideas. Preferences are readily visible to others and are usually the basis of first impressions.

When we are working to our preferences we set up conditions where our psychic energy can flow freely. If we are more extroverted we like work where there are lots of interactions with others, both inside and outside the organization. If we are more introverted, then we like conditions where we can work on our own with few interruptions and a minimal requirement for meetings. Under these conditions our energy can flow freely with little resistance. Just as electrical energy generates heat when it meets resistance, so our psychic energy generates tension and stress when it has to flow through areas that are not our preference. This leads to wasted energy and eventually lower performance, reduced productivity and even poorer health.

The main difference between preferences (apex) and values (base) is that preferences are enduring dispositions whereas values are enduring goals. Preferences vary in the frequency and intensity of their occurrence whereas values vary in their importance as guiding principles of behaviour. People believe that their values are desirable, at least to a significant reference group, whereas preferences may be considered by them to be positive or negative. People may explain their behaviour by referring to either their preferences or values, but they refer to their values when they wish to justify choices or actions as legitimate or worthy.

Although all three levels are important in the TMS coaching approach, I shall focus mainly on the apex of the Pyramid as an example of the TMS process, which is replicated when working with the middle and base levels of the Pyramid.

THE NATURE OF WORK

In order to understand the concept of work preferences it is first necessary to understand the nature of work in a modern organization. Some years ago

Charles Margerison and I researched the nature of work carried out in successful teams. Our job analytic approach looked at the activities of team members that made a difference between good and poor performance in their jobs. The data fell naturally into eight work functions, described in Table 4.1.

Table 4.1 Types of work functions

Advising	Gathering and reporting information
Innovating	Creating and experimenting with ideas
Promoting	Exploring and presenting opportunities
Developing	Assessing and developing the applicability of new approaches
Organizing	Establishing and implementing ways of making things work
Producing	Concluding and delivering outputs
Inspecting	Controlling and auditing the working of systems
Maintaining	Upholding and safeguarding standards and processes

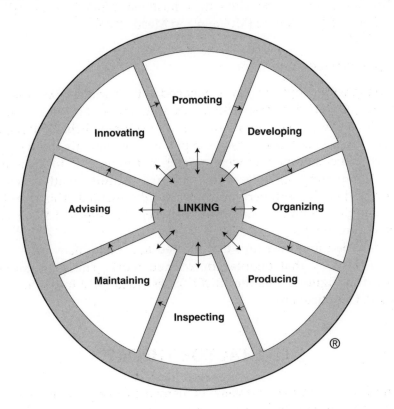

Figure 4.4 Margerison–McCann Types of Work Wheel

Confirmatory factor analysis on large samples by the Institute of Team Management Studies (McCann and Mead, 2008) has shown the existence of four main factors in this model, which when combined can describe the critical work functions of most jobs. Innovating, Promoting and Developing load mainly onto Factor 1, Organizing loads mainly onto Factor 2, Producing and Inspecting load mainly onto Factor 3, and Advising and Maintaining load mainly onto Factor 4.

The centre part of the wheel defines Linking – a process of coordinating and integrating the work of others. Linking needs to be applied to all work tasks regardless of their content. For example, those who have Inspecting as a critical function within the team must do it in a linking way to avoid being labelled a 'police interrogator'. Those who have Organizing as a critical function must do it in a linking way to avoid being seen as 'too pushy'.

The theory of the Types of Work Wheel postulates that differing jobs have different critical functions, and these require people of the requisite skills and competencies in order to perform them to a high level. For example, a job analysis of 587 finance and accounting positions shows the top three work functions to be Organizing, Producing and Inspecting. Compare this with 310 design/R&D jobs where the critical work functions are Advising, Innovating and Developing (McCann and Mead, 2008).

Work preferences

In speaking with people primarily engaged in the various work functions – Promoting, Organizing, Inspecting, Advising and so on – we found that those who really enjoyed their work showed common behavioural characteristics. 'Promoting' people, for example, were commonly more outgoing whereas 'inspecting' people were quieter and more able to focus on the detail. 'Innovating' people were obviously quite creative, whereas 'producing' people were very much practically oriented. This then led us into attempting to find a relationship between the 'Types of Work Wheel' and work preferences.

We identified four measures that seemed to explain many of the differences in the way that people approached work. These measures are presented in Figure 4.5 as the RIDO scales (Relationships, Information, Decisions, Organization).

FIVE-FACTOR THEORY

Over the last 20 years or so the views of many personality psychologists have converged regarding the structure and concepts of personality. Generally,

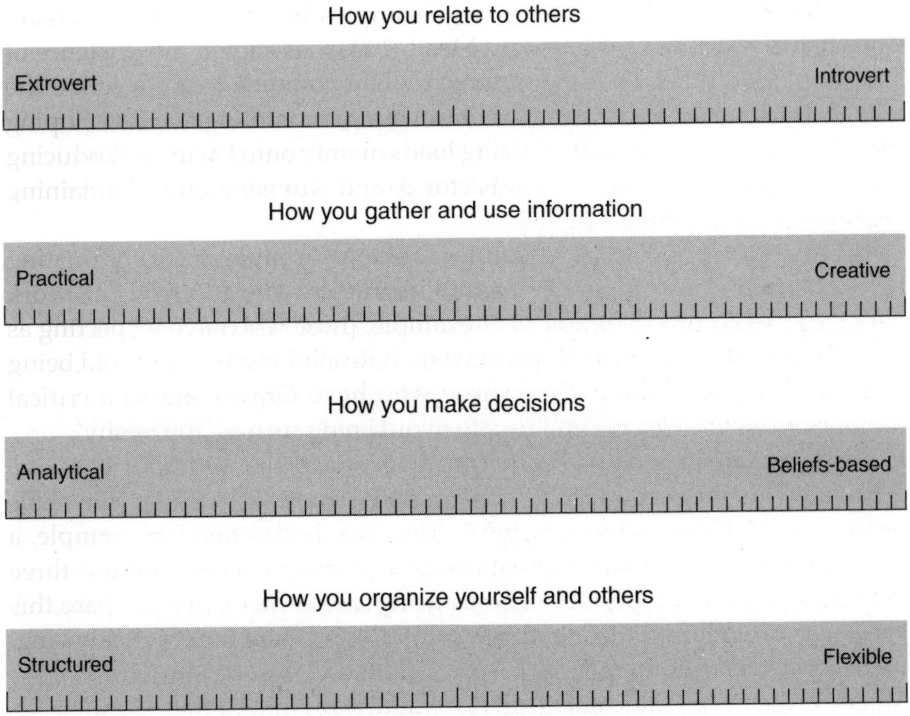

How you relate to others

Extrovert		Introvert

How you gather and use information

Practical		Creative

How you make decisions

Analytical		Beliefs-based

How you organize yourself and others

Structured		Flexible

Figure 4.5   The RIDO work preference scales

researchers agree that there are five robust factors of personality that can serve as a meaningful taxonomy for classifying personal attributes. A good summary of the various approaches is given by Barrick and Mount (1991).

It is widely agreed that the first factor is Extroversion/Introversion. Characteristics frequently associated with Extroversion include being sociable, gregarious, assertive, talkative and active.

There is also general agreement about the second factor, which has most frequently been called Emotional Stability, Stability, Emotionality or Neuroticism (McCrae and Costa, 1985; Noller, Law and Comrey, 1987; Norman, 1963; Smith, 1967). High scorers are defined by characteristics such as anxiety, angry hostility, depression, self-conscientiousness, impulsiveness and vulnerability. Low scorers tend to be calm, poised and emotionally stable.

The third factor has generally been interpreted as Agreeableness or Likeability (McCrae and Costa, 1985; Norman, 1963; Smith, 1967). Characteristics often associated with this dimension are being courteous, flexible, trusting, good-natured, cooperative, forgiving, soft-hearted and tolerant.

The fourth factor has most frequently been called Conscientiousness or Conscience (McCrae and Costa, 1985; Noller, Law and Comrey, 1987; Norman; 1963) although some researchers have referred to it as Conformity or Dependability or even Will to Achieve. As the variation in labels suggests, there is some disagreement in the content of this dimension, although the concepts seem to embrace the ideas of being careful, thorough, responsible, organized and planning-oriented.

The last factor has been the most difficult to identify. It has sometimes been interpreted as Intellect or Intelligence (Borgatta, 1964; Peabody and Goldberg, 1989) or Openness to Experience (McCrae and Costa, 1985) or even Culture (Hakel, 1974; Norman, 1963). Digman (1990) points out that it is most likely all of these. Characteristics commonly associated with this dimension include being imaginative, cultured, curious, original, broad-minded, intelligent and artistically sensitive.

Probably the most common five-factor model used is the NEO Personality Inventory (McCrae and Costa, 1997). The five factors here are defined as Extroversion, Neuroticism, Agreeableness, Conscientiousness and Openness to Experience. This model is not based on any single theory of personality but has been derived from the identification of independent factors that psychometrically describe large data sets. Another popular measure – the Myers–Briggs Type Indicator® (MBTI)® – addresses four of these factors, and both are explored more deeply in the chapters on Wave and MBTI.[2]

In relating the five factors to work preferences, the first factor is clearly a measure of work preference, describing the way people like to relate with others.

The second factor (Neuroticism) is clearly not a work preference but is incorporated into the middle section of the Workplace Pyramid where risk-orientation is assessed.

The third factor shows many of the characteristics impacting decision making and was adapted to the Analytical-Beliefs work preference scale.

The fourth factor has a wide content domain but the aspects that seemed to relate to work preferences were embodied in the measure of how people like to approach information – looking for the ideas, theories and concepts (the 'big picture') rather than the 'down-to-earth' data that applies to the real world.

The fifth factor is clearly a preference associated with organization and led to the identification of the work preference scale of Structure-Flexible.

THE TEAM MANAGEMENT WHEEL

The unique contribution of our research has been to combine the model of the nature of work to the four work preferences measures, creating the Team

Management Wheel. People with preferences for extroverted relationships and creative information gathering mapped most often into the Promoting area of the Types of Work Wheel. Those who tended towards introverted relationships and practical information-gathering most often preferred Inspecting work. Those who liked analytical decision making and who preferred to work in a structured way showed a bias for Organizing work, whereas those with beliefs in decision making and a more flexible approach to the way they organize themselves and others enjoyed Advising work. The development of this relationship is explained in the TMS Research Manual (McCann and Mead, 2008).

The model combining the RIDO scales and the work functions (Figure 4.6) was visually simplified to produce the Team Management Wheel, shown in Figure 4.7 (Margerison and McCann, 1995). Because 'people characteristics' were combined with a definition of work functions, double-barrelled words were used to create a description of 'role preferences'. Brief descriptions of these are given in Table 4.2.

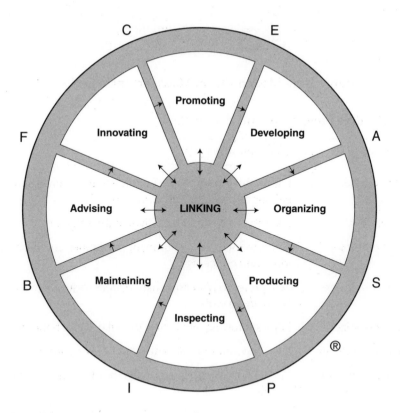

Figure 4.6 Mapping of the work preferences onto the Types of Work Wheel

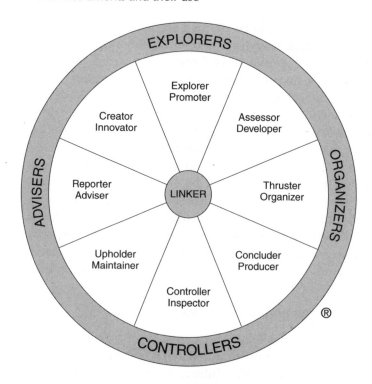

Figure 4.7   Margerison–McCann Team Management Wheel

Table 4.2   Role preferences and characteristics

Role preference	Characteristics
Reporter–adviser	Enjoys the reporting function in a team by giving and gaining as much information as possible
Creator–innovator	Likes to create ideas and diverge their thinking
Explorer–promoter	Tends to focus on exploring opportunities and promoting ideas and concepts
Assessor–developer	Will prefer to plan and analyse ideas to see how they can be made to work
Thruster–organizer	Enjoys thrusting into action to make things happen
Concluder–producer	Likes to work systematically and deliver outputs
Controller–inspector	Prefers control processes where he/she can focus on details
Upholder–maintainer	Likes to put principles first by upholding and maintaining standards

Each role preference can be divided further into two sub-groups, highlighting the different ways that people tend to approach their preferred work function. For example, some Creator-Innovators will work quietly on their own ideas, using their preference for analytical decision making to move from one idea to the next. Others may gather many of their ideas from other people or through conversation, evaluating the possibilities against their beliefs. Further breakdowns of the model show 208 distinct areas, with subtle changes occurring in the interplay between major and related roles.

The location of a person's major and related role preferences on the Team Management Wheel is identified by his or her responses to the Team Management Profile Questionnaire. The resulting feedback report – the Team Management Profile (TMP) – is the basis for a coaching session where the coachee's work preferences form the basis of a 'Who am I?' discussion, placed within a framework of the relationship between the coachee and the rest of the team.

The Team Management Profile Questionnaire

The development of the Team Management Profile Questionnaire (TMPQ) entailed the collation of more than 100 items that a priori seemed to measure the four constructs Extroversion-Introversion, Practical-Creative, Analytical-Beliefs and Structured-Flexible. The majority of these items were gleaned from statements either written down on flip charts or spoken by managers participating in discussions during management workshops. Other items were added from time to time that, from previous research and further experience, seemed to reflect the relevant construct. These items therefore represented a broad sample of the behaviour and cognitive styles of managers that could best and most economically explain the differences in work preferences. The original item-bank was subject to eight or nine revisions in the early stages as items were revised, dropped or added on the basis of expert judgement and testing trials. The items were eventually thinned to 15 measuring each of the four constructs, and these 60 items became the development form of the Team Management Profile Questionnaire. This was then refined by further testing to create a commercial version of the questionnaire (Margerison and McCann, 1984–2005).

Many samples have been analysed as various language versions of the questionnaire were created. There are currently 16 different language versions of the TMPQ in European, Asian, North America and South American languages. For example, one English sample of 275 (McCann and Mead, 2008) gave Cronbach alphas all above 0.8, test–retest coefficients above 0.76 and intercorrelation coefficients (Pearson Product Moment) all below 0.32 (absolute value).

Similar research processes were used in the development of the question-naires (McCann, 2000, 2002b) that measure approach to risk and personal work values.

Using TMS with coaches

We all live in a world containing thousands of different people and objects – the so-called 'real world'. Yet we do not operate directly on that real world but create our own model through perceptions and experiences. It is through this model that we value and assess our interactions with the world.

We can see some of these differences when we examine the Team Management Wheel. Those in opposite parts of the wheel will approach their work differently. In the case of Risk we see those whose model of the world is one of 'opportunities' while others mainly see 'obstacles'. In the values area we have again a variety of patterns around an eight-sector model.

When people from different parts of the Team Management Wheel interact, there is potential for conflict to arise, as different models of the world are interacting. When opposites come together, there is a great potential for things to go wrong and any discussion or conversation may well be doomed before the first word has been uttered.

This is particularly important in the interaction between coach and coachee. This interaction is a cybernetic process where a feedback loop between the two people will either lead to a rapport or become unstable and lead to an ineffective outcome. Cybernetic theory shows that those elements in a loop that have the greatest adaptability will gain control of the dynamics. An experienced coach will know this and design the coaching process to allow for the dynamics of the 'loop' that exists between coach and coachee. In TMS terms this is known as the concept of Pacing – a technique for temporarily modifying your model of the world so that it matches the other person's. This matching shows the other person that you understand and appreciate 'where they are coming from'.

As an example, consider a coachee with a role preference of Concluder-Producer. Each TMP will have a section on Linking which indicates the way that person likes others to interact with him or her. The coachee's profile (Concluder-Producer) may contain the following advice on how the coach might best interact with them. The word 'you' below implies the 'coachee'.

The coach should:

▌ suggest practical rather than theoretical solutions;
▌ give you time to think things through;
▌ allow you to finish your point and not interrupt, particularly if you like to choose your words to avoid ambiguity;

- ask for clarification if they don't understand what you are saying;
- back their arguments with facts;
- converge towards actions and results rather than rambling and wasting time;
- preferably make an appointment to see you, rather than just 'dropping in';
- be punctual to meetings;
- stick to agendas;
- use a whiteboard to record the details discussed, thus helping you to capture key points and keep on top of the details;
- help you to see the 'big picture', where necessary;
- summarize the content of conversations, making sure the summaries are succinct and factual, rather than the coach's opinions;
- give you one or two options rather than a long list, when wanting a decision from you.

This helps the coach to plan the best way of interacting with the coachee. If the coach is a strong Creator-Innovator with a preference for opening up and exploring issues and a reluctance to close things down and focus on small detail, then this information can help the coach plan a session that is more structured and one that converges on action and results rather that being vague and 'big picture', as is often the tendency with Creator-Innovators.

The coach's profile will also contain advice that may be very useful to the coachee in getting the best from the coach. At the start of the coaching session the coach can use the TMP to show how work preferences vary from person to person. By sharing his or her profile results with the coachee, the coach sets up the conditions for open and honest interaction.

The other TMS tools give similar information. For example, the Opportunities-Obstacles (QO2(r)) Profile will give useful information to the coach about a coachee with a high QO2(r). Table 4.3 gives appropriate 'Dos and Don'ts' for this situation.

Work values can also affect the relationship between coach and coachee and the Windows on Work Values will bring this out. Coachees who strongly value Individualism, Authority and Compliance may be more difficult to deal with, particularly if the coach is driven by Empowerment and Equality.

Using TMS with coachees

The full TMS suite of coaching tools contains eight profiles covering personal and leadership coaching, team coaching and organizational development. All profiles are linked to visual models, which we have found to be very important in facilitating coachee learning.

Table 4.3 Pacing the High QO2 Person

Dos

▮ Be initially supportive and listen.

▮ Try to sound positive about their ideas even if you disagree.

▮ Focus on the good part of their proposal before you explain what the difficulties are.

▮ Encourage them to describe the changes that might need to be made to implement their ideas, then point out any obstacles that might arise.

▮ Be prepared for their ideas to be unrealistic but look for the 'kernel' of a good idea.

Don'ts

▮ Don't tell them why their ideas won't work; help them to see this themselves.

▮ Don't dwell on the past.

▮ Don't criticize them personally.

▮ Don't appear negative or lacking in enthusiasm.

There are many possible processes to follow when using TMS tools but they all start with the establishment of clear goals and outcomes. This will involve a three-way discussion between coach, coachee and the organizational client. In this way a benchmark can be established for a later ROI (return on investment) evaluation – something that has become critical to most HR interventions in recent times.

Personal/leadership coaching

Here we tend to use a framework based around eight questions:

▮ What is expected of me?
▮ Who am I?
▮ Where am I now?
▮ Where am I going?
▮ How will I get there?
▮ What support do I need?
▮ How effective am I?
▮ What recognition do I get?

It is in the first three questions that TMS tools have a particular role to play in personal and leadership development.

Often the Types of Work Wheel is first presented as a work-based model and discussions are held to relate the umbrella descriptions of the work functions to the content of the coachee's tasks. It is explained to the coachee that all of these functions are probably done in the execution of his or her job but that usually two or three of the functions are critical to success. The discussion focuses on determining these critical success factors.

The next question is whether the coachee's supervisor(s) would have a similar view of the critical success factors. Coachees then start to realize that alignment between their view of the critical success factors and those of key stakeholders in the organization is fundamental to future success. If they are uncertain, we might suggest that a Types of Work Profile is administered. This is a multi-rater profile that compares the views of jobholder with those of the supervisor and other key stakeholders.

The process may then move on to addressing the question of 'Who am I?' and this usually starts with work preference feedback using the Team Management Profile. In this profile, some 4,000 words cover key areas of Work Preferences, Leadership Strengths, Interpersonal Skills, Decision Making, Team Building and Linking. At this stage the coach may share his or her own TMP with the coachee as a way of establishing a closer rapport. Usually the coachee is given time to digest the report and the discussion continued at the next meeting.

At this meeting coachees are encouraged to talk about those aspects of the report they agreed with by expanding on the comments and relating them to specific scenarios at work. Those areas they disagree with are also discussed and logged for revisiting later in the process. The TMP is written in positive terms, highlighting the strengths of the coachees' role preferences and how they relate to the critical functions on the Types of Work Wheel.

The next step focuses on 'Where am I now?' and this involves mapping the Team Management Profile onto the Types of Work Wheel. An example of the mapping process is shown in Figure 4.8. Here Mary Johnson's work preference distribution from the Team Management Profile is shown on the right-hand Wheel and her assessment of the critical functions in her job are given on the left-hand side. These can than be overlaid to produce the match data in Figure 4.9.

Figure 4.9 shows that Mary is happy with the Developing functions of her job but would prefer to be doing significantly less Organizing and Maintaining, and significantly more Promoting. If Mary's supervisor had been asked to rate the critical aspects of her job, then Mary's view could be compared with her supervisor's view. This data might then initiate a substantial discussion around the questions of 'Who am I?' and how this relates to 'What is expected of me?'

JOB DEMAND/WORK PREFERENCE MATCH DATA

Name: Mary Johnson

Rating Group: Job Holder

Job Title: Human Resources Manager

TMP Net Scores: E:18 C:17 B:8 F:1

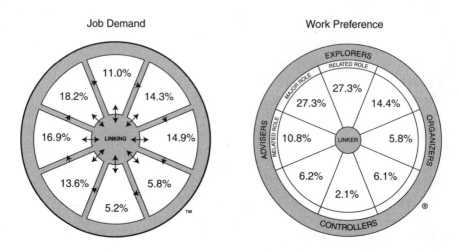

Figure 4.8 Sample job demand/work preference match

The data from the Team Management Profile and Types of Work Profile help establish the picture of 'Where am I now?' A similar process can be used with the Opportunities-Obstacles (QO2) Profile and the Values Profiles. From here the coach can help the coachee move to the future – 'Where am I going?'

Here coachees might talk about the things they would like to be doing in the future that would give them increased success and satisfaction. The profile information makes this discussion easy for the coach as it enables the gaps between the future and the present to be related to the TMS models. If the coachee has a strong preference for the Concluder-Producer role and wants to move to a future job focusing on the areas of Promoting and Developing, then the coach is able to point out those areas of personal development that might hasten this move.

For example, a career that focuses mainly on the Promoting work function requires an emphasis on finding things out by interacting and sharing ideas with others. There is a focus on exploring new ideas, asking questions and networking. Jobs that are strongly oriented to Promoting require a high degree of contact with people both inside and outside of the organization.

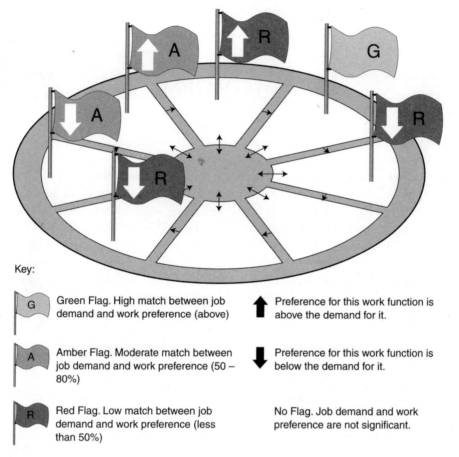

Key:

G — Green Flag. High match between job demand and work preference (above)

⬆ Preference for this work function is above the demand for it.

A — Amber Flag. Moderate match between job demand and work preference (50 – 80%)

⬇ Preference for this work function is below the demand for it.

R — Red Flag. Low match between job demand and work preference (less than 50%)

No Flag. Job demand and work preference are not significant.

Figure 4.9 Sample flagged match of job demand to work preferences

Many Promoting jobs have a high 'communications' component where involvement may be required in several different activities at the same time. The coachee would therefore need to be comfortable with 'multi-tracking', and in general enjoy being with people.

This then moves the coaching process into the question of 'How will I get there?' Among other things, the coach may focus on the coachee's extroversion score and how this might be increased to better match the requirements of Promoting.

The remaining questions of 'What support do I need?', 'How effective am I?' and 'What recognition do I get?' are often built into the Personal Learning Action Plan – the PLAP. Here the coachee addresses the issues of:

▌ What do I want to learn?
▌ What resources do I need?

▌ Who can help me?
▌ How will I know I am on the right track?

TEAM COACHING

Team coaching is a fast-growing area as many people realize that huge increases in performance can be obtained by involving the whole team (not just the leader) in an action-coaching process. A good place to start is with a benchmark that measures current team performance. The Team Performance Profile is the tool we use for this as it measures the team performance perceptions of all team members, supervisors and other key stakeholders against the nine factors of the Types of Work Wheel. This addresses any issues of 'group think' that may currently reside in the team psyche.

A priorities checklist based on the Types of Work Wheel is sometimes a good starting point and the team coach may propose the following checklist for discussion:

▌ What information does the team need that it is currently lacking?
▌ Are we doing things in the best way?
▌ Who are the key stakeholders that we need to influence?
▌ Are we developing products/services that the stakeholders want?
▌ Are we well enough organized?
▌ Are our products/services clearly defined in terms of outputs and outcomes?
▌ What details need checking more thoroughly?
▌ Are we maintaining our standards?
▌ Are we well enough linked together?
▌ What external links do we need to develop?

Each team member also completes a Team Management Profile and this is compared against the critical work functions of each person's job. A team-mapping process will then show the degree of team balance in terms of work function performance and collective work preference. Many teams are unbalanced in terms of role preference and this is often responsible for a lack of focus on some work functions. The principles involved in this part of team coaching are highlighted in the case study below.

AN ACTION-PACKED TEAM

The directors of a large industrial contracting organization requested help as they were having problems with their decision-making process.

This company was a family business that had grown rapidly and now had five directors. They had built up a reputation for being efficient project managers. Their contracts were invariably completed to time and within budget. This reputation won them many large contracts even when their tender had been higher than their competitors'.

THE PROBLEM

After two years, they began to experience problems. They were securing contracts that they would implement as usual, but the costs were increasing unexpectedly and the jobs took longer than planned. Their reputation was becoming tarnished and they wanted to reverse this before any more damage was done.

The five directors completed a Team Management Profile Questionnaire and the results were given to them during their monthly meeting. They were introduced to the concepts of TMS, and when they received their Team Management Profiles the reason for their problems became apparent. All five directors had Thruster-Organizer preferences.

Their strength in the Organizing part of the Types of Work Wheel was good and was the reason that their project management skills were so highly praised. However, this meant that the Advising part of the wheel was not receiving as much attention as was necessary.

Gathering information is an important part of the decision-making process. As none of the directors had a preference for this area of the wheel, problems started to occur. All the directors had strong preferences for Organizing so they preferred to get into action rather than gather more information.

THE SOLUTION

Once they were aware of this and the implications, they resolved to pay attention to the Advising area of the wheel. They began to structure their meetings to pay more attention to the other work functions.

Green meetings

They started off by having a 'green' meeting that concentrated on the Advising and Innovating work functions. (In the coloured version of the Types of Work

Wheel these sectors are different shades of green.) In this meeting they decided on what information was needed, who would gather it and from where they would get it. Once this information was gathered they looked at different and new ways of doing things rather than continuing as they had always done.

Yellow meetings

From here, they would concentrate on 'yellow' meetings (Promoting sector). The directors contacted their customers, clients and new prospects to promote their ideas and make sure that these new services were acceptable. Feedback from the customers was incorporated into the plans and the project moved to a development stage.

Red meetings

Of course, they enjoyed their 'red' (Organizing) meetings the most as they could plan their projects and organize the people and resources to put the ideas into action. Producing was the next area of focus and this was again an area that they preferred. Producing the project was one of their strengths and they would all enjoy seeing the outputs.

Blue meetings

The 'blue' meetings (Inspecting and Maintaining) were again out of their preference area but they realized the value of revisiting the project and seeing if everything went to plan. This was a time for reflection on the process they had used and for making sure that their high standards had been maintained.

It took a few months for the directors to settle into the habit of always auditing the eight Types of Work but the time spent in those meetings paid dividends down the track. The company regained its reputation for high standards of effectiveness and efficiency and gained extra recognition for always being innovative.

This case study shows that even if you are a member of an unbalanced team which prefers action and quick decisions, your team can become a high-performing one, provided it allocates time for innovation and reflection.

Linking is also an important part of the team-coaching process. Many people don't realize that 'communication' is a dynamic process that should reflect the work preferences, approach to risk and values of the person on the other side of the loop. The concept of Pacing is an important part of team coaching and sharing and comparing Team Management Profile reports helps develop action plans in this area.

SUMMARY

The TMS coaching approach provides a suite of feedback tools that give coach and coachee a framework to understand individual, team and organizational workplace behaviour. Eight profile reports based on six visual models are available to coaches, giving them a variety of entry points to deal with the desired goals of the coachee and the organizational client. Individual and team behaviour are largely influenced by work preferences, approach to risk and personal values. TMS provides well-researched tools to measure these characteristics. Once coachees understand why they and others behave the way they do, it makes the journey to a better future easier to chart.

References

Barrick, MR and Mount, MK (1991) The big five personality dimensions and job performance: a meta-analysis, *Personnel Psychology*, **44**, pp 1–26

Borgatta, EF (1964) The structure of personality characteristics, *Behavioral Science*, **12**, pp 8–17

Digman, JM (1990) Personality structure: emergence of the five-factor model, *Annual Review of Psychology*, **41**, pp 417–40

Hakel, MD (1974) Normative personality factors recovered from scalings of personality descriptors: the beholder's eyes, Personnel Psychology, **27**, pp 409–22

Margerison, CJ and McCann, DJ (1984–2005) *The Team Management Profile Questionnaire*, TMSDI York and Team Management Systems, Brisbane, Australia

Margerison, CJ and McCann, DJ (1995) *Team Management: Practical new approaches*, Management Books 2000, Chalford, Glos

McCann, DJ (2000) *The QO2 Profile Questionnaire*, TMSDI York and Team Management Systems, Brisbane, Australia

McCann, DJ (2002a) *The Workplace Wizard*, Gwent Publishing, Team Management Systems, Brisbane, Australia

McCann, DJ (2002b) *The Window on Work Values Profile Questionnaire*, TMSDI York and Team Management Systems, Brisbane, Australia

McCann, DJ and Mead, NHS (eds) (2008) *The Team Management Systems Research Manual*, 4th edn, TMSDI, York

McCrae, RR and Costa, PT Jr (1985) Updating Norman's adequate taxonomy: intelligence and personality dimensions in natural language and in questionnaires, *Journal of Personality and Social Psychology*, **49**, pp 710–21

McCrae, RR and Costa, PT (1997) Personality trait structure as a human universal, *American Psychologist*, **52**, pp 509–16

Noller, P, Law, H and Comrey, AL (1987) Cattell, Comrey, and Eysenck personality factors compared: more evidence for the five robust factors? *Journal of Personality and Social Psychology*, **53**, pp 775–82

Norman, WT (1963) Towards an adequate taxonomy of personality attributes: replicated factor structure in peer nomination personality ratings, *Journal of Abnormal and Social Psychology*, **66**, pp 574–83

Peabody, D and Goldberg, LR (1989) Some determinates of factor structure from personality trait descriptors, *Journal of Personality and Social Psychology*, **4**, pp 681–91

Smith, GM (1967) Usefulness of peer ratings in educational research, *Educational and Psychological Measurement*, **27**, pp 967–84

NOTES

1. Unless otherwise indicated trademarks referred to in this chapter are owned either by the TMS organizations or the author.
2. Myers Briggs Type Indicator and MBTI are registered trademarks of Consulting Psychologists Press Inc. Oxford Psychologists Press Ltd. has exclusive rights to the trademarks in the UK.

5

Coaching with OPQ

Eugene Burke

INTRODUCTION

This chapter introduces the reader to the OPQ32, its structure and its use as an indicator of competency potential, to enable the reader to consider its use in coaching and development. The reader will find information on the OPQ32's versions, the constructs and scales covered, as well as the validity data supporting the OPQ32. The chapter gives an overview of the SHL Universal Competency Framework (UCF), offering an integrative framework for using OPQ32 with behavioural competencies to provide a powerful diagnostic of strengths and development needs as well as possible derailers and potential for role misfit. Finally, a number of specific reports are described that cover leadership, team working, learning styles and competencies, as well as Emotional Intelligence.

HOW THE OPQ HELPS IN UNDERSTANDING PERSONALITY

While the Big Five model dominates as a theoretical structure for personality at the time of writing, OPQ32 was designed specifically with the world of work in mind and to provide coverage of personality dimensions shown by research and practice to be relevant to job performance. The OPQ32 is a very transparent instrument and does not propose a rigid or deterministic view of personality, but the model underlying it does propose that current and future behaviour is influenced by the personality of individuals and work groups. In short, the OPQ32 provides a straightforward work-related view of a person's personality today that can be used to provide a practical framework for coaching and development of individuals and groups.

THEORETICAL PERSPECTIVES

In writing this chapter, I have not adopted a particular model for coaching or development interventions. However, the types of applications of OPQ32 reports described in the second half of the chapter are aligned with models such as that described by Klein (1989). That is, measures of personality can be used to understand the drivers for individual or team behaviours and provide an insight into the factors influencing the choices and intentions that underlie those behaviours.

The proposition given in this chapter for how the OPQ32 can facilitate understanding of behaviour follows the distinctions made by Kanfer (1990) between distal and proximal measures, and the importance attached by Zaccaro (2007) to using distal measures for understanding the potential for behavioural change and for development. Kanfer distinguishes between distal measures as measures of those factors affecting goal choices and intended future effort. She defines proximal measures as mechanisms that control the initiation and execution of actions during the actual engagement with a task. Reports from the OPQ32 provide information through a variety of lenses on how dispositions (distal measures) are likely to influence learning and the present or future manifestation of desired behaviours in a given organizational or role context (proximal measures).

THE OPQ32 QUESTIONNAIRE

The Occupational Personality Questionnaire (OPQ) is available in 36 languages at the time of writing, and is widely used in the selection, development, succession and transition of potential and current employees in both public and private sector organizations across a range of job levels. The OPQ has over 23 years of development history and is supported by a continuous R&D programme including a wide range of reports that have increasingly moved towards SHL's Universal Competency Framework (UCF) as the basis for their design.

2006 saw the launch of a revised OPQ32 manual which provides extensive technical and user information, in addition to two technical supplements showing how the OPQ32 measures Big Five personality constructs, and the relationships between the OPQ32 and the highest level of the UCF, The Great Eight. Links to this manual, which is available free as a download, are provided at the end of this chapter.

The OPQ32 model describes 32 dimensions or scales of people's preferred or typical style of behaviour at work and follows the general OPQ model of personality. This breaks personality down into three domains: Relationships with People, Thinking Styles and Feelings and Emotions. The three domains are joined by a potential fourth – the Dynamism domain – which is composed of scales such as Vigorous, Achieving and Competitive that relate to sources of energy (Figure 5.1).

The OPQ32 R&D effort was of an international nature from the start ensuring that the questionnaire could be readily adapted for use in many languages and countries. Particular emphasis has also been given to ensuring that OPQ32 is appropriate for use with people from different ethnic and gender groups.

Versions of the OPQ32

There are two versions of the OPQ32 available: normative, OPQ32n, and ipsative, OPQ32i. The ipsative version of the OPQ32, OPQ32i, asks respondents to consider four statements and to choose the statement that they

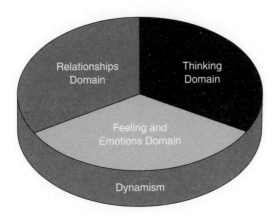

Figure 5.1 The OPQ model of personality

consider 'most' like them and the statement they consider 'least' like them. This is a forced choice (ipsative) format. There are 104 blocks of four items to complete (416 statements altogether). Here is an example of a block of four statements:

▋ I like helping people.
▋ I enjoy competitive activities.
▋ I view things positively.
▋ I like to follow procedures.

In addition to the main 32 scales, the OPQ32i questionnaire includes a Consistency scale. The Consistency scale is a measure of how consistently a person responds to questions in terms of the extent to which they systematically choose certain traits as being more or less like them across the items that are presented. Random responding would generate a very low consistency score, thus highlighting a potential problem with the interpretation. The ipsative version is particularly useful for high-stakes situations, such as assessment for selection, as the forced-choice format makes it more difficult to convey a socially desirable image.

The second, normative, version of the OPQ32, OPQ32n, asks respondents to rate each item (or statement) on a 1 to 5 scale, ranging through Strongly Disagree (1), Disagree (2), Unsure (3), Agree (4) to Strongly Agree (5). This is sometimes called a Likert scale. The questionnaire consists of 230 statements, an average of seven per scale. Here are two examples of statements:

▋ I enjoy talking to new people.
▋ I usually keep things tidy.

In addition to the main 32 scales the OPQ32n questionnaire includes a Social Desirability scale. The Social Desirability scale reflects the extent to which a candidate gives socially desirable answers. It can therefore provide an indication that a person is 'faking' responses to the questionnaire.

What the OPQ32 measures

Summary descriptions of the 32 scales of the Occupational Personality Questionnaire are presented in Table 5.1.

Table 5.1 OPQ32 scale descriptions

Domain	Scale	Lower scores	Higher scores
Relationships with people	Persuasive	rarely pressures others to change their views, dislikes selling, less comfortable using negotiation	enjoys selling, comfortable using negotiation, likes to change other people's views
	Controlling	happy to let others take charge, dislikes telling people what to do, unlikely to take the lead	likes to be in charge, takes the lead, tells others what to do, takes control
	Outspoken	holds back from criticizing others, may not express own views, unprepared to put forward own opinions	freely expresses opinions, makes disagreement clear, prepared to criticize others
	Independent minded	accepts majority decisions, prepared to follow the consensus	prefers to follow own approach, prepared to disregard majority decisions
	Outgoing	quiet and reserved in groups, dislikes being centre of attention	lively and animated in groups, talkative, enjoys attention
	Affiliative	comfortable spending time away from people, values time spent alone, seldom misses the company of others	enjoys others' company, likes to be around people, can miss the company of others
	Socially confident	feels more comfortable in less formal situations, can feel awkward when first meeting people	feels comfortable when first meeting people, at ease in formal situations
	Modest	makes strengths and achievements known, talks about personal success	dislikes discussing achievements, keeps quiet about personal success

Domain	Scale	Lower scores	Higher scores
Relationships with people	Democratic	prepared to make decisions without consultation, prefers to make decisions alone	consults widely, involves others in decision making, less likely to make decisions alone
	Caring	selective with sympathy and support, remains detached from others' personal problems	sympathetic and considerate towards others, helpful and supportive, gets involved in others' problems
Thinking style	Data rational	prefers dealing with opinions and feelings rather than facts and figures, likely to avoid using statistics	likes working with numbers, enjoys analysing statistical information, bases decisions on facts and figures
	Evaluative	does not focus on potential limitations, dislikes critically analysing information, rarely looks for errors or mistakes	critically evaluates information, looks for potential limitations, focuses upon errors
	Behavioural	does not question the reasons for people's behaviour, tends not to analyse people	tries to understand motives and behaviour, enjoys analysing people
	Conventional	favours changes to work methods, prefers new approaches, less conventional	prefers well-established methods, favours a more conventional approach
	Conceptual	prefers to deal with practical rather than theoretical issues, dislikes abstract concepts	interested in theories, enjoys discussing abstract concepts
	Innovative	more likely to build on than generate ideas, less inclined to be creative and inventive	generates new ideas, enjoys being creative, thinks of original solutions

Domain	Scale	Lower scores	Higher scores
	Variety seeking	prefers routine, is prepared to do repetitive work, does not seek variety	prefers variety, tries out new things, likes changes to regular routine, can become bored by repetitive work
	Adaptable	behaves consistently across situations, unlikely to behave differently with different people	changes behaviour to suit the situation, adapts approach to different people
	Forward thinking	more likely to focus upon immediate than long-term issues, less likely to take a strategic perspective	takes a long-term view, sets goals for the future, more likely to take a strategic perspective
	Detail conscious	unlikely to become preoccupied with detail, less organized and systematic, dislikes tasks involving detail	focuses on detail, likes to be methodical, organized and systematic, may become preoccupied with detail
	Conscientious	sees deadlines as flexible, prepared to leave some tasks unfinished	focuses on getting things finished, persists until the job is done
	Rule following	not restricted by rules and procedures, prepared to break rules, tends to dislike bureaucracy	follows rules and regulations, prefers clear guidelines, finds it difficult to break rules
Feelings and emotions	*Relaxed*	tends to feel tense, finds it difficult to relax, can find it hard to unwind after work	finds it easy to relax, rarely feels tense, generally calm and untroubled
	Worrying	feels calm before important occasions, less affected by key events	feels nervous before important occasions, worries about things going wrong
	Tough minded	sensitive, easily hurt by criticism, upset by unfair comments or insults	not easily offended, can ignore insults, may be insensitive to personal criticism

Domain	Scale	Lower scores	Higher scores
Feelings and emotions	Optimistic	concerned about the future, expects things to go wrong, focuses on negative aspects of a situation	expects things will turn out well, looks to the positive aspects of a situation, has an optimistic view of the future
	Trusting	wary of others' intentions, finds it difficult to trust others, unlikely to be fooled by people	trusts people, sees others as reliable and honest, believes what others say
	Emotionally controlled	openly expresses feelings, finds it difficult to conceal feelings, displays emotion clearly	can conceal feelings from others, rarely displays emotion
	Vigorous	likes to take things at a steady pace, dislikes excessive work demands	thrives on activity, likes to be busy, enjoys having a lot to do
	Competitive	dislikes competing with others, feels that taking part is more important than winning	has a need to win, enjoys competitive activities, dislikes losing
	Achieving	sees career progression as less important, looks for achievable rather than highly ambitious targets	ambitious and career-centred, likes to work to demanding goals and targets
	Decisive	tends to be cautions when making decisions, likes to take time to reach conclusions	makes fast decisions, reaches conclusions quickly, less cautious

Norms for the OPQ32

The user has a wide selection of norm groups to select from. The 2006 manual presents 86 regional norm groups for both OPQ32n and OPQ32i, with the largest group having 17,368 people while the smallest sample is 273.

The reliability of the OPQ32

The accuracy of the OPQ32 scores can be gauged from the reliability data supporting the instrument. While there are a few individual scales with reliabilities close to 0.7, the overall median internal consistency of OPQ32 scales are in the range 0.75 to 0.80. Median retest reliabilities within one month of the initial testing for OPQ32n scales are 0.79.

Validity evidence supporting OPQ32

Validations of the OPQ in predicting work behaviours now amount to a total of more than 8,000 people across work contexts and countries. This large database shows the OPQ32 to have validities between 0.40 and 0.50, matching and exceeding validities reported for Big Five constructs.

Qualifications required for use of OPQ32

In line with best practice in assessment, access to the OPQ32 is governed by either training of those who have no previous qualifications in the use of personality questionnaires, or conversion courses for those who have experience or qualifications in the use of other personality instruments. Please contact your local SHL office for information on access requirements.

Administering OPQ32

Administration and scoring of the OPQ32 is facilitated by a variety of modes through which the instrument can be delivered. As well as traditional paper and pencil formats for the OPQ32n, both versions of the OPQ32 can be administered via the internet. Research on large samples comparing scores from the internet with paper and pencil administrations shows that scores are equivalent across both modes. Given its design, internet administration with automated scoring is the best option for the use of OPQ32i. Indeed, the facility to set up a web administration in advance that enables the selection of OPQ32 versions and languages, norms as well as reports, offers a considerable saving in terms of preparing for a coaching and development session with an individual client or team.

THE OPQ32 AND COACHES

To paraphrase La Fontaine, the 17th-century French poet, every person is three people: the person they think they are, the person others think they are and the one they really are. The principal purpose of the OPQ32, and its widest use, is to help people understand their personality and, thereby, key influences on their behaviour in the workplace. The OPQ32 offers value to coaches in helping them understand themselves and to reflect on their approach to coaching and how it could be improved. Table 5.1 provides a description of the personality scales covered by OPQ32, for which scores are provided on a profile sheet. We will now consider a few of these scales to describe how the OPQ32 can help coaches gain insight into their approach to coaching and coachees. Later, we will describe a range of reports available from the OPQ32 that utilize all OPQ32 scales to provide powerful insights into a range of competencies.

Framing and setting up a coaching intervention

OPQ32 has four thinking-style scales related to structure, a facet of conscientiousness in the Big Five model, which speak to planfulness (Forward Thinking), attention to detail (Detail Conscious) and persistence (Conscientiousness) as well as a need for procedures (Rule Following). Scores on these scales can help the coach to consider (a) their need for structure and (b) the coachee's need for structure. Knowing their own preferred style on these four scales, coaches can then look to the needs of the coachee and identify specific areas they, the coach, will need to adapt to help develop a successful coaching relationship. If, for example, a coach prefers a less structured approach to coaching while a coachee would benefit from a more structured and detailed approach, the use of OPQ32 to highlight these differences can help the coach develop a strategy for managing his or her own natural preferences and adapt to the coachee's needs.

The coach's approach to gaining understanding and insight

A number of Thinking Style scales – Data Rational, Evaluative, Behavioural, Conceptual and Innovative – provide powerful information on a coach's approach to identifying priorities and solving problems. A more data-driven approach is indicated by higher scores on Data Rational (bases decisions on facts) and Evaluative (critically evaluates information), while lower scores on these scales would suggest a more intuitive and instinctual approach to making decisions. Again, knowing their preferred style will help coaches to reflect on areas they need to attend to in their general approach to coaching (eg, are there occasions when gathering more tangible information and taking time to evaluate that information would have resulted in a more successful coaching intervention?).

Three of these Thinking Style scales – Behavioural (an interest in what motivates people), Conceptual (an interest in the world of ideas and theories) and Innovative (creativity and new ideas) – have been found from research with OPQ32 to relate to insightfulness and the facility to consider another person's perspective. However, those that score higher on the Conceptual scale may need to consider when they need to move from a more theoretical view to a more concrete one when working with coachees, particularly if the coachee is reported as scoring lower on the Conceptual scale.

Engaging and developing empathy with the coachee

The three Relationships with People scales of Modest, Democratic and Caring relate to developing and maintaining a sense of empathy and engagement with others. A specific competency that the Modest (dislikes talking about own achievements) and Democratic (consults widely) scales relate to is that of listening, with those who are lower on these scales having a higher likelihood of being people who tend to 'transmit' information rather than operating as 'receivers' of information. The Caring (gets involved in others' problems) scale also provides information on a potential problem area for coaches, with those scoring extremely high on Caring having a potential need to manage how involved they become in a coachee's problems.

Scores on the Outgoing (lively in groups), Affiliative (enjoys others' company) and Socially Confident (at ease with others) scales provide information on how easily a coach can adjust to different social contexts, as well as on first impressions the coach may create when they first meet clients and coachees. This is not to suggest that good coaches necessarily have to have high scores on all three scales. As mentioned earlier, knowledge of highs and lows on the OPQ32 provides potential insight into areas that the coach needs to invest more effort in and develop more.

Managing and communicating emotions

Emotions play a very powerful role in relationships, and four scales in the Feelings and Emotions domain of OPQ32 speak directly to emotionality. The more obvious scales are Relaxed (generally calm and untroubled) and Worrying (feels nervous before important occasions), with Relaxed being a trait (a deeply ingrained aspect of a person's make up) and Worrying being a state scale (a response to specific situations and stimuli). As such, it is possible to obtain high scores on both these scales. Someone who is low on Relaxed and high on Worrying is more likely to be reactive to emotional situations; that is, to react strongly when confronted with emotional situations. Someone who is high on Relaxed and low on Worrying might be seen as having a more 'laid back' approach to life, but in the coaching context this might also be interpreted as a blasé attitude, emphasizing the importance of understanding one's own emotional image in the eyes of others.

Two other Feelings and Emotions scales, Optimistic and Emotionally Controlled, also provide useful information related to the communication of emotions. Research on Emotional Intelligence (EI) and leadership suggests that positive emotions are important in people's perceptions of others and their interactions with them. Research on OPQ32 and EI measures shows that higher Optimistic (expects things will turn out well) and lower Emotionally Controlled (openly expresses feelings) scores are correlated with higher EI and positive perceptions of engagement with others.

OPQ32 reports that will support the coach

OPQ32 research and development has focused in recent years on capturing the insights from scales as just described and putting this information into context to make it more accessible and more relevant to the workplace. These reports also use the validity research on the OPQ32 to ensure that the guidance provided is based on empirically supported relationships between OPQ32 and behaviours. Two such reports are the *Maximizing Your Learning* and the *Emotional Intelligence (EI)* reports which are described next.

OPQ32 Maximizing Your Learning Report

This report is an integration of preferred styles of learning (eg, Honey and Mumford, 1982; Kolb, 1984) with models of action and organizational learning (Argyris, Putnam and McLain Smith, 1985; Argyris and Schön, 1978; McGill and Beaty, 1995). The report is organized into two sections.

The first section covers how the individual prefers to engage in learning and provides feedback on two dimensions. The first is analytical versus intuitive. Those with a strong preference for taking an analytical approach like to use reasoning in their learning, and approach learning opportunities from a more rational and objective perspective. Those with a stronger preference for the intuitive approach are more likely to follow their instincts in the way they engage in learning, and their perception of the learning process will be influenced by how they feel about a learning event and the other people involved in it. The second dimension is hands-on versus observation. People with a hands-on approach prefer taking an active and involved approach to learning. They discover by doing and seeing. The tangible results of an action provide the opportunity to learn from the outside-in: that is, by internalizing and remembering those actions that have been shown from direct experience to work in the external world. Those with a strong preference for observation are more likely to seek opportunities to watch and listen to others before getting involved in a learning activity or experience. People with this preference tend to learn from the inside-out: by first gaining an understanding of what is involved in an activity before directly engaging in it. An example is provided in Figure 5.2.

The second part of the report, 'Maximize your learning', provides feedback on four learning competencies that have been framed to reflect the simple fact that most learning experiences will take place in the context of work through acquiring and developing skills to meet workplace challenges. The competencies explore how well equipped the individual is for experiential learning. Each competency is broken down by specific areas of potential strength (green), scope for development (grey) and area for development (red), along with suggested development tips. The four competencies are: Seeking Opportunities to Learn, or how active the individual is likely to be in identifying learning opportunities and being creative in taking advantage of them; Seizing Opportunities to Learn, or how open the

Your preferred approach to learning Based on your responses to the OPQ32, the following graphs summarize your learning preferences.

	Potential under-use	Active preference	Strong preference
Analytical			
Intuitive			

	Potential under-use	Active preference	Strong preference
Hands On			
Observe			

Analytical/intuitive Your responses suggest that, while this is not strongly characteristic of your approach to learning, you may take the time to reflect on what you want to achieve from your learning, and how you will realize whether or not you have reached the learning objectives you set yourself. Your learning is more likely to be guided by what you think rather than what you feel. How you can involve others and incorporate feedback from others in your learning may be factors for you to consider in planning your personal development.

Hands on/observation Your responses suggest that there may be occasions when a hands-on approach to learning will appeal to you, particularly when you expect a learning experience to have a positive outcome. However, there may be occasions when you prefer a more cautious approach and when you will prefer to observe and listen to others before directly engaging in a learning activity.

Figure 5.2 Example results for maximizing your learning, part 1

individual is likely to be to trying things out and taking on challenges, even if they involve some risk; Planning your Learning, or whether the individual is likely to take a pro-active approach to planning and structuring learning; and Learning from Feedback, or how open the individual is likely to be to seeking and building on feedback from others (see Figure 5.3).

Readers familiar with 360-degree instruments will see the potential value of this report in preparing for 360-degree feedback and considering options for developmental actions in advance of initial discussions with a coachee. From the coaching perspective, the information provided by this report can be used by coaches to consider results for themselves on these competencies when seen from their mirrors: namely, Creating Opportunities to Learn, Providing Opportunities to Learn, Managing and Guiding Learning and Giving Feedback.

OPQ32 Emotional Intelligence Report

We have already looked at some of the scales in the Feelings and Emotions domain of OPQ32. These and other OPQ32 scales have been combined into the OPQ32 Emotional Intelligence (EI) report. This report is modelled after Goleman's (1998, 2000) model of Emotional Intelligence (EI) although strong relationships between OPQ32 and EI have also been shown for the Bar-On EQ measure and for the Salovey and Mayer (1990) model. The model used in the OPQ32 report is shown in Figure 5.4.

The example in Figure 5.5 from the OPQ32 EI report shows how the individual understands and manages his or her own emotional worlds.

While the first section of the EI report talks to the internal world of the coach, the second part of the report talks to how the coach may relate to others. The following provides an example of the information available from this part of the EI report.

We have looked at information that coaches can obtain from OPQ32 to develop their understanding of factors influencing their own behaviour as well as identifying potential areas they can focus on to improve their coaching skills. This knowledge is potentially powerful in interpreting a coachee's OPQ32 scores, enabling the coach to consider differences in their own profiles with that of coachee, and areas where they may need to adjust their behaviour to improve the success of the coaching intervention (or, indeed, whether to take on the intervention at all). The two reports we have just considered in the context of the coach are, of course, useful in providing information on a coachee and in helping the coach to prepare for a coaching intervention. We will now consider some other OPQ32 reports that can be used to identify development areas.

Seeking Opportunities to Learn   `SCOPE FOR FURTHER DEVELOPMENT`

To maximize your learning potential, it is important to identify opportunities that might change your perspective or provide the opportunity to learn new things.

■ ■ ■ Likely to welcome opportunities to come up with creative solutions so very likely to generate, for yourself, ideas and alternatives for how to meet your learning and development needs.

■ More comfortable with conventional approaches so less likely to recognize learning opportunities outside formal training and development programmes.

■ Less likely to be comfortable with change and to experiment with new and different learning experiences.

Seizing Opportunities to Learn   `SCOPE FOR FURTHER DEVELOPMENT`

Seizing opportunities to learn involves taking risks and sometimes making mistakes. This is critical to learning, introducing challenges and providing an invaluable insight into what leads to success as well as understanding what doesn't work as well.

■ ■ Likely to strike a balance between accepting and disregarding decisions made by others so may sometimes set your own agenda for your personal development and act upon it.

■ Prefer to be realistic so likely to set objectives that are easily achievable in your personal development.

Planning Your Learning   `SCOPE FOR FURTHER DEVELOPMENT`

To get the most from your learning, it is important to take a planned approach, setting out both how and when you will achieve milestones and objectives in your development.

■ Tend to deal with things as they happen, so less likely to set deadlines and timescales for your personal development.

■ Tend not to get immersed in details so unlikely to work through the specifics of how you will achieve learning and development objectives.

■ ■ ■ Seek to meet deadlines so likely to persevere with a learning plan or personal development programme.

Learning from Feedback   `AREA OF STRENGTH`

Getting feedback on performance is one of the most powerful ways of learning about personal effectiveness and of identifying further opportunities to learn and develop.

■ ■ Tend to strike a balance between being sensitive and tough-minded so may see feedback for its information value rather than as a possible source of criticism.

■ ■ ■ Likely to modify your behaviour to suit the situation so also likely to adapt your approach to learning and development as a result of feedback from others.

Note: Development tips available from this report have not been shown in this example for the sake of brevity and space. ■ indicates an area of potential weakness; ■ ■ indicates an area for potential development; ■ ■ ■ indicates a potential area of strength.

Figure 5.3   Example results for maximizing your learning, part 2

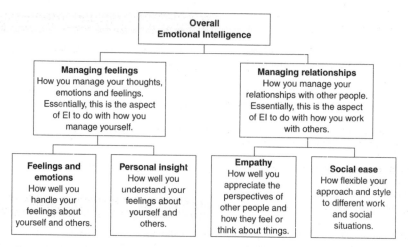

Figure 5.4   Model underpinning the OPQ32 EI report

Managing feelings			
Competency	Potential development need	Scope for development	Potential strength
Feelings and emotions			
Personal insight			

Feelings and emotions Your scores suggest that, while you have the capacity to channel your emotions positively, there are also times when you may find it difficult to do so, and times when the way in which you share your feelings with others could have a more positive impact.

▮ When you find things difficult to progress, when you have concerns about how a situation might turn out, or when you experience problems with other people, how do you express the emotions that you feel? Do you make the time and space to allow your emotions to settle, and to consider how and when your feelings could be shared with others to positive effect?

▮ How open are you with others about your feelings? If you like to express your feelings openly, how aware are you of the impact on others of the way that you express yourself emotionally? If you are someone who is more guarded in sharing your feelings, have you considered ways in which sharing emotions constructively can strengthen relationships, and opportunities you may be missing for others to share their thoughts and feelings with you?

Personal insight Although you have the capacity to effect personal change when committed to doing so, your scores also suggest that you need to think through how to maintain your commitment and deal with the frustrations that you may experience in pursuing your personal development.

▮ Do you find that you tend to act before fully thinking through the consequences of your actions? Have there been occasions recently when thinking before acting might have led to a more positive outcome sooner, and/or have enabled you to better manage the emotions involved in resolving issues? Think back to such occasions and consider how thinking issues through and reflecting on your own feelings in advance of acting could have helped you, and how you might apply those insights in the future.

▮ Are you someone who finds it difficult to stay motivated or committed to a course of action when things prove difficult or frustrating? Has your experience in setting yourself personal goals in the past led to you avoiding difficult goals? How do you adapt to change? Do you see change as motivating or demotivating, and why? Are there others that you know who seem to achieve the goals they set themselves, are able to overcome difficulties and seem to adapt easily to change? Have you discussed these issues with them, and what insights have these discussions given you?

Figure 5.5   Example from OPQ EI report on managing feelings

Managing relationships			
Competency	Potential development need	Scope for development	Potential strength
Empathy	████████████		
Social ease	████████████		

Empathy Your scores suggest that there are times when expressing a more direct interest in the views and feelings of others would strengthen the positive impact that you have on others.

▌ Consider a time when encouraging others to express their thoughts, feelings or opinions, and making the time to hear them out, would have helped to resolve a situation or to enable you to get greater buy-in to your own views and suggestions. Actively listening to others and offering them opportunities to contribute to discussions is something that will encourage a positive view of you as a team member or as a group leader.

▌ Refer to your score under Personal Insight (PI). If this is low, then this suggests a potential blind spot in that the true impact you have on other people may be something that is hidden from your view. If others are not encouraged to share their thoughts and feelings with you, then you may miss opportunities for feedback on your strengths and important areas of self-development.

Social ease While you are someone who is approachable and sociable with others, it may also take you some time to adjust to new people and groups.

▌ The extent to which you feel uncomfortable when meeting new people or becoming involved with groups of people will be indicated by your Feelings and Emotions (F&E) score (the lower this score then the greater your likely discomfort). If your F&E score is low, follow the advice given under F&E on how to manage your concerns, to allow yourself the time to adjust to the situation and to allow more positive emotions to surface.

▌ Compare those situations in which you feel at ease with others and those in which you do not. Is it possible for you to allow yourself to transfer the more positive feelings and thoughts from those situations in which you are more at ease to those situations in which you feel less comfortable? In those situations in which you feel less comfortable, do you allow yourself the time to relax into the situation and adjust to the people that you are with, allowing them the time to adjust to you?

Figure 5.6 Example from OPQ EI report on managing relationships

THE OPQ AND COACHEES

Before we look at reports that can assist the coach in the coaching intervention, we shall consider some basic issues in using the OPQ32 in coaching.

When to use the OPQ32 in coaching

While there is no prescription for using the OPQ32 in coaching, the most obvious value from its use is at the front end of a coaching assignment to bring coaches quickly up to speed in terms of their understanding of coachees, how to approach the coachee and starting points for developing a dialogue in the first meeting, as well as areas that can be discussed to create a development plan and concrete development actions.

Introducing OPQ32

The coachees' understanding of why they are being asked to complete the OPQ32, what it measures and how the information will be used is crucial to ensuring that the information obtained through the OPQ32 is valid, as well as ensuring that the use of the OPQ32 scores in coaching will be positively received by the coachee. As mentioned earlier, the OPQ32 is an instrument that was developed specifically for the world of work. This clearly distinguishes it from clinical measures of personality functioning. It does not have wrong or right answers and provides information on the preferences and dispositions to help people improve their understanding of themselves and their behaviour in the workplace. Therefore, it is not judgemental in the information that it offers on coachees.

Confidentiality of OPQ32 scores is an issue that needs to be addressed at the outset. Answers to questions such as whether the scores be restricted to the coach and coachee or be shared with, say, the coachee's boss or members of a company's HR department will need to have been worked through prior to OPQ32 administration.

The Universal Competency Framework (UCF), OPQ32 reports and working with coachees

The OPQ32 provides a wealth of information in the 32 individual scales and in the various combinations of scores across scales. To channel this information and facilitate its use to identify potential areas of strength or development need, OPQ32 scales have been combined using various algorithms to produce a range of reports looking at areas such as leadership and teamwork. This has been made possible through the extensive OPQ32 validation programmes as well as the development of a competency framework, the UCF, that directly links behaviours in the form of competencies to personality (as well as motivation and ability).

The UCF is the result of several years of research into the integration of SHL and non-SHL competency models, as well as client and other general models, such as the Lominger model (Lombardo and Eichinger, 2004), into a unifying structure. A unique feature of this research is the investigation of the relationships between observed behaviours, as represented by competency models, and measures of personality, ability and motivation (see Bartram, 2005; Bartram and Brown, 2005). The UCF operates at three levels of description, with eight factors, known as the Great Eight, 20 dimensions with each dimension linked to a specific Great Eight factor, and 112 specific behaviours linked to specific UCF dimensions. Table 5.2 describes the Great Eight and shows how these link to personality as described by the Big Five (Wiggins and Trapnell, 1997), motivation and cognitive ability.

Table 5.2 The Great Eight from the SHL Universal Competency Framework

Factor	Description	Big 5, Motivation and ability (g) relationship
Leading and deciding	Takes control and exercises leadership. Initiates action, gives direction and takes responsibility.	Need for Power and Control, Extroversion
Supporting and cooperating	Supports others and shows respect and positive regard for them in social situations. Puts people first, working effectively with individuals and teams, clients and staff. Behaves consistently with clear personal values that complement those of the organization.	Agreeableness
Interacting and presenting	Communicates and networks effectively. Successfully persuades and influences others. Relates to others in a confident and relaxed manner.	Extroversion, General Mental Ability (g)
Analysing and interpreting	Shows evidence of clear analytical thinking. Gets to the heart of complex problems and issues. Applies own expertise effectively. Quickly takes on new technology. Communicates well in writing.	Openness to Experience, General Mental Ability (g)
Creating and conceptualizing	Works well in situations requiring openness to new ideas and experiences. Seeks out learning opportunities. Handles situations and problems with innovation and creativity. Thinks broadly and strategically. Supports and drives organizational change.	Openness to Experience, General Mental Ability (g)
Organizing and executing	Plans ahead and works in a systematic and organized way. Follows directions and procedures. Focuses on customer satisfaction and delivers a quality service or product to the agreed standards.	Conscientiousness, General Mental Ability (g)

Factor	Description	Big 5, Motivation and ability (g) relationship
Adapting and coping	Adapts and responds well to change. Manages pressure effectively and copes well with setbacks.	Emotional Stability
Enterprising and performing	Focuses on results and achieving personal work objectives. Works best when work is related closely to results and the impact of personal efforts is obvious. Shows an understanding of business, commerce and finance. Seeks opportunities for self-development and career advancement.	Need for Achievement, Negative Agreeableness

There are a number of analytic tools that can be used to diagnose performance in terms of UCF behaviours. These enable existing competency models to be mapped to the UCF and, through the UCF, to the OPQ32. In addition to OPQ32 indicators, 360 appraisals can also be designed using the UCF, giving the user a choice of assessment and diagnostic models. The UCF can also be used to design interviews with significant others in the workplace and development centres. Both forms of assessment (competency potential from the OPQ32 and actual competency from 360 and/or interviews or development centres) can be used to offer a very powerful diagnosis combining actual and potential competency.

We shall now explore two reports that can be used to shape the coaching intervention and establish development goals and options for achieving those goals.

OPQ32 leadership Report

Management and leadership are addressed in the SHL Leadership Model in terms of the widely recognized distinction between transactional and transformational styles (Burns, 1978), in which management is about keeping the system running efficiently and effectively, while leadership is about creating it, developing it or changing its direction. While conceptually distinct, management and leadership are essential and in practice interdependent.

The SHL Leadership Model covers four functions critical to leadership effectiveness in any organization:

- *Developing the vision.* Leaders need to analyse the facts accurately and to establish a sense of urgency where change is required. They also need to establish a mission, develop a convincing and appealing vision of the future, and outline the strategy by which the vision can be achieved.
- *Sharing the goals.* Corporate leaders need to communicate the vision, set goals and objectives and take decisions that embody the strategic direction of the organization. In presenting their strategy they need to interact with internal and external stakeholders and get buy-in.
- *Gaining support.* Leaders need to support others in order to gain their trust and support. This requires leaders to recognize concerns and reconcile them with the change agenda.
- *Delivering success.* The effective implementation of strategy requires operational efficiency and commercial acumen. The economic viability of the vision needs to be ensured through operational efficiency and by winning business to grow the organization.

The core of the report is the Great Eight described earlier which have been mapped to the above four leadership functions as shown in Table 5.3.

The report provides a breakdown of where the individual lies when plotted on the transactional and transformational axes under each leadership function. For example, Figure 5.7 shows an individual being considered for a leadership development programme who has taken the OPQ32i online. Scores have been plotted for Analysing and Interpreting (transactional) and Creating and Conceptualizing (transformational) for the leadership function 'Developing the Vision'. As shown, each cell in the two-by-two plot is labelled by a type to characterize likely behaviours under a leadership function and as an overall leader/manager. In the case shown, this individual lies between a Creator and a Visionary. There are five two-by-two plots, one for each leadership function and one for the overall summary of leader/manager potential (Figure 5.8).

Table 5.3 The SHL leadership model

Leadership function	Management focus (transactional)	Leadership focus (transformational)
Developing the vision	Analysing and interpreting	Creating and conceptualizing
Sharing the goals	Interacting and presenting	Leading and deciding
Gaining support	Supporting and cooperating	Adapting and coping
Delivering success	Organizing and executing	Enterprising and performing

Table 5.4 shows an example of the narrative summary available in the report, in this case for the individual being considered for the leadership development programme.

This report can be used with a leadership pipeline, and at a relatively early stage of that pipeline, to identify and meet development needs, as well as with coachees in leadership positions. It can be used to frame a dialogue around coachees' perceptions of their leadership style and to explore their expectations of future leadership roles. If the coach is dealing with a cohort or tier of

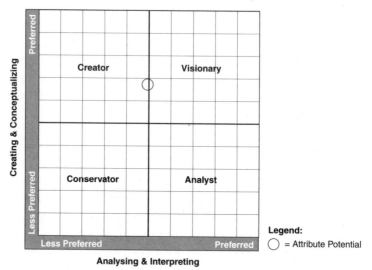

Figure 5.7 Example plot for 'Developing the Vision'

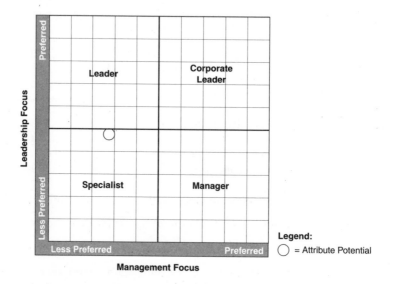

Figure 5.8 Example plot of overall leadership potential

Table 5.4 Example Narrative Summary from the OPQ32 leadership report

Management focus vs leadership focus

Leader/Specialist — Effective leaders manage to transform organizations through a combination of innovation, drive, personal resilience and entrepreneurial flair. However, their efforts may be rendered less effective if they overlook transactional aspects associated with effective management.

Developing the vision

Creator/Visionary — Individuals combining the Creator and Visionary styles work well in situations requiring openness to new ideas and experiences. They typically handle situations and problems with innovation and creativity, and support and drive organizational change. Such individuals adopt a flexible approach to problem solving, balancing logical analytical approaches alongside the lessons of practical experience. In their enthusiasm for change they may be inclined to overlook the positive aspects of the status quo.

Sharing the goals

Decision Maker/ Supporter — Individuals who combine the Decision Maker and Supporter styles are as comfortable as most when called upon to take control of the group and to exercise a more directive style. Generally they prefer to work independently and to involve others only when it is essential to do so, choosing when to exercise decisiveness and personal control. They tend to be somewhat private and socially reserved and to value time for personal thought and reflection. Consequently, they may miss opportunities to network and build business contacts.

Gaining support

Adventurer — Adventurers respond well to the challenges of change and do not worry too much about the possible consequences of trying new approaches. They are strongly focused on pragmatic, task-related aspects of the job and feel uncomfortable engaging with the personal issues and concerns of others. While their personal confidence can provide others with stability and security they tend to underestimate the personal challenges experienced by others in adapting to change and can unintentionally hurt others or fail to get their buy-in.

Delivering success

Implementer/Idealist	Individuals who combine the Implementer and Idealist styles are less driven by commercial considerations or by the need for personal recognition or achievement. As a consequence they may fail to recognize or capitalize on potential commercial opportunities. They derive satisfaction by applying a steady and consistent focus to the task at hand, and balance the need to adopt a planned and structured approach against that of responding to contingencies as they emerge.

leaders within an organization, then reviewing reports on everyone to be involved in coaching will help to identify common areas of need and themes to be discussed with coachees. The aggregation of data to look at work groups leads naturally to how the OPQ32 could be used in a team building setting or to address development needs across a team as well as with individual members of a team. To show how the OPQ32 can help with such assignments, we shall now explore the Team Impact Report from the OPQ32.

OPQ32 Team Impact Report

The OPQ32 team impact report is grounded in an input–process–output model of work groups and teams. It focuses on eight key team processes identified from a review of the literature (examples being Forsyth, 1999; Gladstein, 1984; Goodman, 1986; Janis, 1982; McGrath, 1984 and 1991; Swezey and Salas, 1992) and from SHL's own consultancy experiences. The eight team processes are organized around four key functions for effective teams, as summarized in Table 5.5.

Results are shown in Figure 5.9 for an example technology team involved in new product development at a time of significant technology and business process change (this report was commissioned by the team leader to evaluate how well this team was equipped to undergo the change, and prior to a team coaching intervention). Team impacts are classified according to whether they are team strengths (green), areas for development (amber) or potential development needs (red). While this team's overall profile did not show any development needs, this group view was used to set the scene for giving feedback to individual team members for whom development needs were identified.

The team impact report provides development tips broken down by whether the behaviours to be addressed are task focused and/or people focused. The box following describes some of the development tips for the example team under the impact 'Using Networks'. More specifically, we will look at some tips for the team leader to help address behaviours under this team impact.

Table 5.5 Functions, impacts and behaviours covered by the OPQ32 Team Impact Report

Team function	Team impact	Critical behaviours for this team impact
Creating	Exploring possibilities	Producing new ideas, approaches and insights, taking account of a wide range of issues across, and related to, the task or project.
	Evaluating options	Probing for further information and greater understanding of a problem. Making rational judgements from the available information. Evaluating ideas quickly to determine feasibility.
Managing	Setting direction	Providing others with a clear direction. Motivating and empowering others. Tasking team members according to their performance level. Managing team activities.
	Committing to action	Making prompt decisions, which may involve considered risks. Taking responsibility for actions and people. Acting under own direction. Initiating and promoting activity.
Resourcing	Using networks	Establishing strong relationships with staff at all levels. Building effective networks inside and outside the organization. Knowing how to tap into resources outside your own team.
	Maintaining cohesion	Adapting personal approach to the team's needs and contributing positively to team spirit. Listening and communicating actively. Supporting and caring for others.
Delivering	Staying focused	Working in a systematic, methodical and orderly way. Following procedures and policies. Keeping to schedules. Producing high-quality output in a timely manner.
	Resisting pressure	Keeping emotions under control even in difficult situations. Modifying approach in face of new demands. Staying optimistic and resilient. Being unaffected by pressure.

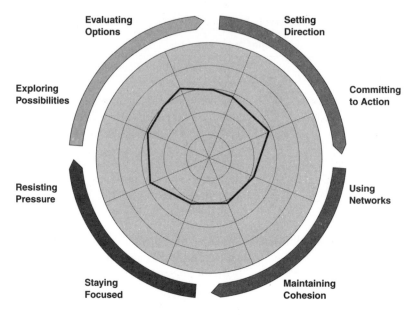

Figure 5.9 Examples of information provided by the OPQ32 team impact report (team view)

Team impact	Team's strength rating	Associated team function
Exploring possibilities	Adequate behaviour	Creating
Evaluating options	Strength	
Setting direction	Adequate behaviour	Managing
Committing to action	Adequate behaviour	
Using networks	Adequate behaviour	Resourcing
Maintaining cohesion	Adequate behaviour	
Staying focused	Adequate behaviour	Delivering
Resisting pressure	Adequate behaviour	

DEVELOPMENT TIPS FOR 'USING NETWORKS' IMPACT

Desired behaviours: Establishing strong relationships with staff at all levels. Building effective networks inside and outside the organization. Knowing how to tap into resources outside the team.

▌ Techniques for the team leader to use with the team:
  - Explain and stress the importance to the team of contacts within the organization and beyond.

- Ask team members to look for ideas and people with useful experience within their networks that may benefit this team.
- Identify ways in which the team can increase its profile within the organization; try to create some curiosity about the team. Support the team in exploiting this interest in building a network of useful contacts.
- Encourage team members to join professional organizations and to take advantage of their networking offerings.

▌ Coaching activities for the team leader
- Explain and stress the importance of contacts within the organization and beyond.
- Consider approaching a team that is very well connected in the organization to have a joint 'night out'. Make sure your team uses this opportunity to expand their network and to tap into that team's connection pool.
- Join networking groups that are organized by your professional organization.
- Find an opportunity where you can present the success of your team to the management body of your organization.

SUMMARY

This chapter has provided the reader with an introduction to the OPQ32 and described how it can be used in the coaching and development of individuals, teams and work groups. Based on the UCF, a variety of reports are available from OPQ32 to enable the user to readily translate scores from personality scales into competency potential scores, and to gather information on factors underlying effective performance against leadership and team functions. These contextualized reports can be used with more general reports on learning and emotional intelligence to gain a deeper understanding of factors influencing behaviour and to identify starting points for coaching dialogues and development planning, as well as for identifying potential blocks to behavioural change and for identifying potential derailers for individuals, teams and organizations.

The OPQ32 can also be used alongside other assessments such as ability tests and measures of motivation as well as 360 measures of behaviour to provide powerful and in-depth diagnostics. There are also a range of other reports available from the OPQ32 that offer potential value to coaches (such as the Universal Competency Report (UCR)). The language versions available for the OPQ32 also allow for multilingual and multi-geography assignments. The reader can access information on the OPQ32 and free downloads of technical manuals and supplements via the URL http://www.shl.com/SHL/en-int/Products/, and information on local SHL offices through whom information regarding access to OPQ32 products can be obtained are provided on SHL's main website, www.shl.com.

References

Argyris, C, Putnam, R and McLain Smith, D (1985) *Action Science: Concepts, methods, and skills for research and intervention*, Jossey-Bass, San Francisco

Argyris, C and Schön, D (1978) *Organizational Learning: A theory of action perspective*, Addison Wesley, Reading, MA

Bartram, D (2005) The Great Eight competencies: a criterion-centric approach to validation, *Journal of Applied Psychology*, **90**, pp 1185–1203

Bartram, D and Brown, A (2005) *Great Eight Factor Model OPQ32 Report: OPQ32 Technical Manual Supplement*, SHL, Thames Ditton

Burns, JM (1978) *Leadership*, Harper and Row, New York

Forsyth, DR (1999) *Group dynamics*, Brooks/Cole/Wadsworth, Belmont

Gladstein, DL (1984) Groups in context: a model of task group differences, *Administrative Science Quarterly*, **29**, pp 499–517

Goleman, D (1998) *Working with emotional intelligence*, Bantam Books, New York

Goleman, D (2000) Leadership that gets results, *Harvard Business Review*, March–April

Goodman, PS (1986) The impact of task and technology on group performance, in *Designing Effective Work Groups*, ed PS Goodman, Jossey-Bass, San Francisco

Honey, P and Mumford, A (1982) *Manual of Learning Styles*, P Honey, London

Janis, IL (1982) Groupthink: A Study of Foreign Policy Decisions and Fiascos, Houghton Mifflin, Boston

Kanfer, R (1990) Motivation theory and industrial and organizational psychology, in *Handbook of Industrial and Organizational Psychology* (Volume 1), ed MD Dunette and LM Hough, Consulting Psychologists Press, Palo Alto

Klein, HJ (1989) An integrated view model of work motivation, *Academy of Management Review*, 14, pp 150–72

Kolb, DA (1984) *Experiential Learning*, Prentice Hall, Englewood Cliffs, NJ

Lombardo, KM and Eichinger, RW (2004) *For Your Improvement: A guide for development and coaching* (4th edn), Lominger, Minneapolis

McCauley, CD and Hezlett, SA (2001) Individual development in the workplace, in *Handbook of Industrial, Work and Organizational Psychology* (Vol 1), ed N Anderson, DS Ones, HK Sinangil and C Viswesvaran, Sage, Thousand Oaks, CA

McGill, I and Beaty, L (1995) *Action Learning: A Guide for Professional, Management and Educational Development*, Kogan Page, London

McGrath, JE (1984) *Groups, Interaction and Performance*, Prentice Hall, Englewood Cliffs, NJ

McGrath, JE (1991) Time, interaction and performance: a theory of groups, *Small Groups Research*, **22**, pp 147–74

Salovey, P and Mayer, JD (1990) Emotional intelligence, *Imagination, Cognition, and Personality*, **9**, pp 185–211

Swezey, RW and Salas, E (1992) Guidelines for use in team-training development, in *Teams, Their Training and Performance*, ed R Swezey and E Salas, Ablex, Stamford

Wiggins, JS and Trapnell, PD (1997) Personality structure: the return of the Big Five, in *Handbook of Personality Psychology*, ed R Hogan, J Johnson and S Briggs, Academic Press, San Diego

Zaccaro, SJ (2007) Trait-based perspectives of leadership, *American Psychologist*, **62**, pp 6–16

6

Coaching with the Motivation Questionnaire (MQ)

Professor Dave Bartram, Dr Alexander Fradera and Helen Marsh

INTRODUCTION

In this chapter we consider the importance of understanding patterns of motivation for the coaching process. A general overview of the concept and theories of motivation is followed by a description of the Motivation Questionnaire (MQ). These sections draw heavily on more extended discussions from the *MQ Manual* (SHL, 2002), and the reader is referred there for details of the instrument and guidance on scale interpretation. The remainder of the chapter focuses on how use of the MQ can raise self-awareness of motivation patterns and help facilitate learning and behavioural change, for both the coach and client.

UNDERSTANDING HUMAN MOTIVATION

Motivation is the driving force behind job success. It determines how much energy will be channelled into job performance, for how long, and under what circumstances effort will be maintained. Motivation is typically defined as that which:

∎ energizes behaviour;
∎ channels or directs behaviour;
∎ sustains and maintains (or suspends) behaviour.

A perennial challenge for management is thus to motivate employees to act not as recipients but as active seekers of personal and organizational goals and objectives. In trying to predict people's performance and to facilitate their development, it is not sufficient to know only about their abilities (what they can do), interests (what they find stimulating), and personality (their preferred ways of behaving). Motivation (the energizing or driving force, the 'why' of behaviour) is also an essential part of the equation, and being able to assess people's motivation assumes vital importance.

Theoretical perspectives

In this section, we focus specifically on (psychological) theories that are relevant to understanding motivation in the workplace. Broadly speaking these theories can be grouped into three main categories: need-based theories, drive and reinforcement theories, and cognitive theories.

Need theories

A number of influential theorists have posited the existence of internal states, or needs, within the individual, which function to energize and direct behaviour. Henry Murray's (1938) approach identified a list of 20 major needs and an elaborate system for categorizing them. His studies identified psychological needs that included autonomy, deference, aggression, dominance, power, achievement and affiliation. The last three in particular have been the subject of quite extensive investigation.

Maslow (1954, 1970) proposed a set of five universal, innate needs, ordered in a hierarchy from the most basic physiological needs, such as to satisfy hunger and thirst, through those for safety, belongingness and love, to the need for self-esteem and, at the very top, the need for 'self-actualization': that is, the realization of one's full potential. Needs at the lower levels must be satisfied before those at higher levels can assume prominence.

Although empirical support is generally weak (Wahba and Bridwell, 1976; Cherrington, 1991; McCormick and Ilgen, 1987), Maslow's theory has proved popular as a descriptive model and has frequently been used as a basis for organizational development programmes.

Alderfer (1969, 1972) used findings from a series of studies to reduce Maslow's hierarchy of needs from five to three categories:

∎ existence needs (material as well as physiological factors necessary for survival);
∎ relatedness needs (all socially orientated needs);
∎ growth needs (ones related to the development of potential).

Herzberg (1966) drew a distinction between needs relating to self-actualization and those stemming from people's assumed need to avoid pain. The first set come only from distinct events in the workplace and are termed 'motivators': achievement, responsibility, advancement. The second set, 'hygiene' factors, are associated more with job context and are concerned with pain reduction rather than positive satisfaction. While the independence of these types of factors is not strongly supported by research, the approach has had a major impact on organizational psychology, acting as a stimulus for job enrichment programmes and creating interest in 'intrinsic motivation'.

Intrinsic motivation, promoted by Deci (1972; Deci and Ryan, 1985) proposes that needs for competence and self-determination underpin an ongoing process of seeking, and attempting to conquer, 'optimal challenges' – situations that stretch one's abilities – and lead ultimately to greater effectiveness. High levels of intrinsic motivation come from 'task involvement': interest in the task for its own sake rather than for the external rewards it may yield. The theory holds that individuals differ substantially in terms of the extent to which they are intrinsically, as opposed to extrinsically, motivated.

In contrast to the notion of innate needs, McClelland and his associates (McClelland, 1987) advocate that needs are learned or acquired through experience, and motivate individuals to pursue particular goals. The three that have received most attention in research have been:

∎ *Need for achievement*: 'behaviour directed towards competition with a standard of excellence'.
∎ *Need for affiliation*: the 'desire to establish and maintain warm relations with other individuals'.
∎ *Need for power*: a 'need to control others, to influence their behaviour and be responsible for them'.

Drive and reinforcement theories

Reinforcement theories assume that behaviour is controlled primarily by its consequences, in terms of how it was rewarded or punished in the past. Strictly speaking, this cannot be regarded as a theory of motivation since it ignores the energizing factor; however, it does provide a means of analysing how behaviour is shaped. As simplistic as these explanations of behaviour are considered, reinforcement techniques can be very effective for eliciting desired behaviour. A seminal article by Kerr (1975), 'On the folly of rewarding A, while hoping for B', discusses the way reward structures can work against organizational goals, for instance by rewarding managers for short-term sales gains, when longer-term thinking is desired.

Cognitive theories

These theories argue that the crucial workplace motivations are not automatic but are mediated by the contents of the mind. Consequently, they focus on elements of meaning, such as thoughts, beliefs and values, and account for how these impact on people's decisions and motivations in the workplace.

Equity theory, as developed by Adams (1963, 1965), revolves around the judgements and comparisons people make regarding 'inputs' to and 'outcomes' from jobs. 'Inputs' refer to everything the individual brings to the situation, including qualifications, experiences and effort; 'outcomes' include pay and other benefits of the job, such as status and interest value. According to Adams, individuals use their own priorities to derive an overall value for output and for input, and thus a ratio between the two. According to the theory, individuals somehow compare their own output–input ratio with that of a relevant other person or group of persons. 'Equity' is said to exist if the two ratios are equal; 'inequity' if they are not. Perceived inequity leads to an attempt to change elements of the ratio, such as the amount of effort contributed; this is the basis of motivation for action.

Expectancy, valence or instrumentality theory has its roots in psychological theorizing dating back some 60 years (Lewin, 1938; Tolman, 1932). It was first elaborated in relation to work motivation by Vroom (1964). It claims that people's expectations about future reinforcements are the main motivational impetus for behaviour, with actions chosen that are anticipated to be maximally advantageous. In Vroom's terms, both choice of action and the amount of effort a person is prepared to expend will be a joint function of:

▮ his or her 'expectancies' regarding the probability of a particular outcome;

▌ the belief that a particular activity will be 'instrumental' in (ie, will lead to) a particular outcome;
▌ the 'valences' or attractiveness of the outcome to the individual concerned.

Managerial approaches

The management literature has always seen employee motivation as key, but has tended to approach it outside a psychological framework. The traditional management model emphasized external controls and financial incentives. The human relations model also viewed the relationship in terms of management extracting work from staff, while emphasizing satisfaction of social needs, being sympathetic to staff and providing them with recognition, as the primary means of motivating people. Later work (following Drucker, 1954) identified the intention of achieving a goal (eg, completing a task well) as the motivation for doing so. This evolved into 'goal setting theory', and current work seeks to identify the most effective types of goals: specific rather than vague, and challenging rather than straightforward.

In the 1960s and 1970s the human resources approach developed, recognizing the fact that people are motivated by a complex set of interrelated factors and that different employees often have different goals and a diversity of talent to offer. This view sees employees in terms of abilities and talents for management to make best use of. Dating from this period is McGregor's (1960) 'Theory Y', conceiving of employees as sources of untapped creativity eager for responsibility, as opposed to lazy and avoidant of responsibility as seen by the default 'Theory X'.

MOTIVATIONAL QUESTIONNAIRE

The importance of individual differences – whether these be in needs, values, beliefs, expectancies, drive level or habits – is implicit if not explicit in each and every one of the psychological theories of motivation outlined above, as well as in contemporary managerial ('human resources') approaches to the topic.

In developing the MQ, we saw it as a prime objective to provide a means of systematically assessing the nature of those differences between individuals in motivational patterns and strengths. In short, the MQ is concerned with the assessment of individual differences in the factors that energize, direct and sustain behaviour in the workplace.

The purpose of the MQ is to assess the energy with which a person approaches tasks and identify situations that are likely to increase or reduce an individual's motivation. The information it provides can help in maximizing the motivation people bring to their jobs and their potential output. The MQ.M5 version is a normative questionnaire designed for use with managerial, professional, supervisory or similar level staff. It is best used to complement the information obtained from the Occupational Personality Questionnaire (OPQ32) or other personality measures.

The MQ presents a picture of the motivations of an individual, which can be compared with job demands, management style, company culture, values and so on to predict how he or she is likely to function in a given position. Managers will find the results valuable in helping them to understand and motivate their teams. In development centres, the MQ can be used in accurate job–person matching. In coaching situations, it can reveal why someone is either performing well or underperforming and help in analysing work relationships. At the organizational level, pooling the information derived from the MQ across a department or the whole organization can provide a perspective on staff morale and achievement. Such a review can be particularly useful prior to changes in company culture, or to assess the impact of such a change.

Structure of the MQ

The 18 scales of the MQ are clustered into four domains (see Table 6.1 for full descriptions). The scales loading onto the Energy and Dynamism factor provide an indication of the main sources of energy and drive for the individual concerned, and of how much energy a person is likely to apply in the work situation.

In contrast to the Energy and Dynamism scales, those in the other categories tend to focus on more specific motivators and demotivators. The scales in the Synergy group relate to feeling comfortable and in harmony with the work environment. These factors are often extrinsic to the task itself, but may be intrinsic to the company culture, such as the upholding of ethical standards, an emphasis on teamwork, and mutually supportive interactions with others. The intrinsic scales relate to features of jobs and tasks which individuals may find inherently satisfying, such as variety and interest value. The fourth group of scales relate to extrinsic rewards, motivating factors like material benefits, which are not integral to the task itself, but which might be gained as a result of performing well.

Table 6.1 Interpretation of the MQ dimensions

Dimension	Summary description	Factors related to drive and success
Energy and dynamism		
Level of activity	The extent to which people are motivated by having to work under pressure, cope with multiple demands and cope with tight timeframes	Being on the go Multi-tasking
Achievement	The extent to which people are motivated by being given challenging targets and feeling that their abilities are stretched	Being challenged Getting ahead Hitting targets
Competition	The extent to which people are motivated by the impact of working in a competitive environment	Being the best Comparison with others
Fear of failure	The extent to which people are motivated by the need to avoid failure, criticism and negative judgements by others and the possible loss of self-esteem that might accompany this	Not living up to expectations Prospect of failure
Power	The extent to which people are motivated by the opportunities for exercising authority, taking responsibility, negotiating and being able to influence others	Having authority Taking responsibility
Immersion	The extent to which people are motivated by work which requires commitment way beyond 'normal' working hours	Enjoy heavy work demands Long hours not an issue
Commercial outlook	The extent to which people are commercially or profits focused	Effort impacting on profits Commercial focus
Synergy		
Affiliation	The extent to which individuals are motivated by opportunities for interaction with other people in their work	Nice people to work with Social contact
Recognition	The extent to which people are motivated by praise and other outward signs of recognition for their achievements	Getting a pat on the back Being praised

Dimension	Summary description	Factors related to drive and success
Personal principles	The extent to which people need to be able to uphold ideals and conform to high ethical and quality standards	Being ethical Quality and reputation
Ease and security	The extent to which people are motivated by contextual factors such as pleasant working conditions and job security	Nice place to work Job security
Personal growth	The extent to which people are motivated by opportunities for further training and development and the acquisition of new skills	Personal development Opportunity for learning
Intrinsic		
Interest	The extent to which people are motivated by jobs providing them with variety, interest and stimulation	Variety, interest, stimulation
Flexibility	The extent to which people are motivated by a fluid environment and the absence of clearly defined structures and procedures for managing tasks	Fluidity Tolerate ambiguity and change
Autonomy	The extent to which people are motivated by being given scope for organizing their work as they see fit	Being independent Having empowerment
Extrinsic		
Material reward	The extent to which people are motivated by financial reward	Financial rewards
Progression	The extent to which people are motivated by having good promotion prospects	Promotion Career focused
Status	The extent to which people are motivated by outward signs of position and status and due regard for rank	Being respected Reputation

THE MQ AND COACHES

The benefits to coaches of exploring their own motivation profile are twofold. First, it provides an opportunity to become familiar with the questionnaire and profile before facilitating its use with clients. Second, it provides an opportunity for self-reflection, a chance to raise personal awareness of key sources of motivation and demotivation, and how these factors may influence our approach to coaching.

In principle, a trained user of the MQ is able to self-administer, score and appraise their own profile; however, receiving feedback from another trained feedback provider is perhaps more powerful, and will result in an experience more closely mirroring that of future clients. While there is no scientific evidence on the benefit of feedback provided by another trained person, it is widely accepted in practice that a well-trained feedback provider can add considerable value to what self-reflection alone would produce. He or she can take a more objective view and can also challenge assumptions that might otherwise be glossed over in a self-appraisal, even when the self-appraiser is an expert in the interpretation of the instrument.

Informing the use of MQ in coaching

Receiving feedback on the MQ benefits the coach by increasing familiarity with the tool and its interpretations. Exploration of the profile enhances the level of understanding of its structure with the four domains and 18 dimensions, the use of descriptors, interpretations of colours (indication of strength and direction of motivator) and 'sten' positions (comparison against the norm group). Uptake of information is often easier when introduced in a meaningful context, in this case through interpretation of one's own profile.

Self-administration also provides an experiential perspective to the MQ. What does it feel like to be delivered information about your own workplace motivations? What responses might descriptors evoke from a recipient? Are there ways in which you might prefer to receive this information? Individuals will differ in their reactions and preferences. Nevertheless, personal experience of the tool allows coaches to empathize with their clients when the MQ tool is introduced.

Informing our approach to coaching

Raising self-awareness is likely to lead to enhanced performance in the role of coach. For this purpose, the MQ is a highly effective tool. Exploring one's own motivation profile provides an opportunity to step back, reflect on and recognize why it is that we coach, the form of personal satisfaction we seek, and which coaching settings we are likely to find most rewarding or challenging. For instance, as a coach how motivated am I by the opportunity to help others? What personal principles and ethical standards are at play, and to what extent will these dictate the type of coaching contracts that I will be motivated by, or deem appropriate to pursue? What will be the most motivating format for my continued professional development as a coach?

As well as these general reflections, the MQ may also help the coach prepare for more specific coaching scenarios. As coaches we can ask ourselves how particular dimensions of our own profiles impact on the coaching experience, for both coach and client. How does my profile help or hinder my coaching style? Are there times when I may find it more easy or difficult to understand my client's viewpoint? When might I hold implicit views or be making value judgements of which motivators are right or wrong? Are there aspects of the profile that are so prominent for me that I may be at risk of colluding with the client when discussing that source of motivation? This process of self-reflection can help to raise our awareness of the role we play and the impact we have on the dynamic of the coaching relationship, and allows us to put our own agenda aside in order to focus on that of the client. To help us illustrate this point, we will explore a subset of dimensions in more detail.

- ▍ *Flexibility*: If I hold a preference for structure and am demotivated by ambiguity, how might I adapt the coaching process to meet the needs of a client who is motivated by a fluid environment? Similarly, if I usually work in a looser manner and am more energized under flexible working conditions, what steps might I take to ensure the client who needs structure can clearly see the way ahead in our coaching relation?
- ▍ *Affiliation*: Being motivated by the opportunity to interact with and help others would suggest a level of alignment with the work of a coach. Affiliation is also about being motivated by harmonious teamwork. Where this is a strong driver, might this lead at times to a softening of critical feedback or a tendency to avoid confronting development issues? Increased awareness allows the coach to adopt a more objective, detached persona where appropriate, offering both support and challenge.
- ▍ *Power*: If motivated by scope to influence and exercise authority, how might this manifest itself in the coaching context? Have there been times when my drive to control has led me to follow my own agenda as opposed to that of the client? The coach may choose to put up strong boundaries around the coaching environment, designating this environment as a 'safe space' where, as a matter of professionalism, considerations of control and authority should figure only minimally, as and when the relationship demands it.
- ▍ *Need for achievement and fear of failure*: If I have a strong desire to succeed and to overcome difficult challenges, and I am spurred on by the prospect of failure, how does this manifest itself in my approach to coaching? Being motivated by a fear of failure may make a coach

extremely averse to terminating coaching sessions, even where the evidence may point to this being the best course of action. The coach may choose to regularly reflect upon the progress of sessions and be open to the possibility that continuing the process may not always be in the best interest of the client.

In summary, this process of self-reflection around the MQ is an individually tailored process where coaches may ask themselves a number of important questions. Through the use of the MQ, these and other questions will be available to the coach both before and during a coaching relationship.

THE MQ AND COACHING CLIENTS

When to use the MQ in coaching

The most appropriate application of the Motivation Questionnaire will depend on the unique demands of each coaching situation, whether it is a performance, transactional or transformational coaching relationship. Typically, the MQ is used as an upfront diagnostic, and feedback is given sooner rather than later in the coaching process. As motivation can be hard for people to assess objectively, the MQ can provide a useful framework and vocabulary to the coaching client, and in this way acts as a springboard for discussion.

A further benefit of using the tool as a diagnostic early on is in achieving immediate insight and impact to meet the expectations of senior executives. Exploration of psychometric tools such as the MQ can demonstrate a robust, scientific approach, and is an effective way of establishing the credibility of the coaching relationship. There may, however, be some instances in which one would defer use of the MQ and other psychometrics, for example if the client first needs to build a greater level of trust in the coaching process overall.

Exploration of the MQ can act as a catalyst, generating many lines of discussion to pursue with the coaching client independently of the profile. In some cases, there may be no need to return to the profile at all, while other clients may benefit from using the tool as a touchstone, returning to the profile and specific dimensions over the course of the coaching relationship. The client's understanding of the dimensions is likely to become more sophisticated over time, yielding insights and perspectives that might have initially been inaccessible. Moreover, clients may experience significant changes or life events over the course of the coaching that may make it appropriate to review their motivation profile or to complete the questionnaire anew.

INTRODUCING THE MQ PROFILE

The manner in which the MQ is deployed is highly flexible, and coaches may adopt the approach best suited to the needs of both coach and client. In preparation it is useful to look to the clients' profiles for clues as to the approach that may best engage them: What are their levels of motivation generally (looking at their profile across the energy and dynamism function)? How motivated are they by opportunities for personal growth and development? How important is it for them to feel in control of the situation? To what extent are they motivated by clear structures and process or by a fluid environment?

Before introducing the profile, the coach might ask open, general questions on the topic of motivation. What do clients consider to be key motivators in their current role? What aspects of their work do they find most demotivating? When have they felt most motivated at work? Why was that? When have they felt most demotivated at work? When introducing the profile it is useful to provide the client with a brief overview of the four domains and 18 dimensions, and an explanation of how the colours represent motivators (green) and demotivators (blue).

The Energy and Dynamism function can provide a useful starting point for understanding their overall levels of motivation, followed by exploration of dimensions from across the profile that stand out as key motivators or demotivators. In facilitating the discussion, a number of questions may be useful: How accurate is this picture of their key drivers? To what extent are these needs met in their current circumstances/role? How does the approach to management align with their motivational drivers? How does their motivation profile align with the company culture and values? What happens in situations where a particular motivator is absent or, if the dimension is a demotivator, where it is present? What coping strategies have they in place/considered? What action might they want to take?

INTERPRETING THE MQ PROFILE

When looking to interpret MQ profiles there are a number of broad patterns that may be worthy of attention. An extreme profile, with a mix of very high and very low stens across dimensions suggests that the client may need a very particular working milieu to perform at his or her best. Conversely, uniform scores may be interesting to explore: uniformly high stens may suggest a degree of eagerness to please and social desirability; uniformly mid-range stens may suggest some caution or unwillingness to engage with the enterprise. Uniformly low stens can be an indicator that the individual may be currently demotivated at work. In all cases the coach may seek further information: What energizes the individual? What motivates them more or less? A profile that falls outside of these patterns may still raise questions when it suggests a dissonance between the client and his or her working environment.

Table 6.1 provides a summary of the MQ dimensions and their interpretations. What follows is a more detailed exploration of a subset of these dimensions.

▌ *Achievement and competition*: These dimensions reflect very different motivations. Achievement is rooted in internal goals and benchmarks, and relates to certain standards that are demanded relatively independently of the changing climate. Competition, meanwhile, is measured against external benchmarks either within or outside the immediate working environment, and is consequently much more sensitive to these changes.

▌ *Immersion and level of activity*: Level of activity reflects general energy levels for work and the need to be busy, whereas Immersion represents the degree to which individuals are prepared to commit themselves to the role. Both can lead to working long hours; one is habitual while the other reflects an attitude to the role. Some highly immersive individuals may not enjoy being hurried, and may invest a lot of time to achieve their output. This may be related to their decision-making style – the degree to which they make fast decisions and reach conclusions quickly.

▌ *Fear of failure*: Individuals may resist the notion of a fear of failure, and may suggest this represents their need to achieve. In fact, Achievement typically reflects a focus upon occupational success, and hence a willingness to recognize and reward this, whereas those motivated by failure are likely to disregard or minimize successes. Given the link between fear of failure and maintainance of self-esteem, care should be taken that the extent to which this is explored is appropriate to the professional boundaries and skill set of the coaching practitioner involved.

▌ *Personal principles*: The profile will indicate whether upholding personal principles is important to the individual; if so, the nature of these principles will be of interest. Clients who show a very flexible approach to these ethical or quality issues may encounter resistance if they work within an atmosphere of high compliance. Conversely, for an individual committed to upholding a set of standards, working in an environment which conflicts with this may be demotivating. In an international climate, the principles may include religious and cultural beliefs.

▌ *Material reward, progression and status*: While these elements are closely linked it is useful to explore each in turn. Status is concerned above all with rank, material reward with financial benefits, and progression with justice and equity. A client concerned with progress and fair treatment may be motivated if given greater responsibility or an increase in the scope of their role, perhaps even more so than if offered a hierarchical promotion or increase in salary.

APPLICATIONS OF THE MQ

The MQ may be applied at the level of the individual, team and/or organization. An organization might review aggregate data, looking for organizational trends in levels and sources of motivation, and drawing on this insight by way of assessing the impact of corporate change. The focus in the remainder of this section will be on the client as an individual, and the client as a team manager.

The MQ may offer the client interesting insights at various levels of the leadership pipeline (Charan, Drotter, and Noel, 2000): How well aligned are the individual's sources of motivation to the expectations of the role, either in managing him or herself, in managing others or in managing an area of the business? In many cases the MQ will be completed alongside other psychometric tools to build a holistic understanding of an individual. In particular, personality questionnaires such as the Occupational Personality Questionnaire (OPQ) are used to complement the motivational responses with data on preference and style. Both personality and motivation may be seen as measures of an individual's potential (also relevant here are abilities, interests and values).

Measures of potential are often powerful in supporting and making sense of competency-based performance data from assessment or development centres, 360-degree or performance appraisal: If individuals perform well in the competency of 'Building Team Capability', and their preferred style and motivation are also aligned to this area, it is likely to be an area of natural strength. If they perform less well in the area of 'Commercial Decision making', what explanation might be found in their underlying preferred style and motivation profiles? Equally, there may be areas where individuals are spurred on by a particular activity and their natural style suggests an affinity to the area, but they have not had the opportunity to demonstrate this as-yet untapped potential.

Some elements, simply by being known, can result in improvements in working conditions. If a client has never articulated the fact that recognition is a prime motivator, knowing and then sharing this fact with colleagues and managers can result in improved job satisfaction and performance. For other elements, awareness of a motivational need, where that source of motivation is lacking, may lead the individual to consider and identify appropriate coping strategies.

In goal-centred coaching it is important to assess the individual's level of buy-in and commitment to the goals identified, and to his or her subsequent development action plans. Goals are only likely to be achieved if the individuals are inspired to achieve them – that is, if the motivation for the goal is high. If goals have been identified that are necessary but that do not inspire the people concerned, then it can be useful to revisit their motivation profiles to explore how key motivators might be used to determine a perspective from which the goal will engage them. For example, if the goal is to increase commercial acumen, but the coachees are demotivated by an over-emphasis on profits and finance, they may choose to reframe the goal as an opportunity for personal growth (what skills or expertise may be acquired from it), or to focus on how reaching the goal can be communicated to colleagues (a source of recognition from senior management).

Exploration of the MQ can also be powerful in helping the client in the role of team manager. The framework can help managers to understand how individual team members are motivated, that there are a variety of sources of motivation and that it is unlikely that all of their team members will be motivated in the same way. It also helps managers to recognize that team members may have different sources of motivation from their own. If attempts to motivate their teams in the past have consistently failed, or have been counter-productive, might it be that a different approach is needed? With an understanding of their teams' motivation profiles, managers may also more accurately assess the likely impact of any organizational initiatives in the extent to which they are likely to motivate their team.

Perhaps the most powerful application of the MQ is in helping a manager understand and explain conflict within a team. Conflict may be founded in differences in need for harmonious teamwork, need for autonomy or tolerance of ambiguity. While personality profiles explain differences in the team members' styles of working, the MQ helps to explain lapses in energy due to these conflicts in working styles. It may be appropriate for the client/manager and the team to participate in facilitated team development. This may involve individual feedbacks followed by a team-building session with the opportunity for each team member to share aspects of his or her motivation profile, for the team to consider what works well/less well within the team, and what they will do differently as a result.

SUMMARY

This chapter has sought to illustrate how the MQ can be used to support the coaching process as a tool for both coaches and clients to better understand their own patterns of motivation. As a result, the coach is in a better position to understand how to help clients direct their behaviour into productive areas for development. Psychometric assessments provide a very cost-effective way of quickly obtaining a wealth of information in an objective way. What is more, this information has built-in benchmarking that helps people understand how their own patterns of motivation may differ from those of others.

References

Adams, JS (1963) Towards an understanding of inequity, *Journal of Abnormal and Social Psychology*, **67**, pp 422–36

Adams, JS (1965) Inequity in social exchange, in *Advances in Experimental Social Psychology*, Volume 2, ed L Berkowitz, pp 267–99, Academic Press, New York

Alderfer, CP (1969) An empirical test of a new theory of human needs, *Organizational Behaviour and Human Performance*, **4**, pp 142–75

Alderfer, CP (1972) *Existence, Relatedness and Growth: Human needs in organizational settings*, Free Press, New York

Charan, R, Drotter, S and Noel, J (2000) *The Leadership Pipeline: How to build the leadership powered company*, Jossey-Bass, San Francisco

Cherrington, DJ (1991) Need theories of motivation, pp 31–43 in *Motivation and Work Behaviour*, ed RL Steers and LW Porter, McGraw Hill, New York

Deci, EL (1972) The effects of contingent and non-contingent rewards and controls on intrinsic motivation, *Organizational Behaviour and Human Performance*, **8**, pp 217–29

Deci, EL and Ryan, RM (1985) *Intrinsic Motivation and Self-Determination in Human Behaviour*, Plenum Press, New York

Drucker, PF (1954) *The Practice of Management*, Harper, New York

Herzberg, F (1966) *Work and the Nature of Man*, World Publishing, Cleveland

Kerr, S (1975) On the folly of rewarding A, while hoping for B, *Academy of Management Journal*, **18**, pp 769–82

Lewin, K (1938) *The Conceptual Representation and the Measurement of Psychological Forces*, Duke University Press, Durham, NC

Locke, EA, Shaw, KM, Saari, LM and Latham, GP (1981) Goal setting and task performance, *Psychological Bulletin*, **90**, pp 125–52

Maslow, AH (1954) *Motivation and Personality*, Harper and Row, New York

Maslow, AH (1970) *Motivation and Personality*, 2nd edn, Harper and Row, New York

McClelland, DC (1987) *Human Motivation*, Cambridge University Press, Cambridge, UK

McCormick, EJ and Ilgen, D (1987) *Industrial and Organizational Psychology*, McGraw Hill, New York

McGregor, D (1960) *The Human Side of Enterprise*, McGraw Hill, New York

Murray, HA (1938) *Explorations in Personality*, Oxford University Press, New York

SHL (2002) *Motivation Questionnaire: Manual and user's guide*, Version 11, SHL Group Ltd, Thames Ditton

Steers, RM, Porter, L and Bigley, GA (1996) *Motivation and Leadership at Work*, 6th edn, McGraw Hill, New York

Tolman, EC (1932) *Purposive Behaviour in Animals and Men*, Appleton-Century-Crofts, New York

Vroom, VJ (1964) *Work and Motivation*, Wiley, New York

Wahba, MA and Bridwell, LG (1976) Maslow reconsidered: a review of research on the need hierarchy theory, *Organizational Behaviour and Human Performance*, **15**, pp 212–40

7

Coaching with Saville Consulting Wave®

Dr Rainer Kurz, Rab MacIver and Professor Peter Saville

INTRODUCTION

For many years personality assessment has played an important part in enhancing the coaching process. The days of irrelevant and embarrassing personality questions are largely over. Today, job-relevant questionnaires can make a useful contribution by providing insights for the coachee and the coach. The technology of personality measurement is moving forward and a new generation of instruments has been designed with high levels of computer-assisted expert interpretation. Behind these new developments lies the crucial issue of 'validity'. It is now possible to show much stronger links between personality scales and job performance. This enables a much more precise focus on the aspects of personality that really matter in improving performance and motivation. The first half of this chapter provides an overview of Saville Consulting Wave®, its theoretical foundation based on recent developments in the field and the unique measurement features of the tools. The second half covers the practical use of

Saville Consulting Wave™ with coaches and coachees, illustrating how the deep levels of analysis afforded by the Professional Styles questionnaire can be utilized by the coach.

THE SAVILLE CONSULTING WAVE® MODEL

The goal at the outset of the development of the Saville Consulting Wave® range was to build on the past century of self-report questionnaire assessment practice and to innovate, utilizing the latest technological advances, in order to create an integrated suite of tools for the assessment of individual, organizational and work variables.

The cluster, section, dimension and facet hierarchy

The model is hierarchical, providing four levels of detail that can be deployed as required. Figure 7.1 shows the four clusters at the apex that provide a broad overview of the key characteristics that underpin work performance. Each cluster comprises three sections that consist of three dimensions that measure at the level of detail expected by experienced psychometric test users. Each dimension breaks down into three facets that jointly define the dimension. These facets provide breadth of measurement while maintaining clarity of meaning.

The model structure was developed from three perspectives simultaneously (MacIver *et al*, 2006). Inductive theorizing led to the a-priori four-cluster model; deductive 'bottom-up' modelling initially created 214 unique styles facets; and validation against 44 rationally derived work criteria (11 per cluster) provided the basis for selecting the 108 facets that became the final model. The Saville Consulting Wave® model applies to three sets of variables:

▐ Organizational variables are measured through 'preferred and actual culture' surveys that enable gap analysis, and a 'climate' survey that captures the impact of person-work fit.
▐ Work-role evaluation and work-performance evaluation multi-rater inventories enable profiling of work requirements and appraisal of work performance by gathering 360-degree stakeholder perspectives.
▐ Individual characteristics are measured through the Professional Styles suite of questionnaires and the shorter Focus Styles assessment.

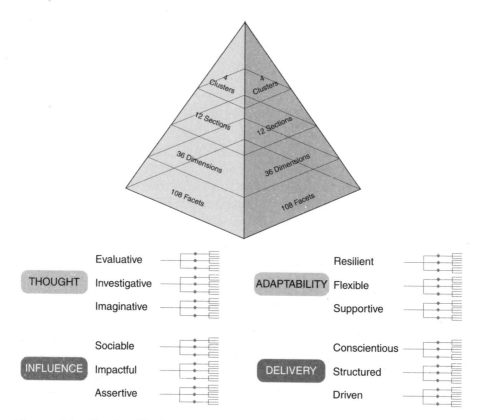

Figure 7.1 The Saville Consulting Wave® Model showing cluster, section, dimension and facet hierarchy

The 'Wave Wheel'

The Thought, Influence, Adaptability and Delivery clusters are designed to account for all major behaviour aspects of performance at work. The clusters and sections build on the global research base of the Big Five personality factors as well as the Great Eight competency model, and are transparently mapped in the Wave Wheel to their underlying constructs as shown in Figure 7.2.

The Wave Wheel arranges sections in a circumplex order where opposing sections tend to have lower correlations than neighbouring sections. The upper half represents characteristics that are less observable while the lower half represents characteristics that are more observable. The sections on the left broadly cover protective behaviours, while the sections on the right from Investigative to Driven broadly cover proactive behaviours. The circular arrangement aids exploration of neighbouring sections as well as those positioned at opposing positions.

Figure 7.2   The Wave Wheel mapping the relationship of four assessment models from the Big Five personality factors at the centre, through the Great Eight competencies to the Terrific Twelve sections and the Fab Four clusters of Saville Consulting Wave® at the periphery

The 'Big Five' personality factors

The broad-trait factors known as Openness to Experience, Conscientiousness, Extroversion, Agreeableness and Neuroticism (remembered by OCEAN mnemonic) form the Big Five personality model. Barrick and Mount (1991) outlined the research base for these broad-trait factors, and traced back their origins to the work of Norman (1963). Over the years different names have been used for what is now understood to be essentially the same construct set. Neuroticism is increasingly referred to in the wake of Positive Psychology as Emotional Stability or Confidence, while Agreeableness and Openness to Experience are sometimes measured through their opposite poles: Independence and Conventionality respectively. The NEO-PI-R questionnaire (Costa and McCrae, 1992) is the most commonly used benchmark measure for the Big Five.

The 'Great Eight' competencies

Kurz and Bartram (2002) expanded the Big Five personality model by adding three new categories (Intelligence, Need for Power and Need for Achievement) to designate the Great Eight competencies that are designed to account for individual differences in work performance rather than personality per se. They defined competencies in relation to their significance for performance at work as 'sets of behaviours that are instrumental in the achievement of desired results or outcomes'.

The origins of the model can be traced back to the meta-analysis work of Robertson and Kinder (1993), who created a criterion taxonomy to classify a variety of 'local' performance criteria. This led to the development of a range of competency inventories enabling large scale validation work like the international validation study by Nyfield *et al* (1995). On the basis of this database, Kurz (1999) developed expert system equations that link standardized psychological predictor scales and competency criteria to power interpretative reports and show consistently high validities in the prediction of competencies from personality and ability predictor scales. The same a-priori equations have been cross-validated on Korean and Japanese samples, demonstrating robust validities across cultures (Gotoh, 1999).

The 'Terrific Twelve' sections

The sections in Saville Consulting Wave® are transparently mapped to the Big Five and Great Eight constructs, yet provide wider and more detailed coverage that reflects the true complexity of people and jobs. In the Focus Styles questionnaire, each section is measured through three facets while the Professional Styles sections feature three dimensions comprising three facets. Kurz (2006) applied a-priori predictions by Crebbin (2005) about the relationship between NEO and Professional Styles sections and found for all Big Five factors significant correlations averaging about 0.50.

The 'Fab Four' clusters

The clusters bring together a diverse range of theories and assessment approaches.

Digman (1997) investigated the higher-order factor structure of the Big Five and found that Agreeableness and Conscientiousness (usually together with Emotional Stability) formed a higher-order factor he called 'Alpha', while Extroversion and Openness to Experience formed his 'Beta' factor. The sections on the left of the Wave Wheel from Structured to Evaluative broadly cover the Alpha supra-factor, and the sections on the right from Investigative to Driven broadly cover the Beta supra-factor.

Bartram, Baron and Kurz (2003) outlined four Leadership Functions that could be viewed as a higher-order structure of the Great Eight. Kurz (2005) measured the Leadership Functions by aggregating relevant competency ratings and identified what ability, interest, motivation and styles variables underpin them. He challenged the distinction of transformational and transactional components in the SHL Corporate Leadership Model (Bartram, 2002) as factor analysis results showed that a better account of the data was provided by a top-level distinction akin to Digman's Alpha vs Beta factors in conjunction with the classic People vs Task orientation well known from leadership research.

The Fab Four clusters effectively parallel the four Leadership Functions but serve as a generic model of work performance across all levels of work complexity and job level. Fullman (2005) factor analysed Professional Styles predictor and criterion data and found good convergence between the a-priori model and statistical four factor solutions.

On the Wave Wheel the Thought and Delivery clusters form the Task Axis while Influence and Adaptability form the People Axis. Comparing the scores on an axis can lead to interesting contrasts or insights into the likely behaviour of an individual and the potential impact on the coaching relationship as outlined below.

The clusters are utilized in the Types Report where Influence and Adaptability combine to define four People Types, and Thought and Delivery to define four Task Types. In combination, they define 16 types that chart transformational and transactional aspects of performance. The 'Transformer–Transactor' type is the most prevalent and effective type in managerial and leadership roles with high staff and resource responsibilities.

SAVILLE CONSULTING WAVE® 'DEEP DIVE' MEASUREMENT FEATURES

The Styles questionnaires and the corresponding expert reports feature three key measurement innovations.

New depths of measurement in coaching

Where the three facet scores for a dimension in the expert reports have a range of three or more stens, their facet range is highlighted. Figure 7.3 shows a facet range for the Abstract dimension in an excerpt from the expert report that shows a high inclination towards conceptualization and learning by reflecting on underlying principles; this contrasts with a fairly low inclination to apply theories. By reflecting the idiosyncrasies and complexities of real individuals through facet ranges, both coach and coachee are able to see the uniqueness of each individual and what sets each one apart.

Combined normative and ipsative assessment in coaching

A new feature of the Styles assessments is the dynamic online Rate–Rank technique where respondents rate their responses on a nine-point Likert scale, and are re-presented with tied items in a forced choice format. This approach builds on the strengths of each response format while minimizing

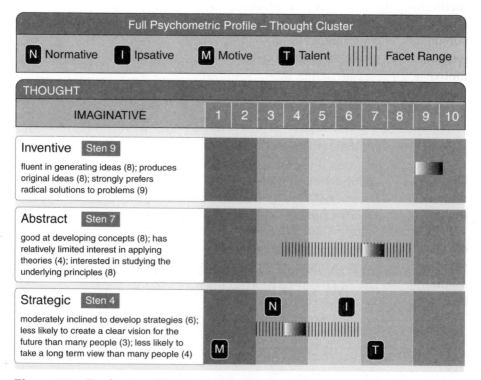

Figure 7.3   Professional Styles report section illustrating Facet range, Normative–Ipsative split and Motive–Talent split display in the Full Psychometric Profile

the weaknesses of each. This dynamic response format has been developed to capitalize on the opportunities afforded by internet technology and bring the normative–ipsative debate (Saville and Willson, 1991; Saville and Sik, 1991) to a natural conclusion.

When comparison of their respective sten scores highlights a difference of three or more stens, the normative–ipsative split is displayed. Such a difference is primarily due to high or low acquiescence on the normative rating, or extreme rankings of a set of dimension items over other areas. In the expert report visual (Figure 7.3), the coachee is fairly disinclined to pursue strategic work. This tendency is particularly pronounced in the normative ratings, and is aligned to a low score on acquiescence: that is, self-critical responding. On the ranking, however, the score is slightly above average, indicating that under pressure the individual may well rise to the challenge and work strategically.

Combined motive and talent assessment in coaching

A unique feature of the Styles assessment is the measurement of behavioural inclinations through Motive (needs and preferences) and Talent (self-efficacy beliefs and skills) items. Motive items are closer to conventional personality and preference items while Talent items are closer to competency items. Each of the 108 Professional Styles facets is composed of one motive and one talent item.

▌ Example items for 'Control Seeking' facet:
  – *Motive*: I want to take control of things.
  – *Talent*: I am good at taking control of things.

Discrepancies between Motive and Talent dimension scores reaching three or more stens scores are graphically highlighted in the profile report through motive–talent splits for further exploration in the feedback interview.

If Motive is higher than Talent on a particular dimension, the coachee effectively acknowledges this area as a development need that he or she wants to do something about, such as wanting to be more Analytical or Self-assured. If Talent is higher than Motive, then competent behaviour may not be backed up by an underlying motivation to perform.

USING PROFESSIONAL STYLES WITH COACHES

The ultimate purpose of coaching is broadly to maximize performance as well as satisfaction, happiness and well-being at the work place.

Self-awareness is at the heart of the coaching process and can be raised for coach and coachee alike through well-constructed self-report questionnaires. Coaches can greatly benefit from questionnaire profiles as they can rapidly gain an overview of their coachees' characteristics. Coaches can form hypotheses from questionnaire results that can be explored interactively. Tools that cover the Big Five naturally provide more comprehensive coverage than those missing out on some of the factors. Those that go beyond the Big Five can create a better understanding, especially if they have been constructed with an occupational frame of reference. Professional Styles has a number of unique features that are useful in deepening the self-awareness of the coach, and could potentially be used as part of an enhanced supervision process.

The scales in Professional Styles have been selected on the basis of their proven validity in predicting related work outcomes, and provide an accessible terminology for talking about potential, either in trait terms through the full psychometric profile or in competency terms through the Competency Potential Profile. The tool avoids the ambivalence of bi-polar scales that are supposedly neutral and non-evaluative when the validation evidence that exists clearly favours one end – at least in use with managerial and professional populations.

Scores show areas of relative strengths and weakness that help coaches to understand how they may be perceived by their coachees. For example, coaches with high scores on Assertive and low scores on Supportive may have to work very hard to avoid domineering their sessions, and to allow coachees to express themselves. Conversely, a coach with the opposite score pattern will have to work hard to prevent domineering senior managers from steamrollering them.

The Competency Potential Profile (see Figure 7.4) highlights relative strengths and weaknesses through a red–amber–green 'traffic light' scheme (see McDowall and Kurz, 2006) backed by large-scale validation research. It displays scores graphically and can be interpreted in conjunction with the rest of the Styles report or alongside work performance evaluation 360-degree feedback to compare potential with actual performance. It can also be used on its own without prior psychometric training, for example by line managers.

High scores on the Competency Potential Profile indicate relative strengths that are likely to lead to superior performance in that area. Extremely high scores, however, which may have served the coachee well for many years in climbing the career ladder, may lead to over-reliance on a strength that may backfire, and potentially lead to derailment. The report enables exploration of genuine strengths as well as over-played strengths that may be detrimental to success.

Competency Description	Potential	

	Evaluating Problems Examining Information; Documenting Facts; Interpreting Data	■■■■□ 6 □□□□	**Above Average** higher potential than about 60% of the comparison group
SOLVING PROBLEMS	**Investigating Issues** Developing Expertise; Adopting Practical Approaches; Providing Insights	■■■■■ 7 □□□	**Fairly High** higher potential than about 75% of the comparison group
	Creating Innovation Generating Ideas; Exploring Possibilities; Developing Strategies	■■■■□ 6 □□□□	**Above Average** higher potential than about 60% of the comparison group

Figure 7.4   Competency Potential Profile Report

Coaches need to watch out that 'red areas' in their own profile do not undermine their own coaching performance. Processing Details is probably the least important of the 12 sections in professional and managerial work, but getting a critical detail wrong can seriously derail coaches as well as their coachees. The expert report enables exploration of personal weaknesses and to what extent they are under-managed.

Over-played strengths and under-managed weaknesses at opposing positions of the Wave Wheel are particularly dangerous combinations, while wide behavioural repertoires spanning opposing positions can lead to extraordinary accomplishments.

Are you an entrepreneurial scientist?

A coach with very high scores on Thought and high scores on Delivery can be viewed as an 'entrepreneurial scientist' (or scientific entrepreneur if Delivery scores are slightly higher than Evaluative scores) who can come up with breakthrough insights that can trigger step-change behaviour shifts and completely change the outlook of the coachee. Breaking this constellation down to the section level below illustrates how low scores may negatively impact the coaching relationship and outcome.

Highly imaginative coaches are often less conscientious; without delivery and follow-up on coachee goal achievement, the best ideas will remain just that, rather than turn into realities. Conversely, a highly conscientious coach may bring structure and strict guidelines to the coaching intervention but may resent unconventional coachee ideas and any deviations from the protocol. Coaches who appreciate 'big' ideas yet also guide towards step-by-step implementation are thus very valuable.

Investigative coaches who lack structure in their approach may miss clues in coachee behaviour and background that help to explain the coachee's situation and shape his or her future. Structured coaches who lack curiosity may overly rely on traditional approaches and are at risk of having their expertise seen as 'old hat'. Coaches who are up-to-date about the latest trends but selective and organized in what they adopt are most likely to uncover critical information and organize it so that it can be put to good use.

Highly driven coaches who lack evaluative acumen may jump impulsively to conclusions without analysing the coachee's situation properly. Highly evaluative coaches on the other hand may, through 'analysis to paralysis', miss opportunities. Coaches with strengths in both areas are hard to find but extraordinarily gifted in judging opportunities and risks.

Are you a caring coordinator?

Very high Influence scores combined with high Adaptability scores characterize the 'caring coordinator' (or coordinating carer if Adaptability is slightly higher than Influence) coach who excels in building lasting relationships. The section level breakdown below illustrates the impact of this constellation.

Sociable coaches may be too talkative and self-centred to fully take in coachee feelings and concerns, unless they are also supportive. Quietly supportive coaches on the other hand may be listening attentively but may fail to make a substantial difference by failing to assert strict guidance.

Assertive coaches who lack inner confidence may show a rather volatile coaching style predicated more on controlling the coachee than respecting the coachee's right to self-determination. In extreme situations this may lead to a breakdown of the coaching relationship, or to dysfunctional relationships. Resilient coaches who lack outer confidence may take things in their stride but may be perceived as 'too laid-back' and lacking motivation. Coaches who calmly but firmly discuss coachee views and actions are most likely to achieve the outcomes desired from the coaching relationship.

Impactful coaches who lack flexibility may overestimate their power in what is essentially an advisory capacity, and may well argue themselves out of their jobs. Flexible coaches who lack conviction, however, will not impress coachees either. Coaches who flexibly challenge coachees combine pointed arguments with a behavioural flexibility that may at times be baffling, but is effective in drawing out and reconciling conflicting views on the coachee's situation.

USING PROFESSIONAL STYLES WITH COACHEES

Any well-developed personality questionnaire can be successfully used in coaching, yet individual coaches, and indeed coachees, will have their natural and/or historical preferences. Professional Styles features job-relevant uni-polar scales that have been validated against specific as well as global performance criteria. The terminology is straightforward and easily accessible so that as a consequence personal reports can be provided to respondents as automated debrief in selection situations, or as a precursor to a developmental coaching session. Only the expert report, however, provides the full depth of psychometric and application information that informs an in-depth feedback (following which the expert report can be given to the coachee at the discretion of the coach).

Response summary

In a coaching feedback session, a useful starting point would be for the coach to review the four response summary indicators that provide an overview allowing extrapolation of likely features of the report that follows and provide clues to the validity of the profile.

The Ratings Acquiescence score captures how generous or self-critical coachees have been in describing themselves. The score itself predicts overall success, showing that in general, positive self-efficacy beliefs translate into performance behaviours as judged by others. High acquiescence reflects lenient self-ratings and strong self-beliefs, but extremely high scores can be indicative of inflated views of self-importance to the point of 'delusion'. Low scores may reflect self-criticism and self-doubts, or frequent use of the 'Unsure' answer option.

Consistency of rankings is derived from the ipsative rank-order data and shows how consistent the rankings were across the questionnaire. Coachees with a very varied 'modal' profile tend to have high consistency scores as it is easy for them to rank order the items, while individuals with a 'flat' profile tend to have low consistency scores as they find it very difficult to rank items. Extremely low scores can be indicative of faking or random answering, but more likely reflect an undifferentiated profile or the mind set differences when completing the online questionnaire across several sittings in different mood states (eg, work, home, internet café).

Normative–ipsative agreement is a direct function of the previous two scales where extremely low or high scores on acquiescence lead to low normative–ipsative agreement with many 'splits' in the report, and moderate scores lead to high normative–ipsative agreement with few splits.

Motive–talent agreement indicates the degree of alignment of scores on the Motive and Talent items across all dimensions. Low scores indicate misalignment between coachees and their environment, which may be at the root of stress and dissatisfaction. Extreme cases may show motive–talent splits even in their Ratings Acquiescence.

The response summary provides overall trends across the whole profile, while normative–ipsative and motive–talent splits together with facet ranges define specific dimensions to probe. Just like any other self-report questionnaire, Professional Styles should be corroborated against other independent evidence such as feedback interviews, 360-degree feedback or behavioural simulations.

Full psychometric profile

Coaches will want to review in depth the full psychometric profile, which features one page for each of the four clusters, as it forms the basis for in-depth feedback and exploration. Coaches who are novice users of Professional Styles are advised to work through the four pages in the order presented as the clusters are arranged in a logical sequence that applies to most work assignments: that is, tackling problems, influencing people to accept a solution, adapting own approaches in the light of feedback and finally delivering results.

Thought cluster

The Thought cluster covers stylistic characteristics that underpin problem solving behaviour. The Evaluative section covers analytical, factual and rational dimensions that relate to 'convergent thinking' aspects of thinking. Results from this section can be fruitfully cross-referenced to results on aptitude tests measuring verbal, numerical and diagrammatic/abstract reasoning. The Imaginative section covers inventive, conceptual and strategic dimensions that relate to 'divergent thinking'. The Investigative section covers a heterogeneous set of dimensions called 'insightful', 'practically minded' and 'learning oriented' that are linked through the 'learning' theme.

Coachees are frequently senior managers and leaders who are expected to be imaginative in coming forward with solutions, but also evaluative in reality, checking their proposals. To what extent a learning orientation helps problem solving depends very much on the company culture (which can be measured through the matched Saville Consulting Performance Culture surveys). Imbalance of Imaginative and Evaluative section scores can be indicative of derailment risk areas. Pursuing fantastic ideas that lack realism can be fatal to an organization just as much as excessive analysis that misses the bigger picture.

The various facets concerned with learning (learning by doing / reading / thinking; open to learning; quick learning) paint a picture of the coachee's learning style. This in turn helps to explain session dynamics and may lead to recommendations on learning strategy. Aptitude test performance levels and profile patterns are also very helpful in this context.

Influence cluster

The Influence cluster covers characteristics that underpin successful Influencing in the work place. The Sociable section covers interactive, engaging and self-promoting dimensions that measure classic Big Five Extroversion personality characteristics. High-scoring coachees will naturally be well-connected and talkative, while low scorers will have to work much harder at communication to establish and develop relationships. The Assertive section covers purposeful, directing and empowering dimensions that are critically related to leadership. Scores on these are statistically strongly related to Sociable (Extroversion) and Driven (Need for Achievement) areas on the profile. The Impact section features convincing, challenging and articulate dimensions related to the communication of information, with clear links to the Thought cluster.

Assertive inclinations are likely to be required for any coachee in the boardroom, given that the facet 'Leadership Oriented' is one of the most universally valid facets. Coachees who score high on all three sections are likely to be very influential, but could at times over-play their strengths by showing, for example, domineering behaviours. Coachees who score low may find it difficult to climb the managerial career ladder in traditional ways, but may nevertheless succeed if creating an impact and career progression based on expertise rather than assertiveness.

Adaptability cluster

The Adaptability cluster is the most heterogeneous of the clusters in Professional Styles as it integrates the Big Five factors Emotional Stability and Agreeableness, as well as the softer aspects of Openness as featured in emotional intelligence research. Emotional, behavioural and social adaptability are covered through the Resilient, Flexible and Supportive sections respectively.

Resilient comprises self-assured, composed and resolving dimensions, all of which underpin emotional adaptability. Self-assured facets cover self-confidence, self-valuing and internal locus of control. Composed facets cover stress tolerance, worries and anxieties. Low scores on these two dimensions indicate neurotic tendencies, and reveal an internal life state of the coachee that may be in sharp contrast to his or her outside behaviour. Many coachees in senior positions compensate for feelings of insecurity through assertive and driven behaviours. However, over-compensation may lead to derailment if volatility is under-managed. Volatile coachees are also disinclined to show resolving behaviours as they find dealing with angry or upset individuals difficult – especially if their own domineering actions may have caused those negative emotions in the first place. The profile helps to break down problems into manageable chunks and thus supports anger and stress management interventions designed to increase coachee effectiveness in this arena.

Flexibility is measured through the receptive, positive and change-oriented dimensions that reflect behavioural adaptability. In times of constant change, all coachees will find challenges and setbacks in their environments. The cognitive mindset for dealing with change will ultimately determine whether the coachee can successfully adapt to such changes or has to leave the changed environment.

Supportive covers social adaptability through the involving, attentive and accepting dimensions. They capture only the work relevant aspects of Agreeableness that were found to be predictive of job performance. High scorers will be well attuned to the feelings and concerns of those around them. Coachees in senior roles, however, tend to score fairly low on these scales, which tend to correlate slightly negatively with Driven and Assertive sections. It seems to be difficult but not impossible to be cooperative and competitive simultaneously! Within a stable and predictable environment, unsupportive coachees may succeed by building relationships with more senior people who often value their task orientation. However, if the environment changes, such coachees may easily become derailed as their deeds become apparent and victims of their selfish actions start to unmask them.

How scores in the Adaptability section translate into actions depends a lot on the context. Coachees may appear supportive, resilient and flexible to their bosses, yet self-centred, emotional and firm (or even rigid) to their subordinates. 360-degree feedback such as Saville Consulting's Work Performance Evaluation can help to glean an accurate picture of a coachee's behaviour with a range of stakeholders.

Delivery cluster

Conscientious in Professional Styles is composed of reliable, meticulous and compliant dimensions. They are important dimensions for job roles where accurate and timely processing of details is of paramount importance (primarily in administrative and operational roles). Coachees occupying managerial and leadership roles often have subordinates to whom they can delegate detail and routine work. However, when weaknesses in these areas are under-managed and combine with low scores on resilient and supportive measures, then coachees may become derailed as their behaviour becomes more and more erratic and unpredictable, with an increasing divergence of 'talk' and 'action'.

Structured covers organized, principled and activity-oriented dimensions. These scales relate to resource allocation and task completion. If time and resources are unlimited it is fairly easy to behave in an ethical manner. If, however, the pressure for results is on, cutting corners or undermining opponents promises quick results. Integrity often tops the list of key attributes required for high-level roles, yet individuals vary widely in what they consider this to be. On the Work Performance Evaluation inventory, observer ratings on Upholding Standards tend to have the highest mean with low variance, indicating that ineffective performance in this area is rarely observed – by those invited by the respondent to rate their behaviour. The activity oriented score has frequently been shown to be an excellent predictor of success at work: those who like a busy environment and get things done are popular with bosses and peers.

Finally Driven covers the need-for-achievement construct through the dynamic, striving and enterprising dimensions. When compared with other professionals, coachees in senior positions will almost inevitably come across as highly driven as otherwise they would not have made it to the top. However, success can also breed complacency and prejudice, or a hunger for greater challenges that may urge a coachee to move on to greater things. Coachees in junior positions with low scores on driven and assertive measures will find it difficult to climb the career ladder, and may need to consider deepening their own area of expertise or using lateral moves as the springboard for their career success.

Competency Potential Profile

The third area which the coach should review and explore in the coaching session is the Competency Potential Profile page, which transforms scores on the psychometric profile through sophisticated algorithms that optimize criterion-related validity into easy-to-understand outputs that at a glance highlight areas of relative strengths and weaknesses. This page effectively translates psychological construct language into line-manager-friendly competency language that is easily accessible to coachees who lack formal training in psychometrics. Experienced coaches may wish to review this page at the outset of the session to emphasize the performance orientation of the tool.

The coaching process can draw on relative strengths and explore how they can be fully exploited without turning into over-played strengths that are deployed at the expense of other important areas. Extreme strengths that have served well in the past can have a 'dark side' that turns them into 'career stallers' or 'derailers' if they are not counterbalanced in other areas.

Relative weaknesses matter only if the work environment requires use of particular behaviours; for example, if processing details is of no importance in the role then there is no need to coach someone to improve in that area. The vast majority of areas, however, will matter for most senior roles. Coachees need to become aware of the impact that under-managed weaknesses have on their own performance and career, and what their impact on others may be.

Predicted Culture/Environment Fit – performance enhancers and inhibitors

A final area to review is the list of performance enhancers and their corresponding performance inhibitors. Identifying enhancers helps coachees to understand how well their current work demands are in line with their stylistic preferences. The list of inhibitors helps to check whether a new environment would really fit the coachee's needs. This page can also help the coach and coachee to have a perspective on how the environment and job demands could change to better reflect the individual's style, rather than simply looking at how to change the individual coachee to fit the current work demands and environment.

SUMMARY

Personality questionnaires have evolved into a new generation of tools that potentially assist both coach and coachee. It is important for coaches to understand their applications, and how they relate to the leading academic models. Advances in questionnaire design and delivery can give the 'coaching' user much more information and confidence in the accuracy of the data and much greater time efficiency.

Saville Consulting Wave® assesses individual and organizational as well as performance variables. The tools for assessment of these three kinds of variables were developed in parallel to offer coaches a coherent model. The benefits of this approach are that coaches can compare current and desired culture, and facilitate culture change initiatives that are behaviourally framed in terms of competency.

The Professional Styles questionnaire provides a detailed assessment of the coachee's characteristics across 4 clusters, 12 sections, 36 dimensions and 108 facets with strong psychometric and psychological credentials. The reporting uniquely features facet ranges, normative–ipsative splits and the motive–talent split. The Competency Potential Profile enables coach and coachee to discuss the link between self-report and actual performance, with scope for exploring the extremes of over-used strengths and under-managed weaknesses. The Predicted Culture / Environment Fit report facilitates exploration of likely fit against various culture and environment demand characteristics. The Types report provides a high-level view of the data in a highly graphical report geared towards leadership and team development.

References and further reading

Barrick, MR and Mount, MK (1991) The Big Five personality dimensions and job performance: a meta-analysis, *Personnel Psychology*, **44**, pp 1–26

Bartram, D (2002) *The SHL Corporate Leadership Model SHL Research White Paper*, SHL Group, Thames Ditton

Bartram, D (2005) The Great Eight competencies: a criterion-centric approach to validation, *Journal of Applied Psychology*, **90**, pp 1185–1203

Bartram, D, Baron, H and Kurz, R (2003) Let's turn validation on its head, *Proceedings of the BPS DOP Conference*, pp 75–78, BPS, Leicester

Bartram, D, Kurz, R and Baron, H (2003) The Great Eight competencies: meta-analysis using a criterion-centric approach to validation, paper presented at SIOP, Orlando, May

Costa, PT Jr and McCrae, RR (1992) *Revised NEO Personality Inventory (NEO-PI-R) and NEO Five-Factor Inventory (NEO-FFI): Professional Manual*, Psychological Assessment Resources, Odessa, FL

Crebbin, K (2005) *A Construct Validity Investigation into the Relationship between Personality, Motivation, Values and Organizational Culture Preferences*, unpublished MSc thesis, Northumbria University

Digman, JM (1997) Higher-order factors of the Big Five, *Journal of Personality and Social Psychology*, **73**, pp 1246–56

Fullman, C (2005) *An Empirical Investigation of the Criterion-Related Validity of the Professional Styles Personality Questionnaire*, unpublished MSc dissertation, University of London, Goldsmiths College

Gotoh, A (1999) *The Evaluation of Competencies Predictors across Nine Studies in Five Countries*, unpublished MSc dissertation, London, Goldsmith College

Kurz, R (1999) Automated prediction of management competencies from personality and ability variables, *Proceedings of the Test User Conference*, pp 96–101, BPS, Leicester

Kurz, R (2005) Convivence of personality, motivation, interest and ability theories in competency, paper presented at EAWOP Congress, Istanbul, May 2005

Kurz, R (2006) Personality, motivation and culture preference, paper presented at the Work Psychology Congress in Leipzig

Kurz, R and Bartram, D (2002) Competency and individual performance: modelling the world of work, in *Organizational Effectiveness: The role of psychology*, ed Robertson, Callinan and Bartram, Wiley

McDowall, A and Kurz, R (2006) Making the most of psychometric profiles: effective integration into the coaching process, skills-based session at the 1st International Coaching Psychology Conference in London, 18 December 2006, BPS Special Group in Coaching Psychology

MacIver, R, Saville, P, Kurz, R, Mitchener, A, Mariscal, K, Parry, G, Becker, S Saville, W, O'Connor, K, Patterson, R and Oxley, H (2006) Making waves: Saville Consulting Wave Styles questionnaires, *Selection and Development Review*, **22**(2), pp 17–23

Norman, WT (1963) Towards an adequate taxonomy of personality attributes: replicated factors structure in peer nomination personality ratings, *Journal of Abnormal Social Psychology*, **66**, pp 574–83

Nyfield, G, Gibbons, PJ, Baron, H and Robertson, I (1995) The cross cultural validity of management assessment methods, paper presented at the 10th Annual SIOP Conference, Orlando, May 1995

Robertson, IT and Kinder, A (1993) Personality and job competences: an examination of the criterion-related validity of some personality variables, *Journal of Occupational and Organizational Psychology*, **65**, pp 225–44

Saville, P and Sik, G (1991) Ipsative scaling: a comedy of measures, As You Like it or Much Ado About Nothing? *Guidance and Assessment Review*, **7** (3), pp 1–4

Saville, P, Sik, G, Nyfield, G, Hackston, J and MacIver, R (1996) A demonstration of the validity of the Occupational Personality Questionnaire (OPQ) in the measurement of job competencies across time and in separate organizations, *Applied Psychology*, **45**, pp 243–62

Saville, P and Willson, E (1991) The reliability and validity of normative and ipsative approaches in the measurement of personality, *Journal of Occupational Psychology*, **64**, pp 219–38

8

Coaching for emotional intelligence

MSCEIT

Dr David R Caruso and Professor Peter Salovey

INTRODUCTION

This chapter describes emotional intelligence (EI), focusing on the scientific concept as distinct from those that appear in the popular press. EI is the ability to accurately and adaptively perceive, use, understand and manage emotions. People differ in this ability, and the ability can be measured through performance-based tests.

There are alternative approaches to EI that define it as a set of personality traits such as assertiveness or optimism. These approaches are best considered as models of personality dispositions rather than as the competencies and capacities that underlie emotional intelligence. There remains real excitement and promise for EI, when EI is defined and measured as a standard intelligence. There are several reasons for this excitement. First, this ability-based EI is a new concept. Second, the skills-oriented EI model is ideal for training and development. Third, the model itself can be used as a generic coaching model. And fourth, we can measure these emotional abilities in an objective fashion, and such measurement yields fascinating and unique results for both coaches and their coachees.

THEORY OF EMOTIONAL INTELLIGENCE

The best-selling book *Emotional Intelligence* (Goleman, 1995) motivated a large amount of assessment and training under the broad category of EI. Many such approaches took existing personality traits and relabelled them as EI, and others defined EI as a set of traditional leadership competencies. Any positive trait or ability that was not measured by a general intelligence test was fair game to be considered EI by some.

Attention was drawn to EI by claims that it could predict up to 80 per cent of the variance in important outcomes, for life outcomes generally speaking and workplace outcomes specifically. People were fascinated by EI due to these, and other, claims, seeking to better understand this quality that was purported to be 'twice as important as IQ', and the 'best predictor of success in life' (Gibbs, 1995). Although the claims made in the popular press are what originally fuelled the excitement and widespread interest in EI (or 'EQ' as it is sometimes referred to), these pronouncements are, for the most part, unsubstantiated.

When we take a look at what is left of EI, after stripping away the veneer of such over-optimistic claims, we find that there is indeed a valid, scientific model that presents reasonable evidence of its importance. But this scientific EI, unlike the popular notions of EQ, does not predict 80 per cent of the variance in outcomes. Instead, EI predicts outcomes at levels similar to other psychological traits (for a summary, see Mayer, Salovey and Caruso, 2004).

Although the concept was brought into the public eye in 1995, EI was initially presented in a series of journal articles in 1990 and 1993 (Salovey and Mayer, 1990; Mayer and Salovey, 1993). In these and later articles, EI was defined as the ability to identify emotions accurately, to use emotions to enhance thinking, to understand the causes of emotions, and to manage emotions to promote growth (Mayer and Salovey, 1997). It is this ability-based concept of EI that is the focus of this chapter.

INTELLIGENCE AND EMOTIONS

This ability model of EI represents the intersection of intelligence and emotion. Intelligence, even after 100 years of scientific study, still lacks a consensus definition (see Neisser *et al*, 1996), but for our purposes it is sufficient to define intelligence as the ability to learn, acquire knowledge and solve problems. Emotion theories abound, from basic emotion models to social constructionist approaches (see for example Ekman, 1992; Russell, 2003). We view emotions as containing information: they are not extraneous experiences that come upon us without good reason. Emotions do not interfere with good decision making; they are, in fact, necessary and critical for effective decisions (eg Damasio, 1994).

At the most basic level, emotions can be viewed as (see Caruso and Salovey, 2004):

▌ occurring as a result of some sort of change in the internal (imagined) or external world;
▌ starting automatically, and quickly;
▌ generating certain physiological changes and feelings;
▌ altering your attention and thinking;
▌ preparing you for action;
▌ quickly dissipating.

The basic function of an emotion is to help people to cope, survive and thrive in their environment. Without access to the data provided by the emotions, one misses critical information, and decisions will be suboptimal.

THE ABILITY MODEL OF EI

This intersection of intelligence and emotion includes a number of abilities, and the ability model of EI described by Salovey and Mayer (Salovey and Mayer, 1990; Mayer and Salovey, 1997) includes four related emotional skills. Their theoretical model is hierarchical, which means that each ability grows out of the previous one. It is also postulated that it is a developmental model where these abilities grow as we mature. We next review each of these four abilities.

Identifying emotions

The most basic ability is identifying emotions. This ability begins with awareness of emotions, but it focuses on the accuracy of perceptions of emotions in self and others, as well as in the environment. Emotions are often viewed as signals of people's intentions and therefore communicate meaning (Plutchik, 1980). Picking up on these signals enhances the quality of people's relationships. In addition, however, emotions arise from elements of the environment around us as we can have an emotion episode when there is a perceived threat, or even an emotional reaction to a warm, sunny day.

Using emotions to facilitate thought

How we feel influences the way we think and what we think about. The interaction of emotion and cognition means that emotions can facilitate different types of thinking: positive emotions, generally speaking, enhance creative problem solving whereas negative emotions may facilitate the search for errors or analysis of details (eg Isen, 2001). People differ in their ability to generate and use emotions to assist thinking.

Understanding emotions

Just as there exists a vocabulary for different fields of study, there exists an emotion vocabulary. The understanding emotions ability includes the knowledge of how emotions change, progress and transition from one state to another. A number of emotion taxonomies exist, with numbers of identified emotions ranging from two basic dimensions of affect to 10 discrete emotions (see, for example, Ortony, Clore and Collins, 1988). Table 8.1 lists some of the more well-known emotion taxonomies.

Table 8.1 Various emotion taxonomies

Watson	Plutchik	Ekman	Tomkins	Izard
Positive Affect	Joy Acceptance	Happiness	Enjoyment	Joy
Negative Affect	Fear Surprise Sadness Disgust Anger Anticipation	Fear Surprise Sadness Disgust Anger	Fear Surprise Distress Anger Interest Shame	Fear Surprise Distress Disgust Anger Interest Shame Guilt
		Contempt	Contempt	Contempt

Managing emotions

Finally, managing emotions is the ability that allows one to stay open to emotions, to extract the data from emotions and to integrate such data into decisions and behaviours. This ability does not preclude one from 'getting emotional'; rather it can assist people to confront and deal with difficult emotional situations. This ability can apply both to intrapersonal conflict and to interpersonal situations. Various coping strategies are more, or less, effective in dealing with emotional problems (Thayer, 1996).

DEVELOPING EI

Can EI be improved? The assumed answer to this question is often a rousing 'yes', and it is puzzling to many people when we indicate that the answer, theoretically, is either 'no' or 'maybe', and possibly a 'yes'. After all, EQ is learned, goes the popular wisdom. Theoretically, there is little reason to assume that an intelligence can be 'learned', so therefore, why should one expect EI to be learned? Unless, of course, one was just using the term 'intelligence' as a foil. But our approach to EI is rooted in the intelligence literature, and so, we begin our reasoning about the development of EI from that point of view.

A recent intervention study found that students in an EI-based course did indeed increase their EI scores (as measured by the Mayer–Salovey–Caruso Emotional Intelligence Test[MSCEIT]) compared with a control group (Chang, 2006). It is, however, a relatively simple task to obtain increases in self-report test scores. Studies of actual changes in skills are few, and therefore we urge caution regarding drawing firm conclusions about the development of EI.

Coaches might be puzzled by this approach. After all, if EI cannot be learned, why bother including it in coaching? There are two reasons for doing so. First, awareness of one's emotional strengths and weaknesses is enormously helpful. Learning that one's 'read' of others' emotions is often inaccurate can lead a manager to question some of his or her assumptions and conclusions about people. Second, one can develop compensatory strategies to offset a deficit in an emotional ability. The manager in the previous example can learn how to better read faces, body language and tone of voice, or can learn to verify reads by asking other people how they feel. Third, it may prove – in the end – that EI is, in fact, learnable. Ongoing studies involving schoolchildren, for instance, provide further evidence that this may be the case (Brackett and Rivers, 2007).

The issue of increasing EI is important for another reason, which is to demonstrate the efficacy of the individual's coaching practice. The focus of EI coaching evaluation should be around demonstrating certain behavioural changes, such as leaders who are better able to influence others, or client managers who demonstrate greater concern for customers.

THE MSCEIT ASSESSMENT

The Mayer–Salovey–Caruso Emotional Intelligence Test (MSCEIT) operationalizes the four-branch ability model of emotional intelligence (Mayer, Salovey and Caruso, 2002) in a battery that takes 30 to 40 minutes to administer. It includes eight tasks and the test-taker's responses to these emotional problems are scored objectively. A standard score is then computed, based upon comparing the test-taker's performance with that of a normative sample of 5,000 individuals or an expert sample of 21 emotion researchers. The MSCEIT yields 17 separate scores: a total score, two area scores, four branch scores, eight task scores, a positive–negative bias score and a scatter score.

There are two 'tasks' or subtests for each of the four abilities in the EI model. Each is based on research and theory in the area of emotion (eg Ekman, 1973; Isen, 2001; Ortony, Clore and Collins, 1988; Thayer, 1996).

Identifying emotions is measured with the Faces and Pictures tasks. In the Faces task, the test-taker views four faces and indicates how likely it is that each emotion listed is present in a photograph of a person's face. The Pictures task presents test-takers with six designs or photos of an outdoor scene and asks them to identify the emotions that are conveyed by that design.

Using emotions is measured by the Sensations and Facilitation tasks. In the Sensations task people indicate how various emotions feel by identifying and describing the direction and degree of several physical sensations that accompany that emotion. (For example, 'Does happiness feel warm, cold, sharp or soft?'). The set of questions for the Facilitation task measures the ability to determine how different moods affect thinking and decision making. Test-takers indicate how effective different emotions are in helping people to solve a specific problem. (For example, 'How helpful are each of the following moods when you are making plans for a picnic: (a) happiness; (b) frustration; (c) surprise; (d) fear.')

The understanding emotions ability is measured by the Changes and Blends tasks. The Changes task measures an understanding of how emotions transform over time. These test items are multiple-choice questions. (For example, 'When anger intensifies, it turns into: (a) rage; (b) frustration; (c) sadness; (d) joy.) The Blends task is a multiple-choice format and taps knowledge of complex emotional states people may experience. (For example, 'Optimism is a combination of: (a) happiness and anticipation; (b) fear and sadness; (c) happiness and joy; (d) sadness and happiness.')

Managing emotions is measured with the Emotion Management and Emotional Relationships tasks. Figure 8.1 illustrates a sample emotional management MSCEIT item. Emotion management presents test-takers with hypothetical personal situations. The test-taker indicates the effectiveness of various emotional strategies in achieving a specific outcome. Emotional Relationships tests the ability to motivate a certain emotional outcome in interpersonal situations. Effective strategies are those that result in the desired outcome, for both individuals. (For example, 'Jane was asked to lead a new project team that Joe wanted to be in charge of. How effective would each of the following actions be in getting Joe to cooperate with Jill: (a) Jill recognizes Joe's feelings but requests his help; (b) Jill threatens to fire Joe if he does not help the team; (c) Jill points out Joe's many weaknesses to the team.')

The MSCEIT was developed as both a clinical and a research assessment instrument, and for that reason, we devised two different scoring methods. In practice, we employ the expert consensus method, which uses the judgements of emotions experts to create a scoring key. In this case, 21 members of the International Society for Research on Emotions were asked for their responses to each MSCEIT question. Their consensus scores were then used to construct the expert scoring key.

The MSCEIT Resource Report provides detailed feedback based on the ability model of EI and the MSCEIT. Coachees' test scores are reported using bar graphs, but rather than show the standard scores, the report indicates

INSTRUCTIONS: Rate how effective each action below would be in achieving the desired outcome.

Debbie just came back from vacation. She was feeling peaceful and content. Which action would best preserve her mood?

Action	Ineffective			Effective	
a. Starting to make a list of things at home that she needed to do.	O	O	O	O	O
b. Reflecting on the nicest parts of the vacation she had just been on.	O	O	O	O	O
c. Deciding it was best to ignore the feeling since it wouldn't last anyway.	O	O	O	O	O

Figure 8.1 A sample MSCEIT item from the emotion management task

levels of performance using verbal descriptors: Develop, Consider Developing, Competent, Skilled or Expert. When we developed the reports for the MSCEIT we felt that it was important not to over-emphasize a numerical score for fear that people would rely too heavily upon it.

Perhaps the greatest challenge in using the MSCEIT is the fact that people are very poor estimators of their own EI ability. We asked a sample of 82 managers to take the MSCEIT and then immediately afterwards they were asked how well they performed on the MSCEIT. The correlation between their total EI self-estimate and the MSCEIT was 0.15. This lack of correspondence between self-concept and test results provides the MSCEIT with unique challenges, as well as unique strengths.

One of the limitations of the MSCEIT is that it does not look at differences in the capacity to process various kinds of emotions. However, it does include a measure of emotion bias. This score, the Positive–Negative Bias Score (PNBS), is computed on the basis of the test-taker's raw responses to the Faces and Pictures tasks. A low score indicates that the test-taker endorsed negative emotions more than other people, whereas a high score indicates that he or she selected positive emotions for these test items. The PNBS can be used to generate hypotheses about which sort of emotions the test-taker identifies, uses, understands and manages.

PSYCHOMETRICS

The MSCEIT has adequate internal and test–retest reliability (Mayer, Salovey and Caruso 2002; Mayer *et al*, 2003). Although the face validity of the MSCEIT has been demonstrated empirically, some executives and coaches struggle with the test. Coaches can easily address this issue through the pre-test preparation they provide to their coachees.

Most importantly, the MSCEIT has adequate discriminant validity, as it is not strongly associated with classic personality traits and only modestly related to standard intelligence (IQ). However, despite the promises in the popular press, the MSCEIT does not predict 80 per cent of the variance in any outcome. Instead, the MSCEIT provides modest incremental validity in certain areas of functioning. These areas most notably include pro-social behaviour, less aggression and better-quality relationships. (For a detailed review of these results, see Mayer, Salovey and Caruso, 2004; Salovey and Grewal, 2005.)

EI AND COACHES

The idea that people are not good at estimating their own EI proves to be challenging when the MSCEIT is administered to coaches themselves. Coaches, who come from a dizzying array of backgrounds, may or may not score high on the MSCEIT. Coaching backgrounds, training and skill sets vary widely, and even coaches with clinical training and experience do not necessarily receive overall scores that are above average on the MSCEIT. One exception is that psychologists, as a group, tend to score higher than the average (Boone and DiGiuseppe, 2002).

The question arises, therefore, whether coaches can help coachees develop their EI skills if the coaches themselves do not have well-developed EI skills. The answer is 'yes', and coaches with lower EI, or at least lower scores on the MSCEIT, can be superb developers of EI skills in their coachees if they are aware of their level of skill.

Coaches scoring lower on identifying emotions may need context to figure out how their coachees are feeling. We have seen coaches who employ some simple, but effective, remedial strategies such as confirming their perceptions with the coachee. Coaches lower in using emotions tend to have less emotional empathy for coachees, and sometimes claim that such lack of empathy helps them to avoid the consequences of job burnout and coachee over-involvement. They may wish to consider whether they connect emotionally with coachees, and if not, whether such a relationship-based interaction would assist them in their coaching. Understanding emotions, as noted above, is the language of emotions, and coaches with lower scores in this ability area may not be seen as possessing keen insight into their coachees. These coaches may be extremely insightful, but their vocabulary does not communicate this to others. Acquiring emotional language is a relatively simple task, as many texts on emotion taxonomies exist. Finally, coaches lower in managing emotions may at times be overwhelmed by their feelings, or may coach in a more abstract and logical way, and not always consider the emotional causes of coachee difficulties. Learning an emotional point of view and acquiring emotion management strategies can help coaches in their coachee work as well as with coping in general. Table 8.2 summarizes the influence of each EI ability on the coaching process. Coaches with a high level of emotional intelligence should leverage this ability by attending to their emotions, processing these signals and trusting their judgements and observations.

Table 8.2 Impact of low and high EI ability on coaching

EI ability	Low	High
Identify	May miss certain cues.	Aware of coachee's feelings and accurately identifies them.
Use	Lacks emotional empathy for coachee or may not be able to easily connect with coachee.	Feels what the coachee feels, can see different perspectives.
Understanding	Finds it difficult to describe his or her insights. May struggle to predict emotional reactions.	Expresses emotional insights with great sophistication. May describe the coachee's emotions and behaviours in an analytical manner.
Manage	May get overwhelmed by feelings or fail to integrate emotions into problem solving.	Handles difficult emotions well. Includes emotional data in coaching process.

Particular coach EI profiles

There are also particular EI profiles that provide special challenges to coaches. Coaches whose identifying emotions ability is weak may have excellent emotional problem-solving skills but their input is inaccurate. Thus, their assumptions about the coachee are faulty. We also see coaches who score higher on understanding emotions than they do on using emotions. This profile often results in a coach with excellent clinical insights into coachees, but lacking in emotional empathy for them. Such interpersonal distance might be the conscious choice of some coaches, but a MSCEIT profile like this is not a choice – it is an ability differential.

Another difficult profile is the coach who is high on using emotions and lower (relatively) on managing emotions. Such people feel things deeply and can connect readily with their coachees. However, these feelings and experiences can 'get' to the coach after a time. The coach can become overwhelmed and fail to process information adequately. These kinds of coaches sometimes ask whether they feel too much, and the answer is not to disconnect from their rich emotional life but instead to develop better emotion coping strategies.

All coaches, no matter their level of EI, can use the EI ability model to help them prepare for and conduct an effective coaching programme. They can ask themselves questions based on the model:

▌ How am I feeling right now, and how do I feel about this coaching session?

▌ How do these feelings influence my thinking?

▌ Why do I feel this way and how might these feelings change?

▌ How will I manage these feelings?

Often, coaches take themselves out of the equation, and fail to identify how they are feeling about the coachee or about a specific coaching session. What happens, for example, if the coach is anxious about providing difficult feedback to the coachee? How does this anxiety influence the coaching session, and in the longer term, the coaching relationship? Use of the ability model can assist coaches in being more mindful of the role that their emotions have on the coaching relationship. Once this approach is mastered, the next step is to include the coachee in this analysis. In addition to a self-analysis using these questions, the coach should attempt to answer the questions for the coachee. Of course, if the coach's ability in any of the four areas is limited, then the coach will need to develop methods to answer these questions accurately.

USING EI WITH COACHEES

Providing feedback to coachees

We typically provide MSCEIT feedback to the coachee by explaining what EI is, describing the nature of the MSCEIT, using the model, and then, reporting the assessment results. If coachees understand the nature of both EI and the unusualness of the MSCEIT, they will be better able to understand and to interpret their EI assessment results. Ideally, one can use the EI model itself to explain the model. In other words, the coach can engage the coachee by asking a set of questions modelled on the four-step blueprint.

Figure 8.2 describes this Emotional Blueprint. The coach can first ask coachees to describe their current mood in a simple, two-dimensional representation of mood using valence (positive–negative, or pleasant–unpleasant) and arousal (low energy–high energy). Second, coachees are asked how these feelings are affecting their thinking. Several dimensions of thought can be tapped, such as how closed or open minded they are, whether they are focused on details or the big picture, and how distracted or focused they are at the moment. Third, the coach can ask their coachees to consider two 'emotional what-if' questions: how will their coachees react to negative assessment results and how will they react to positive results. We find that the answers to these two questions are independent of each other.

Finally, the coach can enlist the coachees to be active participants in the feedback process by asking how their coachees will manage their reactions to receiving both positive and negative results in order to learn from and benefit from the feedback experience.

The feedback process should then begin by explaining the ability model of EI, relating each of the four abilities to the set of questions asked above. Next, the nature of MSCEIT scoring and results is explained. After explaining EI and the MSCEIT the coach can then begin discussing actual MSCEIT results with coachees in such a way as to enlist the coachees in drawing their own hypotheses and conclusions.

Emotional Blueprint

We can use the Emotional Blueprint as a general, emotion-focused problem-solving process:

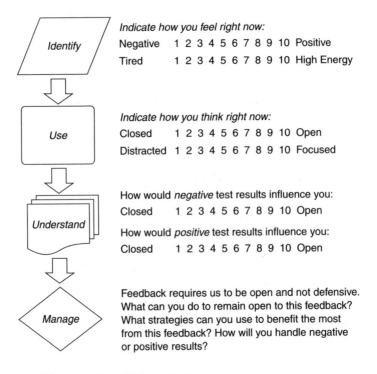

Identify

Indicate how you feel right now:
Negative   1 2 3 4 5 6 7 8 9 10 Positive
Tired   1 2 3 4 5 6 7 8 9 10 High Energy

Use

Indicate how you think right now:
Closed   1 2 3 4 5 6 7 8 9 10 Open
Distracted 1 2 3 4 5 6 7 8 9 10 Focused

Understand

How would *negative* test results influence you:
Closed   1 2 3 4 5 6 7 8 9 10 Open

How would *positive* test results influence you:
Closed   1 2 3 4 5 6 7 8 9 10 Open

Manage

Feedback requires us to be open and not defensive. What can you do to remain open to this feedback? What strategies can you use to benefit the most from this feedback? How will you handle negative or positive results?

Figure 8.2   The emotional blueprint

Developing EI in coachees

Identifying emotions

The most fundamental of the four EI abilities, the ability to identify emotions, is critical to successful interpersonal interactions. Emotions, it has been argued, communicate intentions. Misinterpreting the intent of others means that the raw data, or inputs, for emotional reasoning are faulty. Coaching this ability begins by teaching coachees to be aware of emotional cues. Next, they need to learn how different cues signal, or are associated with, different emotions. Compensatory strategies, such as checking one's conclusions with the target person, can be taught as well.

Using emotions

The ability to generate emotions on demand so as to assist thinking is difficult to develop. Coaching this ability can start with discussions regarding the influence that various emotions have on thinking. For example, you might ask coachees who score low on this ability whether it matters how people feel. A more pointed question might be, 'Would you ask your boss for a pay raise if s/he were in a bad mood?' Teaching these coachees the connection between emotion and thinking can proceed from that point. Additional strategies may be introduced to help such coachees generate various emotions, such as imagery, visualization and storytelling.

Understanding emotions

Arguably the easiest ability to coach, understanding emotions at its most basic consists of vocabulary. Reading about emotions can enhance the coachee's ability in this area. Emotion theories and taxonomies, such as Plutchik's emotion circumplex (1980), provide an excellent visual summary of the topography of emotions. In addition, analytical coachees can utilize their ability and apply it to emotional reasoning. Recent situations can be analysed, looking for ways in which an emotion has intensified and changed over time, and uncovering reasons for these emotional changes and transitions. Coaches can also encourage their coachees to use what-if planning by asking them how a person will react to a certain event.

Managing emotions

The most critical of the four abilities in many ways, managing emotions can also be difficult to develop. Coaches can discuss the efficacy of various strategies and promote the use of both preventative and responsive emotion management strategies. Preventive strategies include:

▮ selecting an alternative situation such as deciding to work somewhere besides the noisy office;
▮ modifying the situation by, for example, changing the agenda for a meeting to focus on positive steps that can be taken to achieve team goals;
▮ modifying the emotion or mood (recognizing low energy and changing to an energetic, enthusiastic mood);
▮ reappraising the situation (reframing a situation to make it more positive).

Responsive emotion management strategies kick in after a difficult situation begins. Some of these strategies include:

▮ self-talk ('Everything is going to be OK');
▮ physical activity (take a quick walk);
▮ behavioural strategies (apologize to a person who you treated poorly);
▮ socio-emotional support (talk with a friend or trusted colleague about a problem);
▮ distraction (read the news, check messages, do something to get your mind off the topic disturbing you).

LEVERAGING THE FULL RANGE OF EMOTIONS

There is another aspect to emotional abilities that coaches and coachees need to consider: their access to the full range of emotions. We find, for example, that some people are masterful at identifying some, but not all, emotions. Or they are able to tap into anger and fear but have a more difficult time being able to feel sadness or joy. And this pattern has worked for them, as illustrated by the case of the founder and CEO of a fast-growing company who was superb at identifying and using anger, fear and surprise. He was challenged when it came to the emotion of joy, and to some extent, with sadness. As a coachee, the CEO was assessed with the MSCEIT, and he scored well on identifying, using and understanding, and lower on managing emotions. Further discussion helped to discover which emotions the CEO was better able to process (as illustrated in Table 8.3).

During the start-up and growth phases of his computer services company, tapping into fear and surprise was effective for him, and for the company. But when they reached the level at which they needed to continue their

Table 8.3 CEO's emotional abilities profile

Emotion/Ability	Identify	Use	Understand	Manage
Anger	✓	✓	✓	
Sadness			✓	
Fear	✓	✓	✓	✓
Disgust		✓	✓	✓
Surprise	✓	✓	✓	✓
Joy				

amazing record of growth, the CEO faltered. It was easy for him to motivate himself and others through the use of anger, fear and surprise, but now that the company needed to maintain its customer base, continue to innovate and to examine the possibility of going public, the mindset, or feeling set, of the CEO did not change to reflect these new realities.

Coaching focused on two areas: accessing and leveraging the specific emotions of joy and sadness, and in addition, how to utilize the four-step emotional blueprint. Teaching emotional identification was relatively straightforward: first, pay attention to the clues that people display, although fleetingly. Next, match those clues to the correct emotion. In fact, the physical clues that differentiate one basic emotion from another are fairly straightforward and easy to learn. Using emotion is much more difficult, and for this area, we had to motivate this CEO actually to feel joy. We did this through storytelling, asking the CEO when he had felt the emotion, and what the physical sensations were like, how he viewed the world, and what the experience was like. Then, we increased the intensity, asking the CEO to recall a time when he felt happy, repeating the cycle until he was able to generate, and utilize, feelings of joy. It was a long, difficult, and for the CEO often embarrassing, experience. But once he had achieved a modest level of success, he was able to relate better to a wide range of people, people who were content, and to feel more at home with his own emotions.

There was an immediate, and noticeable, benefit: the CEO was better able to 'connect' with certain key executives and customers. He seemed more approachable and in-touch with others. Emotional understanding was easy to address, as such knowledge is in written form. So, we quickly progressed to managing emotions, which first required us to make the point that emotions contain data and do not need to be controlled or suppressed. Instead, we worked on basic emotion management strategies that allowed the CEO to feel sad or joyful, and then to express these emotions in a profes-sional and a productive manner. More importantly, we taught him basic anger management strategies that gave him 'permission' to feel angry when it was justified but to express it in a constructive manner. Thus, when the CFO failed to live up to a promise, the CEO was justifiably angry. Rather than scream at him at the next executive meeting, his usual style, the CEO called the CFO to his office and expressed his displeasure and anger. The CFO received the message, apologized, and then corrected the error. More importantly, the CFO did not repeat that behaviour in the future.

Not all of us can, or should, fully develop our EI and our full range of emotions. Those in senior leadership positions can be successful with a limited emotional repertoire: but being fully emotionally intelligent may provide leaders with an advantage in uncertain, unpredictable times. Remember the premise that emotions contain data and that they are adaptive. It is the role of coaches to help their coachees develop their entire emotional repertoire, allowing them to thrive in many ways.

EI BLUEPRINT

The ability model of EI and the MSCEIT can help a coach to develop questions, or hypotheses, about a coachee. Each of the four key MSCEIT scores can generate discussion of key coaching objectives. These are summarized in Table 8.4. In addition, executives readily understand, and can apply, their MSCEIT results broadly through the use of the emotional blueprint.

Many managers, leaders and coaches believe that we should 'take emotion out of it' for critical interactions and decisions. As we have tried to make clear in this chapter, emotions are data and ignoring such data can lead to suboptimal decisions and actions. The blueprint can serve as an analytical tool to help coaches teach their coachees to better manage difficult, emotion-charged situations by asking a series of linked questions.

Coaches can apply the EI blueprint to their coaching practice with relative ease. They can begin by walking a coachee through a recent conflict by using the outline in Table 8.5 and supplement their coaching session by asking

Table 8.4 Hypotheses to examine MSCEIT scores

MSCEIT Score	Questions to ask
Identifying	Do coachees 'read' others well?
Using	Do they emotionally connect? Are they idea-oriented?
Understanding	Do they perform adequate what-if analyses regarding people?
Managing	Are they effective decision makers?

Table 8.5 A generic emotional blueprint

What is the desired goal for each person?

1:

2:

How did each person feel?

1:

2:

What was each person paying attention to and thinking about?

1:

2:

What caused each person to feel this way?

1:

2:

What did each person do to manage his or her own and the other person's feelings?

1:

2:

What strategies of emotion management might have been more effective?

1.

2.

questions listed in Table 8.6. Of course, it is critical that the coaches be aware of their own EI abilities as they conduct such work.

The blueprint process begins with a critical question: what is the desired outcome or goal? This needs to be kept firmly in mind, as various strategies that the coach helps the coachee generate should be evaluated on the basis of their chances of achieving that desired outcome. The blueprint process itself starts with accurate identification of the emotions of the key parties involved: the coachee and others. It is absolutely critical that coachees be trained to become accurately aware of how they feel, and to begin to separate out the effects of specific emotions (which contain data) and more diffuse moods. Next, whether mood or emotion, the coachees have to determine how these feelings influence their thinking: is the mood helpful in that it focuses the person on the task, or is it distracting and counterproductive? Third, an analytical understanding of the underlying causes of the

Table 8.6 Emotional blueprint questions and probes

Identify

Did you know how you felt at the time?
How did you feel during this interaction?
How do you feel about it right now?
Did you express your feelings? Appropriately so?
How do you think the other person/people felt at the time?

Use

Did it help you to feel this way? Why or why not?
Were you able to feel what the other person was feeling?
How did the other person feel and think?

Understand

Why did you feel this way?
Why did the other feel the way he/she felt?
How did your feelings change, and why?
How did the other person's feeling change? Why?
What if you do not address the situation, how will each person feel?

Manage

What did happen?
What did you want to happen?
Was there a better way to have handled it?
How satisfied were you with the outcome?
How satisfied do you think the other person was with the outcome?
What did you learn from this situation?
Did your feelings guide you in the right direction? Did you ignore them or pay attention to your gut feel?

---

feelings needs to be gained. It is here that the coachee can be taught to generate emotional 'what-if' analyses, such as 'What if I ignore that nasty e-mail, will the sender back off, or will he get further inflamed?' The key of the blueprint is in managing emotions. Rather than ignoring emotions, and rather than taking emotions out of it – if that were even possible – we manage emotions so that the most effective and helpful emotions assist our thinking and help direct us towards the best actions to take.

Many coaches, and some of the coachees, probably engage in a similar process, but in our experience, few follow a process template with an explicit focus on emotions and their meaning. The EI blueprint is a fairly generic process that coaches can use in a wide variety of situations.

SUMMARY

Emotional intelligence, defined as an ability and measured objectively, holds promise for coaches and their coachees. Assessing a coachee's abilities to accurately read others, utilize emotions to assist thinking, understand the causes of emotions, and manage emotions can help to devise more effective coaching plans. Coachees with strengths in any or all of these abilities can be assisted in leveraging these abilities in their behaviours, whereas coachees demonstrating difficulties can receive a skills-based approach to development. Objective EI assessment can be a powerful coaching tool as it provides new insights into the functioning of a coachee, and information that is not likely to be captured with other assessment tools. EI assessment results can stimulate deep, productive and difficult conversations in the coaching relationship as many people are poorly equipped to gauge their own emotional abilities.

The ability model of EI described in this chapter also serves as a generic problem-solving template that can be applied in a variety of settings. Coaches can teach their coachees how to employ the EI Blueprint, emphasizing their strengths and teaching them how to compensate for ability deficits. The ability model of EI also allows coaches to understand and develop their own coaching skills. Although EI may not be the entire basis for 'success' in life, it is a factor that can play a role in many important outcomes.

References

Barrett, LF and Russell, JA (1999) The structure of current affect: controversies and emerging consensus, *Current Directions in Psychological Science*, **8**, pp 10–14

Boone, RT and DiGiuseppe, R (2002) Emotional intelligence and success in professional graduate programmes in psychology, paper presented at International Society for Research on Emotions, Cuenca, Spain, 20–24 July 2002

Brackett, MA and Rivers, SE (2007) What is emotional literacy? In *Emotional Literacy in the Elementary School: Six steps to Promote Social Competence and Academic Performance*, ed MA Brackett, JP Kremenitzer, M Maurer, MD Carpenter, SE Rivers and NA Katulak, National Professional Resources, Port Chester, NY

Caruso, DR and Salovey, P (2004) *The Emotionally Intelligent Manager*, Jossey-Bass, San Francisco

Chang, KBT (2006) *Can We Teach Emotional Intelligence*? Dissertation submitted to University of Hawaii

Damasio, A (1994) *Descartes' Error: Emotion, Reason, and the Human Brain*, Putnam, New York

Ekman, P (1973) *Darwin and Facial Expression: A Century of Research in Review*, Academic Press, New York

Ekman, P (1992) Are there basic emotions? *Psychological Review*, **99**, pp 550–53

Gibbs, N (1995) The EQ factor, *Time*, **146** (October 2), pp 60–8

Goleman, D (1995) *Emotional intelligence*, Bantam, New York

Isen, AM (2001) An influence of positive affect on decision making in complex situations: theoretical issues with practical implications, *Journal of Consumer Psychology*, **11**, pp 75–86

Mayer, JD and Salovey, P (1993) The intelligence of emotional intelligence, *Intelligence*, **17**, pp 433–42

Mayer, JD and Salovey, P (1997) What is emotional intelligence? In *Emotional Development and Emotional Intelligence: Educational Implications*, ed P Salovey and D Sluyter, pp 3–31, Basic Books, New York

Mayer, JD, Salovey, P and Caruso, DR (2002) *Mayer–Salovey–Caruso Emotional Intelligence Test (MSCEIT) User's Manual*, MHS Publishers, Toronto

Mayer, JD, Salovey, P and Caruso, DR (2004) Emotional intelligence: theory, findings, and implications, *Psychological Inquiry*, **60**, pp 197–215

Mayer, JD, Salovey, P, Caruso, DR and Sitarenios, G (2001) Emotional intelligence as a standard intelligence, *Emotion*, **1**, pp 232–42

Mayer, JD, Salovey, P, Caruso, DR and Sitarenios, G (2003) Measuring emotional intelligence with the MSCEIT V20, *Emotion*, Summary, pp 97–105

Neisser, U, Boodoo, G, Bouchard, TJ, Boykin, AW, Brody, N, Ceci, SJ, Halpern, DF, Loehlin, JC, Perloff, R, Sternberg, RJ and Urbina, S (1996) Intelligence: knowns and unknowns, *American Psychologist*, **51**, pp 77–101

Ortony, A, Clore, GL and Collins, AM (1988) *The Cognitive Structure of Emotions*, Cambridge University Press, Cambridge

Plutchik, R (1980) *Emotion: A Psychoevolutionary Synthesis*, Harper and Row, New York

Russell, JA (2003) Core affect and the psychological construction of emotion, *Psychological Review*, **110**, pp 145–72

Salovey, P and Grewal, D (2005) The science of emotional intelligence, *Current Directions in Psychological Science*, **14**, pp 281–85

Salovey, P and Mayer, JD (1990) Emotional intelligence, *Imagination, Cognition, and Personality*, **9**, pp 185–211

Thayer, RE (1996) *The Origin of Everyday Moods*, Oxford University Press, New York

ACKNOWLEDGEMENT

We thank Susan Kornacki for her comments on a draft of this chapter.

9

Identifying potential derailing behaviours

Hogan Development Survey

Dr James M Fico, Richard Brady and
Professor Robert Hogan

INTRODUCTION

All psychological practice, including organizational coaching, requires measurement tools. Executive coaching tends to attract assessment instruments that are less incisive and more self-congratulatory in nature (Dotlich and Cairo, 2003). Coaches and their coachees often avoid assessment tools that are more likely to identify risk of derailing because the coachees fear a loss of privacy, and because coaches prefer to use their personal analytical skills rather than depend more heavily on objective assessment. However, coaches who use scientifically validated assessments of the bright side as well as the dark side of personality (Hogan, 2007) find that those assessments accelerate the coaching process, improve the professional relationship between the coach and coachee, and improve the coachee's satisfaction with the coaching experience.

Since business leadership is best described as the ability to build a team that will work together successfully and outperform the competition (Hogan, 2007), the relationships between the leader and the followers are critical to the leader's success. Any tool that allows the leader to build more constructive relationships and to avoid habits that will derail him or her will be valuable to the coaching experience.

This chapter will review our approach to using objective assessment to enhance the coaching experience. The Hogan Development Survey (HDS) is a measure of 11 different personality dimensions, with the dimensions organized into psychometrically sound clusters that can be understood by coachees. The HDS specifically identifies personal and interpersonal strengths and derailers that have substantial impacts on the coachee's success with his or her team. The chapter will introduce the coach to interpretation of the HDS results and begin to illustrate ways to use those results for the benefit of the coachee.

HOGAN'S SOCIO-ANALYTICAL THEORY OF HUMAN BEHAVIOUR

We believe that getting along (acceptance by others), getting ahead (being trusted by others enough that they will help us reach our goals) and having meaning in our lives (so that we can understand an order and a pathway for our lives) are the cornerstones of interpersonal relationships (Hogan and Roberts, 2000). All 'bright side' and all 'dark side' personality dimensions can be seen from the perspective of how they either enhance or interfere with our acceptance by others, how they promote or prevent other people from liking us, and how they enhance our understanding of how our lives fit with the larger whole. We also believe that the 'dark side' dimensions are best viewed, as suggested by Benjamin (1996), as unsuccessful attempts to achieve acceptance and trust, or at least as a natural reaction to the absence of acceptance and trust.

For example, people who are worried that they might offend others, who are intensely embarrassed by mistakes, and who actively avoid taking even calculated risks are trying to get along with, and be accepted by, other people. Their colleagues, friends and family, however, find that they are so intent on managing some of the components of being accepted (avoiding embarrassing statements or actions) that they rob the relationship of its spontaneity and the opportunity for forgiveness. In other words, the strategy has become stronger than its original purpose, namely to be accepted.

We also believe that it is critical for managers to understand this process of how their most practised coping strategies are, in the eyes of others, jeopardizing trust and acceptance (Hogan and Hogan, 2001). For example, some managers may intend to be astute and aware of difficult problems ahead, while others find that they push away friends and allies with their suspicion and mistrust.

All 11 dimensions of the HDS assess specific personal and interpersonal dimensions that affect the individual's success. Hogan believes that the derailers that have impacts on our lives come in the form of attempts to intimidate, seduce or control other people. The strategies of intimidation, seduction and control form the basis of the HDS clusters that are explained later in this chapter. Since the people with whom we work grow weary of being intimidated, seduced or controlled, our penchant for using those strategies to excess interferes with our abilities to get along, get ahead and have meaning in our lives.

It is the job of the coach, then, to help coachees identify their specific derailers, discover the intensity with which they use those derailing strategies, and learn how to reduce the negative impact of their derailers.

THE HOGAN QUESTIONNAIRE

The Hogan Development Survey (HDS) measures enduring personality qualities that can interfere with professional success and relationships on the job. The HDS is most commonly used for job selection and career development. In the latter application, reports based on the HDS help people recognize the interpersonal factors that derail them at work, especially when they are in leadership roles or when their technical skills allow them to use a good deal of discretion on the job. The HDS outlines dysfunctional habits and styles apparent to people who know the individual well, when the individual is in distress, or when the person is not paying attention.

Specifically, the HDS is an objective measure of how people affect others, especially those people who know them well enough to have seen them both at their best and at their worst. It is intended to help managers understand how their enduring behaviour patterns impact their relationships with their closest colleagues on the job. The HDS is useful both during the consulting relationship and afterwards, because the individual's strengths and advisory tips in the report are useful as a reference tool.

The HDS is a 168-item true–false objective measure of enduring personal and interpersonal patterns that impair people's abilities to be accepted and/or trusted by colleagues. It has been shown to predict descriptions made by other people (including co-workers, supervisors, spouses and coaches) of the test-taker's typical behaviour. In essence, the results of the HDS predict people's reputations with those who are closest and most important to them. Coachees who have completed and reviewed the results of the HDS have described the experience positively (Fico, Hogan, and Hogan, 2000).

In contrast with measures of psychopathology, the HDS predicts how the test-taker is viewed by those people with whom he or she is most likely to interact, including co-workers, supervisors and customers. Coachees are given, in both written and oral form, descriptions of their strengths as seen by others, summaries of potential problems, and tips on how to use that information in their daily work lives.

Because it focuses on the everyday interpersonal habits and problems experienced by the people with whom the coachee works, the HDS can be used to help select the critical, job-related themes that are important for many different coaching models. For example, many executive coaches speak about the necessity of identifying interpersonal themes (being overly optimistic, a penchant for rebelling against any structure, lack of clarity of instructions to direct reports and so on) that the coachees can understand and that have relevance in their professional lives. When coaches do not use objective assessment in the early stages of the coaching experience, the interpersonal themes emerge gradually during the coaching process, as the coachee's characteristic adaptive and maladaptive patterns become clear. These themes then become the anchor points of the coaching process.

Specific coaching themes are often selected because they represent some of the coachee's strengths or greatest areas of risk, and those themes can be used as specific anchors to be shaped into more effective interaction strategies. The HDS is intended to help the coachee at the very onset of the coaching experience to select and describe these patterns or themes, because they usually represent some of the most powerful components of the coachee's problems. The HDS reports specifically outline the coachee's patterns of strength, and also suggest some tips that may help reduce the negative impacts of the coachee's patterns.

HDS AND COACHES

Coaches can use their own HDS results to identify their personal strengths and potential derailers. Coachees are likely to notice the qualities that are reflected in HDS scores, especially during an ongoing business relationship, and so awareness of significant HDS dimensions will improve the chances of success. We have illustrated a few of the dimensions here.

Excitable

Coaches with very high (above 90) scores on Excitable have a great deal of spirit, and their coachees will appreciate their initial enthusiasm. Highly Excitable coaches are at risk, though, of becoming quickly disappointed. They are more likely to denigrate coachees' colleagues and business rivals and to create rather than reduce conflict among team members. Excitable coaches often encourage coachees to vent their irritation about 'impossible' or 'incompetent' colleagues, at the risk of alienating those colleagues and also at the risk of damaging the coaching relationship.

Sceptical

Coaches who score above 90 on Sceptical are more likely than their colleagues to create lengthy debates with their coachees and coachees' colleagues. Sceptical coaches are often highly astute and are skilled at detecting workplace political problems. Their wariness can alienate coachees and make the coach unwelcome in team meetings. If your Sceptical score is high, you will need to be especially careful to avoid distancing yourself from customers with your hunches and suspicions. Look for coaching opportunities in organizations that require lots of negotiation, for example for mergers and acquisitions.

Cautious

Highly Cautious (above 90) coaches earn their coaching reputations by making certain that coachees and their team never commit a fateful error. They consider all possible implications of decisions before they are made. If you have a high Cautious score, you will be a good complement for most entrepreneurs, who tend to 'ready, fire, aim', and who spend resources running headlong down blind alleys. Make sure you don't say 'no' to the entrepreneur coachee. Instead, give the coachee a list of options together with a risk–benefit analysis. And remember to check your second-guessing at the door.

Reserved

Coaches scoring high (above 90) on Reserved are often tough, thick-skinned, and not easily thrown by temperamental coachees' tirades. Your niche may well be the coachee who alienates other people with tantrums and rash decisions. Because you only listen to selected portions of what people say rather than the whole message, you can remain a good advisor despite the coachee's mood. You will need to concentrate, though, on communicating your ideas more fully, because you are at risk of giving an important topic a 'once-over', assuming the coachee already knows what you are thinking.

Leisurely

High Leisurely scores are obtained by diplomats, people who can do a 'slow burn' when frustrated, but keep their irritation largely to themselves. You risk concluding too quickly that your coachee does not measure up to your expectations. Part of your irritation with the coachee is due to your penchant for providing indirect, diplomatic feedback rather than candid and detailed information. Desirable industries for you are those in which harmony is sometimes valued over effectiveness, or where the coachee wants support and validation rather than change.

Bold

Coaches with high (90 or above) Bold scores are highly confident and goal-directed, and are eager to get into action. Bold coaches, however, risk failing to respond to situational changes or to their own mistakes, which they often do not recognize. Bold coaches believe that their tenacity will always trump caution, and they will spend lots of time taking their teams in the wrong direction. If you have a high Bold score, make certain that you have someone on your team who enjoys spotting pitfalls, and try to accept their advice. Your customers will enjoy your 'can-do' attitude. However, you are at risk of losing credibility if they get burned following your lead into an unanticipated error.

Mischievous

Highly Mischievous coaches are very influential. They can get customers and their coachees over barriers, and they motivate people to take risks. Sometimes, though, coachees will regard Mischievous coaches as insincere and a bit too willing to take risks just to keep things exciting. If you have a high Mischievous score, your niche may be with companies that are either in highly volatile industries, or in ones that must make changes quickly in order to compete successfully. When your coachee has feet of clay, make sure that he or she gets only small, gradual doses of your expectations for rapid change, or you will risk derailing the relationship.

Colourful

Highly Colourful (above 90) coaches have an advantage when creating the coaching contract. They are charming, good company, and will attract lots of eager associates. Many coachees and organizations will work with them in part because they simply enjoy the relationship. If you have a high Colourful score, be careful not to think that activity automatically translates to productivity. You will be inclined to take on too many projects that head in too many different directions. Use some of your charm to attract team members who do not mind making sure that each step in the project gets completed before moving on to the next set of tasks.

Imaginative

Coaches with high Imaginative scores make certain that change will occur. They like to look at problems in ways that their more conventional partners might never see, and so they will occasionally develop brilliant ideas. They are also skilled at demonstrating to coachees that old methods and products have had their day and must adapt to a changing reality. However, highly Imaginative coaches are easily distracted and risk developing a large number of good ideas that never get implemented. Their niche is likely to be either with creative teams, where the occasional stellar idea makes up for the number of mis-directions taken, or with a coachee whose survival depends on quickly finding a new business model.

Diligent

Highly Diligent (90 or above) coaches are taskmasters. They make certain that performance standards and schedules are addressed during every step of a project. These coaches can also be judgemental, giving the coachee the impression that he or she will never be able to perform the task as well as the coach. The coachee will be at risk of appearing to be the coach's assistant, or of becoming dependent on the coach. Highly Diligent coaches are best suited for long-term coaching relationships in which the coach becomes an advisor who is also integrated into the organization and seen as a resource by all the team members.

Dutiful

Coaches with high (90 or above) scores on Dutiful are valued for their loyalty. They are well suited for coaching relationships with coachees who are intent on maintaining and enhancing their own power, and who, possibly because of the changes they are trying to make, need to know that even their coach is 'on board' and will not be critical. If you are Dutiful, it will be important to consciously look for times when the coachee is going the wrong direction or is alienating team members or customers. Your loyalty increases the risk that your coachee will derail because he or she is not paying attention to warning signs being noticed by more critical colleagues who have assessed the situation more accurately.

USING HDS WITH COACHEES

The HDS is useful for coachees whose job performance is affected by enduring troubles with interpersonal relationships. Whether coaching is conducted individually or as part of a working team, the HDS's contributions include helping coachees see how they are perceived by others, from the point of view both of interpersonal strengths and of potential risks to their relationships. Coachees have the opportunity to learn fresh and possibly more positive ways of thinking and speaking about themselves. They also can learn to recognize when their customary coping mechanisms (strengths) are becoming more severe, and as a result more problematic.

Introducing the HDS to the coachee

When introducing the HDS to the coachee, consider emphasizing its role in identifying strengths. Coachees often believe that they are seeking professional consultation because they have problems, and that once the problems are resolved, there is no longer a need for involvement. Few coachees conceptualize their problems as strengths taken to the extreme, for example when caution has become fear or diplomacy has become passive-aggressiveness. Nor do they see the identification of strengths as necessary to the coaching process. Coachees usually believe that they are well aware of their own positive qualities, and do not need to spend time on the endeavour. Most coaches will attest, however, to the common experience of the coachee's habits of dwelling on problems in the hope of finding a solution. Coachees seldom actively pursue the development and expansion of their strengths unless prompted to do so.

When proposing the use of the HDS, we usually say, 'People who know you well probably have more positive things to say about you than you say about yourself. In fact, I think that if you could be more aware of your strengths, you might be at your best more often.'

Another option is to say, 'You've probably noticed that I often ask you to remember a time when things were going better for you than they are now. It might be easier for you to find those times if you and I knew more about your positive qualities, about those appealing parts of you that other people notice but that you have forgotten.'

When the coachee is being coached as part of a working team, or is having specific interpersonal problems, such as troubles with specific supervisors or direct reports, consider saying something like 'You've been getting lots of feedback about yourself lately, some of which is unwelcome because you believe it is not accurate. We might want to consider taking a more objective look at how you relate to other people, especially from the point of view of your best qualities.'

The coachee's assessment goals

The next step is to ask the coachees what they would like to know about their relationships with colleagues, supervisors and direct reports. Consider asking them, 'What specific questions do you have about how you get along with people you interact with on the job? If you could get an honest answer from the people you know, what would you ask them regarding their feelings and opinions about you?' It is important here to stimulate an attitude of discovery rather than one of examination. It is also important for coachees to overcome the fear of learning about themselves. The coach can help the coachee develop the courage to ask candid questions about their reputations and their habits. It is sometimes useful to remind the coachee about past frustrations mentioned in coaching sessions, times when the coachee could not understand a friend's, colleague's or direct report's reactions. Some examples are set out in Table 9.1.

After listing a few of these questions and comments in Table 9.1, ask about problems that arise from other people's impressions of the coachee. Consider asking your coachee, 'What questions do you think people have about you? You often mention your (supervisor, colleague, direct report) and how you get irritated with them. What do you think they believe about you that is either wrong or, if true, is just not that important?'

Emphasizing the strengths

The most critical aspect of feedback is reviewing the Strengths section of the HDS. It is important to review the Strengths section slowly, devoting plenty of time to look into the coachee's life to find examples that illustrate the strengths listed in the report. Coachees are often in a hurry to find anything that could be interpreted as criticism, and therefore beginning with the section on strengths is important. Focusing on the negative is natural for most clinical coachees because they, more often than organizational coaching

Table 9.1 Illustrating the HDS dimensions

Excitable	'Why are people always disappointing me?' 'As soon as I get to know people, I find that they are not who they claimed to be. Why do I keep ending up with these people?'
Sceptical	'Don't they know I can tell when they are betraying me?' 'I can see through them. Why do they keep doing the same things that they know have always irritated me?'
Cautious	'Why am I so alone? I used to try to approach people, but I'll never forget that time when I was so embarrassed.'
Reserved	'What's the difference between empathy and apathy? I don't know and I don't care.' 'My administrative assistant always says that I don't listen, but I think that I'm listening to everything she says.'
Leisurely	'Why don't these incompetent people just do their jobs?' 'Why don't people just leave me alone and mind their own business? If they would take care of their own problems, they wouldn't have to pester me.'
Bold	'Why do people make such a big thing out of a few simple mistakes? I'm not going to apologize for something that wasn't my fault. Why can't they just get over it? After all, if it weren't for me, nothing would get done around here.'
Mischievous	'I'll get them to see things my way, and they won't even notice.'
Colourful	'Give me a few minutes with them and I'll get them motivated.'
Imaginative	'Let's not just think outside the box. Let's pretend there is no box.'
Diligent	'I'm not controlling, I just want things done right. It takes less time if I just do it in the first place than have to redo everything that everyone else messes up.'
Dutiful	'When you are deciding on that promotion, remember all the times that I have supported you.' 'Employees have no respect any more. When I was just starting my career, I could never get away with the things my employees do. They treat me and all supervisors as if we don't matter to them.'

coachees, have high scores on the first five scales of the HDS (see section on 'Cluster A' below). Remember that such scores occur in people who wish to 'know the bad news right away'. Because it is so difficult for coachees to look closely at their strengths, devoting extra time to building some positive self-reference habits through the framework of the HDS will be necessary.

When strengths become deficits

Strengths turn to deficits when they are at their extreme, usually when the person is under duress, not paying attention, or dealing with a long-term, conflicted relationship (Hogan and Warrenfeltz, 2003). People who are often stimulating can become volatile when they are disappointed with their partners. Analytical coachees can become sceptical when they believe they have been betrayed. Conscientious parents can become diligent when they are afraid their teenagers are becoming too independent.

Keeping positive qualities from becoming deficits is a central theme when providing executive coaching with the help of the HDS. The process that we take with nearly every coachee is to help them recognize when they are at their best, and also realize when their dominant coping strategies have become enduring negative patterns. Whenever possible, as the coachee describes a frustrating situation, consider asking the person to identify which coping strategy he or she was using, and decide whether that strategy had become a liability because it was used in the extreme, or was the right solution for the wrong problem.

Of course, the coach's function is to help the coachees see what their strengths are, to identify the signs of 'going too far' in the direction of their problems, and learning to keep themselves in check. We need to put up some road signs so that they will know when they are causing trouble, and they also need to be able to appreciate feedback from colleagues and direct reports.

The implications listed here are abstracted from observers' descriptions of high scorers. Coachees need to first understand that there will be contrasts between their identities (how they see themselves) and their reputations, or who they are from the observer's point of view. An objective view of their reputations is especially important in executive coaching for two reasons. First, the HDS identifies strengths that are probably recognized by others, including by their colleagues during the hiring process. For example, Excitable coachees will probably have been seen by their colleagues as stimulating, Dutiful coachees as loyal, and so on. In fact, in coaching it is important for the coach and each coachee to keep these strengths in mind during intervention. Second, each coachee's strengths are likely to have been lost during the duress that led to the request for coaching.

Coachees often wish that they were part of a company that might see them as they see themselves. They want to be seen as having, for example, a strong sense of urgency rather than as habitually over-reacting to minor problems (Excitable), or expedient rather than manipulative (Mischievous). It is important to help them understand that the point of view of the observer (which is the function of the HDS) is probably different from their own.

When introducing the HDS to coachees, it is important to emphasize that its central purpose is to identify positive qualities as well as potential derailers of their careers. It is best to explain that most positive qualities, though adaptive when moderate, can be troublesome when they are used at the wrong time or in excess.

Cluster A

This cluster consists of Excitable, Sceptical, Cautious, Reserved and Leisurely. High scorers on the first five scales of the HDS reframe events in their lives in a negative way. Facts and experiences are seen in their dimmest light. High scorers on Cluster A screen out encouraging information and emphasize misfortune, past, present and future. Loss and disappointment are, to these high scorers, facts of life. More importantly, these losses are largely beyond their control, and so the best these high scorers can do is cope with the problems that are inevitable. The dance between their managers and direct reports is usually one of these high scorers pointing out a tragedy, with the direct report trying to show that the tragedy either could have been averted or was not as tragic as described. Cluster A people can draw others into a downhill spiral, as so often happens on internet chatrooms where people share their stories of woe without an effort toward resolution of the problems. The more positive colleague is then often accused of failing to understand or simply being insensitive.

High scorers on this cluster are ordinarily risk-averse, anticipating worst-case scenarios in order to avoid disappointment and embarrassment. As a result, they can lose credibility when involved with others in making decisions, because they are so prone to take a 'no action' position.

People whose Cluster A scores dominate their profile have a penchant for more planning and regret than do other people, and they tend to be more aware of the negative implications of decisions. Their common impact on a project is to tend to slow it down, and to reduce the chances of rash decisions being made.

Excitable

Excitable employees are, above all, unpredictable. They can be enthusiastic one minute and profoundly disappointed the next. When under stress, Excitable scorers believe that their employees and colleagues have let them down. As managers, Excitable people are hard to please. They are tense, moody and quick to anger and to raising their voices. Their colleagues and direct reports often try to encourage and cheer them up, but those efforts are usually thwarted. The more optimistic team members may try to demonstrate to their Excitable colleague that actions or decisions that led to the current crisis either could have been avoided or could now be escaped. Excitable managers, however, believe that misfortune is inevitable. There is always plenty of data to support either an optimistic or a pessimistic view, and so disagreements about the future with Excitable people can be never-ending. If anyone insists that the Excitable manager is being negative, ample support for discouragement will be found. Past traumas can also be used to illustrate the futility of effort and the reasons for pessimism.

Sceptical

Highly Sceptical managers frequently feel mistreated and are easily hurt by criticism. They are constantly alert for signs of being betrayed. Sceptical coachees question other people's loyalty or concern. They tend to start arguments with accusations that their colleagues are not sufficiently attentive, or that they are purposely doing something to thwart or injure the Sceptical individual. These people often aggressively justify their own ideas, and appear to enjoy the conflict. It is important to remember that this scale is highest among the profiles of maximum security prisoners. That fact does not, of course, mean that a high Sceptical score predicts violent behaviour. Instead, it points out the cycle of argument and self-justification.

Cautious

People with high Cautious scores have serious doubts about themselves and their colleagues. They are often tense, pessimistic and irrational, believing that even the most positive evidence of success is a sign of ultimate failure. They avoid making decisions, often by arguing both sides of the question. Because of a powerful aversion toward embarrassment or shame, they stick with stereotypic patterns of interaction and problem solving, if for no other reason than because the problems associated with those methods are familiar. For example, when trying to decide on a course of action, they look intently at the potential problems that could result from any decision, and forget to assess the cost of a delayed decision or of making no decision at all. For example, a Cautious manager will often decide to delay a decision whose potential problems are small, but be oblivious to the fact that by failing to decide they cause major conflict on the team.

Reserved

The colleagues of Reserved managers complain that they don't listen. Especially in times of distress, they become more distant and uncaring.

Reserved managers need little nurturance and reassurance, and they provide little to others.

When Reserved coachees bother to listen instead of tuning out the other person, they are usually 'listening for' what they want to hear, and are not 'listening to' their colleagues' entire messages. They seem not to care as much for their partners' welfare as do most people. Reserved managers communicate less often and less completely than their partners. Most Reserved managers have the kind of toughness that helps them be resilient, but they are also not likely to understand things from their colleagues' points of view. They give the impression of being independent, and expect that others should be the same. Reserved managers are not particularly considerate of others, and seem self-centred.

Leisurely

Highly Leisurely managers are often very socially skilled. Their colleagues complain, however, that they want to do things their own way and at their own pace. They do not want to share decisions that affect colleagues, and will procrastinate to avoid working together with them. Though they are only occasionally openly angry, colleagues of Leisurely managers say that they are not particularly helpful, except on their own terms. They wish to be left alone when busy, and get quietly irritated, wishing that others would do their own work and leave them alone. They don't like to be hurried or to get advice.

Cluster B

This cluster consists of Bold, Mischievous, Colourful and Imaginative.

Managers whose highest scores lie in Cluster B are risk takers. They ignore negative information about themselves and their actions, and try to avoid people who are negative or cautious. When scores on this cluster are dominant, colleagues and associates can count on being entertained. Some of the most important risks of this cluster of scales, however, include self-absorption and unwillingness to profit from their mistakes. Conflicts often arise because high Cluster B scorers are more likely to consider their own short-term interests first, sometimes sacrificing team relationships for the sake of personal priorities.

Bold

Bold managers are very confident. They often have a strong presence, and see themselves as multi-talented. They are not easily discouraged because they tune out negative information. They interpret problems as 'glitches' or 'false starts', but often do not accept personal responsibility for failures. It is common for them to blame others for their mistakes in judgement. Bold managers are often arrogant, and quickly grow weary of people who point out the dark side of decisions and actions. They reject negative information, and are indignant when their colleagues identify their failures. Bold managers are often self-centred and demand a great deal from the team members and the organization, but are not as inclined to give back. Their colleagues complain that Bold managers are too willing to take risks because of their high levels of self-confidence and their expectation of being treated as if they are special.

Mischievous

Mischievous managers like to stir things up. They enjoy 'the chase', in both relationships and projects. They enjoy defying rules and being the Devil's advocates. They make decisions that are expedient and exciting. Their statements, decisions and actions are often devoted to the achievement of short-term goals, sometimes at the expense of long-term stability.

Colourful

Colourful managers are entertaining and active. Many people find them to be charming and attractive. Like many people who score high on Cluster B, they are more willing to take risks and to act without planning than are most people.

Imaginative

Imaginative managers are creative and unpredictable. Moments of insight and innovation are accompanied by the individual being sufficiently off-task to be disruptive. Very high scorers often have unusual ideas and behaviours, some of which are brilliant while others can be off-putting. Colleagues of high scorers must grow accustomed to the likelihood that Imaginative managers will get bored quickly. They do not like to take care of details except in tasks that are of the highest interest to them. Colleagues of Imaginative managers often feel insecure about the future because their colleague is not focused on planning or thinking strategically. Team members of Imaginative managers believe that they must hold the team and its fortunes together, because their Imaginative colleagues are unpredictable and lack common sense.

Cluster C

The Diligent and Dutiful scales are generally more benign than the other scales, in that moderate scores (75 to 85) bring with them less risk for creating conflict. High scores on Factor C scales usually reflect a positive side of an individual that will tend to moderate the impact of more troublesome scales. In other words, if two people have the same scores on Factors A and B, the person with the higher scores on Factor C will often function better in organizations.

Conscientiousness and devotion to pleasing other people can have positive short-term implications in most organizational situations more often than is true for Clusters A and B. At higher score elevations (85 to 100), however, Diligent and Dutiful managers bring substantial risk for interpersonal conflict, as will be described below. The behaviour patterns represented by these high scores also bring the risk of losing one's identity for the sake of unbridled devotion to the task (Diligent), or to people in authority (Dutiful).

Two fundamental principles that are vital in supervising teams include the abilities of the managers to provide structure and support. Managers scoring high on Cluster A (Excitable, Sceptical, Cautious, Reserved and Leisurely) are at risk of having trouble providing either structure or warmth, while high scores on Cluster B (Bold, Mischievous, Colourful, Imaginative) provide warmth, but insufficient structure. People with elevated scores on Cluster C (Diligent, Dutiful) will often provide the structure that is needed, especially high Diligent scorers, and especially when they have particularly challenging or troublesome team members. When a high score on Diligent is balanced with a similar elevation on Dutiful, the manager will often be able to provide the acceptance and wish to please that team members experience as warmth.

Diligent

Highly Diligent managers are often the 'responsible' members of the team. They attempt to set the standards of conduct for everyone else. They make sure that everyone is aware of the schedule, and are inclined to take care of details like taxes and bills. They can also be quite critical of other team members, and sometimes describe their colleagues as 'careless and sloppy'. They often feel overworked because they have trouble delegating, fearing that other members of the team will not 'do it right'. In fact, they are often overworked, because their team-mates will know that whatever they do, the Diligent manager will redo and be critical of the initial effort.

Diligent managers become so involved in the details of projects that they do not attend to or discuss the big picture. They do not like to reflect on their choices, and are at risk of failing to abandon an idea or course of action that has outlived its usefulness. As a result, they can make great strides in a project that should never have been done at all.

Dutiful

As the name of the scale suggests, Dutiful managers are not likely to challenge their supervisors. They are reluctant to express their opinions in risky situations because of the potential of taking a position contrary to that of the person to whom they look for support.

Dutiful managers can be very predictable, but are often not very rewarding. They are a comforting constant after all the decisions are made and the policies set, but make little contribution to innovation or to changing the status quo.

SUMMARY

The senior author once asked a talented but cynical psychiatrist friend, 'What is the one quality you would like to give your patients?' He answered: 'I would like to give them an intramuscular injection of maturity.' When we embark on a coaching experience, all of us must have a picture of what we are trying to accomplish, and many of us think of different aspects of maturity. For us, mature people are supportive, encouraging and even-tempered. They have the courage to make decisions without undue second-guessing or regret. They do not betray confidences and do not betray business relationships. They follow rules, honour their contracts, and are concerned about the welfare of their partners. Mature business people take pride in contributing to the organization as a whole and they hold the welfare of their colleagues above their own. The worst business leaders intimidate, manipulate and control their peers, subordinates, and if possible their supervisors. They create crises to keep people off balance. They argue and accuse, and are vigilant to anyone seeming to cross them. They spend their workdays giving their colleagues warnings, so that if something goes wrong they can avoid blame. Some just do not care about their colleagues or organizations, and are not easily influenced. If other people are in trouble, they cannot be bothered to help.

We have tried to show that the HDS is a useful tool in coaching, because more than many other tools, it identifies the nature and relationships among 11 different critical qualities of managers. Each of these qualities has a desirable side, for example, with people scoring high on Excitable being spirited, Colourful managers being charming and entertaining, and Diligent people being conscientious. We have also argued that at the extremes of these 11 dimensions lie the manager's dark side, the side that close associates see every day and hope they can avoid. Sceptical people argue about trivia, Leisurely people procrastinate, and Mischievous people manipulate. We showed how these 11 dimensions form three clusters, and how people who score highly on these clusters influence people in unwelcome ways. People in Cluster A try to intimidate, those in Cluster B try to seduce or distract, and managers in Cluster C try to control through being over-committed to the mission and organization.

The 11 dimensions examined with the HDS are those most likely to cause a manager to derail, and so being able to coach the leader to avoid the dark sides of those dimensions is a valuable service to the individual and the organization. Many colleagues of these people do not have the courage or the mandate to give this kind of direct, critical feedback, so the coach's ability to outline and intervene with these qualities is especially valuable.

References

Benjamin, LS (1996) *Interpersonal Diagnosis and Treatment of Personality Disorders*, 2nd edn, Guilford Press, New York

Dotlich, DL and Cairo, PP (2003) *Why CEOs Fail*, Jossey-Bass, San Francisco

Fico, JM, Hogan, R and Hogan, J (2000) *Interpersonal Compass Manual*, Hogan Assessment Systems, Tulsa, OK

Hogan, R (2007) *Personality and the Fate of Organizations*, Lawrence Erlbaum, Mahwah, NJ

Hogan, R and Hogan, J (2001) Assessing leadership: a view from the dark side, *International Journal of Selection and Assessment*, **9**, pp 1–12

Hogan, R and Roberts, B (2000) A socioanalytic perspective on person/environment interaction, in *New Directions in Person–Environment Psychology*, ed WB Walsh, KH Kraik and RH Price, pp 1–24, Lawrence Erlbaum, Mahwah, NJ

Hogan, R and Warrenfeltz, R (2003) Educating the modern manager, *Academy of Management Learning and Education*, **2**, pp 74–84

10

Coaching for transformational leadership

ELQ™ (Formerly TLQ)

Beverly Alimo-Metcalfe and Peter Pritchett

INTRODUCTION

The Engaging Leadership Questionnaire™ (ELQ™) is a 360-degree feedback instrument designed specifically to provide individuals with feedback on their leadership behaviour as perceived by others, and the impact on staff motivation, job satisfaction, commitment and well-being. Its reliability and validity as a leadership assessment instrument has been described in several academic peer-reviewed papers.

Given the plethora of 360-degree instruments on the market, the provenance of the ELQ sets it apart from others, particularly within the context of changing models of leadership. The ELQ emerged from the findings of the largest single investigation of leadership ever undertaken, and the first to be deliberately inclusive in terms of gender, ethnicity and the level of individuals involved. The emergent model provides coaches with guidance as to how to approach the '360-process' in this increasingly important field, so as to maximize the value of the process for coachees and to ensure the integrity of the instrument.

THE CHANGING NATURE OF LEADERSHIP

Leadership research has been concerned with what characterizes those individuals who have the greatest positive impact on the behaviour, performance and well-being of the staff whom they manage, and on organizational performance (Alimo-Metcalfe and Alban-Metcalfe, 2001).

Notions of leadership change over time, being affected by factors including social, political, technological and economic change, which have significantly impacted on how organizations operate, are structured, are managed and are led. Not surprising, models of leadership are influenced by variables such as:

▌ when the research was originally undertaken;
▌ who funded it, and for what purpose;
▌ how the data were gathered.

The study of leadership can be seen to have gone through five main stages. The first three – the Trait approach, which focused on personality characteristics; the Behaviour approach, which focused on observable behaviours; and the Situational/contingency approach, which focused on interactions between leader and context – were criticized for not being applicable in times of continuing change, and have now come to be regarded as models of 'management' (Wright, 1996).

These gave way, in the late 1970s to 'new paradigm' thinking in leadership, its best known advocate being Bass (eg 1998), who distinguished between:

▌ 'transformational' – achieving the 'greater good' and adhering to principles and values;
▌ 'transactional' – exchanging rewards and punishments;
▌ 'laissez-faire' – abrogation of responsibility.

While Bass's influence has been enormous, the underlying model is one of a 'distant' leader, often a 'hero'.

RECENT DEVELOPMENTS IN LEADERSHIP RESEARCH

The 'new paradigm' models, also referred to as the 'heroic' models, which dominated the 1980s and 1990s, have in the last few years come under increasing attack, affected by major changes in society. There appears to be a growing cynicism about 'heroic' models of leadership that place the responsibility for leadership in the hands of a few of the most senior managers. This is partly because of recent spectacular corporate scandals, such as the demise of Enron and WorldCom, and cynicism about political leaders (World Economic Forum, 2007).

Also, there is a burgeoning of articles denouncing 'the dark side of charisma' (eg Hogan, Raskin and Fazzini, 1990; Yukl, 1999), coupled with promotion of 'quietly leading' and 'moral leadership' (Badaracco, 2002), and 'managing quietly' (Mintzberg, 1999).

There is now the recognition of 'leaderful' organizations (Raelin, 2005), and 'distributed' leadership, whereby 'Rather than seeing leadership practice as solely a function of an individual's ability, skill, charisma and cognition... it is best understood as a practice distributed over leaders, followers and their situation' (Spillane, Halverson and Diamond, 2001: 13). This is coupled with the realization that the 'engagement' of employees' discretionary effort is crucial for survival and success in an increasingly competitive world.

THE IMPORTANCE OF EMPLOYEE 'ENGAGEMENT'

The benefits to organizations of high engagement are considerable in terms of financial performance (Sirota Survey Intelligence, 2006; Watson-Wyatt, 2006). This is consistent with our own research which shows a significant relationship between quality of leadership, staff attitudes and well-being, and organizational performance (Alimo-Metcalfe *et al*, 2007).

Thus, the new direction for leadership research, is to understand what exactly are the behaviours and approaches that increase staff motivation, morale and well-being – ie 'engagement' – since manager–direct report relationship has been identified as the crucial determining factor.

THE DEVELOPMENT OF THE ENGAGING LEADERSHIP QUESTIONNAIRE (ELQ)

It is important for potential users of the ELQ to understand why and how the instrument was developed, and how it differs from the range of other leadership development 360-feedback instruments.

In essence, the ELQ is a refined version of the 'Transformational Leadership Questionnaire' (TLQ), developed through subsequent empirical research. The TLQ assesses nearby leadership, based on an 'engaging' or 'post-heroic transformational' model. As such, it is a model of 'distributed' leadership. A defining feature of the methodology adopted was to elicit 'constructs' of leadership from the ways direct reports perceived their current or a previous line manager to act, rather than what managers say of themselves; this was augmented by reviews of the literature.

Our methodology differed significantly from previous research, which sought to 'fit' the examples of behaviour studied into pre-existing categories of leadership behaviour. Our intention was to 'see' leadership through the personal perceptions and experiences of individuals, rather than to 'interpret' the impact of certain behaviours we might observe in those who happen to occupy formal leadership roles. This is extremely important in the context of personal coaching since respect for each individual's subjective experience of his or her world is regarded as central to both processes. Also, by adopting a 'grounded theory' approach we ensured content validity.

More than 2,000 elicited constructs were content analysed and a pilot questionnaire was developed that included statements describing a manager's behaviours. This was distributed among over 800 organizations. Responses from over 3,500 managers rating their line manager anonymously were analysed and 14 dimensions of 'nearby', 'engaging' leadership were identified (eg, Alimo-Metcalfe and Alban-Metcalfe, 2001). These dimensions form the basis of the 360-degree feedback instrument, the TLQ, from which the ELQ was developed.

The original research, undertaken in the NHS and local government, has been replicated in the prison service and education, in an independent study conducted by the Home Office (Dobby *et al*, 2004), and in three FTSE100 companies (Alban-Metcalfe and Alimo-Metcalfe, 2007).

The 14 ELQ leadership dimensions, which form four clusters, are shown in Figure 10.1.

THE 10 LEADERSHIP IMPACT MEASURES

Unlike most other 360-feedback instruments, the ELQ also contains 10 'Leadership Impact Measures', which gather information of the impact of the leadership behaviours on staff of the person being rated, including those factors that affect 'engagement'. These include the impact on staff's:

▌ motivation;
▌ job satisfaction;
▌ job commitment;
▌ organization commitment;
▌ work-related stress;
▌ self-confidence;
▌ self-fulfilment.

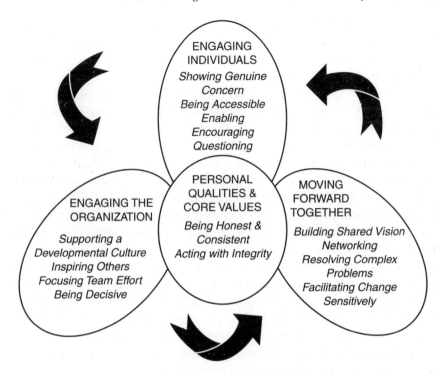

Figure 10.1 The Structure of the Engaging Leadership Questionnaire (ELQ)

This enabled us to demonstrate the convergent and discriminant validity of the instrument, reported in several peer-reviewed journals (Alban-Metcalfe and Alimo-Metcalfe, 2000, 2007; Alimo-Metcalfe and Alban-Metcalfe, 2001; Kelly *et al*, 2006; Alimo-Metcalfe *et al*, 2007). ELQ scores are significant predictors of 'attitudes to work' and 'well-being at work', which have been shown to impact significantly on staff turnover, productivity and profitability.

Evidence of the relationship between ratings of managers on specific ELQ dimensions, and the impact they have on staff managed, has been found to be of particular value in post-360 coaching sessions, since it reinforces the importance of how particular behaviours do affect the motivation, stress and commitment of staff, and organizational performance.

THE ELQ MODEL

The Engaging Leadership Questionnaire (ELQ) is a 360-degree feedback instrument, designed to assess the leadership development needs of managers and professionals working in private, public and voluntary sector organizations. As is typical with 360-degree instruments, the process involves individuals being rated by their direct reports, boss, peers and others (eg clients), as well as completing self-assessments. This allows for the collection of multiple perspectives and perceptions of individuals' leadership behaviour and its impact.

The ELQ highlights the crucial distinction between management and leadership. Managerial or leadership competencies form the foundation of successful performance within a role, but they are not sufficient for leadership.

We are probably familiar with individuals who are highly competent, but are not the easiest people to work with. Leadership is about how people enact their competencies so that they exert a positive influence on the motivation, self-confidence and performance of their staff and colleagues, and on increasing organizational success. Figure 10.2 shows this relationship.

The ELQ can be used in a variety of diagnostic developmental situations, ranging from the identification of individuals' leadership strengths and development needs to the identification of team and larger organizational group profiles. It can thus form the basis for the construction of extensive leadership development interventions, such as leadership programmes, workshops, team-building activities, personal, executive and career development coaching, and organization development initiatives.

It is also useful for evaluating individual and/or group developmental changes over time, and the impact of particular interventions.

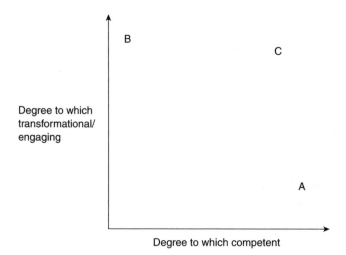

Key
Individual A is highly competent but has a style that is not at all engaging.
Individual B is highly engaging, but not competent.
Individual C represents the ideal, in being highly competent, and enacting his/her competencies in a highly engaging way.

Figure 10.2 Leadership: showing the relationship between being competent and adopting an engaging approach

For the individual, it can be invaluable as an activity undertaken some time before a developmental review, at which manager and individual construct a joint development action plan based on feedback the individual may wish to share with their manager, and for which the individual may seek support. It does not, however, replace an individual's appraisal/performance review. Another use is in individual coaching and mentoring activities.

Fundamental to the 360-feedback process is the intention to provide the individual with feedback as to others' perceptions of his or her effectiveness, and to compare these with the person's self-perceptions. While we believe that it is essential for those in leadership roles to seek feedback about their impact on others, we are very aware of the potentially damaging effect that insensitive use of 360-feedback can have on individuals undertaking the process. This is why we impose certain conditions on its use, which can be in no way compromised (Alimo-Metcalfe, 1998). These conditions, which are consistent with the British Psychological Society's guidelines for the ethical use of 360-feedback, include requirements that:

▌ the ELQ be used solely for development purposes;
▌ the process be voluntary;
▌ an individual's choice to use the ELQ be based on an understanding of what it measures, and its provenance;
▌ the data be confidential to the particular individual;
▌ the individual select their own raters;
▌ raters' scores be represented anonymously;
▌ no organization have a right to see any individual's report;
▌ the choice of sharing report data with another person, including a coach – something that we would encourage – be made only by the individual concerned;
▌ there be support for the individual in interpreting the data by someone accredited and licensed to use the ELQ;
▌ the individual's line manager discuss how s/he will support the individual's personal development plan (PDP);
▌ there be some organizational support for the individual's development.

A MODEL FOR EXPLORING ENGAGING LEADERSHIP

Since the feedback session is an exploration of engaging leadership behaviours, and information included in the ELQ is rich and detailed, a diagnostic process has been developed to help the coach guide the coachee through the information in order to gather accurate information from the cluster scales and specific behaviours contained within them.

Cluster A: personal qualities

Underpinning all the dimensions of the ELQ are the two scales that comprise this central cluster – 'Acting with integrity' and 'Being honest and consistent'. Transparency and principled behaviours are reflected in these scales.

Cluster B: engaging individuals

▮ 'Showing genuine concern' – genuine interest in staff as individuals; valuing their contribution; developing their strengths; coaching, mentoring; having positive expectations of what their staff can achieve. Irrespective of whether public or private sector, level, gender and ethnicity of staff with whom used, statistical analyses reveal that ratings of managers on this scale significantly predicts all leadership impact measures (Alimo-Metcalfe and Alban-Metcalfe, 2001, 2007).

▮ 'Enabling' – trusting staff to take decisions/initiatives on important issues; delegating effectively; developing staff's potential.

▮ 'Being accessible' – approachable and not status-conscious; preferring face-to-face communication; accessible and in-touch.

▮ 'Encouraging questioning' – encouraging questioning traditional approaches to the job; encouraging new approaches/solutions to a problem; encouraging strategic thinking.

Cluster C: engaging the organization

▮ 'Being decisive' – decisive when required; prepared to take difficult decisions, and risks when appropriate.

▮ 'Inspiring others' – exceptional communicator; inspiring others to join them.

▮ 'Focusing team effort' – clarifying objectives and boundaries; team-orientated to problem solving and decision making, and to identifying values.

▮ 'Supporting a developmental culture' – supportive when mistakes are made; encouraging critical feedback on her/himself and the service provided.

Cluster D: moving forward together

This cluster contains strong elements of connecting different stakeholders in working collaboratively towards a shared vision.

▮ 'Networking' – inspiring communicator of the vision of the organization/service to a wide network of internal and external stakeholders; gaining the confidence and support of various groups through sensitivity to needs, and by achieving organizational goals.

▮ 'Building shared vision' – having a clear vision and strategic direction in which s/he engages various internal and external stakeholders in developing; drawing others together in achieving the vision.

▮ 'Resolving complex issues' – capacity to deal with a range of complex issues; creative problem solving.

▮ 'Facilitating change sensitively' – sensitivity to the impact of change on different parts of the organization; maintaining a balance between change and stability.

ELQ AND COACHES

Owing to the nature of the ELQ, it is vital that the coach giving feedback be trained in its use. The sensitive nature of the feedback demands that a detailed and precise exploration of the information take place with the coachee. For the tool to be of maximum value as a developmental opportunity for the coachee, the coach needs to be skilled in helping the coachee to explore and to make sense of the themes and patterns that emerge.

It is also very important that coaches are aware of the impact that they are having on the coachees. Coaches should at all times model the behaviours found in the ELQ and should be self-aware and sensitive enough to be able to guide coachees towards making links for themselves between the results and their leadership style.

It takes a very skilled coach to be able to assist coachees in drawing conclusions for themselves with regards to the feedback, as opposed to offering advice and instruction. Fundamentally, the ability of coaches to engage at this higher level will depend upon their own capacity to engage with, and incorporate, transformational behaviours into their own practices and to demonstrate these in the coaching session.

Two examples of dimensions and scales within the ELQ that coaches should be able to demonstrate as being core to their own coaching practice and ethical value base are described below.

Authentic ELQ coaching behaviours: the necessity for engaging with 'showing genuine concern' and being 'enabling'

Showing genuine concern

For coaches using the ELQ, it is vital that this scale be incorporated into personal practice, particularly when offering feedback to coachees during the ELQ feedback session.

With regards to showing genuine concern, coaches should be able to demonstrate:

❚ sensitivity to the coachee's needs and aspirations;
❚ sensitivity and empathy towards the coachee's feelings about his or her working situation;
❚ ability to recognize the importance of using the session to raise morale;
❚ a positive approach to the coachee's development;
❚ a focus on developing the coachee's potential;
❚ a strong sense of loyalty and commitment to the relationship;
❚ ability to help the coachee make sense of the current situation;
❚ ability to support the coachee in making sense of data for him or herself, rather than interpreting it for the coachee;
❚ willingness to take time to listen and empathize with the coachee's working context.

If coaches engage in this way in the feedback session and model genuine concern behaviours, coachees will experience the extent to which transformational or engaging behaviours can assist with the process of positive change and thus affect in a positive manner the individuals' development towards being a more capable and integrated transformational engaging leader.

Enabling

Another key set of behaviours for coaches to model and incorporate into their coaching practice refers to 'enabling'. Within the ELQ scales, enabling is seen as a vital area of development for the engaging transformational leader, and therefore coaches need to be highly skilled in this respect in the way they conduct coaching sessions. Again, it is vital that they be able to display and demonstrate the behaviours in the coach/coachee relationship. 'Enabling' refers to the extent to which coaches, during the sessions, allow coachees to arrive at their own conclusions about the feedback, while exploring the information and patterns in the ELQ report in a thorough way.

With regards to enabling behaviours, coaches should have an integrated coaching approach that demonstrates:

❚ an involvement with coachees in setting their outcomes and objectives;
❚ empowering coachees to return to their organization and begin conversations with colleagues and others, in order to better understand themselves and their leadership approach, and its impact on others;
❚ building trust in the relationship with the coachee;
❚ an acknowledgement that the process may be sensitive, and possibly difficult for the coachee, and offering appropriate support during this time;
❚ a shared ownership of the process.

In terms of coaching practice, it is vital that the coach be able to engage with the leadership model and incorporate (as a minimum) these two areas into their practice. The coaching sessions that follow the completion of the ELQ™ are not feedback sessions in the traditional sense of giving scores back to the coachee. They are about making sense of the perceptions others have of one's behaviour and its impact, and exploring possible development needs in terms of becoming more transformational and engaging. Thus, the coach should be as sensitive to the process as to the outcome of this coaching event.

USING THE ELQ WITH COACHEES

We believe strongly that the use of the ELQ 360-feedback process should form part of an integrated approach to developing a transformational organization: that is, to embedding a culture of engaging transformational leadership.

Not only is this the underlying purpose for which the instrument was developed, but we believe this to be of ethical importance, since supporting individuals in becoming more aware of the impact of their behaviour on the morale, motivation, satisfaction and well-being of others will typically involve encouraging them to reflect on the personal experiences of working with a manager and/or in an organization that has had a negative impact on their motivation and well-being. It is our experience that coachees inevitably become more sensitive to the culture of their organization and/or line manager, and how they are being treated. We also have evidence of positive behavioural change.

If the ELQ is being used as part of an organizational culture change process, the coaching sessions should always take account of the wider organizational change context with respect to the development that is to take place. Coaches should familiarize themselves with the wider organizational issues as part of the preparation for the sessions so as to be able to fully understand their coachees' working contexts.

It is vital that the coach understand the reasons for the coaching sessions and what is to be their focus. When using 360-feedback instruments other than the ELQ™, coaching sessions often focus on the transactional competence components of the coachee's development needs, that is on competencies. Coachees can often arrive believing the sessions will be about developing competence-based skills, rather than about adopting an engaging approach to how they enact their competencies in their daily role, along with the attitudes and values that underpin them. The focus of ELQ™ feedback sessions, however, is to evaluate and explore the extent to which the coachee currently applies a transformational engaging approach, and to identify how the current approach can be enhanced to have a greater positive impact in his or her leadership role. The coach will need to focus on this continually as the session develops in order for it to be successful.

There should be an exploration of how the coachee currently attempts to achieve an engaging style with staff, and to what extent his or her objectives are being met. Emergent themes for development will flow from this.

Overall, the coach should always be focused on outcomes that have an impact broadly on the following areas:

▮ how developing an engaging style will impact on the staff's motivation, job satisfaction, effectiveness and development;
▮ how engaging behaviours will enhance the capacity of the team in adopting an engaging leadership approach;
▮ how engaging behaviours will enhance team and departmental effectiveness;
▮ the extent to which coachees as leaders will have an impact on their team's and(depending on their role) their organization's culture;
▮ how the coachees will put in place actions to continually develop their own leadership capacity.

This forms the basis of the necessary requirements and conditions of the coach when approaching an ELQ feedback session.

USING THE ELQ: THE COACH'S ROLE

It is vital that the coach engages with the feedback process from the perspective of exploration. It is not the role of the coach to interpret the information for the coachee.

In order for engaging behaviours to become integrated and embedded into leadership practice, coaches should explore the emergent themes from the perspectives and framework of reference of the coachees. Coachees should be encouraged to begin to make links between the scales and the responses received from their raters.

A major factor in the use of the ELQ 360-degree process is that it allows extensive information to be gained about perceptions that colleagues (and possibly others with whom the individual comes into contact) have of an individual's current leadership style and the impact that this has on them. The coach should encourage the coachee to see the completion of the ELQ as the beginning of the process of his or her leadership development, and not the process itself. The coach should be strongly encouraging the coachee to follow the initial post-360 coaching session with gathering more specific information from those who have responded to the questionnaire, by arranging a series of follow-up discussions with individual raters. There are a variety of reasons for this, apart from gathering specific examples of behaviours that are regarded by raters (including, importantly, direct reports) as effective or not, by seeking more feedback from his or her colleagues the individual is enacting one of the most important characteristics of engaging leaders, which is to understand their impact on individuals and teams.

Some individuals feel comfortable to discuss their 360 report openly with their team, and we have known some people to show their reports to their team. However, while this is encouraging in that it reflects a very open leadership style, we would urge caution in adopting this approach, because an individual who is not confident in conducting such group sessions might become uncomfortable and defensive in response to questions. This might have a deleterious effect on relationships with the team. It might also make it more difficult for some team members to offer specific feedback because of their discomfort in the situation.

The coach should be looking to affirm the positive aspects of the results in the report as well as helping the coachee to explore developmental needs. Some individuals are more likely to under-rate than over-rate their effectiveness. Research suggests that in general this is more typical of women than of men. It is important for the coach to encourage the coachee to focus on dimensions of leadership that are areas of positive 'blind spots'.

Since even unexpected positive feedback from others challenges, to some degree, an individual's self-concept, it is important for coaches to encourage their coachees to reflect on the information, and on why any differences emerge. As is the case with unexpected negative feedback, it will be important to encourage coachees to consider arranging discussions with their raters to seek more specific examples of the behaviours that relate to the dimension under scrutiny. This is as important for under-raters as over-raters.

INTEGRATING THE ELQ DIMENSIONS

Various ways of linking the 14 dimensions can emerge in a coaching session, depending on particular themes emerging in relation to the coachee's data, but as an overall model we propose the model shown in Figure 10.3.

The coaching session following the receipt by the coachee of his or her ELQ report is a process of shared exploration. In approaching the discussion it is important to be prepared for a wide range of different responses – anxiety, defensiveness, surprise, pleasure and so on.

The aims for the coachee are:

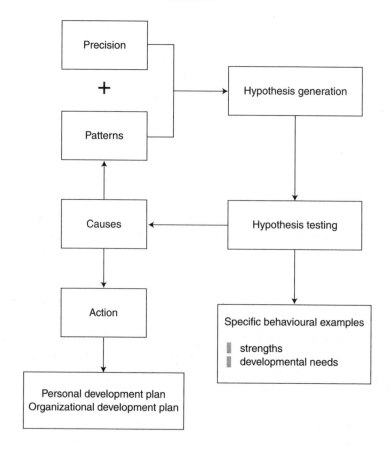

Figure 10.3 A model for approaching the diagnostic process of the coaching session

▮ to be as active as possible in understanding the questionnaire profile and the implications to be drawn from it;
▮ to be open rather than defensive to what is emerging;
▮ to be involved in bringing into the discussion, relevant data from their past experiences;
▮ to emerge better able to take action in relation to his or her situation.

THE DIAGNOSTIC PROCESS

The diagnostic process can be thought of as comprising the three components of precision, patterns and causes, which lead to the generation of hypotheses to be tested in post-coaching discussions held by the coachee with her/his raters. These are shown in Figure 10.3, and described in more detail below.

The structure and content of the ELQ is such that identifiable patterns exist between scales, between items on the same scale, and between items on different scales.

Relationships between scales

Fundamental to the concept of the ELQ model is authenticity. Thus, the leadership behaviours that are assessed are predicated on the qualities and values articulated in Cluster A. Furthermore, taking 'acting with integrity' and 'showing genuine concern' as two starting points, it is possible to suggest ways in which each of the 14 scales are linked. Such a pattern of relationships is shown in Figure 10.4, in which 'facilitating change sensitively' is seen as a kind of end-point, though other patterns can be proposed.

Relationships between items on the same scale

While some coachees find looking at relationships between scales to be valuable, more commonly the relationships between items within scales are most informative. Here we strongly encourage the coachee to draw attention to direct reports' ratings, where these are available.

In many cases, the process of encouraging coachees to look for which items have the highest ratings (precise information), and then asking them whether they can see a pattern between the items, provides them with valuable insights into their behaviour. It is also the first stage in generating a hypothesis. The corresponding process of encouraging coachees to see whether there are any patterns among the items on which they were rated lowest can be equally informative, and enable them to confirm, refine or modify their hypothesis. Consideration by the coachees of the other, intermediately rated, items can lead to further confirmation, refinement or modification.

Where the pattern of relationships is not self-evident, two alternative strategies can be adopted. One is for the coach to identify the ways in which the different items could be related. This pattern of relationships – which it is important to emphasize is (a) theoretical, and (b) based on the coach's construction of the world – can be drawn in the form of a diagram similar to that in Figure 10.4, but with the scales replaced by items. An exercise of this kind is a training exercise that forms part of the ELQ Accreditation Workshop, and the reason why such diagrams can be produced is that, on each scale, the items can be interrelated in a logical way.

Using the diagram as a template, the coachee is asked first of all to write the average ratings made by, say, their direct reports on each of the items. The next stage is to ask the coachee to indicate which of these scores are the highest, and to record this, on the diagram, with a 'tick' or two 'ticks', or an

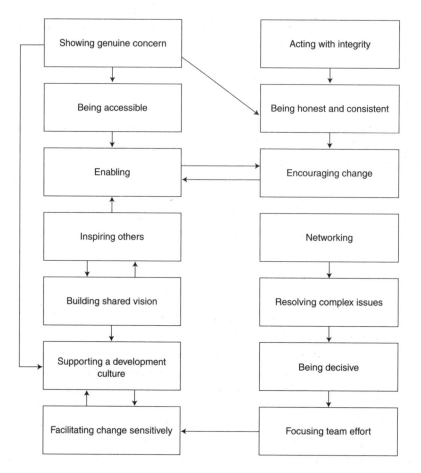

Figure 10.4 Relationships between the scales of the Engaging Leadership Questionnaire (ELQ)

'H' for high. Next the same process is repeated, in this case recording the lowest scores with an 'x' or an 'L' for low; the intermediate scores are recorded as a '?' or an 'M' for medium. It is important to remember that these scores are relative or 'ipsative', and not normative – even though extensive normative data are available for individuals working in different public and private sector organizations. Therefore, for one coachee, a rating of 3.5 or 4.0 may be recorded as an 'H', whereas for another, it would be recorded as an 'L' or 'M'. It is also important to emphasize that the decision on what is a high, medium or low score must rest with the coachee.

This strategy is open to the criticism that the coachee's thinking about the way in which the different behaviours (items) measured on a scale are inter-related may be influenced by the coach's construction of reality.

The alternative strategy, which addresses this criticism, is for the coach to prepare a series of small laminated cards, each with one of the items of the relevant scale printed on it. Here, the coachee is encouraged to arrange the cards in a way that it is meaningful to them. This process, inevitably, stimulates discussion, and may lead to the cards being rearranged at least once. Thereafter the process is similar to that outlined above, with the coachee being encouraged to record (a) the ratings they have been given on the laminated cards (using a felt tip pen), and (b) whether he or she rates the score as 'H', 'M' or 'L'.

Two patterns commonly emerge within 'showing genuine concern'. One is that coachees are rated highly in terms of 'being loyal to their staff' and 'being sensitive to others' needs and aspirations', which are, as it were, prerequisite behaviours, but low in 'taking time to listen to staff, even when they themselves are busy' or 'being active in coaching or mentoring'. In other words, their high level of commitment and sensitivity does not result in the appropriate action!

Another is where coachees are rated highly in terms of 'being loyal to their staff', 'being sensitive to others' needs and aspirations', and in 'taking time to listen to staff, even when they themselves are busy', but not in 'coaching or mentoring' or in 'setting aside time for team building'. Here, the coachee may be interpreted as responding appropriately when asked for help (reactive behaviour), but not being proactive in providing developmental support.

Relationships between items on different scales

An example of links between different scales is where coachees recognize that the low rating they have been given on 'empowering their staff' in the 'enabling' scale can be related to a low rating on 'delegation' on the same scale, and to 'being sensitive to others' needs and aspirations' on the 'showing genuine concern' scale. A moment's reflection enables them to recognize that they can hardly expect staff to feel empowered if tasks are either not delegated properly or not delegated at all; and that effective delegation requires knowledge not only of staff's needs, but also their aspirations.

SUMMARY

Without doubt, leadership is becoming a topic of increasing importance to organizations and individuals who work within them. The challenges being faced are becoming more complex and demanding, while at the same time there is a need to be 'lean', and to rely on proportionally fewer resources. This inevitably places increasing pressure on managers to 'get more for less', and the cost in human terms of high levels of stress can be incalculable. This will eventually have a negative impact on performance. There is, therefore, a crucial need to support those with leadership responsibilities, so that they achieve the greatest benefit from the feedback offered from their colleagues and others with whom they work, but also that they reflect on the impact of their behaviour.

Not surprisingly, the market is responding with a confusing array of 360-feedback instruments, many of which have virtually no evidence that they are effectively measuring those aspects of behaviour that are most critical for effectiveness. The ELQ emerged from probably the largest investigation of leadership, and has been validated in an increasing number of studies, and this research is ongoing.

While we believe that we must ensure the rigorous academic foundations of the instrument at all times, our passion to develop the instrument was to make a real and wholesome difference to the experiences of people working in organizations, which in turn will reap benefits for their organization.

Supporting users of the ELQ with high-quality coaching can multiply the potential benefits exponentially, which is why the activity is so important and such a privilege for those undertaking this role. However, we are also very aware that 360-degree assessment can be used inappropriately and insensitively, and its effect can be devastating. We hope that this chapter helps in some way to ensure that all those who are involved in using the ELQ find the experience enriching.

References

Alban-Metcalfe, B and Alimo-Metcalfe, J (2006) Leadership culture and its impact on job satisfaction, motivation, commitment and well-being at work, paper presented at the British Academy of Management, 12–14 September, Belfast

Alban-Metcalfe, B and Alimo-Metcalfe, J (2007)'The development of the (engaging) Transformational Leadership Questionnaire (private sector version), *Leadership and Organization Development Journal*, **28**, pp 104–21

Alban-Metcalfe, RJ and Alimo-Metcalfe, B (2000) An analysis of the convergent and discriminant validity of the Transformational Leadership Questionnaire, *International Journal of Selection and Assessment*, **8** (3), pp 158–75

Alimo-Metcalfe, B (1998) 360 degree feedback and leadership development, *International Journal of Selection and Assessment*, **6** (1), pp 35–44

Alimo-Metcalfe, B and Alban-Metcalfe, J (2002) The great and the good, *People Management*, 10 January, pp 32–34

Alimo-Metcalfe, B and Alban-Metcalfe, J (2003) Under the influence, *People Management*, 6 March, pp 32–35

Alimo-Metcalfe, B and Alban-Metcalfe, J (2005) Leadership: time for a new direction? *Leadership*, **1** (1), pp 51–71

Alimo-Metcalfe, B and Alban-Metcalfe, J (2007) The development of the Transformational Leadership Questionnaire (Private Sector version), *Leadership & Organisational Development Journal*, 28 (2), pp 104–21

Alimo-Metcalfe, B, Alban-Metcalfe, J, Bradley, M, Mariathason, J and Samele, C (2007) Leadership quality, attitudes to work and well-being at work, and organizational performance: a longitudinal study, *Journal of Health and Organizational Management* (accepted for publication)

Alimo-Metcalfe, B and Alban-Metcalfe, RJ (2001) The development of a new Transformational Leadership Questionnaire, *The Journal of Occupational and Organizational Psychology*, 74, pp 1–27

Badaracco, JL (2002) *Leading Quietly: An Unorthodox Guide to Doing the Right Thing*, Harvard Business School, Harvard, MA

Bass, BM (1998) Transformational Leadership: Industrial, Military, and Educational Impact, Lawrence Erlbaum, Mahwah, NJ:

Dobby, J, Anscombe, J and Tuffin R (2004) *Police Leadership: Expectations and Impact*, Home Office Online Report 20/04

Hogan, R, Raskin, R and Fazzini, D (1990) The dark side of charisma in, *Measures of Leadership*, ed KE Clark, MB Clark and RR Albright, pp 343–354, Leadership Library of America, West Orange, NJ

Kelly, A, Robertson, P and Gill, R (2006) Time for a change: a UK model of transformational leadership, paper presented at the Annual Conference of the British Academy of Management, Belfast, 12–14 September

Mintzberg, H (1999) 'Managing quietly', *Leader to Leader*, 12, Spring, pp 24–30

Raelin, JR (2005) We the leaders: in order to form a leaderful organization, *Journal of Leadership and Organizational Studies*, 12 (2), pp 18–30

Sirota Survey Intelligence (2006) 'High morale again pays off in stock market gains', Purchase, New York, www.sirota.com

Spillane, J, Halverson, R and Diamond, J (2001) *Towards a Theory of Leadership Practice: A Distributed Perspective*, Northwestern University, Institute for Policy Research Working Paper, Evanston IL

Watson-Wyatt Research Report (2006) Effective Communication: a Leading Indicator of Financial performance – 2005/2006 Communication ROI Study™

World Economic Forum (2007) Gallup International Voice of the People© Survey http://www.weforum.org/en/media/Latest%20Press%20Releases/voiceofthe peoplesurvey

Wright, PL (1996) *Managerial Leadership*, Routledge, London

Yukl, G (1999) An evaluation of conceptual weakness in transformational and charismatic leadership theories, *Leadership Quarterly*, 10, pp 285–30

11

Developing resilience through coaching

MTQ48

Dr Peter Clough, Keith Earle and Doug Strycharczyk

INTRODUCTION

This chapter focuses on the concept of mental toughness and the work carried out at the University of Hull in developing the Mental Toughness Questionnaire (MTQ). Mental toughness is widely referred to but until now has been a rather vague concept. A user-friendly model has been developed that, in conjunction with the construction of a reliable and valid scale, has enabled coaches to both assess mental toughness and offer developmental advice. The model identifies four important elements of mental toughness: challenge, control, commitment and confidence. These core dimensions are described in detail and their use as part of a coaching intervention is discussed. It has been found that a number of aspects of mental toughness can be enhanced by identifying clear and specific development needs and coupling these with specific interventions drawn from a wide array of applied psychology fields.

THE THEORETICAL MODEL

From a theoretical perspective, the concept of mental toughness can only be fully understood by placing it within the context of related constructs. The two key constructs are arguably resilience (Dyer and McGuinness, 1996) and hardiness (Kobasa, 1979). While both of these have their roots firmly in the area of health psychology they have clear relevance to the fields of occupational and sport psychology.

Recent research in the field of occupational psychology has been undertaken examining the concept of resilience, its impact on performance at work and the development of resilience within individuals (Jackson and Watkin, 2004). They suggest that our internal thinking processes can both moderate the impact of adversities and provide a valuable resource in moving forward from them, focusing on the things we can control rather than those we cannot.

The other main thrust of theoretical development relates to hardiness (Kobasa, 1979). There has been a plethora of research investigating the concept of hardiness or the 'hardy personality' (Funk, 1992). Kobasa proposed that hardiness consists of three interrelated concepts: control, challenge and commitment. This concept of hardiness is considered to have a buffering effect between stressful life events and illness.

Recently the use of the term 'mental toughness' has become increasingly common across a number of domains, including sporting and occupational contexts, and has tended to replace resilience and hardiness in the public's consciousness. Within the context of the psychology literature, the use of this term can be traced back to the work of Loehr (1982), who was a sports psychologist working with athletes with the principal goal of improving sporting performance. In this capacity he found that athletes and coaches were beginning to use the term mental toughness to describe a desired trait. This led Loehr to investigate the construct and attempt to identify what this 'mental toughness' actually was. In his book *Mental Toughness Training for Sport: Achieving athletic excellence* (1986), he defined mental toughness as 'the ability to consistently perform toward the upper range of your talent and skill regardless of competitive circumstances'.

However, it should be noted that Loehr's model of mental toughness and the resulting questionnaire were both generated from informal interactions with athletes, and Loehr made no attempt to scientifically test the model or develop his questionnaire into a psychometric instrument.

The current plethora of definitions of mental toughness have served to confuse the area and inhibited the development of an operational concept. These definitions range from an ability to rebound from failures (Dennis, 1981; Gould *et al*, 1987; Taylor, 1989; Woods, Hocton and Desmond, 1995), acquisition of superior mental skills (Bull, Albinson and Shambrook, 1996; Loehr, 1995), an ability to cope with pressure, stress, and adversity (Goldberg, 1998); and an insensitivity to severe pressure (Alderman, 1974; Tutko and Richards, 1976).

It was apparent that mental toughness was indeed a widely used and discussed topic but there were few, if any, reliable psychometric tests to measure it. It was therefore decided to develop a reliable and valid instrument to measure this potentially important concept.

THE MENTAL TOUGHNESS QUESTIONNAIRE (MTQ48)

The initial development work revolved around interviews. From these a working definition of mental toughness was developed, and in turn this was used to construct a robust test of the concept. The working definition developed was:

> Mentally tough individuals tend to be sociable and outgoing as they are able to remain calm and relaxed, they are competitive in many situations and have lower anxiety levels than others. With a high sense of self-belief and an unshakeable faith that they control their own destiny, these individuals can remain relatively unaffected by competition or adversity. (Clough, Earle and Sewell, 2002: 38.)

On the basis of this definition, a range of items were written. The aim was to develop items that could encapsulate each of the four components of the model (challenge, commitment, confidence and control). Each item consisted of a statement followed by a five-point Likert scale with verbal anchors ranging from (1) strongly disagree to (5) strongly agree.

A series of factor analyses were carried out which identified four key core, independent scales of mental toughness:

▌ control;
▌ challenge;
▌ commitment;
▌ confidence.

Two of the scales – control and confidence –are also found to have sub-scales. These are briefly described below.

Control

Individuals who score high on this scale feel that they are in control of their work and of the environment in which they work. They are capable of exerting more influence on their working environment and are more confident about working in complex or multi-tasked situations. This means for example that, at one end of the scale, individuals are able to handle lots of things at the same time. At the other end, they may only be comfortable handling one thing at a time. Ongoing development of MTQ48 has enabled the identification of two subscales to this scale: emotional control and life control.

▌ *Control (emotion)*: Individuals scoring highly on this scale are better able to control their emotions. They are able to keep anxieties in check and are less likely to reveal their emotional state to other people.
▌ *Control (life)*: Individuals scoring higher on this scale are more likely to believe that they control their lives. They feel that their plans will not be thwarted and that they can make a difference.

Challenge

This scale describes the extent to which individuals see challenges as opportunities. Individuals who see them as opportunities will actively seek them out and will identify problems as ways for self-development. At the other end challenges are perceived as problems and threats. So, for example, at one end of the scale we find those who thrive in continually changing environments. At the other end we find those who prefer to minimize their exposure to change and the problems that come with that – and will strongly prefer to work in stable predictable environments.

Commitment

Sometimes described as 'stickability', this scale describes the ability of an individual to carry out tasks successfully despite any problems or obstacles that arise while achieving the goal. Consequently an individual who scores at the high end of the scale will be able to handle and achieve things to tough unyielding deadlines. In contrast, an individual at the other end will need to be free from those kind of demands to perform satisfactorily.

Confidence

Individuals who are high in confidence have the self-belief to successfully complete tasks that might be considered too difficult by individuals with similar abilities but with lower confidence. Less confident individuals are also likely to be less persistent and may make more errors. For example, individuals at one end of the scale will be able to take setbacks (whether generated externally or caused by themselves) in their stride. They keep their heads when things go wrong and difficulties may even strengthen their resolve to do something. At the other end individuals will be unsettled by setbacks and will feel undermined by these. Their heads are said to 'drop'. As with the control dimension, further analysis revealed two sub-scales within the confidence dimension:

▐ *Confidence (abilities)*: Individuals scoring highly on this scale are more likely to believe that they are a truly worthwhile person. They are less dependent on external validation and tend to be more optimistic about life in general.
▐ *Confidence (interpersonal)*: Individuals scoring highly on this scale tend to be more assertive. They are less likely to be intimidated in social settings and are more likely to push themselves forward in groups and to express their views. They are also better able to cope with difficult or awkward people.

The software related to the MTQ48 has the ability to generate four types of report: (a) a candidate report, (b) an assessor report, (c) a development (candidate report + development ideas) report and (d) a coaching report. This latter report will form the basis of the next section of this chapter.

THE MTQ AND COACHES

There is significant benefit for the coach in embracing the mental toughness model and examining its application to themselves and their work. The work of a coach is challenging and has its own sources of stress – not least the need to make a difference with another person who may not always be receptive to what a coach can offer.

The MTQ48 can be extremely valuable to coaches in provoking thinking about their own qualities in this area – and guiding them towards developing their skills, behaviours and attributes.

Coaches who are mentally tough have the capability to withstand a significant amount of pressure. They have confidence in their abilities and are often willing to take on demanding tasks, believing they will succeed. They can usually shrug off criticism and not take others' comments to heart. They are likely to speak their mind when working in groups and are usually comfortable in many different social and work contexts. This positive approach to the coaching encounter is more likely to put the coachee at ease and allow the coaches themselves to have far more control.

More specifically coaches scoring high on mental toughness will tend to:

▌ set realistic goals, allowing them to avoid overwhelming coachees, or perhaps under-challenging the coachee;
▌ happily accept the more challenging encounters which offer them the opportunity to truly demonstrate their own abilities;
▌ feel in control, maintaining the belief that they can truly make a difference, despite setbacks.

Basically it can be argued that the coachee will respond better to a coach who is more confident, in control, committed and who is appropriately challenging. Therefore mental toughness and mental toughness development are as important for the coach as for the coachee. It is literally a matter of 'practise what you preach'.

For coaches who are not particularly tough a number of tools and techniques can be used to facilitate the achievement of a successful coaching session. These include:

▌ *Visualization*: being able to envisage what a successful outcome to the coaching session will look like.
▌ *Positive thinking*: being able to develop the inner belief that the coach can make a real difference. This will allow the coach to deal more effectively with the inevitable setbacks. Techniques like listing 'five positives about oneself' and 'mentally revisiting successes' are valuable here.
▌ *Attentional control*: being able to allow everything to emerge in your work with the coachee while retaining the ability to focus on the core issues.
▌ *Goal setting*: being able to set 'SMARTER' goals and targets – particularly in being able to identify milestones and actions which need to be achieved as part of the coachee's journey to improved performance. As we know from the sports world, 'success breeds success'. Creating a sense of progress and achievement works for the coach and the coachee.

Finally it is acknowledged that mental toughness is not a universal panacea. The mentally tough coach will be better able to deal with the cut and thrust of challenging encounters but may not be as sensitive as some to the emotional content of their discussions. It is hard for a truly mentally tough individual to fully empathize with the plight of someone who is, for example, very sensitive. However, again, an understanding of your own toughness can be helpful. For example, a tough coach may need to clearly recognize that clients may not instantly have the resources to move their lives forward. It is indeed useful for such coaches to remind themselves of the fact that 'if it appears to be a problem to the coachee, it is a problem'. Driving too hard, or failing to acknowledge the coachees' feelings will severely impact on the coaching process.

USING THE MTQ48 WITH COACHEES

The MTQ48 measures how people respond to the world around them – more specifically how they respond to stressors, challenge and pressure. And as we have seen, it does so through four scales (two of which have two subscales each). This enables the coach to undertake a reasonable degree of analysis and feedback in an area important for the development and performance of many individuals.

The coachees' scores are reported on a sten scale. Although the scales are bi-polar, when we are looking at mental toughness we can make a simplifying assumption that the scales have a low end (usually stens 1–3), a high end (usually stens 8–10) and a middle (stens 4–7) where individuals behave like most people and demonstrate characteristics of people at the high and the low end.

What follows provides general descriptions of the characteristics of people scoring above average, around the average and below average on overall mental toughness – together with a commentary for the coach. There is then a general description of high and low scores on each of the four component scales. Each description attempts to capture the typical and distinctive characteristics of people in each group. However, there will be some variation within each of these groups.

It should be noted that the descriptions produced by the MTQ48 software make finer distinctions between the score levels than those given here.

As with all feedback, the first step is to ensure that the use of the MTQ48 is relevant to the particular case. Mental toughness is a quality that is not always needed in a particular role – and many people will have the 'right' level of mental toughness to carry out their roles and lead a reasonably comfortable life.

In working with a coachee it is important, at the outset, to:

▌ provide feedback about the scores and what they indicate;
▌ check that the coachees are comfortable with that description of them at the present time – coachees will frequently challenge the picture that is being offered;
▌ confirm that the description has or has not changed in recent times;
▌ if a change has occurred, to fully explore this.

Prior to a feedback session the coach should:

▌ plan the schedule to ensure that the coachee is given adequate time;
▌ read the relevant reports thoroughly and construct an outline plan for the session;

▌ identify ways of illustrating what he or she wishes to say;

▌ provide the coachee with a copy of the (candidate or development) report or with sufficient time to read it before the discussion.

The following is a brief overview of what MTQ48 scores mean and their implications for the coachee.

Overall mental toughness

High overall mental toughness

High-scoring individuals have the capability to withstand a significant amount of pressure. They have confidence in their abilities and are often willing to take on demanding tasks, believing they will succeed. They can usually shrug off criticism and not take others' comments to heart. They are likely to speak their mind when working in groups and are usually comfortable in many different social and work contexts.

They are normally committed to the task in hand. They tend to be tenacious and resolute and likely to complete what they start. They can deal with unforeseen circumstances without undue stress. When problems arise, they are unlikely to give up, and typically view such events as challenges and opportunities for personal development, rather than threats to their security.

They believe that they are in control of their lives. They feel that they are responsible for their own destinies and that they are influential in their own environments. They tend to be in control of their emotions and can cope with difficult events. They are usually calm and stable under pressure.

Issues which may arise derive from the observation that these individuals may emerge as mentally or emotionally insensitive. Problems do not exist – they are easily shrugged off. This can lead to difficulties in several areas:

▌ being (un)aware of their impact on others – either causing offence or simply trampling over people's feelings;

▌ being intolerant of those who are not like them – even though they may be effective in their own ways;

▌ being unable to deal effectively with others who are like them but who may challenge them in some way.

In most situations the effect is that they can become ineffective as managers or leaders even though they have many of the characteristics of a good leader or manager. This can lead to frustration because they are not achieving what they expect to achieve, which in turn can result in a reduction in mental toughness or in more extreme behaviour. Coaching here will normally focus on the coachees' impact on the people around them – and how they can become more effective through dealing with others more sensitively.

Low overall mental toughness

People with low overall toughness may find it difficult to cope with stressful and really demanding environments and, on some occasions, suffer from a lack of self-belief. They may find it hard to deal with criticism and will probably take others' comments too much to heart. In addition, they may be overly self-critical at times. They may not be willing to push themselves forward enough, possibly as a result of worrying that they will not succeed.

On occasions they may not speak their mind, even when they feel strongly about a particular issue. They may be slightly uncomfortable in groups and a little apprehensive in social settings.

When facing problems and difficult circumstances, they may feel nervous and threatened. They may avoid some challenging situations for fear of failure, and hence may not take all their opportunities for personal development. They may worry about things unduly, sometimes getting problems out of perspective. Unexpected events may completely throw them on occasions.

Such coachees may be very sensitive. It takes little to bring them to a grinding halt – they are generally unable to deal with setbacks, complexity or even modest targets, and are unable to express themselves when pressured in this way.

The coach could examine the four scales to identify where the greatest sensitivities lie and plan to deal with these in a logical manner. More specifically the coach could identify situations that the coachee habitually finds difficult, and develop strategies and tactics to deal with each in turn.

Average overall mental toughness

People of average toughness are able to cope with most of life's challenges, although, when facing some difficult circumstances they may feel nervous and a little threatened. They are quite confident in their abilities, but their self-belief may be affected by others' criticism. When opportunities for development present themselves, they are likely to accept the challenge, although the potential for failure may concern them. They are likely to be comfortable in most social situations, and will usually contribute to group activities.

They will usually achieve their goals, although they may occasionally become distracted when facing difficult circumstances. They are likely to feel in control in most situations and feel that they have some power to influence what goes on around them. However, they may occasionally feel that events have overtaken them.

Issues that can arise include dealing with or understanding people at the extremes. A more mentally tough person may prove difficult to be with and will begin to wear someone down – affecting the coachee's own mental toughness. Coachees with low mental toughness may prove equally difficult in a different way – it may prove challenging to get them to respond in a way their coach wants them to respond

Consequently, coaches may need to confirm not only that the score reflects the current state but that the score also represents a move from a previous (usually) higher (or lower) state. Coachees will recognize the change if they are less effective than before and more things seem to trouble them, so that the coach's role may be to restore the previous state where desired.

Mental toughness confidence

There is some indication that this is the most 'fluid' scale within MTQ48. The confidence of individuals can vary widely over a comparatively short period of time usually as a result of some significant and traumatic event or a repeated exposure to setbacks. However, this is the scale where an intervention like coaching or counselling can make the biggest impact in the shortest time.

From the coach's perspective this may be a good place to start with a coaching programme. Confidence is a key issue in developing mental toughness – it is more difficult to work with someone whose confidence is low.

High mental toughness confidence score

These individuals have high levels of self-confidence and are self-assured. Typically they are seen as high achievers and will often succeed where others will give up or fail – but they may 'go for it' when commitment is not really warranted. They can be determined to try to succeed even when the task is unachievable.

When dealing with tasks, self-confident individuals deal comfortably with setbacks and problems – they are not fazed by them. The issue for people with high confidence is likely to be more to do with their relationship with others – they may be intolerant and unforgiving of those who do not respond to adversity in the same stoic way, thereby making life more difficult for someone who may already see the downside to life and work.

The challenge for the coach is to help such coachees to understand the characteristics of the people around them and, first, adjust the way they deal with them and, second, work out how they can support them better.

Low mental toughness confidence score

Individuals with low scores are not particularly confident and may lack a degree of self-belief. In the workplace these will often be people with skills and qualities who underachieve and will avoid putting themselves forward for tasks and responsibility.

They may blindly carry out work – to the issued instruction – but will not always communicate problems along the way, which might mean that the work will not be completed satisfactorily. They may wait to be told what to do next.

Typically these individuals will react poorly to adversity and setback. They are more likely to shrug their shoulders, say 'I gave it my best shot – I can't do any more' and give up when the going gets tough. They may even shy away from attempting anything which looks difficult (even though it may not be difficult at all).

The challenge for the coach is to work in two areas: enhancing the coachees' confidence in their abilities and their interpersonal confidence (the confidence to express themselves to others).

To develop their confidence in their abilities, the coach could work with the coachees to put their self-assessment into perspective and help them understand better what qualities they do 'bring to the party', and to outline their achievements and value them properly. It is not uncommon (especially when working with young people) to find that individuals understate and undervalue what they can offer.

Developing interpersonal confidence may involve working with the coachees to enable them to assert themselves. Enabling them to understand how and when to make a mark, to learn how to speak with people and within groups. Again it is not uncommon to find individuals who underachieve – even though they are knowledgeable and skilled, they are unable to express themselves and make others aware that they too can make a valuable contribution.

Challenge

High mental toughness challenge score

High-scoring individuals will tend to see a challenge as an opportunity rather than a threat, often using it as a way to achieve personal development.

They are not intimidated by changes in their routine and may be actively drawn to fast-moving, challenging environments. They will tend to be 'quick on their feet', having an ability to quickly deal with unexpected events.

They may be quickly bored by repetitive tasks, becoming frustrated by what they see as mundane. They will probably appreciate an unstructured environment that allows them scope to be flexible.

They might take on too many tasks or projects – because each one seems interesting. In turn this might mean that some work is not completed properly or is forgotten. Similarly, when in authority, they may create initiatives and stimulate change for change's sake. Such managers can create what is known as 'initiative overload' – and find that their effectiveness plummets.

The coach may need to work in two areas. The first is getting these coachees to understand their impact on others and their need for routine and structure. The second may be getting the coachees to learn to value completion as well as starting things off.

Low mental toughness challenge score

Low-scoring individuals may feel a little daunted when facing challenging situations. They will tend to be a little uncomfortable in unstable environments and are likely to try to minimize their exposure to change where possible.

They may prefer to work with established routines and will probably perform best in stable environments. They have quite a strong preference for the predictable over the unpredictable, and may be quite slow to react to unexpected changes. Typically this might mean that the individual is reluctant to take on new work or challenge – particularly where it upsets the 'status quo'.

The coach's quest here is to help the coachees understand the need to respond positively to change and challenge. These individuals are more comfortable where there is structure, order and routine. For them, this puts what they do into perspective – they understand its place in the scheme of things.

The coach can work in two areas. The first is getting the coachees to understand the need for change – why it occurs and why it is beneficial. The second is getting them to learn how to take more risk and to understand some of the benefits of change. Encourage them to take small risks and to reflect on what this has brought to them in widening horizons.

Control

High mental toughness control score

High-scoring individuals will tend to feel in overall control of their lives and have a belief that they can make things happen. Their overall control orientation can be split into two distinct areas: life control and emotional control.

In the workplace they may typically be seen as unflappable and believe that they can always make a difference. However, there are occasionally situations where the organization or events do not allow this to happen. Often, these individuals will not recognize this is occurring and will become frustrated – 'knocking their heads against a brick wall' – or they will simply react negatively to the obstruction.

Typically, issues for the coachee will either be about impact on others or one's own inability to deal with an adverse situation.

The coachee may have a negative impact on colleagues where he or she fails to accept that others can feel less in control than the coachee, or even takes over when something needs to be done and undermines the people who should be doing it. Both can have a detrimental impact on productive working or personal relationships.

Low mental toughness control score

Individuals with low scores may feel they are not really in control of their destiny, but are more at the mercy of the things and the people around them. Their control orientation can be split into two distinct areas: life control and emotional control.

Typically these individuals will be tense and anxious, and may demonstrate that to others. They may unsettle others around them if their anxiety takes over. They may often undervalue their contribution to the organization and dismiss their achievements.

These individuals are comfortable doing one thing at a time – working within a fairly tight comfort zone. The work of the coach will focus on developing coping strategies, enabling the coachee to deal with anxiety as it arises.

Commitment

High mental toughness commitment score

Individuals with high levels of commitment will usually complete their tasks even under difficult conditions, finding different ways to motivate themselves. They will have substantial internal resources, which allow them to sustain high levels of effort.

They are resilient and tenacious. Once they have begun a task they will usually see it through to the end, tending to go round, or occasionally through, obstacles that are blocking the achievement of their end goal. Typically in the workplace this is the kind of person to whom you would be likely to entrust a key project. There may be occasions where the high degree of focus may mean that others may be bruised by this individual's commitment to achieve – particularly where weaknesses are ruthlessly criticized and strengths and achievements taken for granted.

The coach will most likely be concerned with dealing with two groups of issues: impact on others and impact on self. Where people who are high on commitment are stopped in their tracks, they may demonstrate extreme reactions such as showing anger and frustration, walking away from the task or project, or undoing what they have done. The coach should provide coping strategies. Issues relating to impact on others commonly lie in two areas. First there is the obvious impact on others when the individual shows frustration and anger. However, anyone who is high on commitment is likely to be someone for whom a statement of a target or goal is enough – that's all such people need to get going and they will work out what to do for themselves. If they are managing or guiding others they may deal with them in the same way – simply stating the goal and expecting the recipient to respond accordingly. This is the classic 'managing by numbers'. Most people and most teams do not just need to know what to do – they need to know how and why they have to do it. The coach may find it effective to work with coachees to develop their awareness of how people respond to them.

Low mental toughness commitment score

Low-scoring individuals may become easily diverted from the task at hand. They may find it difficult to complete tasks when facing significant adverse circumstances and may consequently give up too easily. They may become unwilling to sustain effort if they believe that they cannot overcome the obstacles in their way. In general, they may find it hard to summon up enthusiasm for some tasks.

This may manifest itself in uncompleted tasks and increasing levels of stress where individuals become more and more demotivated – particularly when the unexpected happens. They may 'stop in their tracks' and may not seek help or support.

These individuals may offer apparently plausible excuses for why things don't happen – they will overemphasize the negatives of a situation. They can convince themselves that something is not possible when it is in fact perfectly achievable.

One way of looking at low scorers on this scale is to imagine that they are inhibited or are intimidated by goals and targets. The maxim that 'if it ain't measured it doesn't get done' (Henry Ford) is only true up to a point. This is increasingly significant as performance management (appraisal) systems begin to apply to most people in the workplace.

People with low scores may need a greater degree of explanation and a greater degree of support if they are to achieve goals that are set for them. The coach may need to show the coachee how to scope a goal and how to break it up into manageable and achievable chunks. Visualization may also be effective. The low scorer's first instinct is to imagine that the task cannot be achieved – a visualization of failure.

SUMMARY

In this chapter the usefulness of the concept of mental toughness in the coaching arena has been discussed. It is often argued that stress is endemic in modern society. While this emphasis on stress may over-inflate its importance, it is none the less obvious that many coaching sessions are instigated by clients under the umbrella of stress management.

There has been a considerable debate in the research literature as to what mental toughness actually is. It is obviously related to concepts such as reliance and hardiness, but provides a more specific hook onto which you can hang coaching interventions. The more mentally tough individual is better able to deal with the pressures of life and prosper within a competitive environment (eg Earle and Clough, 2001).

We believe the model of mental toughness and MTQ48 is a robust and useable tool. It has four main components: Control, Challenge, Commitment and Confidence. Our view that mental toughness can be developed is driven both by personal experience of working as coaches and clear empirical evidence.

In conclusion, mental toughness coaching offers the coachee the ability to deal with performance pressures better. It also provides the coach the opportunity to deal more effectively with the stresses that are often associated with this particular role.

References and further reading

Alderman, RB (1974) *Psychological Behaviour in Sport*, WB Saunders, Toronto

Bull, SJ, Albinson, JG and Shambrook, CJ (1996) *The Mental Game Plan: Getting psyched for sport*, Sports Dynamics, Eastbourne

Clough, PJ, Earle, F and Earle, K (2005) Can training toughen you up? Division of Occupational Psychology, paper delivered at the BPS conference, Warwick, UK, 12–14 January 2005

Clough, PJ, Earle, K and Sewell, D (2002) Mental toughness: the concept and its measurement, in *Solutions in Sport Psychology*, ed I Cockerill, pp 32–45, Thomson, London

Dennis, PW (1981) Mental toughness and the athlete, *Ontario Physical and Health Education Association*, **7**, pp 37–40

Dyer, JG and McGuinness, TM (1996) Resilience analysis of the concept, *Archives of Psychiatric Nursing*, **10** (5), October, pp 276–82

Earle, K and Clough, PJ (2001) When the going gets tough: a study of the impact of mental toughness on perceived demands, *Journal of Sport Science*, **19**, p 61

Funk, FC (1992) Hardiness: a review of theory and research, *Health Psychology*, **11** (5), 335–45

Goldberg, AS (1998) *Sports Slump Busting: 10 steps to mental toughness and peak performance*, Human Kinetics, Champaign, IL

Gould, D, Petlichkoff, L, Simons, J and Vevera, M (1987) Relationship between competitive state anxiety-2 subscales scores and pistol shooting performance, *Journal of Sport Psychology*, **9**, pp 33–42

Hodge, K (1994) Mental toughness in sport: lessons for life. The pursuit of personal excellence, *Journal of Physical Education*, New Zealand, **27**, pp 12–16

Hull, C L (1951) *Essentials of behaviour*, Yale University Press, New Haven, CN

Jackson, R and Watkin, C (2004) The resilience inventory: Seven essential skills for overcoming life's obstacles and determining happiness, *Selection and Development Review*, **20**, (6) pp 9–11

Kobasa, SC (1979) Stressful life events, personality, and health: an inquiry into hardiness, *Journal of Personality and Social Psychology*, **37** (1), pp 1–11

Krane, V, Joyce, D and Rafeld, J (1994) Competitive anxiety, situation criticality, and softball performance, *The Sport Psychologist*, **8**, pp 58–72

Loehr, JE (1982) *Athletic Excellence: Mental Toughness Training for Sport*, Forum, Lexington, MA

Loehr, JE (1986) *Mental Toughness Training for Sport: Achieving athletic excellence*, Stephen Greene Press, Lexington, MA

Loehr, JE (1995) *The New Toughness Training for Sports*, Plume, New York

Taylor, J (1989) Mental toughness (part 2): a simple reminder may be all you need, *Sport Talk*, **18**, pp 2–3

Tutko, TA and Richards, JW (1976) *Psychology of Coaching*, Allyn and Bacon, Boston

Woods, R, Hocton, M and Desmond, R (1995) *Coaching Tennis Successfully*, Human Kinetics, Champaign, IL

12

Using archetypes in coaching

Thomas J Hurley and Jeff Staggs

INTRODUCTION

What supports the development of mastery in coaching?

In our experience, two fundamental shifts are involved in developing mastery. One involves the shift from a focus on 'doing' and the application of skills to the cultivation of presence and a trust in the intuitive intelligence of embodied being; the second involves shifting attention from surface structure (or content) to deeper structures in the coaching relationship. The first shift applies to self, the second to working with the coachee – and both impact on the coaching space. Both enable coach and coachee to be more open to the full range of experience that arises in the coaching process, to work more effectively with the subtle forces that shape perception, choice and action, and to be more vital, authentic and effective.

This chapter starts by reviewing archetypal patterns of experience and action that characterize the transformative learning journey, based on the archetypal practices model (Hurley, 2003). It moves on to describe how to begin using the model, and the distinctions it offers, to support both the personal and professional development of coaches and their work with coachees.

THE MODEL OF ARCHETYPAL PRACTICES

As coaches, we aim to support people in clarifying what they want or need and in developing the capacity to realize their aims. To this end, we help coachees know themselves, discover what supports and what constrains them in moving toward their goals, develop new patterns of behaviour, and create the systems and structures that foster success. In a deeper sense, we want to help coachees become increasingly able to initiate, guide, sustain and evolve their own processes of learning and development (Flaherty, 1999).

Our success thus depends on our ability to help those we work with to know themselves in increasingly powerful ways. This in turn requires both coach and coachee to be comfortable exploring the deeper structures that shape our experience and action. Fundamentally, we work to help coachees come into a living, dynamic relationship with that in their own immediate experience which provides an ever-present source of information and guidance. We also help them learn how to open to, embrace, act on and integrate what emerges. The archetypal practices model is a tool for doing this.

Archetypes represent deep organizing principles that shape the structure of our inner and outer worlds. They are universal patterns or modes of experience that show up as fundamental human roles (such as mother, wise elder, warrior, or lover) or natural phenomena that have profoundly shaped human experience (such as the sun or moon). These are what most people think of when we speak of archetypes, but the term has a broader meaning. For Carl Jung, the father of modern archetypal psychology, they are also manifest in the structure of the psyche (in forms such as the self, the shadow, and the anima or animus) and in regularly repeated patterns of action (Conforti, 1999). Ultimately unknowable in themselves, archetypes are universal in their essence yet unique in how they manifest in each individual, group, community, and culture (Jung, Adler and Hull, 1981).

The archetypal practices model describes 16 elemental patterns, organized in eight complementary pairs. Collectively they form a map of the transformative learning journey – or any creative process – as it moves from inception to completion. These are practices, or capacities, that are integral to coaches' personal and professional development, to the coaching process, and to the learning journeys of our coachees. The archetypal practices are found in Table 12.1.

Table 12.1 Archetypal practices

The practice of:	Complemented by:
Clarifying intent	Inviting guidance
Fearless engagement	Respecting boundaries
Being with all that arises	Taking a stand
Illuminating truth	Engaging in dialogue
Staying in the fire	Surfing the wave
Eating the dark and bitter rind	Uplifting the treasure
Surrendering to love	Acting with power
Sensing the rhythm	Fulfilling our aims

These practices are archetypal in that they are elemental, quintessentially human patterns of experience or behaviour that characterize both individuals and groups engaged in exploring new territory, developing new capacities or innovating. The processes of clarifying intent or engaging in dialogue, for example, are universal patterns of behaviour that, when undertaken consciously, lead us to presence. They are also archetypal in that working with them may evoke archetypal content (meaning-rich images, symbols and ideas that arise from the personal and collective unconscious). They may also catalyze archetypal dynamics – powerful energies, emotions and tendencies that accompany particular elemental patterns of relationship. In the coaching space, these potent images, ideas and interactions carry information, illuminate challenges and reveal opportunities we may not have appreciated before. Sometimes they activate us and orient attention in creative ways, bringing just the insight or knowledge we need. At other times we and our coachees must work with care and imagination to understand what is taking place and to discern the possibilities they represent.

Hence the importance of approaching these archetypes as practices, by which, in this context, we mean disciplined ways of working with consciousness to cultivate different capacities of being. We all tend to settle into habitual ways of seeing, thinking, feeling and relating. Our practices challenge that conditioning, and our tendency to stay within our comfort zone, by continually inviting us to the freshness of experience in the present moment. Importantly, these particular practices do not require specialized training or esoteric knowledge. Rather, they involve using and cultivating the most basic capacities of the mind, heart and spirit in ever more conscious and refined ways.

Archetypal practices as such are necessarily personal and are grounded in the private experience of each individual, yet they also provide a potent framework for understanding and working with fundamental dimensions of the coaching relationship. Ultimately, they orient coach and coachee to the formative fields that shape both our inner and outer worlds. By working with the archetypal practices, we sensitize ourselves to the fields that influence our relationship with self, other and the world. We learn to work more consciously with them, and in doing so come to discover and trust the deeper intelligence, wisdom and creative capacity that becomes available to us.

Each exists in creative tension with its complementary practice, yet each practice also contains its complement in seed form. For example, fearless engagement leads naturally, if we are mindful of the consequences of our actions, to respecting boundaries. Taken to an extreme, or overdeveloped in relation to its sister practices, any of these forms of experience could result in blind spots or maladaptive ways of thinking, feeling or perceiving.

With mastery of the model, we discover the set of archetypal practices as a whole to be endlessly generative, with each capacity appearing organically as it is needed. The model provides a structure that allows our intuitive intelligence about who we are, where we are and what we need for our growth and development to function more freely and powerfully. Loving this process and continually refining our capacity for creative, fluid engagement with all that arises in our life is the key to a final master practice at the heart of the archetypal practices wheel – playing the whole game magically. Figure 12.1 depicts all of the practices in relation to one another.

The names of each practice are meant to evoke the essence of the archetypal structure to which each points. Hence, we have found just the names are sufficient for beginning to work with the model since they themselves express universal experiences we can all call on. For those who wish to explore the definitions of each archetype and the model in more depth, we recommend the article 'Archetypal practices for collective wisdom' (Hurley, 2003).

USING ARCHETYPAL PRACTICES WITH COACHES

We have found the archetypal practices model invaluable in training and developing coaches on their journey from competence to mastery. We use the model to help coaches bring themselves more fully to their coaching and to inform the ways they work with coachees.

In workshops and when supervising coaches, we observe two fundamental shifts that are at the heart of that journey toward mastery. The first is a movement away from a reliance on skills and 'doing' to trust in presence

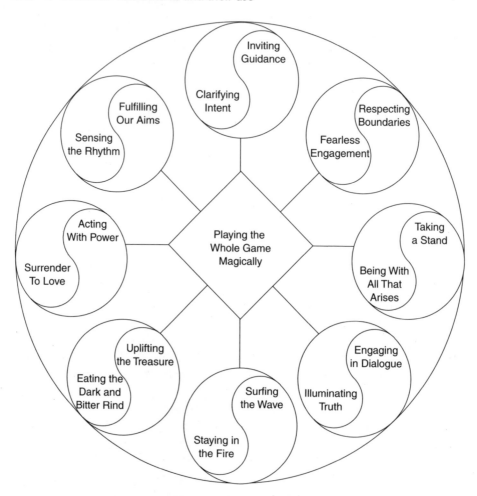

Figure 12.1 Archetypal practices

and how it impacts on us, the coaching space and coachee. The second is a shift in attention from the surface structure of content and behaviour to the deeper structures or processes that give rise to content. We do not mean to imply here that skills and content are not important. On the contrary, they are. Skill building is a key phase of development as coaches, and content is always important as the 'current reality' with which we are working (though what emerges as content may itself change as we begin to work with the archetypal practices). In mastery, though, this phase of development is more integrated and requires less attention. As an analogy, when writing you no longer think about how to form letters or construct sentences, but focus instead on how to convey your ideas in a way that creates a particular experience for your readers. As writers relax into a deeper creative space, richer veins of content, new connections and unexpected insights emerge. Often, the problem in developing oneself as a coach is that the stages of development, and the ways we move from one to another, are not as clear nor the distinctions as refined as in, for example, learning to write.

This is where the archetypal practices model is useful. It provides a more fine-grained set of distinctions having to do with how coaches and coachees actually relate to key dimensions of their experience. They involve how we are being more than what we are doing. Consequently, they enable us to cultivate presence and to refine our capacity for sensing the fields that emerge in the coaching space – the complex of subtle forces that exist in, between and around coach and coachee, and out of which experience arises. Presence has to do with essential qualities of being and how we bring our selves to bear on and within the coaching relationship. Our ability to be present and how we are present have a profound impact on the coaching space and the possibilities alive within it.

In using the archetypal practices with coaches – as, for example, in mastery workshops – we often begin by inviting them to identify strengths and weaknesses in their patterns of engagement with coachees. We each have personal preferences, both generally and with specific coachees, and we tend to rely on our preferred modes of interacting. As a result, we all have strengths as well as blind spots in our coaching. Some of our patterns are conscious and some are not, as anyone who has had supervision can attest. Using each of the archetypes as a lens of inquiry can help make our patterns more visible, our strengths and weaknesses more conscious, and can therefore open them to change or modification. It also helps us learn the model, and of course, to use the model effectively with coachees, we first need to be familiar with it ourselves. Otherwise it remains just another technique.

Our first recommendation then is to use the model to assess your own strengths and weaknesses as a coach. In using the set of archetypal practices in developing your capacity, the first step is to familiarize yourself with each one. This will help ground you in the basic distinctions. Once you become familiar with each of the patterns, use the following questions as a starting point to explore your own patterns of engagement with coachees. You can consider them both from the personal and the professional points of view:

▌ Which practices do you naturally gravitate towards?
▌ Which represent your natural strengths?
▌ Which do you avoid or consider weaknesses?
▌ Which evoke excitement for you? Why?
▌ Which evoke anxiety for you? Why?
▌ Which are you least familiar with?

▮ How would mastery in this archetype impact your coaching presence? (Ask this of yourself for each of the archetypes.)

One of the first questions we ask in exploring the model is: 'Which practices do you have a natural affinity for?' These are usually people's strengths. As they go more deeply into those patterns, they uncover further dimensions of meaning associated with the qualities and capacities they most value. For example, one coach found that 'being with all that arises' came naturally to her. She found it very easy to be present to whatever was brought up by her coachees. She had a high level of empathy and could hold a lot of strong emotion when a coachee was feeling challenged. The next question was: 'Why was this important and what was effective for coachees?' She found her own response illuminating, for it gave her much deeper insight into her own motivation. Specifically, she saw that, for her, the capacity to be with all that arises came from deeply held beliefs about who her coachees were, what it is to be human, and how her receptivity supported them in developing self-knowledge and self-mastery. These beliefs gave her a presence that created a very safe space within which her coachees were willing to take risks they never dreamed possible.

There are usually several archetypal processes that people are comfortable with or naturally gravitate to. Once they explore and have a deeper understanding of their strengths and their roots, they start to become more conscious of how and when they are appropriate and when they represent a 'comfort zone' that may not provide what is truly needed. They also begin to see which practices they avoid, are uncomfortable with, or perhaps do not understand or identify with. These are usually areas of weakness that are not part of their ways of being with coachees. One of the practices people most frequently avoid is 'staying in the fire'. This archetype has to do with moving into and staying with discomfort, not fleeing places we feel might burn or consume us, or for which we do not have stamina. This practice often needs to be consciously developed since we are internally wired to move away from pain. People do not like to be burned (or overwhelmed by anxiety or frustration) and it is counter-intuitive to stay in the fire. However, with practice, we learn that staying in the fire also has transformational power that can liberate us. We learn, too, what issues tend to bring up the fire for us personally; this will obviously differ for each person.

What is significant about the archetypal practices that are less developed in us, or that we avoid, is that we effectively withhold permission to explore these within the coaching relationship. This can impede the insight and learning that might otherwise be possible, and consequently has a powerful impact on the overall course of the coaching process. When we do not give ourselves permission, or do not have the range, we effectively withhold permission from our coachees as well. For example, in supervising one coach it became clear she had a blind spot. The women she was coaching brought up several times, and in different ways, that she wanted to explore an area related to her sexuality. Each time, it was as if the coach could literally not hear her. She would ask a question that led in a different direction, change the topic, or do something that moved away from the subject of sexuality. When the tape was stopped and she was asked about this pattern, it was completely outside of her awareness. As we explored it further, her discomfort with her own sexuality became evident. This was the fire for her – and it was something she could not be with when it was arising in the coaching relationship. Her inability to be present in this area significantly limited her effectiveness with coachees.

Often, as in this example, noticing the absence of a particular archetypal pattern – such as the ability to stay in the fire – can open up exploration and discovery at a deeper level. The distinction (or new 'handle') becomes instrumental in initiating a fresh and deeper line of inquiry. Then one moves through other phases of the archetypal learning cycle. Because this particular coach was committed to her own development, her willingness to stay in the fire fostered both personal and professional transformation.

As coaches inquire into each practice as it relates to their coaching, their experience and understanding of the practice move from the purely cognitive realm to embodied mastery. As this development occurs, coaches develop greater sensitivity to qualities of the field in the coaching space and to when archetypal energies or patterns are arising, including aspects of presence like strength, tenderness, or wisdom. In our use of the word 'field' we are referring to the dynamic background that underlies and is formative to all our experience. By analogy, if we hold a magnet under a piece of white paper and then sprinkle iron filings on the paper, they arrange themselves in line with the magnetic field. The pattern of the field that had been invisible is now seen. We intuitively recognize the existence of the field when we say things like 'the tension was so thick you could cut it with a knife'. This field is always present, and the distinctions the archetypal practices model offer help make the patterns visible, just as the iron filings on the paper make the magnetic field visible.

Another simple application of the model to promote mastery involves using each archetype as a lens of inquiry and personal practice. For example, start with 'clarifying intent'. For a day, or perhaps a week, practise being clear about your intention for each coaching session. Pay exquisite attention to the clarity of your intent. Notice the impact this has on you and your sessions. Notice what is easy for you and what is hard. Be aware of how clear your coachee's intent is. After a day or week, choose another archetype and do the same thing. Over time, explore your coaching through the lens each one provides.

The net result of working with the archetypal practices will be a greater flexibility and freedom in your coaching as well as stronger, deeper and more fluid presence. In truth, we engage in these processes all the time to one degree or another, but when we practise them consciously and with intent, they lead to a continuous deepening of presence. They can in fact be understood as forms of presence in action.

By first working with each practice in relation to your own personal development, you will refine your own distinctions for these archetypal patterns. You will soon be able to recognize them when they arise within the space of the coaching relationship and your coachees' lives. Ultimately this is what we want to be able to do – to use these distinctions in the service of those we serve.

USING ARCHETYPAL PRACTICES WITH COACHEES

We stated earlier that the second shift we observed in developing mastery involved moving our attention from the surface structure of content and behaviour to the deeper structures or processes that give rise to content. The prerequisite for being able to listen and attend at this level is presence, and our ability to be present as a coach depends on at least two variables. First, we must have sufficiently integrated the fundamental coaching skills to be able to place most of our attention on the coachee. Second, we need to be open and fluid enough to embrace all that may arise within the coaching space, as well as what the coachee brings to each session.

Work on our personal development as coaches also opens up a deeper field of inquiry and practice with our coachees. In exploring the archetypal practices ourselves, we begin to form our own inner map of the fields of experience to which the archetypes are pointing. This inner map includes more refined distinctions that we can articulate (and which become part of the mental models that inform our work), and it also includes more refined capacities for sensing (or other forms of knowing) that are difficult to articulate clearly. We begin to discover the depths from which our patterns arise and how we experience and respond to them. These distinctions in turn can open us to listening and working at greater depth within the coaching space. They heighten our awareness of what is happening beyond the content of what the coachee is saying. They orient us to the deeper structures that give rise to our own and our coachees' experience. And as we said earlier, this shift in moving our attention from the surface structure – content – to the deeper structures is one of the developmental stages of mastery.

With the 'handles' the archetypes give us, we then listen with more precision. We need to rely on surface structure and content unless we are aware of what is below the surface, are willing to engage with it, and can work to make sense of it. This is usually a gradual process of trial and error. However, once we own the archetypal distinctions this process can be much more immediate and more precise. As our listening moves outward into the coaching space and into the heart of what is happening with our coachees, the archetypes can serve as a reference.

In using the archetypal practices with coachees, then, the first step involves learning to listen at depth, sensing deeper structures and what is present or emerging before it has been explicitly stated. As 'handles', they help us interpret and make sense of what is arising within the field of the coaching relationship and inform our discernment of where we are and what is called for.

It takes practice to hear what is happening at depth – to have a full, felt sense of what is occurring. It goes beyond just listening with our ears to sensing with the whole of ourselves. When we learn to listen with our whole being, we start to become aware of the field that is always present within the coaching space – whether we are aware of it or not. Sometimes we experience it as resonant; at others we are more aware of the discord present in it.

We all have experiences of this field. Recall a time when you entered a room of people and could feel the thick tension of unspoken anger or the uplift of collective joy. Think of times when a group naturally falls silent because everyone senses that something is about to emerge but isn't quite there yet. Anticipation permeates the group field. Think, too, of coaching sessions in which you ask a powerful question and suddenly there is a pregnant pause, with the tension growing as something is quickened within the coachee. In such moments, uncomfortable in the intensity of that space, beginning coaches often jump in too soon rather than holding the field, allowing the tension to build. If the coach can keep his or her attention at depth, trusting the power of presence, it helps the coachee open to new depths and allows what is seeking to emerge to do so with less obstruction. 'Sensing the rhythm' is important at such times.

These phenomena suggest we have an intuitive awareness and experience of the field in our daily lives, though most of us only become conscious on occasion. Yet if as coaches we can attune our listening at this level, we become more masterful in our work with coachees. We move from general awareness of the underlying emotion within the field – which we might broadly call happiness, sadness, anger or joy – to the discernment of more nuanced feelings and deeper truths. We discover that surface content or expressed emotion may actually mask a deeper idea, emotion or energy that is different and which, if invited forward, might change the course of our conversation with the coachee.

Using the archetypal practices model effectively with coachees requires understanding all the patterns (or practices) as integral elements in a larger pattern. These archetypal practices are deeply interrelated and – for the development of mastery in coaching – cannot be taken in isolation from each other. There is a wholeness to the set, which begins with 'clarifying intent' and ends with 'fulfilling our aims'. One question for us as coaches is then, where are coachees in the cycle? Are they in the beginning of a cycle, suggesting our primary concern might be intention and guidance? Or are they farther along and perhaps struggling, suggesting that if they let go and surrendered their work might flow more? By understanding the set and appreciating the part that each practice plays in it, we are better able to allow different patterns to be present at different moments in the coachee's experience.

Because there is an implicit wholeness that the complete set of archetypal practices embodies, we can sense when the balance within the deep structure of the coaching space has shifted or changed. Absence or presence can both be felt. When something is missing, or a step in the dance is off, there is a hole in the implicit order that draws our attention, that can be felt. Similarly, when something is arising within the field, it also creates a felt shift in the coaching space. In this case you can feel that something is emerging that has significance and might fruitfully be explored. The integrity of the set also enables us to sense where we are in the process of coaching. For example, a sense of completion is present when we feel our coachee's aims have been fulfilled and they have come full circle from clarifying intent.

We use a simple set of questions to begin orienting coaches to qualities of the field and characteristics of the deeper structures within the field. They guide attention and help coaches develop a felt set of distinctions, grounded in deep listening and subtle sensing, that can inform their work with coachees. When beginning to work with these questions, we make three recommendations. First, observe a coaching session in progress. This enables you to focus just on what is taking place in the field without having to do the coaching as well. Second, remember to sense into patterns in the field, not content. Third, try listening into the space with your eyes closed so as not to be distracted by visual cues. (You can practise the same kind of observation in meetings at the office, town hall gatherings or family events, too. The same patterns can be found there, shaping and informing our experience.)

The questions are:

▮ What is present or happening within the coaching space?
▮ What is missing within the coaching space?
▮ What is called for within the coaching space?

▌ What wants to emerge?
▌ Where do things want to go next?

Note that these questions do not ask about the coachee. Initially, we are focusing exclusively on the patterns and 'relational intelligence' within the space. In the beginning, this feels like a radical shift to some because both coaches and coachees are so used to relying on the content of a coachee's words and on their macro behaviour. At first, you may only have a vague sense of what is going on and not trust your own intuitions. Working with someone who is familiar with the archetypes can help guide your attention and shape your awareness. Eventually, as coaches stay with these questions and hone their capacity for sensing the field, they develop a more grounded knowing of how to work with their coachees, and come to trust its power and efficacy.

To give you a sense of what you might experience as you pose these questions and listen through the lens of the archetypal practices, here are some of the patterns we observe.

The first pattern we call 'circling Dallas'. You are probably familiar with it if you have done any coaching at all. The felt sense is that things are just not going anywhere. It can feel like you are lost, just circling in a fog without getting anywhere. This pattern is usually a sign that the practice of clarifying intent is called for in the coaching.

When you feel tension or heat along with avoidance or resistance and fear, it may mean the coachee can be encouraged to stay in the fire. As you go into the fire and stay there, a shift may be felt as new energy is released and swells. Coachees may then find themselves 'surfing the wave' as they experience a release and harness their energy to further their aims.

You can feel when someone steps into 'being with all that arises' by a sense of release as well as deepening and opening of the space for the coachee. There is a feeling of integration and connection. At the level of experience, you may observe the coachee gains a new perspective or insight, enabling movement forward.

Sometimes you can feel that it is time to move forward, at others it is clear that it is not time yet or that your coachee is full and needs to stay where he or she is. This knowing exemplifies 'sensing the rhythm'.

A strong upwelling of tenderness, of longing or of tearing up may signal a need to 'surrender to love'. The practice invites ownership of a very potent authentic experience.

These examples illustrate what 'listening into the field' with a sensitivity to archetypal patterns and deeper structures might reveal. As you deepen your awareness and felt sense of how the archetypes manifest themselves, they can be used more directly in the process of coaching – either 'visibly' or 'invisibly.'

When they are used invisibly, the coach draws on distinctions in the model to illuminate areas for the coachee's attention without revealing the full model. For example, you might have a sense of 'circling Dallas'. Simply asking the coachee, 'What is your intent?' can provide an initial break-through. However, we may still need to probe for a deeper level of clarity and persist until we feel a coalescing and shift within the space that marks a readiness to move forward.

Another example shows how several archetypes may come into play. A coachee was exploring how she wanted to support her husband's work. There was a felt sense in the space that there was something she was not saying. Simply asking, 'What is true for you?' had the effect of 'illuminating the truth', which she was not admitting. Once this was explored it shed light on the conversation she was avoiding. This created an easy movement for her in 'taking a stand' and a commitment to action and accountability.

Using the archetypes visibly by explicitly pointing them out to a coachee can also be very powerful. One of the authors was meeting with a coachee who was working hard towards a goal. As he recounted his efforts, progress and accompanying uncertainty, it became evident that he was very clear about his intent and expending great effort, but that his spiritual orientation was nowhere in sight. Explaining the archetypal complementarity of 'clari-fying intent' and 'inviting guidance' provided a new frame of reference for him. The coachee was then asked, 'To what extent are you open to and inviting guidance?' Recognizing that both archetypal practices were essential completely shifted his orientation and transformed his perspective on how to move forward. Further, leaving him with the inquiry, 'How will you invite guidance?' provided a structure for moving his insights into his life.

We have also used the full set of archetypes more formally with coachees by showing them the model or even physically laying it out on the floor. In these cases, we give a brief explanation of the model and then use it to invite coachees to explore a situation or problem they are facing in their life. The exploration usually starts by framing a question.

In working with a coach during a recent course using the archetypal prac-tices for coaching mastery, the question posed was, 'What practice do you need to develop to bring more mastery to your coaching?' The coach began to walk around the model, stopping at different practices to sense and reflect. He stopped on fearless engagement. After exploring what this practice would bring to his coaching and stating what stopped him from fearlessly engaging, he was asked, 'What archetypal practice would enable you to fearlessly engage?' He immediately stepped into being with all that arises. After exploring this archetype and what it provided him, he was asked, 'Where do you need to go next?' After some reflection there was a deep shift in the field. Hesitation and anticipation could both be sensed at the same time. The question was asked again in a very soft, inviting tone of voice. He slowly walked onto the circle representing surrender to love. When asked what this was about, he said he needed to surrender to loving himself. There was a deep welling up of emotion in the whole room with all who were present. The archetypal field that was called forth powerfully carried him and everyone else who was present with it. When asked what he needed to surrender to love, he said, 'Loving myself'. He was asked if he was willing to surrender. He acknowledged he was and as he did so, tears of joy welled up in his eyes and there was a cleansing sensation of released energy. This took a little while to integrate as he stood in silence with a smile of joy. At this point it was important to sense the rhythm and wait for the deep structure cue signalling it was time to move forward. When it came the man was asked where he needed to move next. He stepped first into fulfilling our aims and then came back to fearless engagement. This time when he stood in that space his entire physiology had changed. When asked what was different now he said, 'Everything!' He now trusted himself and said he could count on himself in a fundamentally different way.

This example illustrates the power of the archetypes in bringing us into direct, embodied, living relationship with our experience in the moment. It also shows how they foster insight into our aims, assumptions, and inner patterns of thought and feeling – and how they can help illuminate the many forces acting in and through us. The example demonstrated too, how deeply interrelated the archetypal practices are and how we can use them to call forth our coachees' deep intuition, inner guidance and wisdom about themselves and what they need in their lives. Finally, as we said earlier in this chapter:

> with mastery [in using this form], one may discover this set as a whole to be endlessly generative, with each capacity appearing organically as it is needed. Loving this process and continually refining our capacity for creative, fluid engagement with all that arises in our life is the key to a final master practice at the heart of the archetypal practices wheel – playing the whole game magically.

SUMMARY

The archetypal practices model is a powerful tool for supporting the development of mastery in coaches. Based on the identification of 16 elemental patterns of experience and behaviour that are universally present in learning and development, the model can be used both for the personal and professional development of coaches and in our work with coachees. We recommended that coaches first use the model to assess their own patterns of engagement in coaching and as a personal tool for development. We then illustrated how the model could be applied to working within the coaching space, both as a tool for assessment and as a set of perspectives and practices that can inform work on specific issues.

The qualities that make for mastery can often feel mysterious and elusive as we seek to attain the heights in our chosen field. One of the factors that differentiates the master from the beginner is a more robust and flexible set of distinctions, especially when those distinctions are embodied in practice. We have shown how coaches can use the model of archetypal practices as a set of distinctions to further their development related to two key shifts in gaining mastery in coaching. The first is a shift from doing to being, with trust in the power of presence within the coaching space. The second is a shift from focusing on the surface structures of content and our coachees' manifest behaviour, to sensing the field that permeates the coaching space and working with the deeper structures that shape the experience and choices of both coaches and coachees. As we observed in working with the model, these archetypal patterns are phenomena we can observe, capacities to be developed, and practices to be applied for coaching mastery. As George Leonard (1992) states in his seminal book on mastery, 'The master of any game is generally a master of practice.'

References

Flaherty, J (1999) *Coaching*, Butterworth Heinemann, Boston

Hurley, TJ (2003) Archetypal practices for collective wisdom, unpublished manuscript available at www.collectivewisdominitiative.org/hurley_archetypal.htm

Jung, CG, Adler, G and Hull, RFC (1981) *The Archetypes and the Collective Unconscious (Collected Works of CG Jung, Vol 9, Part 1)*, Princeton University Press, Princeton, NJ

Leonard, G (1992) *Mastery*, Plume, Penguin Group USA, New York

13

Coaching for strengths using VIA

Dr Carol Kauffman, Jordan Silberman and
David Sharpley

INTRODUCTION

Positive psychology has been defined as the 'scientific study of what goes right in life, from birth to death and at all stops in between' (Peterson, 2006a: 4). It is a young and burgeoning movement that scientifically explores the things that make life worth living. This chapter will provide a brief introduction to the Values in Action Institute Inventory of Strengths (IS) (Peterson and Seligman, 2004), the most ambitious project undertaken within the positive psychology (PP) movement. The IS is a well-validated survey that assesses individuals' strengths of character (eg leadership, kindness, creativity). After providing a brief orientation to the instrument, we discuss how it can be used to enhance a strengths-based approach to coaching. We then describe how coaches can identify and apply their own strengths of character, and how they can use the IS to help coachees overcome challenges and enhance psychological well-being.

THE THEORY OF SIGNATURE STRENGTHS

Many coaches are grateful for the turn that academic psychology took in the late 1990s. Before that time, most academic psychologists were primarily concerned with making people less miserable; university psychology departments focused on curing mental disease (Barnett, 2007; Peterson, 2006a: 3–7). Before the recent shift, relatively few academic psychologists addressed anything north of psychological neutral. Some psychologists researched positive mental health before PP was officially launched in 1998, but very few.

The founders of positive psychology – Martin Seligman, Mihaly Csikszentmihalyi and Ed Diener – prompted a shift in the field. These leaders developed theoretical foundations that prompted thousands of academics to begin investigating PP. There has been particular interest from the academic community in positive psychology's three pillars, which are: positive subjective experience (particularly positive emotion, full engagement with challenging activities, and meaning in life), strengths of character (eg leadership, persistence, and kindness), and institutions that help cultivate positive experience and character (Seligman and Csikszentmihalyi, 2000).

The developing body of PP research has provided coaches with a large reservoir of scientific findings and theories that can guide the coaching process. The applicability of PP to coaching is highlighted by Gable and Haidt (2005), who define positive psychology as a field that investigates 'the conditions and processes that contribute to the flourishing or optimal functioning of people, groups, and institutions'. Helping coachees to flourish is often a large part of the coach's goal, and studying the causes of flourishing has revealed many ways to achieve this.

The Inventory of Strengths is perhaps the most ambitious project undertaken within the PP movement. Led by Christopher Peterson, PhD, a group of psychologists reviewed a wide variety of texts from many cultures to identify strengths of character (Peterson and Seligman, 2004: 15–16). The resultant classification included qualities like leadership, persistence, kindness, curiosity and creativity. To be included in the inventory, each quality had to meet specific criteria, which are described in detail elsewhere (Peterson and Seligman, 2004: 16–28).

The strengths included in the IS have been organized into six categories that Peterson and Seligman (2004) call 'virtues', which are: wisdom, courage, humanity, justice, temperance and transcendence. Each virtue encompasses a number of character strengths included in the inventory. Wisdom, for example, might surface as creativity, curiosity or love of learning.

Rigorous studies of character strengths have helped to correct an imbalance that has plagued psychology for years. Psychologists have historically had excellent questionnaires to assess depression, anxiety and other mental illnesses. There have, however, been few measures available to assess constructs that are north of psychological neutral (Snyder *et al*, 2006). As a result we have clearly articulated and agreed-upon language to describe mental illness or 'neurotic' behaviour, but we lack equally clear and differentiated language to describe mental health or character strengths. Only recently – in large part due to the PP movement – has this imbalance begun to shift. By creating a survey to assess character strengths, Peterson and Seligman have made a major contribution toward correcting the imbalance in available psychological measures and language.

THE VIA STRENGTHS QUESTIONNAIRE

In addition to creating a classification of character strengths, Peterson and Seligman (2004) went a step further: they created a self-report measure to assess these qualities. The 240-item questionnaire assesses the 24 character strengths, and requires about 25 minutes to complete. Each strength is measured by 10 scale items, all of which are answered on a scale from 1 (very much unlike me) to 5 (very much like me). The instrument is both valid and reliable (eg, Peterson, 2006a: 153). Peterson and colleagues have also developed alternative methods for assessing character in populations that are young or illiterate, or for those who are unwilling to invest the time necessary for a lengthy questionnaire. A thorough description of alternative strengths assessments is outside the scope of this chapter, and more detail is available elsewhere (Park and Peterson, 2006a, 2006b; Peterson, 2006a: 150–53; Peterson and Seligman, 2004: 638).

Thanks to the generosity of Neal Mayerson of the Mayerson Foundation, the 240-item inventory is available for free online at www.viastrengths.org or www.authentichappiness.sas.upenn.edu. Information is also available at www.CoachingPsych.com. Given the cross-cultural emphasis of the project, it is not surprising that the survey has sparked incredible interest from all over the world. The questionnaire has been translated into Chinese and Spanish, and has been completed by approximately 350,000 people in more than 200 nations (Peterson, 2006a: 150).

The originators of the IS did not anticipate that the instrument would lead directly to interventions; they had intended simply to develop an assessment tool. To their surprise and delight, graduate student Tracy Steen (in Peterson, 2004) noticed that research subjects' well-being seemed to increase after taking the IS and applying their strengths. This observation led to further study, and researchers soon realized that the instrument could be useful in ways that extend far beyond what its developers had envisioned. The following sections describe some of the ways in which the IS can be particularly useful within coaching contexts.

STRENGTHS AND COACHES

Developing expertise with the IS can help coaches more effectively move toward goals and face challenges. Using the inventory can help coaches:

▌ develop a new language to label and access their strengths;
▌ clarify how strengths can be accessed to increase self-efficacy, effectiveness, and enthusiasm in the midst of challenges;
▌ provide information to help coaches create optimal relationships with coaches.

Develop a language of strengths

The first step in using a new measurement tool is to take it oneself. This can help the coach determine whether the information revealed feels valid and expands one's self-knowledge. Feedback from the IS occasionally creates 'aha' moments in which people find new labels for strengths that have not been captured with precise language. When vague personal qualities coalesce into a clear list of personal resources, it becomes easier to access and harness these qualities.

Next, one might ask self-coaching questions regarding how each top strength might further one's practice. For example, coaches might ask questions like these: 'How have my strengths surfaced previously during times of peak performance?' 'How can I harness my strengths to coach more effectively and to market my practice?' 'How can I apply my strengths to create new coaching tools that may benefit the entire field?' More examples of how coaches can apply strengths to face difficult situations are presented in the next section.

Create new avenues to self-efficacy, enthusiasm and effectiveness despite challenges

Identifying one's own strengths, and becoming adept at accessing them, can be particularly useful for overcoming coaching challenges. When addressing difficult or complex problems – especially when the stakes are high for the coachees or their companies – it is common for coaches to feel 'de-skilled', or to feel that they are 'in over their heads'. Reviewing strengths while stressed often triggers a different cascade of cognitive and affective responses from focusing on weaknesses. If one can access a more positive state by focusing on strengths, creativity and cognitive flexibility may increase (Fredrickson, 2001). This is often exactly what a coach needs to find solutions during times of crisis. Reminding oneself of and drawing upon core strengths can also expand the nature of the self-talk that is possible during stressful situations. Positive self-talk can begin to accompany (and perhaps partially replace) negative self-talk. Over time, and as one becomes accustomed to working with strengths of character, the process of accessing strengths during crises becomes second nature. Coaches who are experienced in this process can quickly identify which of their top strengths to deploy in which circumstances, and can often find unique solutions to tough challenges.

For example, suppose that a coachee turns on you and states the following with great intensity: 'You don't understand, if I don't fix this crisis today I will probably be fired!' How can coaches use strengths to access enhanced self-efficacy, enthusiasm and effectiveness in this situation? The pathway to optimal strengths-based performance varies, depending on the unique strengths profile of a particular coach. Someone who is strongest in gratitude, for example, would access different resources from someone strongest in creativity. Coaches with a top strength of gratitude are often able to find something to be grateful for even when circumstances seem negative. These coaches might think to themselves something like: 'This is tough, but helping my coachee overcome this challenge is a privilege and I really want to help him through this.' For those who are strong in gratitude, this kind of thinking can create a surge of energy, which can feed other strengths and skill sets. Having the coachee suddenly 'turn on' the coach might also trigger a negative interpersonal response; the coach might feel attacked. A coach high in gratitude might counteract this by immediately accessing positive feelings about the coachee, perhaps by saying to him/herself: 'Working with this coachee is a privilege. I don't *have* to help this person, I *get* to help this person' (Harnisch, 2005).

If gratitude is not among one's top strengths, however, this approach may feel inauthentic; coaches with different strengths might utilize different approaches. A coach high in creativity, for example, might focus on finding new solutions. When facing an ultimatum from the coachee like the one previously mentioned, a very creative coach might get a kind of 'high'. The coach might ask him/herself: 'How can I use my creativity to beat this problem? I can't imagine that the coachee has tried every possible pathway to success. What creative solution can we find?' This coach would not automatically assume that most roads have been explored, would not be trapped by mundane or linear approaches, and might be more likely to find new ways to overcome complicated challenges.

It is important to note that different coaches will need to use different strengths-based pathways to self-efficacy, enthusiasm and effectiveness;

what works for one coach will not necessarily work for another. Coaches who do not have creativity as a top strength would probably find the afore-mentioned application of creativity unnatural or daunting. They might feel inauthentic if they tried to address a crisis by applying one of their weaknesses. Space does not permit an exhaustive discussion about the application of strengths to coaching challenges, but for an extended discussion or more resources on this issue go to www.coachingpsych.com. Coaches can begin to explore, during times of stress, how they might apply their own unique configurations of strengths in order to rise to the occasion. It can be useful to run through one's strengths to imagine alternate paths to optimal performance. For example, how might somebody with the capacity to love and be loved, or prudence (far-sightedness), or authenticity develop new strategies to meet coaching challenges? Being able to identify strengths and apply them to challenges is an invaluable addition to a coach's toolbox.

Provide information to assist coaches in creating optimal coaching environments and relationships with coachees

Coaches strive to foster optimal environments for and relationships with their coachees. How can coaches improve the quality of these environments and relationships? Awareness of one's strengths may be helpful. Some studies (Clifton and Harter, 2003; Arakawa and Greenberg, 2007) suggest that when managers focus on employees' strengths, employee engagement, productivity and optimism all increase. Coaches, similarly, can foster positive states in coachees by focusing on strengths. Foster and Lloyd (2007) have found that a strengths-based coaching orientation increases hope, makes the coachee feel more energized, increases the coachee's ability to generate solutions, and decreases the coachee's defensiveness. These positive effects of a strengths-based approach can yield a more positive environment in which coach–coachee teams can be enthusiastic and creative.

Evidence suggests that, within psychotherapy contexts, the quality of the therapist–client relationship is often the strongest predictor of psychological outcomes (Peterson, Stober and Kauffman, 2006). The same phenomenon may apply in the coaching context. Most coaches do not believe that there is a one-size-fits-all approach to optimizing the coach–coachee relationship (Kauffman and Scouler, 2004); this crucial partnership must be tailored to the personalities and needs of both coach and coachee. Considering the strengths of both parties can be important as we strive to create an ideal coach–coachee match. When this match seems less than ideal, it can be useful to adjust the interaction style by noticing if you manifest a particular strength in a way that does not resonate with the coachee. Many readers may be familiar with theories about how the MBTI profile affects social behaviour. We can similarly consider how our strengths profiles affect our interaction with coachees, and use different strengths if our current behaviour does not 'click' with the coachee. Consider, for example, a coach whose top strengths include both gratitude and creativity. If a coaching relationship is not clicking, then the coach might shift gears and focus on accessing the former strength rather than the latter. When working with a jaded senior executive, a gratitude-focused social style may be less effective than a focus on creativity. Identifying things to be grateful for in challenging situations may be foreign and awkward to the executive. Solutions-focused creativity, on the other hand, may resonate with an executive who is used to solving challenging problems.

USING THE VIA WITH COACHEES

Align the coachees' work with their strengths

The inventory is a powerful springboard from which we can explore coachees' experiences and help them access their strengths. The first three steps are similar to those described above. They include asking coachees to take the assessment, assisting them as they learn how to label and apply their strengths, and considering how they can use strengths in work and personal relationships. We focus here on one important aspect of strengths-based coaching: helping coachees to bring their strengths and their work into closer alignment. Large-scale surveys suggest that only 17 per cent of the working population believes that they use their strengths at work (Buckingham, 2007). When workers can harness their strengths, they are more productive, engaged and satisfied, and experience greater well-being. Basic strengths coaching with the IS helps coachees shift their approach to work and bring themselves and their jobs into closer alignment with their strengths. Coaches can help coachees alter aspects of their tasks to fit more closely with their strengths, or shift which of their strengths they can harness to negotiate the challenges they face.

Strategies for addressing challenges on the job can be categorized, fundamentally, into two groups: changing the circumstances and changing the approach. The first involves changing one's job description or location. If responsibilities are extremely overwhelming or boring, if colleagues are abusive or if commute times are unbearable, then the coachee might change his or her circumstances by quitting the job or requesting a reassignment. Surveys indicate, however, that only 31 per cent of workers want to leave their jobs, and that the remaining 69 per cent would prefer merely to alter their approaches to their work (Buckingham, 2007). Fortunately, every job offers a lot of wiggle room, and there are often far more ways to effectively complete a set of tasks than what appears obvious at first glance. As the saying goes, 'there are many ways to skin a cat'. It is often possible to transform a challenge by shifting to a strengths-based approach. Coachees can learn to re-craft work: that is, to alter how they approach their goals, work relationships and process aspects of daily work demands. When it is possible to shift their tasks in a way that allows them to use their top strengths, coachees are likely to find greater intrinsic motivation, achieve greater job fulfilment and improve job performance.

Take, for example, three architects who design commercial offices. The first architect's top strength is appreciation of beauty and excellence, and the others' top strengths are the capacity to love and be loved, and creativity. All three strive to provide superb services, but they find different sources of satisfaction from the process. One loves the aesthetic aspect of the work, experiencing immense fulfilment when stepping back to observe how beautiful a design looks. This architect might transform his approach by focusing more on the outcomes than on the specific techniques utilized. The second architect – who finds bursts of energy from interpersonal connections – might focus more on brightening each and every client's day. When feeling drained, she might reconnect with her concern for her clients' happiness, and recall how much past designs have contributed to clients' satisfaction and joy. Remembering their compliments and thanks could be a source of inspiration. The third architect is excited by innovation in building design and technology, and might spend more time developing novel approaches in these domains. Experimenting with new materials and exploring cutting-edge techniques might be exciting and engaging for this person. Each of these individuals can find entirely different ways to re-craft their jobs by applying their strengths of character and focusing on aspects of their work that they enjoy most.

The coaching implications of these examples are straightforward. Coachees can scan their work experience to identify what they find satisfying and energizing. The coach and coachee can then explore how to capitalize on this information. They can discover small choices that can help the coachee tap more fully into strengths. Seligman calls this 're-crafting' one's work (Seligman, 2002: 165–72). Most jobs (or even social occasions) can be tweaked to come into closer alignment with core strengths, which can make experiences more engaging and fulfilling, and can allow one to bring one's best self to new experiences.

Even the most high-powered or high-performance business executives can find ways to enhance their jobs by applying strengths in new ways; there are no limits when applying strengths of character. A CEO with an appreciation of beauty and excellence, for example, might reinvigorate a formerly lacklustre work life by finding ways to move his or her company toward greater levels of excellence. The coachee might strive to transform business practices that are merely adequate into practices that are exceptional. Some executives might apply the character strength of fairness to improve hiring, evaluation and compensation practices, while others might apply creativity by finding new strategies for marketing goods and services.

Using strengths to help business executives or other accomplished individuals re-craft their professional lives can rekindle dwindling vitality. The positive effect that often arises through this process may induce a broadening and building of the coachee's thought–action repertoire (Fredrickson, 2001), which can unleash out-of-the-box and big-picture thinking. A related positive spiral of development may also occur: new insights can lead to bursts of energy, and this energy can prompt more insights.

Strengths-based brainstorming

Some coachees are able to identify strengths applications themselves, but not all coachees are this self-sufficient; many require that coaches gently and purposefully guide them toward strengths applications in a more active manner. For these individuals, 'strengths-based brainstorming' can be helpful. This is a process in which the coach asks thought-provoking questions to help coachees develop their own ideas for applying their character strengths. Coaches might ask things like, 'How could your creativity (or another top strength) help you overcome a challenge? Can you garner inspiration to complete a difficult task by drawing on your love of learning? Can you apply your citizenship strength to motivate you to complete arduous work for the good of the team?' As coaches accrue basic experience with the contours of the strengths, and begin to understand how coachees can harness this potential for energy, questions naturally emerge. Ideal questions prompt coachees to carefully consider how they might apply their strengths in new ways, and ignite their capacity to access core strengths of character.

It is also helpful for some coachees to recall how they have deployed their strengths in the past. It can be powerful to revisit previous successes. Coaches might request that coachees share an experience in which they were at their best despite a challenge that was comparable to the challenge they currently face. Identifying how they overcame previous obstacles by applying strengths – or considering how they might have done so – can yield insight regarding how to apply strengths in the future.

Some coachees also find that visualization or meditative approaches can help them to reconnect with previous successful applications of their strength, and to use these previous applications as a resource for the future. These coachees slow their breathing to meditate on a particular situation, visualize themselves using their strength as a resource, and remind themselves that they have the ability to replicate past successes. Coachees often report that this practice makes them feel calm, centred and restored, which then leads to increased energy and resolve. This approach is somewhat similar to a method developed by Foster and Lloyd (2007), in which coachees examine their state of mind and access positive states through specific self-talk constructed in previous coaching sessions. This positive self-talk is grounded in previous experiences that involved identifying and accessing strengths.

There are two rationales for having coachees recall how strengths have been applied previously. The first is straightforward: considering previous strengths deployments helps coachees connect with and re-apply their strengths. The second, drawn from positive psychology research and theory, is that sharing a victory can incite a positive emotional state. This positive emotion is sometimes necessary to generate a wide enough 'crack in the stress' to facilitate clearer thinking and allow coachees to consider how they can deploy their strengths. As mentioned previously, moreover, positive emotion can help broaden and build the available repertoire of thoughts and actions. This process can be helpful – or even essential – for coachees who are about to delve into new applications of their strengths, which typically involve a slew of new thoughts and actions.

Choosing appropriate deployment strategies

These tools for guiding coachees toward new strengths applications are helpful, but the steps discussed thus far are not yet complete. Not all strengths applications are equally effective, and it is essential to ensure that the coachee select the most effective applications from their 'strengths-based brainstorm'. We want to guide people toward applications of strengths that will work best for each individual's unique challenges and goals. One simple way to explore this issue is to take each top strength and predict how applying it might affect a challenge or goal. The coachee can visualize and use 'futuring' techniques. How might a scenario play out if the coachee decided to focus on deploying one strength rather than another? What would happen, and how would it feel? If the coachee experiences sudden bursts of learning, expanded confidence in his or her own skills, increased energy, or a greater sense of hope, then the strengths application under consideration may be a promising one.

Issues regarding selecting a strengths deployment approach have recently been raised by Peterson (2006c) and Schwartz and Sharpe (2006). Their ideas can help coaches shape a more careful and effective approach to sensing what specific strengths applications might be most helpful for the coachee. Peterson suggests that either a lack or an excess of any strength can be undesirable. Too little or too much social intelligence, for example, can lead to social 'clue-lessness' or to 'psychobabble' (2006c: 39). Schwartz and Sharpe similarly suggest that every strength has a 'golden mean'. For example, we are best served by finding a level of courage that lies somewhere between cowardice and recklessness. As coaches, part of what we might do is help coachees artic-ulate what balance is right for them in light of the specific challenge they face.

Schwartz and Sharpe go on to note that strengths cannot be treated in isolation from one another; people can overdevelop some strengths to the detriment of other strengths, leading to 'deformations of character'. They point out that identifying a good application of strengths also requires that we consider relevance, specificity and conflict. Relevance refers to the appropriateness of a particular strength under unique circumstances. Humour, for example, is probably more appropriate at a bowling alley than it is at a funeral. Specificity refers to the problem of determining what specific actions should be undertaken in the deployment of a particular strength. Should we apply kindness to an ailing patient by sitting at their bedside for hours, or by giving them privacy?

Conflict refers to the problem that arises when multiple strengths would be deployed through different and incompatible actions. When a woman asks how she looks in her new dress, should we apply kindness by flattering her, or apply authenticity by asking her to go upstairs and change? Therefore, when coaching for strengths, one should keep these more nuanced approaches in mind.

Schwartz and Sharpe (2006) present their concerns as a criticism of the strengths approach, but we prefer to view their insights as questions that can guide the growth of coaching acumen. The ability to navigate these questions, which Schwartz and Sharpe dub 'practical wisdom', is a skill that coaches can develop. Considering these issues as part of the strengths-based coaching process can help coaches guide coachees toward the most appropriate applications of their strengths.

Consider an executive trainer who frequently presents new material to employees, and whose character profile leans more heavily toward cognitive than toward interpersonal strengths. This individual may apply character strengths like love of learning to create intellectually sound and thorough presentations. Relying exclusively on 'strengths of the head', however, may lead to ineffective pedagogy. Applying love of learning without co-deployment of interpersonal strengths may prevent the trainer from identifying and responding to the learning needs of his or her students.

If they are toward the top of his or her strengths profile, social intelligence and kindness may be helpful for this executive trainer. The former may help the trainer to better understand students' experiences, and the latter may yield a genuine desire to improve the quality of those experiences. Social intelligence might, for example, help the trainer to notice when lecture material is presented too quickly for audiences to understand. A kind trainer – one who cares about preventing students' frustration – might slow down in response. Applying social intelligence and kindness, a trainer might also provide question-and-answer sessions for students who do not understand lectures, and incorporate humour into otherwise bland material.

In this example, it is imperative to consider the question of relevance. Cognitive strengths can be a blessing in one situation (eg developing thorough training materials) and a curse in another (eg presenting information to students). It sometimes requires exploration and insight to reveal that the strengths being deployed are more of a hindrance than a help. Coaches may, of course, need to address different strengths deployment issues in different situations. Some coachees may need to consider whether they have achieved a balance between excess and deficiency of particular strengths. Others may need to focus on balancing their strengths, or on the aforementioned issues of conflict and specificity. These questions can form a framework to guide coaches as they identify the most appropriate deployment of strengths for unique coachees in unique circumstances. Both helping the coachee generate ideas regarding applications of strengths, and helping him or her select the best of these applications, are essential components of the strengths-based coaching process.

Job fulfilment and performance

Applying strengths to re-craft work can powerfully enhance job performance. When coachees find new ways to apply their strengths, the way that they view their job becomes more aligned with their values. Earlier we took the example of a trainer who valued kindness, and explored how such people's work becomes more consistent with their values when they apply this strength. Taking the time to find what you value in your work, rather than simply struggling through a task you are indifferent about, may increase intrinsic motivation. This, in turn, may enhance performance (Katz *et al*, 2006).

The application of strengths may also enhance performance by helping coachees achieve flow in their work. Flow states, of course, are most likely to arise when challenges balance skills. Applying strengths can be helpful when the skills being drawn upon are not adequate to meet the demands of a task, when there is a need for greater skill. Identifying how to deploy strengths can help correct this imbalance of challenge and skill, facilitating flow experiences. Such experiences, of course, are associated with high levels of performance (Nakamura and Csikszentmihalyi, 2002).

Finally, strengths deployment may enhance performance by enhancing well-being. A growing body of evidence suggests that using signature strengths in new ways can make people happier and less depressed (Seligman *et al*, 2005). Improving psychological well-being, not surprisingly, often improves individuals' performance in a wide variety of contexts (Lyubomirsky, King and Diener, 2005).

Although it is grounded in science, helping coachees to identify and unleash their strengths is a complex art. Among other crucial functions, coaches must help coachees identify and reconnect with strengths, generate ideas for applying strengths in new ways, and select a strength deployment strategy that is most appropriate under unique circumstances. Although we have focused on re-crafting work, much of what has been presented regarding strengths application can be applied to any domains of life. By focusing on effective deployment of strengths, coaches can help coachees access their natural giftedness and find their most direct routes to enhanced job fulfilment, performance and well-being.

The virtuous cycle

As coachees begin to apply their strengths, many enter a self-sustaining cycle of character development. The process begins when they identify and begin developing awareness of their strengths. As discussed previously, coachees then begin to apply their strengths in new ways. Even if the coach and coachee have carefully selected strategies for deploying strengths, they do not always work on the first try. It is of course ideal if the initial attempt is successful, but it is also often necessary to tweak their preliminary approach. Having a coach available to guide coachees when an application of strengths fails can be pivotal. Coaches can encourage coachees to adjust deployment strategies in order to increase the chances of success in the future, which may bolster self-efficacy regarding strengths applications. Simply wallowing in failure, on the other hand, can destroy self-efficacy, which immediately thwarts the Virtuous Cycle shown in Figure 13.1. Failures can prompt people to move into the Virtuous Cycle of strengths application or to abandon their strengths altogether, and coaching can make all the difference. The self-efficacy that arises from deployment and adjustment further enhances awareness of strengths, which completes the cycle depicted below. This cycle may lead coachees to deploy strengths more frequently, and to develop successively greater levels of confidence in their ability to do so.

SUMMARY

The VIA Inventory of Strengths is revolutionary in its combination of positive focus, cross-cultural emphasis and empirical rigor. Although we have already identified many ways in which it can be useful, we have only scratched the surface of the instrument's potential. A relatively young tool, many questions remain regarding how the IS can best be put to use. What other character strengths might be important that are not included in the preliminary classification? What character cultivation tools are most helpful? For whom? Which combinations of strengths are most helpful within business teams, friendships and marriages? These are a few of many questions that, if explored further, may expand the utility of the Inventory of Strengths. Future research – guided by the experience of coaches and coachees – may reveal which questions are most significant, and may hint at

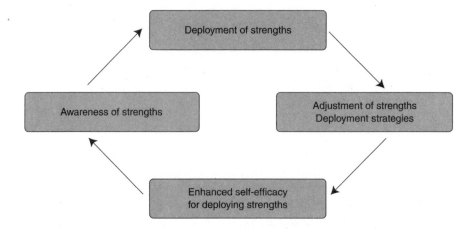

Figure 13.1 The Virtuous Cycle

some of the answers. Applying the IS through the aforementioned suggestions, and further exploring how the IS can be used most effectively, may enhance the capacity of coach–coachee teams to overcome challenges and enhance psychological well-being.

References and further reading

Arakawa, D and Greenberg, M (2007) Optimistic managers and their influence on productivity and employee engagement in a technology organization: Implications for coaching psychologists, *International Coaching Psychology Review*, **2** (1), pp 78–89

Barnett, D (2007) Positive psychology: For growth and well-being [online] from http://www.newlifejournal.com/DecJan07/Barnett.shtml (accessed 26 February 2007)

Buckingham, M (2007) *Go: Put your strengths to work*, Free Press, New York

Clifton, D and Harter, J (2003) Strengths investment, in *Positive Organizational Scholarship*, ed KS Cameron, JE Dutton and RE Quinn, pp 111–21) Berrett-Koehler, San Francisco

Foster, S and Lloyd, P (2007) Positive psychology principles applied to consulting psychology at the individual and group level, *Consulting Psychology*, **59** (1), pp 30–40

Fredrickson, B (2001) The role of positive emotions in positive psychology: the broaden and build theory of positive emotions, *American Psychologist*, **56** (3), pp 218–26

Gable, S and Haidt, J (2005) What (and why) is positive psychology? *Review of General Psychology*, **9** (2), pp 103–10

Harnisch, RA (2005) Personal communication

Katz, I, Assor, A, Kanat-Maymon, Y and Bereby-Meyer, Y (2006) Interest as a motivational resource: feedback and gender matter, but interest makes the difference, *Social Psychology of Education*, **9** (1), pp 27–42

Kauffman, C (2006) Positive psychology: the science at the heart of coaching, in *Evidence Based Coaching Handbook*, ed D Stober and A Green, pp 219–53, John Wiley, Hoboken, NJ

Kauffman, C (2007) Positive psychology coaches, retrieved 19 May 2007, from www.CoachingPsych.com

Kauffman, C and Scouler, A (2004) Towards a positive psychology of executive coaching, in Positive Psychology in Practice, ed A Linley and S Joseph, pp 287–304, John Wiley, Hoboken, NJ

Lyubomirsky, S, King, L and Diener, E (2005) The benefits of frequent positive affect: does happiness lead to success? *Psychological Bulletin*, **131** (6), pp 803–55

Nakamura, J and Csikszentmihalyi, M (2002) The concept of flow, in *Handbook of Positive Psychology*, ed C R Snyder and S J Lopez, pp 89–105, Oxford University Press, New York

Park, N and Peterson, C (2006a) Moral competence and character strengths among adolescents: the development and validation of the Values in Action Inventory of Strengths for Youth, *Journal of Adolescents*, **29** (6), pp 891–909

Park, N, and Peterson, C (2006b) Character strengths and happiness among young children: content analysis of parental descriptions for youth, *Journal of Happiness Studies*, **7** (3), pp 323–41

Petersen, D, Stober, D and Kauffman, C (2006) The coaching relationship, Continuing Education Half Day Workshop presented at the American Psychological Association, New Orleans, August 2006

Peterson C (2004) Values in action, Class 13 of M. Seligman's Authentic *Happiness Coaching* virtual training course. More information at: http://www.mentor-coach.com/AHC/index.htm

Peterson, C (2006a) *A Primer in Positive Psychology*, Oxford University Press, New York

Peterson, C (2006b) Measurement instruments [online] http://www.virtuesin-action.com/index.aspx?ContentID=34 (accessed 18 April 2007)

Peterson, C (2006c) The Values In Action (VIA) classification of strengths, in *A Life Worth Living: Contributions to positive psychology*, ed M Csikszentmihalyi and I Csikszentmihalyi, pp 29–48) Oxford University Press, New York

Peterson, C and Seligman, MEP (2004) *Character Strengths and Virtues*, American Psychological Association, Washington, DC

Schwartz, B and Sharpe, K (2006) Practice wisdom: Aristotle meets positive psychology, *Journal of Happiness Studies*, **7** (3), pp 377–95

Seligman, MEP (2002) *Authentic Happiness*, Free Press, New York

Seligman, MEP and Csikszentmihalyi, M (2000) Positive psychology: an introduction, *American Psychologist*, **55** (1), pp 5–14

Seligman, MEP, Steen, T, Park, N and Peterson, C (2005) Positive psychology progress: empirical validation of interventions, *American Psychologist*, **60** (5), pp 410–21

Snyder, CR, Ritschel, L, Rand, K, and Berg, C (2006) Balancing psychological assessments: strength and hope in client reports, *Journal of Clinical Psychology*, **62** (1), pp 33–46

14

Coaching for stress

StressScan

Dr Kenneth M Nowack

INTRODUCTION

The topic of stress is playing an increasing role in coaching interventions, as evidenced by the chapter 'Coaching and stress' in *Excellence in Coaching* by Maria Alicia Pena and Cary Cooper (Pena and Cooper, 2006). Effectively managing stress and facilitating wellness is important for both the coach and coachee. In this chapter, coaching for stress and health using StressScan, a validated individual stress and health management assessment, will be presented.

The chapter first provides a general overview of an integrative stress and health management model across executive, life, career or health coaching. The theoretical models behind stress and individual behaviour change are then briefly introduced. This is followed by the development and interpretation of StressScan and its link to an online stress management planning system and resource library called Talent Accelerator to help facilitate coachee wellness. This section draws heavily on more extended discussions about StressScan from previous publications (Nowack, 1990, 1991, 1994; Nowack and Pentkowski, 1994). The reader is referred to the manual (Nowack, 1990) for details of the instrument and research, and guidance on scale interpretation. The remainder of the chapter focuses on the use of StressScan with coachees as well as how the concepts behind this assessment can help coaches manage their own work/life stress and avoid job burnout.

THEORETICAL MODELS OF STRESS

Stress coaching

A number of popular stress models exist to help coaches understand the transactional nature of individual perceptions within organizations. Figure 14.1 provides a synthesis of these models including job-strain/support (Karasek and Theorell, 1990), effort-reward balance (Siegrist, 1996), Warr's 'vitamin' model (Warr, 1987) and emotional labour (Hochschild, 1983).

It is common in many coaching engagements to hear coachees share perceptions of work–family balance challenges and work stressors. Perceptions of stress are often quite high, with 40 to 60 per cent of all coachees reporting very high levels caused by both work and home pressures and challenges (Nowack, 2006).

Consultation regarding stress, health and lifestyle behaviours has typically been seen as the domain of physicians, psychologists and other health professionals – not the arena for coaches. It can be argued that helping employees deal more effectively with work and life balance, coping with stress, and facilitating physical and psychological well-being can be a major focus across executive, life, career or health coaching (Palmer, 2003). Additionally, the profession of coaching is not immune to occupational stress. Coaches are equally vulnerable to experiencing high levels of stress and job burnout in light of heavy workloads, challenging assignments and organizational constraints.

Organizational benefits of having healthy employees

Stress has emotional, cognitive, physiological and behavioural effects on the individual as well as important consequences for an organization, including such outcomes as poor concentration and decision making, fatigue, accidents, injuries, absenteeism, presenteeism, physical illness and psychological distress (Nowack, 1994). Improving the total health of the workforce

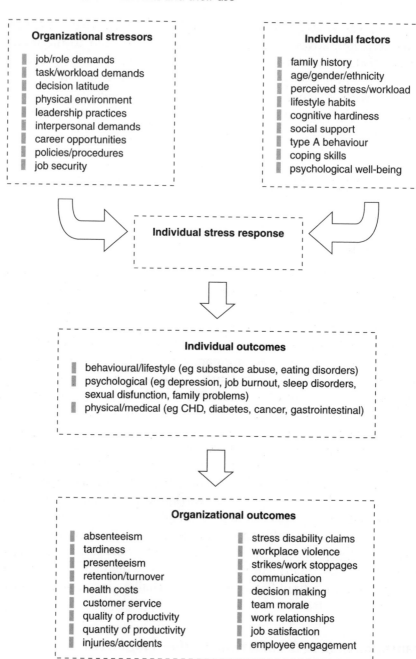

Figure 14.1 Health and productivity management model

(physical and psychological) through formal programmes including coaching would appear to be important for increasing productivity and competitive advantage.

A conservative estimate of business benefits derived from the improvements in health status indicate a likely annual return on investment from such a programme to be £3.73 for every £1 spent (Mills, 2005). In the United States, Aldana (2001) reviewed 13 studies that reported average benefit–cost ratios of $3.48 in reduced health care costs and $5.82 in lower employee absenteeism costs for each dollar invested. Finally, Pelletier (2001) reports on a total of 120 corporate health promotion studies that consistently show cost savings for the organization as well as productivity and health improvement. Although evidence suggests that a focus on individual interventions without addressing the root organizational causes is typically ineffective (Nowack, 2000), the focus of this chapter will be on the impact of coaching on facilitating coachee stress reduction, health, productivity and enhanced well-being.

The stress response or 'fight or flight' reaction is our body's rapid and automatic switch into a protective mode. The purpose of this response is to prepare the individual for activity in response to a perceived or real threat. By itself, this response is normal, healthy and adaptive. We know today that continued arousal and activation of our 'fight or flight' system can affect almost all of our body's processes, diminishing the effectiveness of our immune system, increasing risk of obesity, insomnia, digestive problems, heart disease, depression, memory impairment, physical illnesses, aging, and inflammation.

THE THEORETICAL MODEL FOR STRESSSCAN

StressScan was designed to be an important assessment in a coaching practitioner's 'tool box' to facilitate increased knowledge, skills and behaviour change efforts aimed at reducing stress and improving physical health and quality of life. Together with an integrated online developmental planning/reminder system containing a comprehensive stress/wellness resource library of articles, websites, books, tips and media called Talent Accelerator, the coach can not only help individuals reduce stress and identify wellness resources and risks but can help facilitate the initiation and maintenance of health promoting habits and behaviours.

The major conceptual goals of stress, health and lifestyle modification coaching are summarized in Table 14.1.

Using a variety of tools such as motivational interviewing (Rollnick and Miller, 1995; Passmore and Whybrow, 2007), stress/health assessments and cognitive–behavioural techniques, coaches can help coachees move through

Table 14.1 Stress, health and lifestyle modification coaching goals

Time	Stress/health/lifestyle coaching goals	Core challenge
Past	Understanding, acceptance, forgiveness, satisfaction	Closure
Present	Happiness, engagement, social connectiveness, manageability, self-management skills, practice of health-promoting behaviours	Control
Future	Optimism, legacy, meaningfulness, sustaining of health-promoting behaviours	Hope

the core challenges of reaching acceptance with past issues (eg chronic illness), developing strategies to increase self-management skills and healthy lifestyle behaviours and create a purposefulness and supportive environment for maintenance of key behaviours over time.

Behaviour change theories underlying Talent Accelerator

The goal of StressScan is to facilitate coachee awareness whereas the goal of Talent Accelerator is to enable successful behaviour change. The design of Talent Accelerator is based on the most often applied theories of individual behaviour change including the theory of planned behaviour (Ajzen, 1991), self-efficacy and social cognitive theory (Bandura, 1977), the Health Belief Model (Becker, 1974), and the Transtheoretical Model of Change (TTM; Prochaska and Velicer, 1997). Each of these theories should be useful to all coaches who are attempting to facilitate behaviour change in coaches.

The various features of Talent Accelerator have been specifically designed and developed to support these various individual change theories, including TTM and relapse prevention (Parks and Marlatt, 1999). It was specifically designed to be integrated with StressScan to monitor and track performance on specific stress/wellness goals, being provided with periodic reminder messages about success in completing the coachee's stress/wellness action plan and providing a comprehensive topical resource library for each StressScan scale to facilitate greater understanding, learning and behaviour change.

THE DEVELOPMENT OF STRESSSCAN

StressScan is an assessment to be used by executive, life and health coaches to facilitate stress management and wellness promotion with coachees. The conceptual development of StressScan began in the early 1990s and has been described in detail in several previous publications (Nowack, 1990, 1999). StressScan is an adapted version of the Stress Profile currently published by Western Psychological Services (WPS) in the United States.

StressScan is a 123-item questionnaire that measures important psychosocial factors based on the cognitive-transactional model of stress (Lazarus and Folkman, 1984). StressScan is administered and scored online and takes approximately 15 to 20 minutes to complete. A growing and large international database now exists for StressScan, with the assessment being translated into several other languages including Spanish, German, Danish, Turkish, Hungarian, Greek and Lithuanian.

StressScan results in a comprehensive individual feedback (Figure 14.2) report providing an overview of 14 major scales, a summary of wellness risks and wellness resources and integration with the online developmental planning system called Talent Accelerator to translate awareness into a personal stress and wellness action plan that can be monitored and tracked over time. StressScan also provides feedback on smoking status and excessive use of substances (alcohol and drugs), and includes a response distortion bias scale to identify possible careless or overly desirable responding patterns.

Reliability

StressScan has been shown to possess adequate internal consistency reliabilities (alpha) ranging from 0.51 to 0.91 across all scales. The test–retest reliability of the scales ranges from 0.76 to 0.86 over a three-month period. A principal component analysis has yielded three major factors with eigenvalues greater than or equal to 1.0 (adaptive cognitive and behavioural behaviours, non-adaptive resources and lifestyle habits) accounting for 57 per cent of variance.

Validity

StressScan has been associated with diverse health and productivity outcomes in cross-sectional and longitudinal studies, including immune response, job burnout, depression, absenteeism, physical illness, anxiety, job satisfaction, organizational commitment and performance (cf, Nowack, 2000; Giesser et al, 2007; Beasley, Thompson and Davidson, 2003; Winefield

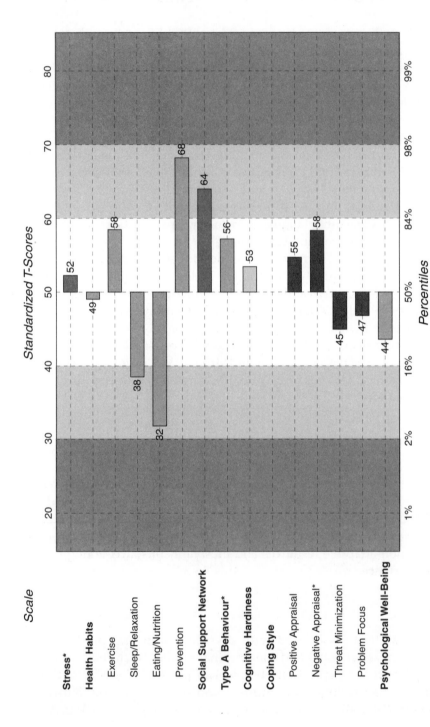

Figure 14.2 StressScan sample report (StressScan is an adapted version of the Stress Profile published by Western Psychological Services)

et al, 2002; Sharpley and Yardley, 1999; Greene and Nowack, 1995; Nowack, 1994; Nowack and Pentkowski, 1994; Schwartz *et al*, 1993).

DESCRIPTION OF THE STRESSSCAN SCALES

Stress (six items)

This scale provides a global index of the appraisal of stress (hassles) over a three-month period and has demonstrated adequate internal consistency reliability (alpha) of 0.68. It is conceptually based on a factor analysis of the Hassles scale (Lazarus, 1984; Kanner *et al*, 1981) and measures self-reported hassles in six distinct work and life areas:

▮ health;
▮ work;
▮ personal finances;
▮ family;
▮ social obligation;
▮ world / environmental concerns.

This provides an overall measure of self-reported stress as well as a ranking of the areas of greatest concern of the respondent, making it very useful for coaching and stress management programmes.

The stress scale has been shown to be associated with immune response (Schwartz *et al*, 1993), job burnout (Nowack 1987; 1991), absenteeism (Greene and Nowack, 1995; Nowack, 1994) and physical illness (Nowack, 1990). This scale also seems to be sensitive to changes in specific interventions designed to teach stress management skills to those with a chronic illness (Giesser *et al*, 2007). This finding has important implications in light of several recent studies indicating the impact of stress management interventions on major chronic conditions and illness (Nowack, 2000).

Global health habits (25 items)

Health habits or global lifestyle practices are measured by a 25-item scale assessing the daily practice of specific behaviours hypothesized to be conducive to both physical and psychological well-being. This scale is a composite of the four subscales below as well as specific items on smoking and substance use. High scores on the health habits scale suggest the frequent practice of lifestyle habits on a regular basis.

Global health habits – exercise (three items)

The exercise scale measures the frequency of physical activity an employee engages in on a regular basis. The questions focus on aerobic activities, stretching/flexibility, strength and leisure activities involving some level of exercise. This scale has shown internal consistency reliability of 0.79 and association with absenteeism in several employee studies (Nowack and Pentkowski, 1994).

Global health habits – sleep/relaxation (five items)

This scale measures the frequency of obtaining adequate rest/relaxation, quality and quantity of sleep on a regular basis. The sleep scale has shown moderately high internal consistency reliability (alpha) of 0.71 and appears to be independent of clinical measures of fatigue (Giesser *et al*, 2007). Sleep-deprived, fatigued and tired employees are actually potential liabilities to their organizations, so having a separate self-report measure in StressScan can be quite valuable for coaching interventions.

Global health habits – nutrition/eating (eight items)

This scale measures the frequency of eating well-balanced meals and a healthy approach to diet on a daily basis. This scale has shown moderately high internal consistency reliability (alpha) of 0.70. The nutrition/eating scale focuses on facilitating healthy eating, rather than weight management.

Global health habits – prevention (six items)

This scale measures the frequency of employing sound health hygiene behaviours on a daily basis, such as avoiding those who are ill and maintaining preventive practices. This scale has shown moderately high internal consistency reliability (alpha) of 0.70. These types of preventive behaviours are a common focus of organizational risk reduction and health promotion programmes.

Social support (18 items)

Social support is measured using an 18-item scale that separately assesses the availability, utility and satisfaction with five separate support groups available to the respondent – co-workers, supervisor/boss, family, friends, and significant others – based on the work of Sarason *et al* (1983). An overall social support score is calculated across all five groups. This scale has demonstrated adequate internal consistency reliability (alpha) of 0.83. High scores on this scale suggest that an employee perceives the availability of social resources at work and home, seeks them out when required and reports a level of satisfaction with the type of support they received (eg emotional, informational, instrumental).

Type A behaviour (10 items)

Type A behaviour is measured in StressScan with a brief 10-item scale conceptually based upon the original Framingham Type A measure (Haynes, Feinleib and Kannel, 1980). High scores on the StressScan scale suggest more frequent use of achievement-striving, hard-driving, competitive, angry and hostile reactions to work and life stressors. This scale has shown adequate internal consistency reliability of 0.82 and convergent validity with both the Jenkins Activity Scale (JAS) and Framingham Type scales (Nowack, 1987, 1990). Elevated scores on this scale suggest a tendency towards cynical mistrust and hostility.

Cognitive hardiness (30 items)

This scale assesses the possession of specific attitudes and beliefs, based upon the concept of personality hardiness attributed to Kobasa (Kobasa, 1979; Kobasa, Maddi and Courington, 1981). This scale measures a set of attitudes and beliefs about work and life that are relatively enduring and include:

▌ *control*: beliefs an individual has self-efficacy and influence over significant outcomes in life;
▌ *challenge*: attitudes around viewing life changes as empowering and challenging as opposed to inducing helplessness and hopelessness;
▌ *involvement*: commitment, as opposed to alienation, with work, family, friendships and self;
▌ *self-confidence/self-esteem*.

Factor analytic analyses in several published and unpublished studies support the uni-dimensional interpretation of this scale (Beasley, Thompson and Davidson, 2003; Nowack, 1999).

The cognitive hardiness scale has demonstrated moderate internal consistency reliability of 0.84 and been shown to predict a variety of physical and psychological health outcomes in recent studies (Greene and Nowack, 1995; Nowack, 1991; Nowack, 1990; Beasley, Thompson and Davidson, 2003). Additionally it has shown convergent validity with measures of optimism

(Goss, 1994) and overall health and low job stress in a study of 1,925 Australian university staff (Sharpley *et al*, 1999) and was significantly associated with absenteeism and self-reported hospitalization for injury/illness in a three-year longitudinal study of police officers (Greene and Nowack, 1995).

Cognitively hardy employees are expected to be more persistent, actively engaged and resilient in the face of work and life challenges. This scale would appear to be a relatively good indicator of coachee success in initiating and maintaining new behaviours, and persisting in the face of work/life obstacles and challenges.

Coping style (20 items)

Coping style is assessed by a 20-item scale composed of four trait coping responses to work and life stressors and challenges. Respondents are asked how frequently they typically use these four techniques to cope with work, family and personal stressors. The four coping style scales are:

▮ *positive appraisal*: realistically emphasizing the positive side of stressful situations through self-talk and cognitively minimizing the importance of the stressor;
▮ *negative appraisal*: self-deprecating statements, catastrophic thinking and focusing on the negative aspects of the situation;
▮ *threat minimization*: actively acknowledging and moving ahead without dwelling excessively on the stressor, and using humour to put things in the proper perspective;
▮ *problem-focused coping*: behavioural attempts to modify one's behaviour or the environment.

High scores on these independent scales suggest frequent use of these coping styles. The coping scales have shown internal consistency reliabilities ranging from 0.68 to 0.79 in previous studies. In both cross-sectional and prospective studies, each of these coping scales have been associated with diverse outcomes such as physical illness, job burnout, absenteeism and depression (Giesser *et al*, 2007; Nowack, 1989, 1999). The pattern and use of specific coping strategies assessed in StressScan can help coaches to better understand how coachees approach specific work and life situations that are perceived to be challenging and stressful.

Psychological well-being (12 items)

Psychological well-being is measured by a 12-item scale assessing overall life satisfaction and absence of psychological distress during the previous three months. High scores suggest low overall distress and emotional negativity (ie greater satisfaction with one's self, greater ability to enjoy life, and feeling happy with family, work, interpersonal relationships and achievements. This scale shows high internal consistency reliability (alpha) of 0.93 and is strongly associated with measures of depression, distress and anxiety (Nowack, 1999).

A three-item Spirituality Index (alpha 0.76) has been derived and validated from this psychological well-being scale and it appears sensitive to psychosocial educational interventions with those with chronic illness (Nowack and Roberts, 2006). At the present time, this Spirituality Index is not currently available as a separate scale in StressScan but shows promise as being sensitive to measuring connection to meaningful activities and relationships in one's life for future research and use by coaches.

Response bias (five items)

This scale assesses the tendency to respond in a manner that might be interpreted as careless, biased or distorted. The items are conceptually based on the Crowne–Marlowe Social Desirability scale (Crowne and Marlowe, 1960). Respondents with high scores on this scale tend to endorse items that would appear uncharacteristic for most individuals, raising the likelihood the respondent was tired, hurried, careless in reading the items or responding in a manner that could be distorted.

USING STRESSSCAN WITH COACHEES

StressScan and Talent Accelerator can play an important role in identifying stress/health risks and resources in coaching interventions. This type of individual assessment is well suited for use with coachees complaining of stress, job burnout, challenges with work and family balance, poor health/lifestyle management and ineffective coping.

Coaches interested in using this type of individual stress and health assessment should have a full understanding of the dynamics of individual behaviour change and the implications for coachees of implementing and maintaining new stress management and lifestyle practices.

Figure 14.3 illustrates a comprehensive stress, health and lifestyle coaching model incorporating the latest theories of successful behaviour change. This new model suggests that successful stress, health and lifestyle modification coaching will lead coachees systematically through three distinct stages – each with specific goals and techniques to ensure successful behaviour change efforts.

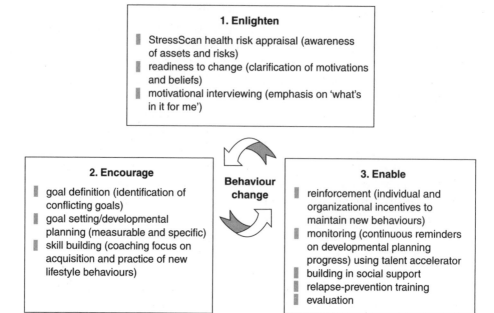

Figure 14.3 Health and productivity management coaching stages

Stress coaching stages

Stage 1: Enlighten

The 'what's in it for me' (WIFM) is a critical leverage point for coaches to be successful in lifestyle modification. Helping coachees to become more aware of personal areas of stress/health risk and resources can be useful to help increase readiness for behaviour change as well as being an important step in successfully setting specific wellness goals.

The use of a personal stress and health assessment like StressScan can be invaluable at this step for coaches to utilize to facilitate awareness and motivation to change behaviour. Such assessments help clarify lifestyle assets and risks that are associated with health, well-being and productivity.

Once coaches have some specific data about possible areas of health resources and risks, they can assist coachees to reflect on resistance to change, ambivalence or unrealistic goals that might interfere with lasting behaviour change. Motivational interviewing (MI) is a useful approach for coaches in working with lifestyle change engagements to assist coachees to reflect and target specific lifestyle goals to work on. It is a style that values and emphasizes the coachee's values, interests and motives and utilizes reflective listening and probing to help the coachee make lasting behaviour changes. MI is a collaborative approach to identifying motivations to change, potential barriers, goal setting and re-appraisal to ensure long-term success without being overly directive with the coachee (Passmore and Whybrow, 2007). The coach must identify the key 'readiness to change' stage from pre-contemplation (no intention to change), contemplation, prepa-ration, action and maintenance, and apply specific strategies and approaches at each stage to help facilitate successful long-term success (Prochaska and Velicer, 1997).

From an MI perspective, coaches would listen carefully to understand professional goals, work/family challenges, self-efficacy, health beliefs and specific attitudes linked to behaviours. As an example, the coach would ask open-ended questions to help the coachee see how one's ability to maintain high energy, be productive and concentrate could be related to eating/nutrition, sleep and physical activity. The coach would help the coachee reflect on the advantages of maintaining optimal wellness and the readiness to begin to set some specific behavioural goals that could be moni-tored and evaluated using Talent Accelerator.

Stage 2: Encourage

The key to successful long-term behaviour change is in the planning process. The coach's role is to ensure the stress, health and lifestyle modifi-cation plan is realistic, specific and measurable. In helping the coachee translate awareness and motivation into actual behaviour change, the coach can begin to ask some critical questions to facilitate a successful behavioural change plan effort, such as: 'What benefits will there be to managing stress and coping more effectively?'

This is the stage where coaches begin to actually help the coachee acquire new knowledge and practise new skills to initiate and maintain important lifestyle practices and behaviours. In general, most coachees are more likely to try new behaviours in which they are confident of a successful outcome and which they feel a sense of mastery in maintaining over time despite some possible setbacks and challenges. If coachees lack confidence in their ability to implement the lifestyle modification plan, the chances that they will maintain it will be low. It is the role of the coach to provide an encour-aging and supportive role with coaches and to explore their feelings about the wellness journey through structured emotional expressive writing or by probing for reactions, reflections and insights in each session.

Online tools like StressScan and Talent Accelerator provide a vehicle for developing personal stress and wellness action plans and monitoring progress over time. The coach's role is to ensure the lifestyle modification plan is realistic, specific and measurable. In helping the coachee translate awareness and motivation into actual behaviour change, Talent Accelerator provides an electronic summary of the coachee's StressScan report and has built in exercises such as a set of reflective questions to help interpret the feedback and facilitate a successful behavioural change plan including:

▌ How can I make my behavioural change goal realistic and achievable?
▌ How can I track and monitor my progress on my behavioural change goal?
▌ What are some possible barriers to successfully changing my behaviour?
▌ What actions and steps can I take to anticipate and prevent these barriers from interfering with my successful behaviour change effort?
▌ How can family members, friends or co-workers help me to successfully change my behaviour?
▌ How will I reward myself for successfully maintaining my behaviour change goal for 30 days?
▌ What can I do to continue to motivate myself to keep a high level of commitment to my wellness goal, even if I temporarily slip back into my old habits?

Talent Accelerator also contains a confidential online journal to facilitate reflection and emotional expressive writing. It also contains an extensive library of stress/wellness suggestions, books, articles, websites, media and other resources to facilitate learning and behaviour change.

Stage 3: Enable

This third phase is critical for the long-term success of any health and lifestyle modification programmes and is often overlooked by many coaches. Where possible, coaches should be working during this stage to help the coachee manage lapses, recognize successes, enlist the power of social support systems, focus on progress through structured reminders and evaluate overall success. In fact, once a coachee sets up a personal stress/wellness development plan within Talent Accelerator, it automatically sends out e-mail reminders about progress towards completion at least once a month to help facilitate successful behaviour change.

The coach's role is to assist the coachee with re-evaluating the importance of the wellness goals and exploring some relapse-prevention strategies to prepare the coachee for the inevitable lapses that accompany any behaviour change effort. For example, the coach could help the coachee anticipate future unavoidable high-risk situations and prepare in advance for inevitable lapses. Encouraging ways for the coachee to reward sustained behaviour is also something the coach can discuss during follow-up meetings along with an analysis of the coachee's social support network and what role it can play in maintaining new behaviours over time.

The strategy of goal reappraisal should be emphasized during the entire coaching process with a coachee. The coach and coachee should mutually define ways to track, monitor and evaluate progress on the specific lifestyle goals that were set. For example, the coach can review with the coachee these steps to evaluate progress and ensure long-term success. Ideally, continuous reminders can be sent to the coachee to highlight progress and successful performance towards his or her lifestyle modification plan.

Interpreting StressScan results

StressScan provides coaches with a comprehensive individual assessment to measure self-perceptions of coachees' stress, current lifestyle habits, social support network, coping style, resilience and current psychological well-being. The comprehensive report generated by StressScan can be useful for coachees to identify specific stress/health resources and risks. Each coachee's individual feedback report will generate a unique profile that can provide coaches with specific points of intervention based on their unique theoretical orientation, training and experience.

Table 14.2 provides a brief overview of possible interventions and approaches that could be taken by coaches using StressScan and Talent Accelerator. Coaches using this assessment should be familiar with both community and organizational resources available to the coachee to facilitate successful stress, health and lifestyle management changes.

STRESSSCAN AND COACHES

StressScan can be useful for coaches both personally and professionally. Since coaches are not uniquely immune to stress, anxiety, depression or job burnout, learning to manage work and life pressures and remain healthy is important professionally. Working with coachees can be emotionally draining and interpersonally challenging even to the most competent coaches.

At a personal level, StressScan provides insight and information to coaches about their own approach to coping with stress and about specific lifestyle areas to focus on to enhance physical and psychological well-being. For those experiencing symptoms of job burnout (eg emotional exhaustion and cynicism) this tool can help renew commitment to taking better care of one's own spiritual, emotional and physical well-being enabling coaches to effectively assist and support coachees.

Table 14.2 Examples of StressScan-based coaching interventions

StressScan scale	Possible implications of undesirable scores	Examples of coaching interventions
Stress	Psychological distress; work/family overload; high anxiety and arousal; emotional exhaustion; exacerbations of existing medical conditions	▮ Daily stress journal ▮ Biofeedback ▮ Mental relaxation (eg ▮ visualization, self-hypnosis, breathing exercises) ▮ Physical relaxation (eg meditation, tai chi, yoga) ▮ Fostering spirituality/religious practices
Health/lifestyle habits	Poor lifestyle and preventive practices; fatigue; eating disorders; obesity and weight management problems; smoking; substance use and abuse; sleep disorders and rhythm problems; physical inactivity	▮ Smoking cessation ▮ Daily exercise/sleep/eating journal ▮ Fostering exercise/physical activity (eg strength, flexibility, cardiovascular) ▮ Referral to dietician/ nutritionist ▮ Weight management ▮ Sleep hygiene ▮ Referral to a sleep disorders clinic ▮ Referral to self-help groups ▮ Relapse-prevention training
Social support	Lonely and isolated; poor support network; socially inhibited and anxious interpersonally	▮ Social network analysis ▮ Personality/style awareness ▮ Forgiveness/compassion exercises ▮ 360-degree feedback ▮ Team building
Type A behaviour	Hostile; cynical and mistrusting of others; hard driving; perfectionist; impatient; possesses hurry sickness; obsessive thoughts; poor behavioural self-control	▮ Anger management ▮ Conflict management ▮ Communication skills (eg assertiveness) ▮ Time management ▮ Mindfulness training ▮ Physical relaxation ▮ Practising and using humour

Cognitive hardiness	Pessimistic; cynical; disengaged; alienated; hopeless; change averse; negative explanatory style	▌ Identifying/employing signature strengths ▌ Gratitude exercises ▌ Values-clarification exercises ▌ Employing passions
Coping style	Neurotic; irrational beliefs; self-defeating thoughts; poor problem solving	▌ Daily journal ▌ Cognitive restructuring ▌ Problem solving
Psychological well-being	Depression; fatigue; suicidal thoughts and tendencies; poor concentration	▌ Referral to employee assistance counselling ▌ Affirmation exercises ▌ Encouraging volunteering

Professionally, for those doing executive, life, career and health coaching, StressScan can be a useful individual assessment to utilize in one's practice. So many coachees are struggling to find adequate work–life balance or to cope with increasing work and family demands. Today, it is unusual when a coachee does not mention being somewhat fatigued, stretched by multiple demands, burned out or pressured by time within a coaching session. The scales in StressScan provide the coach with specific diagnostic areas to address common coachee work and life pressures and, together with Talent Accelerator, some practical ways to ensure successful stress and health management behaviour changes.

StressScan provides another unique individual assessment to use with coachees that can easily be 'added value' to most coaching interventions. Taken together, StressScan and Talent Accelerator can actually increase the value of the coaching services being offered to coachees or organizations by increasing readiness to change behaviour and facilitating lasting stress and health management action plans.

SUMMARY

The negative impact of stress on absenteeism, injuries, accidents, rising health care costs and productivity is a growing concern of organizations. Additionally, employees are also experiencing greater work–life balance challenges than ever before. Coaches are increasingly being asked to play a role in helping both the individual and organization manage stress more effectively.

This chapter has sought to illustrate how using a validated stress/health risk assessment such as StressScan and online development system such as

Talent Accelerator can help coaches facilitate successful and meaningful lifestyle changes and effectively enhance coping with work/life pressures and challenges. As a result, coaches can address stress issues with specific models and techniques to promote both organizational productivity and individual well-being.

References and further reading

Ajzen, I (1991) The theory of planned behaviour, *Organizational Behaviour and Human Decision Processes*, **50**, pp 179–211

Aldana, S (2001) Financial impact of health promotion programs: a comprehensive review of the literature, *American Journal of Health Promotion*, **15**, pp 296–320

Bandura, A (1977) Self-efficacy: toward a unifying theory of behaviour change, *Psychological Review*, **84**, pp 191–215

Beasley, M, Thompson, T and Davidson, J (2003) Resilience in response to life stress: the effects of coping style and cognitive hardiness, *Personality and Individual Differences*, **34**, pp 77–95

Becker, MH (ed) (1974) 'The Health Belief Model and Personal Health Behavior, *Health Education Monographs*, **2**, pp 324–473

Crowne, DP and Marlowe, D (1960) A new scale of social desirability independent of psychopathology, *Journal of Consulting Psychology*, **24**, pp 349–54

Eisenberger, N, Lieberman, MD and Williams, KD (2003) Does rejection hurt? An fMRI study of social exclusion, *Science*, **302**, pp290–92

Giesser, B, Coleman, L, Fisher, S, Guttry, M, Herlihy, E, Nonoguch, S, Nowack, D, Roberts, C and Nowack, K (2007) Living Well with Multiple Sclerosis: Lessons Learned from a 12-Week Community Based Quality of Life Program. Paper presented at 17th Annual Art and Science of Health Promotion Conference, San Francisco, CA, March 2007

Goetzel, R (2001) The financial impact of health promotion and disease management programs: why it is so hard to prove value, *American Journal of Health Promotion*, **15**, pp 277–88

Goss, J (1994) Hardiness and mood disturbances in swimmers while overtraining, *Journal of Sport and Exercise Psychology*, **16** (2), pp 135–49

Greene, R and Nowack, K (1995) Stress, hardiness and absenteeism: results of a three-year longitudinal study, *Work and Stress*, **9**, pp 448–62

Haynes, SG, Feinleib, M and Kannel, WB (1980) The relationship of psychosocial factors to coronary heart disease in the Framingham study, III: eight-year incidence of coronary heart disease, *American Journal of Epidemiology*, **111**, pp 37–58

Heaney, C and Goetzel, R (2001) A review of health-related outcomes of multicomponent worksite promotion programs, *American Journal of Health Promotion*, **11**, pp 290–307

Hochschild, AR (1983) *The Managed Heart: The Commercialization of Human Feeling*, UCP, Berkeley, CA

Kanner, A, Coyne, J, Schaefer, C and Lazarus, R (1981) Comparison of two modes of stress measurement: daily hassles and uplifts versus major life events, *Journal of Behavioural Medicine,* **4** (1), pp 1–39

Karasek, RA and Theorell, T (1990) *Healthy Work,* Basic Books, New York

Kobasa, S (1979) Stressful life events, personality and health: an inquiry into hardiness, *Journal of Personality and Social Psychology,* **37**, pp 7–11

Kobasa, S, Maddi, S and Courington, S (1981) Personality and constitution as mediators in the stress-illness relationship, *Journal of Health and Social Behaviour,* **22**, pp 368–78

Lantz, PM, Stencil, D, Lippert, MA (1995) Breast and cervical cancer screening in a low-income managed care sample: the efficacy of physician letters and phone calls, *American Journal of Public Health,* **85** (6), pp 834–36

Lazarus, RS (1984) Puzzles in the study of daily hassles, *Journal of Behavioural Medicine,* **7** (4), pp 375–89

Lazarus, RS and Folkman, S (1984) *Stress, Appraisal, and Coping,* Springer, New York

Mills, P (2005) Results of the vielife/IHPM Health and performance research study, *European Newsletter of the Institute for Health & Productivity Management,* 1 (5), pp 6–7

Nowack, KM (1987) Health habits, Type A behaviour, and job burnout, *Work and Stress,* **1**, pp 135–42

Nowack, KM (1989) Coping style, cognitive hardiness, and health status, *Journal of Behavioural Medicine,* **12**, pp 145–58

Nowack, KM (1990) Initial development of an inventory to assess stress and health risk, *American Journal of Health Promotion,* **4**, pp 173–80

Nowack, KM (1991) Psychosocial predictors of physical health status, *Work and Stress,* **5**, pp 117–31

Nowack, KM (1994) Psychosocial predictors of health and absenteeism: results of two prospective studies, paper presented at the American Psychological Association Annual Convention, Los Angeles, CA, September,

Nowack, KM (1999) *Stress Profile Manual,* Western Psychological Services, Los Angeles, CA

Nowack, KM (2000) Occupational stress management: Effective or not? in *Occupational Medicine: State of the art reviews,* ed P Schnall, K Belkie, P Landensbergis and D Baker, Hanley and Belfus, Philadelphia, PN, **15** (1), pp 231–33

Nowack, KM (2006) Optimizing employee resilience: coaching to help individuals modify lifestyle stress news, *International Journal of Stress Management,* **18**, pp 9–12

Nowack, KM and Pentkowski, A (1994) Lifestyle habits, substance use, and predictors of job burnout in professional working women, *Work and Stress,* **8**, pp 19–35

Nowack, K and Roberts, C (2006) Chronic illness and spirituality: what do you believe? American Group Psychotherapy Association National Conference, San Francisco, February

Palmer, S (2003) Health coaching to facilitate the promotion of healthy behaviour and achievement of health-related goals, *International Journal of Health Promotion and Education,* **41** (3), pp 91–93

Parks, GA and Marlatt, GA (1999) Relapse prevention therapy for substance-abusing offenders: a cognitive-behavioural approach, in *What Works: Strategic Solutions: The International Community Corrections Association examines substance abuse*, ed E Latessa, pp 161–233, American Correctional Association, Lanham, MD

Passmore, J and Whybrow, A (2007) Motivational interviewing: a new approach for coaching, in *The Handbook of Coaching Psychology*, ed S Palmer and A Whybrow, Routledge, London

Pelletier, K (2001) A review and analysis of the clinical and cost-effectiveness studies of comprehensive health promotion and disease management programs at the worksite: 1998–2000 update, *American Journal of Health Promotion*, **16,** pp 107–16

Pena, MA and Cooper, C (2006) Coaching and stress, in *Excellence in Coaching: The industry guide*, ed J Passmore, Kogan Page, London

Prochaska, JO and Velicer, WF (1997) The transtheoretical model of health behaviour change, *American Journal of Health Promotion*, **12**, pp 38–48

Rollnick S and Miller, WR (1995) What is motivational interviewing? *Behavioural and Cognitive Psychotherapy*, **23**, pp 325–34

Sarason, I, Levine, H, Basham, R and Sarason, B (1983) Assessing social support: the social support questionnaire, *Journal of Social Psychology*, **44**, pp 127–39

Schwartz, GE, Schwartz, JI, Nowack, KM and Eichling, PS (1993) Changes in perceived stress and social support over time are related to changes in immune function, University of Arizona and Canyon Ranch, unpublished manuscript

Sharpley, C, Dua, J, Reynolds, R and Acosta, A (1996) The direct and relative efficacy of cognitive hardiness, Type A behaviour pattern, coping behaviour and social support as predictors of stress and ill-health, *Journal of Behavioural Medicine*, **22** (5), pp 511–27

Sharpley, C, Dua, J, Reynolds, R and Acosta, A (1999) The direct and relative efficacy of cognitive hardiness, Type A behaviour pattern, coping behaviour and social support as predictors of stress and ill-health, *Scandinavian Journal of Behavior Therapy*, **1**, pp 15–29

Sharpley, C and Yardley, P (1999) The relationship between cognitive hardiness, explanatory style, and depression–happiness in post retirement men and women, *Australian Psychologist*, **34**, pp 198–203

Siegrist, J (1996) Adverse health effects of high-effort/low-reward conditions, *Journal of Occupational Health Psychology*, **1**, pp 27–41

vielife/IHPM Health and Performance Research Study (2005)

Warr, P (1987) *Work, Unemployment and Mental Health*, Clarendon Press, Oxford

Winefield, A, Gilliespie, N, Stough, C, Dua, J and Hapuararchchi, J (2002) *Occupational Stress in Australian Universities: A National Survey 2002*. A Report to the Vice Chancellors, National Tertiary Education Union, Faculty and Staff of Australian Universities, and the Ministers for Education and Health, National Tertiary Education Union, Adelaide, Australia, July 2002. Unpublished manuscript.

Zuckerman, M (1990) The psychophysiology of sensation seeking, *Journal of Personality*, **58** (1), pp 313–45

15

Coaching for cultural transformation

CTT

Richard Barrett

INTRODUCTION

Values stand at the very core of human decision making. Our underlying values determine our behaviours. Coaching based on values therefore sheds light on our underlying motivations and helps us to understand what is important in our lives.

This chapter describes the coaching instruments that are part of the Cultural Transformation Tools (CTT)®. The Individual Values Assessment is a self-assessment instrument that compares an individual's top 10 values (personal values) with the top 10 values they see in their organization (current culture) and the top 10 values they would like to see in their organization (desired culture).

The Leadership Values Assessment is a feedback instrument that compares people's perception of the values they believe best describe their management/operational style with their colleagues' perception of their management/operational style. The instrument also compares people's perception of their strengths, and the behaviours that they believe they need to improve or stop, with the assessors' perceptions.

These instruments are based on Seven Levels of Consciousness model (Barrett, 1998 and 2006). The model is shown in Table 15.1, together with the principal characteristics of each level of personal consciousness, leadership consciousness and organizational consciousness.

Table 15.1 Seven Levels of Consciousness model

Seven levels of consciousness	Personal consciousness	Leadership consciousness	Organizational consciousness
7. Service	Leading a life of selfless service to humanity or the planet. At ease with uncertainty. Compassion, humility, wisdom.	Focus on ethics, long-term perspective and global issues. Future generations. Human rights. At ease with uncertainty. Humility, compassion, wisdom.	Long-term perspective. Future generations. Human rights. Ecological awareness. Service to humanity. Humility, compassion, wisdom, ethics.
6. Making a difference	Actualizing your sense of meaning by making a difference in the world or your community. Caring about the environment. Mentoring, coaching.	Focus on strategic alliances, collaboration and partnerships. Employee fulfilment. Environmental awareness. Empathy, mentoring.	Strategic alliances and partnerships. Coaching, mentoring and employee fulfilment. Community involvement. Environmental awareness.
5. Internal cohesion	Finding meaning in existence by activating your soul purpose. Commitment, enthusiasm, passion, integrity.	Focus on vision, mission and values. Commitment, enthusiasm, integrity, honesty, trust, transparency, openness. Focus on the common good.	Shared vision and shared values. Commitment, enthusiasm, passion, creativity, integrity, honesty, trust, transparency, openness.
4. Transformation	Feeling a sense of independence and freedom by overcoming your survival, relationship and	Focus on empowerment, participation, team building and personal growth. Continuous improvement.	Continuous improvement. Continuous renewal. Continuous learning. Teamwork, empowerment,

	self-esteem fears. Courage, adaptability, accountability.	Equality, diversity, continuous learning.	accountability, adaptability, innovation.
3. Self-esteem	Feeling a sense of self-worth. Feeling good about who you are. Feeling respected by peers. Feeling a sense of personal pride.	Focus on performance, productivity, efficiency, quality and results. Systems and processes. Goal orientation. Focus on professional development.	Pride in performance. Best practices. Competency. Efficiency, productivity, systems and processes. Professional growth. Excellence, quality, expertise.
2. Relationship	Feeling a sense of belonging, and friendship. Feeling loved and being part of a family. Open communication. Loyalty.	Focus on customer satisfaction, employee recognition and conflict resolution. Respect. Open communication. Accessible.	Employee and customer satisfaction and loyalty. Sense of camaraderie and fellowship. Open communication. Respect, tradition, caring, supportive.
1. Survival	Satisfying our security, safety and physiological needs.	Focus on profit, shareholder value and organizational growth. Employee health and safety.	Pursuit of profit or shareholder value. Employee health and safety.

THEORETICAL BACKGROUND TO THE CULTURAL TRANSFORMATION TOOLS

The Seven Levels of Consciousness model was created by amalgamating Western and Eastern thinking on human motivations. The model was derived from two primary influences: Abraham Maslow's hierarchy of human needs and the approach to consciousness described in Vedic science.

Abraham Maslow (1968) postulated that healthy motivated people satisfy their needs in a specific order – survival, safety, love/belonging, and self-esteem. Once they have learned how to master these needs they begin the process of self-actualization: they learn how to become viable independent human beings and begin to focus on fulfilling their innate potential by becoming all they can become. They take on a larger sense of identity where their self-interest becomes enfolded within the common good. They seek to find their personal meaning in life and express this meaning by making a difference in the world and being of service to humanity.

Maslow described the first four layers of his hierarchy of human needs – survival, safety, love/belonging and self-esteem – as 'deficiency needs'. An individual gains no sense of lasting satisfaction from being able to meet these needs, but feels a sense of anxiety if these needs are not met. The lower the order of a need in the hierarchy, the more an individual will experience anxiety or fear if he or she is not able to meet that need. Thus, the greatest fears we face have to do with survival.

Maslow described self-actualization as 'growth' or 'being' needs. When these needs are fulfilled they do not go away, they engender deeper levels of motivation and commitment that become more and more potent over time.

During times of crisis the lower order 'deficiency' needs naturally take precedence over the higher order needs. The lower order needs are instinctual and are shared to varying extents by animals. Only humans possess the higher order needs.

The Seven Levels of Consciousness model was created by:

∎ shifting from a focus on needs to a focus on consciousness;
∎ restructuring and relabelling the hierarchy of needs;
∎ giving more structure to self-actualization by integrating the concepts of Vedic science.

Shifting from needs to consciousness

Needs represent the surface level of our motivations. When we state what we want in order to overcome our deficiency needs or satisfy our growth needs, we are expressing our underlying motivations. Healthy individuals find ways of expressing their motivations openly, without harming or hurting others. They are not anxious or impatient about satisfying their needs.

When people have fears about satisfying their deficiency needs, their subconscious remains focused on that need, even though to all intents and purposes it would appear that the need has been satisfied. For example, there are people who are never satisfied with the amount of money they earn. Even though they may be very rich, they cannot get enough. No matter how many assets they have, they always want more. Such people remain subconsciously focused at the survival level of consciousness, because they are holding on to subconscious beliefs about not having enough.

People who have underlying anxieties or subconscious fears about belonging or being loved subconsciously operate from the relationship level of consciousness. They have such a strong need to experience a feeling of affiliation that they may compromise their own integrity to get their needs met. This may cause them to be co-dependent because they want to be liked. They may avoid conflict and sometimes use humour to mask their true feelings. Further, individuals in this group who have underlying anxieties or subconscious fears about their performance or ranking in relation to their peers, subconsciously operate from the self-esteem level of consciousness. Their need for power, authority, status or respect is paramount for their well-being. They can never get enough recognition, praise or acknowledgement. They become perfectionists, workaholics and over achievers. They are driven by their need to be recognized.

Relabelling the lower levels of consciousness

The first two levels of Maslow's hierarchy of needs (the physiological survival level and the safety level) were brought together in the Seven Levels of Consciousness model into a single category known as survival consciousness, and the level of love/belonging, was renamed relationship consciousness. Thus, there are three levels of human consciousness that precede self-actualization – survival consciousness (survival and safety combined), relationship consciousness (replacing love/belonging) and self-esteem consciousness.

Structuring the higher levels of consciousness

The concept of self-actualization was given more definition by integrating the spiritual levels of consciousness described in Vedic science (Alexander and Boyer, 1989). The levels of consciousness described in Vedic science that correspond to self-actualization are known as soul consciousness, cosmic consciousness, God consciousness and unity consciousness. As we progress through each of these levels of consciousness, we feel an increasing sense of connectedness to the world and an expanded sense of identity. We feel a sense of oneness with ourselves, with our family, with our community, with the organization we work for, with our nation, with humanity and the planet, and eventually with the whole of creation.

The Seven Levels of Consciousness model is an evolutionary model that corresponds to the seven life themes that are intrinsic to the human condition (see Table 15.1).

THE SEVEN LEVELS OF LEADERSHIP CONSCIOUSNESS

In this section we provide more detail on the seven levels of leadership consciousness that are summarized in Table 15.1. The characteristics of each level, both healthy and unhealthy, can be used to support the discussions the coach has with the coachee.

Level 1: the crisis director/accountant

Healthy aspect

Level 1 leaders understand the importance of profit and shareholder returns. They manage their budgets meticulously. They look after the health and safety of employees. They are appropriately cautious in complex situations. They maintain a long-term perspective while dealing with short-term issues and goals. They promote a culture of compliance, but normally will go no further than they have to in satisfying legal regulations. One of the most important attributes of level 1 leaders is their ability to handle crises. When the survival of the organization is threatened, they know how to take control. They are calm in the midst of chaos and decisive in the midst of danger. In such situations, the leader needs to take on the mantle of the authoritarian.

Unhealthy aspect

When leaders operate as authoritarians on a regular basis, they quickly lose the trust and commitment of their people. Leaders often use a dictatorial style to get what they want because they find it difficult to relate to people in an open and effective way. They are afraid to let go of the reins of power because they have difficulty trusting others. The greater their existential fears regarding their survival and safety, the more risk-averse they become. Authoritarians can be quick to anger and are unable to discuss emotions. They bottle up their feelings and hide their true selves behind their position of authority. They are very lonely people. If they have insecurities around money, they will exploit others for their own ends. They are greedy in the midst of plenty and enough is never enough. They focus exclusively on short-term results. Fear-driven authoritarians create unhealthy climates in which to work. They hardly ever relax. They are consumed by their subconscious fears.

Level 2: the relationship manager/communicator

Healthy aspect

Relationship managers handle conflicts easily and invest a lot of time in building harmonious working relationships. They do not run away or hide from their emotions. They use their relationship skills to handle difficult interpersonal issues and their communication skills to build loyalty with their employees. They deliver good news and bad news to all staff indiscriminately. They believe in open communication. They acknowledge and praise staff for work well done. They are accessible to their employees and not stingy with their time. They are actively involved with customers and give priority to customer satisfaction.

Unhealthy aspect

When leaders hold subconscious fears about not belonging, they are afraid to deal with their own or others' emotions, they avoid conflicts, are less than truthful in their interpersonal communications, and resort to manipulation to get what they want. They either try to mask their true emotions behind humour or protect themselves by blaming others when things go wrong. Relationship managers are often protective of their people, but demand loyalty, discipline and obedience in return. They are often enamoured by tradition and operate as paternalists. Paternalists find it difficult to trust people who are not part of the 'family'. They are secretive and engage in mafia politics. This lack of trust in outsiders can severely limit the pool of talent that the organization can draw on. Because paternalists demand obedience, they tend to crush the entrepreneurial spirit of employees. Paternalism frequently shows up in family-run businesses.

Level 3: the manager/organizer

Healthy aspect

Managers bring logic and science to their work by using metrics to manage performance. They build systems and processes that create order and efficiency and enhance productivity. They have strong analytical skills. They think strategically and move quickly to capitalize on opportunities. They are rational in decision making. Inwardly focused managers are good at organizing information and monitoring results. Outwardly focused managers anticipate workflow problems and get things done. They plan and prioritize their work and provide stability and continuity. They create schedules and enjoy being in control. They are focused on their careers and willing to learn new skills if it will help them in their professional growth. They want to learn the latest management techniques so they can strive towards quality and excellence. They want to be successful and they want to be the best. They have a healthy pride in their work.

Unhealthy aspect

When managers' self-esteem needs are driven by subconscious fears, they become hungry for power, authority or recognition. They build empires to display their power. They build bureaucracies and hierarchies to demonstrate their authority. They compete with their colleagues so they can come out on top and gain recognition and self-respect. Their self-esteem is derived externally from others. They will play office politics to get what they want. And they will want to show off. They will want to buy a big house, join the best golf club, or drive the flashiest or most exclusive car. They will be meticulous about their wardrobe. They are often more concerned about how things look rather than how they are. Image is everything. They often derive their self-esteem through their work. Consequently, they tend to work long hours and neglect themselves and their families. They lead unhealthy lives because they are out of balance. They become consumed by their work because they are focused only on achievement.

Level 4: the facilitator/influencer

Facilitators readily seek advice, build consensus and empower their staff. They recognize that they do not have to have all the answers. They give people responsibility and freedom, making them accountable for outcomes and results. They research and develop new ideas and consistently evaluate risks before embarking on new ventures. They resist the temptation to micro-manage the work of their direct reports. They promote participation, equality and diversity. They ignore or remove hierarchy. They are adaptable and flexible. They embrace continuous learning. They actively engage in their own personal development and encourage their staff to participate in programmes that promote personal growth. They are looking to find balance in their lives through personal alignment. Balance leads to perspective and independence, and allows them to become objective about their strengths and weaknesses. They are learning to release their fears so they can move from being outer-directed to being inner-directed. They are in the process of self-actualization. They are on a journey of personal growth. As they let go of the need for outer approval, they begin to discover who they really are. They become enablers of others, encouraging them to express themselves and share their ideas. They encourage innovation and focus on team building. They enjoy challenges and are courageous and fearless in their approach to life. Facilitators are shifting from being a manager to becoming a leader.

Level 5: the integrator/inspirer

Integrator/inspirers are self-actualized individuals who build a vision and mission for the organization that inspires employees and customers alike. They promote a shared set of values and exhibit congruent behaviours that guide decision making throughout the organization. They demonstrate integrity and are living examples of values-based leadership. They walk their talk. They build cohesion and focus by bringing values alignment and mission alignment to the whole company. In so doing, they enhance the company's capacity for collective action. They foster opportunities for collaboration. By creating an environment of openness, fairness and transparency, they build trust and commitment among their people. The culture they create unleashes enthusiasm, passion and creativity at all levels of the organization. They are more concerned about getting the best result for everyone rather than their own self-interest. They are focused on the common good. They are creative problem solvers. They view problems from a systems perspective, seeing beyond the narrow boundaries of cause and effect. They are honest and truthful and feel confident in handling any situation. This confidence and openness allows them to reclassify problems as opportunities. They clarify priorities by referring to the vision and mission. They display emotional intelligence as well as intellectual intelligence. Integrator/inspirers are good at bringing the best out of people.

Level 6: mentor/partner

Mentor/partners are motivated by the need to make a difference in the world. They are true servant-leaders. They create mutually beneficial partnerships and strategic alliances with other individuals or groups who share the same goals. They collaborate with customers and suppliers to create win–win situations. They recognize the importance of environmental stewardship, and will go beyond the needs of compliance to make their operations environmentally friendly. They display empathy. They care about their people, seeking ways to help employees find personal fulfilment through their work. They create an environment where people can excel. They are active in building a pool of talent for the organization by mentoring and coaching their subordinates. They are intuitive decision makers. They are inclusive. They are on top of their game. They may also be active in the local community, building relationships that create goodwill.

Level 7: wisdom/visionary

Wisdom/visionary leaders are motivated by the need to be of service to the world. Their vision is global and they have a holistic perspective on life. They are focused on the questions 'How can I help?' and 'What can I do?' They are concerned about the state of the world. They also care about the legacy we are leaving for future generations. They will not compromise long-term outcomes for short-term gains but use their influence to create a better world. They see their own mission and that of their organization from a larger, societal perspective. They are committed to social responsibility. For them, the world is a complex web of interconnectedness, and they know and understand their role. They act with humility and compassion. They are generous in spirit, patient and forgiving in nature. They are at ease with uncertainty and can tolerate ambiguity. They enjoy solitude and can be reclusive and reflective. Level 7 leaders are admired for their wisdom and vision.

THE CULTURAL TRANSFORMATION TOOLS® ASSESSMENT INSTRUMENTS

The key insight that led to the creation of the Cultural Transformation Tools assessment instruments was that every human value/behaviour is motivated by a specific level of consciousness. Thus, if people are able to choose values/behaviours that represent who they are or how they or their organizations operate, the values they choose are a proxy for the levels of consciousness that they or their organizations are operating from. This includes not only positive values such as trust, commitment and open communication but also limiting values such as manipulation, blame and control. The limiting values/behaviours are expressions of unmet deficiency needs and represent fears showing up for the individual or in the organization.

In addition to categorizing by level of consciousness, each value can be categorized as:

■ either a positive or limiting value (used to calculate a Health Index – P/L);
■ an individual, relationship, organizational or societal value (used to calculate a Balance Index – IROS);
■ one of six categories of a business-needs scorecard focusing on specific business areas – finance, fitness (performance), clients/customers, evolution (acceptance of new ideas), culture and societal contribution (for the culture template only).

The coach receives three documents for both an Individual Values Assessment, and a Leadership Values Assessment. These are:

■ a written report that is given to the coachee;
■ a visual set of data plots that is given to the coachee;
■ a confidential report for the coach highlighting the key issues and discussion topics for the coaching session.

Individual Values Assessment

The Individual Values Assessment is a web-based instrument that asks three questions:

▎ *Personal values.* Which of the following values and behaviours most represent who you are, not who you desire to become? Pick 10.
▎ *Current culture values.* Which of the following values and behaviours most represent how your organization currently operates? Pick 10.
▎ *Desired culture values.* Which of the following values and behaviours most represent how you would like your organization to operate? Pick 10.

The template of personal values contains about 60 to 80 words or phrases. The template of cultural values (used for the latter two questions) contains about 80 to 100 words or phrases. The template of personal values differs from the template of cultural values in that it does not contain organizational values such as customer satisfaction, profit and empire building. The personal and cultural values templates are customized to reflect the culture of the country and the operating context of the organization.

The Individual Values Assessment written report contains five sections: personal values, current culture values, desired culture values, business needs scorecard and a summary. The Individual Values Assessment data plots show a visual representation of the individual's personal values, current and desired culture values mapped against the Seven Levels of Consciousness model along with the placement of the current and desired culture values on the six-part business needs scorecard (BNS). An example of the data plots is shown in Figure 15.1a and an example of the BNS is shown in Figure 15.1b.

The section on personal values in the written report contains:

▎ A personality profile based on the individual's choice of values. This profile enables the coach to identify the most important motivations in the personal life of the coachee.
▎ A Health Index (P/L) and commentary indicating the relative weight of positive and limiting values chosen by the individual. When limiting values show up in the top-10 list of personal values this is indicative of underlying subconscious fears that can cause dysfunctional behaviours. These are areas for the coach to explore, eg, being liked.
▎ A Balance Index (IROS) and commentary indicating the relative weight of individual, relationship and societal values chosen by the individual. A strong focus on individual values shows the individual is self-focused. A significant number of relationship values shows the individual is other-focused. Self-actualized individuals have a healthy balance of the three different types of values.

Personal values (PV)

1. Experience
2. Friendship
3. Humour/fun
4. Listening
5. Making a difference
6. **Open communication**
7. Personal growth
8. **Professional growth**
9. Responsibility
10. Trust

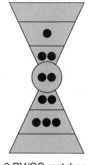

0 PV/CC matches

PL = 10-0
IRS (P) = 5-4-1
IRS (L) = 0-0-0

Current culture values (CC)

1. Bureaucracy **(L)**
2. Caution **(L)**
3. Consensus
4. Control **(L)**
5. *Diversity*
6. Financial stability
7. *Job security* **(L)**
8. Mission focus
9. Short-term orientation (L)
10. Territory **(L)**

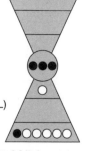

2 CC/DC matches

PL = 4-6
IROS (P) = 0-2-2-0
IROS (L) = 1-1-4-0

Desired culture values (DC)

1. Balance (home/work)
2. Creativity
3. *Diversity*
4. Employee fulfilment
5. Enthusiasm
6. Innovation
7. *Job security (L)*
8. **Open communication**
9. **Professional growth**
10. Wisdom

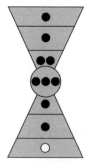

2 DC/PV matches

PL = 9-1
IROS (P) = 4-2-3-0
IROS (L) = 0-0-1-0

Figure 15.1a Individual values assessment

▮ An analysis and commentary on the levels of consciousness that the individual is operating from. When the individual's choice of values are plotted on the seven-levels model, the coach can immediately see a map of the consciousness of the individual. What is important to note is where the values are clustered, and where there are gaps. Gaps in the lower levels of consciousness are indicative of either mastery or blind spots.

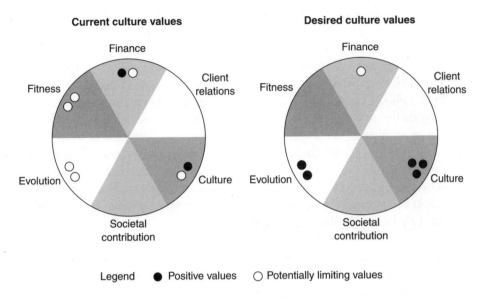

Figure 15.1b Business needs scorecard

Gaps in the higher levels of consciousness are indicative of next levels of growth. A lack of values at the transformation level of consciousness is indicative of an unwillingness or inability to change.

█ An analysis of and commentary on the degree of alignment between the personal values and current culture values (number of matching values). This is indicative of the degree to which the individual is able to bring his or her full self to work.

The section on current culture in the written report contains:

█ A cultural profile of the organization based on the individual's choice of current culture values. This profile enables the coach to identify what the coachee considers to be the most important motivations of the organization.

█ A Health Index (P/L) and commentary indicating the relative weight of positive and limiting values in the current culture. When limiting values show up in the top-10 list of current culture values, this is indicative of underlying subconscious fears that cause dysfunction and inhibit the performance of the organization.

█ A Balance Index (IROS) and commentary indicating the relative weight of individual, relationship, organizational and societal values in the current culture. A strong focus on organizational values shows the organization is internally focused, paying little attention to employee or customer needs. A significant number of relationship values shows the organization is employee or customer focused. A significant number of societal values shows the organization is focused on making a difference in the world.

▐ An analysis and commentary on the levels of consciousness of the current culture. When the individual's choice of current culture values are plotted on the seven-levels model the coach can immediately identify the levels the organization is operating from. What is important to note is how different this plot of values is from the coachee's personal values.

▐ An analysis of and commentary on the degree of alignment between the current culture and the desired culture (number of matching values). This indicates the degree to which the individual thinks the organization is on the right track. The low number of matching values indicates a high level of frustration with the organization, especially when there are many limiting values in the current culture.

The section on desired culture in the written report contains:

▐ A cultural profile of the organization that the individual would like to see, based on the individual's choice of desired culture values. This profile enables the coach to see what the coachee considers to be the most desired cultural values.

▐ A Health Index (P/L) and commentary indicating the relative weight of positive and limiting values in the desired culture. Usually all the values chosen by the coachee are positive.

▐ A Balance Index (IROS) and commentary indicating the relative weight of individual, relationship, organizational and societal values in the desired culture: It is important to compare this Balance Index with the Balance Index of the current culture. Differences indicate important changes the coachee would like to see.

▐ An analysis of and commentary on the levels of consciousness of the desired culture. When the individual's choice of desired culture values are plotted on the seven-levels model and compared to the current culture values, the coach can immediately see what changes the coachee would like to see in the organization. The choice of desired culture values is a reaction to what is happening in the current culture and indicates areas of improvement that the coachee would like to see.

▐ An analysis of and commentary on the degree of alignment between the individual's personal values and the values of the desired culture (number of matching values). Particular attention should be paid to values in the desired culture that are the same as the coachee's personal values, especially if these values are not showing up in the current culture. A high number of matching desired culture and personal values (that are not showing up in the current culture) is a measure of the level of frustration of the coachee with the organization.

The section on the business needs scorecard in the written report contains:

▮ A commentary on the comparison of the current and desired culture values by business category. This commentary highlights the degree of balance between the different areas of business focus and indicates the major shifts that the coachee would like to see between the current and desired culture.

The summary section of the Individual Values Assessment contains:

▮ A descriptive overview of the personality of the individual, the degree to which he or she is aligned with the current culture of the organization, and the degree to which he or she thinks the organization in on the right track. This provides the coachee with a realistic evaluation of his or her relationship to the organization and the degree to which he or she feels empowered or frustrated by the current culture. The comparison of the distribution of values in the personal, current and desired culture immediately shows to what extent the coachee is aligned with the organization.

An annex to the report provides a description of the Seven Levels of Organizational Consciousness.

The coach's Confidential Notes for the Individual Values Assessment contain:

▮ a general set of instructions for the coach for interpreting the results;
▮ specific insights, comments and questions that can be used to direct the coaching session.

THE LEADERSHIP VALUES ASSESSMENT

The Leadership Values Assessment (LVA) is a web-based feedback assessment. Coachees go online and pick 10 values/behaviours from a template of about 60 to 80 words or phrases that represent their operating/management style. They are then asked to indicate three of their key strengths, three things they want to improve or stop, and what, if anything, they are doing to change.

Each person or leader who is being coached is then assessed, usually by 12–15 or more assessors who go online and pick 10 values/behaviours that they believe represent the leader's operating/management style. The same values template is used by the leaders and the assessors. In addition, the assessors are asked to identify three of the leader's strengths, three things they think the leader needs to improve or stop, and any other comments or feedback they want the leader to receive. The assessors are chosen by the leader.

Since organizational transformation starts with the personal transformation of the leaders, this instrument and the coaching that follows the assessment can often be the most powerful of the CTT surveys and the one most able to effect deep and meaningful change.

The written report for the Leadership Values Assessment comprises two sections: a detailed comparison of the leader's and assessors' responses regarding the leader's operating/management style, and the suggested next steps for his or her development.

The data plots for the Leadership Values Assessment shows a visual comparison of the leader's chosen values and the top 10 values chosen by the assessors' mapped against the seven levels of leadership consciousness, together with a distribution chart of all the assessors' values and the leader's values plotted against the seven levels of leadership consciousness.

The distribution chart also shows the level of personal entropy of the leader – the proportion of votes for all limiting values. The level of personal entropy shows the degree to which leaders allow their fears to dominate their decision making. Table 15.2 shows the implications of different levels of personal entropy. An example of the Leadership Values Assessment data plots is shown in Figure 15.2.

Table 15.2 Implications of different levels of personal entropy

Personal entropy	Implications
6% or less	Prime. Such leaders' behaviours are not sourced from their subconscious fears.
7%–10%	Low. A call for leaders to examine how their behaviours and actions are affecting the people around them, their decision-making processes or their degree of balance.
11%–15%	Moderate. An indication that from the assessors' point of view the leaders' behaviours are counterproductive to what they want to achieve.
16%–20%	High. These leaders need to understand how their behaviours may be compromising their personal integrity and their ability to achieve their or their organization's objectives.
21% or more	Very High. Leaders are significantly compromising their personal integrity and the ability of the organization to achieve its objectives.

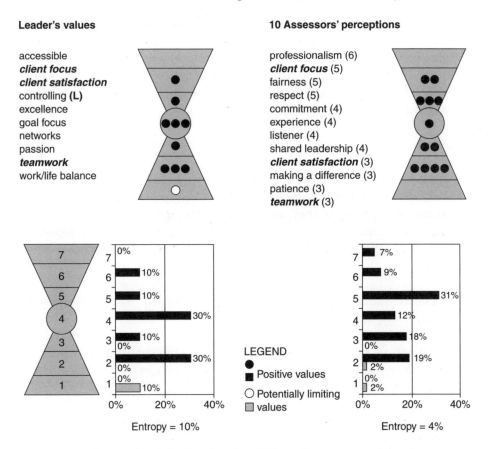

Figure 15.2   Example of the Leadership Values Assessment data plots

The section on the comparison of the leader's and assessors' responses contains:

▌ The assessors' evaluation of the leader's strengths and the leader's evaluation of his or her own strengths. This provides a picture of what the assessors appreciate about the leader and the degree to which the leader understands how he or she is coming across.

▌ The number of values matches between the values chosen by the leader and the top 10 values chosen by the assessors. A high degree of alignment shows the leader has a strong sense of self-awareness. Such leaders are conscious of who they are. A low degree of alignment shows a lack of self-awareness.

▌ A comparison of the leader's and assessors' distribution of values across the levels of consciousness. This provides accurate feedback on the leader's operating styles. If the assessors' and leader's values are clustered around different levels of consciousness, then the leader does not have an accurate perception of how he or she is coming across. When the assessors' values are higher than the leader's values, the leader does not fully appreciate his or her qualities. When the assessor's values are lower than the leader's values, the leader is operating with a false sense of reality.

The section on next steps for the leader's development contains:

▌ The assessors' evaluation of the leader's areas of improvement, the leader's evaluation of his or her areas of improvement, and the leader's comments on what they are doing to change. This section provides significant insights for changing or developing the leader's personal action programme, and a rich area of discussion and interaction with the coach.

The coach's confidential notes for the Leadership Values Assessment contain:

▌ a general set of instructions for the coach for interpreting the results;
▌ specific insights, comments and questions that can be used to direct the coaching session.

An overview of the seven levels of leadership consciousness is shown in Table 15.1.

USING CTT WITH COACHEES

The Individual Values Assessment (IVA) provides significant insights into the alignment of an individual's personal values with those of the organizational culture they are operating in, and the degree to which the individual believes the organization is on the right track. The example in Figure 15.1 shows a significant misalignment in values. You will note in Figure 15.1(a) that the individual has a good spread of personal values from Levels 2 to 6, whereas the organization is strongly focused at Level 1 and Level 4 consciousness. There are six potentially limiting values in the current culture, showing a significant degree of misalignment. One of the interesting anomalies that could be discussed as part of the feedback of this IVA would be the juxtaposition of the value of 'consensus' with the value of 'control'. The large number of potentially limiting values is an indication of a significant amount of fear in the organization, which comes from the leaders' operating style. The culture of an organization is always a reflection of the consciousness of the leaders.

The individual in this assessment wants to see a major shift in the values of the organization, as shown by the desired culture values. He or she wants to see a shift towards full-spectrum consciousness. The only limiting factor is the individual's need for job security. Again, we find an anomaly. If in the current culture the organization has 'financial stability', why would 'job security' be a desired culture value? Another rich arena for discussion with the coach.

The business needs scorecard shown in Figure 15.1(b) indicates regression in the areas of fitness, evolution and culture. The desired culture scorecard indicates that the individual wants to see much more focus on evolution (diversity and innovation) and culture (balance of home and work, employee fulfilment and open communication).

Whereas the IVA is a self-assessment on the degree of alignment of the individual with the culture of his or her organization, the Leadership Values Assessment provides external feedback on the individual's leadership style.

The example in Figure 15.2 shows someone who sees himself as operating from Levels 2 and 4, but comes across to colleagues as operating from Level 5. This can be clearly seen from the distribution diagram. This person does not have an accurate perception of who he is or of his strengths. There are only three matching values between leader's perception of his operating style and the assessors' perception – client focus, client satisfaction and teamwork. Even though the assessors show only three values at Level 5 and four at Level 2, there were many more votes for Level 5 (31 per cent) values than Level 2 (19 per cent). The job of the coach in this situation is to help the leader acknowledge his strengths and also understand why the values that he believes he is operating with are not coming across.

It is interesting that the leader sees himself as 'controlling' whereas this is not coming across to his colleagues. This could be a rich avenue for the coach to explore. Why is this person judging himself so harshly and why does he have a lower opinion of himself than his colleagues do? Is this a self-esteem issue?

It is also interesting to note that there are six relationship values among the values chosen by the assessors – 'fairness', 'respect', 'listener', 'patience', 'shared leadership' and 'teamwork' – whereas the leader gives himself only two relationship values, 'accessible' and 'teamwork'. Why is this person not recognizing his potential as a leader of people?

This leader has strong people skills as well as strong business skills, as shown by the values of 'professionalism' and 'experience'. It is time for him to step up into the fullness of his being. The lack of positive values at Level 1 suggests that the leader may not be as focused on the financial aspects of the organization's business as he should be.

USING CTT WITH COACHES

The Leadership Values Assessment has also been tailored for use by coaches to get feedback from their clients on their coaching style. The assessment process is exactly the same as for the LVA. Coaches go online and pick 10 values/behaviours from a template of about 60 to 80 words or phrases that represent their coaching style, including positive as well as potentially limiting values. They are then asked to indicate three of their key strengths, three things they want to improve or stop, and what, if anything, they are doing to improve or change.

The clients of each coach, usually 12–15 or more, go online and pick 10 values/behaviours that they believe represent the coach's style. The coach's clients are then asked to identify three of the coach's strengths, three things they think the coach needs to improve or stop, and any other comments or feedback they want the coach to receive.

The feedback to the coach is best delivered by another coach who is trained in the CTT approach. The feedback session usually lasts two or three hours. The session begins by affirming the coach's strengths – what the coachees appreciate about him or her. The coach's perception of his or her coaching style is then compared with the coachees' perception of it. The gaps between the coach's perception and the coachees' perception are explored to discover areas of alignment and areas of divergence. This is a fertile area for exploration of the coach's possible blind spots.

Another key area of feedback is the comments made by the coachees on what they consider to be the coach's areas of improvement or things they think the coach should stop. Again, the areas of alignment and divergence provide a rich arena for discussion and an opportunity to explore potential blind spots.

The distribution of the top 10 values chosen by the coachees indicates which levels of consciousness coaches are projecting to the world. This may be different from coaches' perception of the distribution of their consciousness as indicated by the values that they chose for themselves. Some individuals have a higher perception of their values than do those with whom they interact. Sometimes they have a lower perception. In either case the reasons for the misperception should be explored. The most authentic individuals are those who know their values and project these values out into the world; in their case the distribution of their values and the coachees' values would be very similar.

SUMMARY

This chapter describes the coaching instruments that are part of the Cultural Transformation Tools (CTT). The coaching instruments are based on the Seven Levels of Consciousness model. This is an evolutionary model that corresponds to the seven life themes that are intrinsic to the human condition. The unique feature of these instruments is that they provide visual and quantifiable data that can be used to develop time series data to map the progress of an individual or a leader.

References

Alexander, C and Boyer, R (1989) Seven states of consciousness, *Modern Science and Vedic Science*, **2** (4), pp 325–364, Department of Psychology, Maharishi International University, Fairfield, Iowa

Barrett, R (1998) *Liberating the Corporate Soul: Building a visionary organization*, Butterworth-Heinemann, Boston

Barrett, R (2006) *Building a Values-Driven Organization: A whole system approach to cultural transformation*, Butterworth Heinemann, Boston

Maslow, A (1968) *Toward a Psychology of Being*, 2nd edn, Van Nostrand Reinhold, New York

16

Coaching with FIRO Element B

Roy Childs

INTRODUCTION

This chapter introduces the reader to FIRO Theory (Fundamental Interpersonal Relations Orientation), one of the most comprehensive models of interpersonal relationships available. It provides a way to understand and intervene at the core of what has become known as the emotional intelligence domain. FIRO brings depth to our understanding of what drives people and how they manage their hopes and fears. This chapter describes not only what comes out of the FIRO Element B questionnaire, but also how this represents the tip of an iceberg underneath which lies the essence of people's identity, emotional needs and reactions. The implications for coaching are illustrated through a case study and by illustrating the value of each dimension as they were applied in actual coaching sessions.

THEORETICAL AND RESEARCH BACKGROUND

In 1952 Will Schutz was called up by the US Navy to serve in the Korean War. As an academic psychologist, Will began to research the effectiveness and compatibility of the teams that ran ships' and submarines' combat information centres. The main issue was that all these people were highly technically competent, but all too often the atmosphere and interpersonal climate did not yield optimal performance. Will's challenge was to work out what made them incompatible and what to do about it. The result was the first formulation of FIRO theory published in 'The interpersonal under-world' in 1958.

At its heart, the theory states that 'people need people' – in other words that we are essentially social beings with strong interpersonal desires which he defines as inclusion, control and affection (later renamed openness). These desires were proposed according to a strict methodology for devel-oping a formal theory. This included an extensive review of the relevant literature together with statistical requirements to meet what is called antecedent and evidential probability.[1] In effect this means that the theory had to be rational and plausible and then supported by empirical evidence. To gather this evidence he needed a way to quantify the dimensions – which resulted in the original FIRO-B questionnaire, which measured inclusion, control and affection. After 20 years of further research he updated FIRO theory and produced his latest suite of instruments – FIRO Element B (behaviour), FIRO Element F (feelings) and FIRO Element S (self-concept). These questionnaires have better psychometric properties, especially in the ability to separate two of the dimensions: inclusion and affection (which was renamed openness). Additionally, people can now measure the feelings and beliefs that underpin the behaviours, making FIRO theory one of the most comprehensive and powerful approaches to understanding both others and ourselves.

It is worth noting that Will Schutz's starting point for developing FIRO was different than for many other developers of personality questionnaires. Since he was exploring what made for effective teams, he was interested in what we seek to satisfy in our relationships with others. This leads to one of the most significant differences between FIRO and other 'personality ques-tionnaires' – as it invites people to say what they want to receive from others. Other questionnaires ask people to express or describe themselves in terms of some general concept of their identity, behaviour or style (ie, what they do in a typical situation). People answer FIRO with two mind-sets – the 'way it is' and the 'way they want it to be' – giving an immediate framework for exploring compatibility.

THE FIRO ELEMENT B QUESTIONNAIRE

The FIRO model is based on three fundamental interpersonal needs.[2] These needs manifest themselves to the outside world as behaviours but also manifest themselves inside each one of us as feelings and beliefs. At the behavioural level the three dimensions are called Inclusion, Control and Openness[3] and the questionnaire provides four different scores for each dimension which can be summarized as shown in Table 16.1.

Being high or low on any of the scales provides information about a person's perception of their preference. However, much of the interpretative power that is derived from FIRO is based on Will Schutz's concept of rigidity: behaving in a particular way regardless of whether it is appropriate to the situation. This is the signal that the behaviour is a defence mechanism that is managing an underlying fear. What follows is a brief description of each of the dimensions and some of the potential underlying issues that can lead to and explain rigidity when it occurs.

Inclusion

This describes the amount of interaction a person engages in or seeks to achieve. It is driven by a need to connect, belong and feel significant. Other words associated with inclusion are 'engage, invite, meet, join, move towards, participate with, acknowledge and recognize'. When people are rigid around Inclusion the model suggests that they are trying to convince themselves (and others) that they are significant. Some people manage the fear that they are not significant by becoming over-social. This means they are desperate to include others, they accept lots of invitations and behave in a way that ensures they will not be ignored. However, to some, this feels like a high-risk strategy and they prefer to do the opposite: they become under-social. By never inviting others they avoid the fear of their invites being ignored. By refusing the invites of others they never put themselves into

Table 16.1 The four options for each dimension

	What I see happening	What I want to see happening
What I do or initiate	How much I include, control or am open with others	How much I want to include, control or be open with others
What I get or receive	How much people include, control or are open with me	How much I want people to include, control or be open with me

those potentially embarrassing situations where others can ignore them. Inclusion is sometimes misunderstood as another form of extroversion. However, some introverts have a high need for Inclusion – but they express it differently from extroverts and so it can be very illuminating to use the FIRO inclusion scale alongside a measure of extroversion.

Control

This describes the amount of control coachees desire in their interactions with others. It is driven by a need to feel in control, self-determining and competent. Other words associated with control are 'influence, guide, lead, take charge, manage, exercise authority over, provide direction, provide structure and take responsibility'. When people are rigid around control the model suggests that they are trying to manage feelings of being impotent or incompetent. Some people manage the fear that they are not competent by becoming over-controlling. This means insisting that things are done in certain ways, thus keeping events within known boundaries where they can demonstrate a practised and developed level of competence. This reduces the risk of straying into areas where competence could be challenged and exposed, but means that such people can be inappropriately autocratic. Others become rigidly under-controlling. By abdicating responsibility they avoid setting themselves up to fail. To these people, saying 'I can't' is preferable to saying 'I can' and then running the risk of being exposed as incompetent when they fail. The result is that they are too quick to avoid responsibility and challenge. The price we pay for not addressing issues in this area is a reduction in our spontaneity and empowerment.

Openness (originally called affection)[4]

This describes the amount of disclosure and depth people seek in their inter-actions with others. It is driven by a desire for connecting personally, sharing intimacies and being accepted for who we truly are. Other words associated with Openness are 'disclosing, intimate, affectionate, secretive, cautious, truthful and honest'. When people are rigid around Openness the model suggests that they are trying to manage feelings of being unlikeable. Some people manage the fear that they are not likeable by becoming over-disclosing. This means inappropriately giving people lots of personal infor-mation. Since this is the behaviour associated with closeness, it can create the feeling (or illusion) of intimacy. It can also have several other roots. Sometimes it pre-empts the pain of rejection by revealing all the things about me that I know are unlikeable. You can then reject me early in a rela-tionship, which is preferable to rejection after I have got close to you.

Sometimes it is a 'managed openness' whereby people appear to be extremely open because they are disclosing things that others might not – but in fact are keeping their real fears well hidden. Others become rigidly under-disclosing. They try to get people to like them by only revealing the nice things about themselves. The fear that others will discover all their horrible parts makes them over- cautious and selective in what they reveal. The price paid for not addressing issues in this area is a difficulty in making long-term intimate relationships and a loss of energy in keeping the 'authentic self' hidden while trying to manage an image of who we are trying to be.

Overview of the FIRO model

Table 16.2 is an overview of the FIRO model with the three behavioural dimensions (the tip of the iceberg) in the top line and a range of other issues (the hidden part of the iceberg) immediately below.

FIRO ELEMENT B AND COACHES

Coaching involves many definitions and can focus on quite different things. Some coaches focus on purely behavioural and performance goals. Others focus on 'softer' issues to do with life purpose, relationships, well-being and

Table 16.2   Overview of the FIRO model

FIRO Element B	Inclusion	Control	Openness
Interpersonal style – high	Sociable, involved	Directing, confrontational	Revealing, disclosing
Interpersonal style – low	Reserved, withdrawn	Abdicating, accommodating	Private, secret
Wants, needs or desires	To belong, be noticed	To influence, be respected	To share, be liked
Feelings and beliefs	Significance	Competence	Likeability
Intrapersonal benefit	Aliveness; presence	Spontaneity; humility	Awareness; tolerance
Anxiety	I am not important	I am not capable	I am not likeable
Fear	I will be ignored	I will be humiliated	I will be rejected

satisfaction. However, one of the most common dangers for all coaches involves moving too quickly and wanting to find solutions, give advice or take action. Since coaching requires helping coachees to find their own goals and solutions, there are times when they need to move at their own pace and to prepare themselves for learning and changing. Unless the coach has sufficient self-awareness and understanding of the coachee, there are real dangers that the process will be driven by the coach's own needs, issues and style. How these manifest themselves will be illustrated using a case study of a coach who was relatively new to coaching.

A newly qualified coach

This coach had been working in IT but had woken up one morning loathing the idea of going to work. She said that it suddenly struck her like a bolt out of the blue: she was in the wrong job. Her pay and conditions were good but her motivation was rock bottom. Within a year she had left that job and set up as a self-employed coach. She described her excitement at getting her first clients but was currently feeling quite despondent. She explained that one of her coaching sessions was not going as well as she had hoped. When asked why, she said that her coachee never seemed to get enough out of the sessions. When asked how she knew this she explained that he was quite reserved, did not express a great deal and even though she had offered to give him further support on the phone prior to an important negotiation, he had not done so. The coach's 'story' was that she was not useful enough to him.

After discussion with her supervisor, she agreed to get some direct feedback from the coachee. She had asked him before but always face to face at the beginning or end of a session. He always said it was very useful but somehow the coach didn't believe him. Her supervisor suggested that she ask a few more probing questions, but in the form of a 'questionnaire' since this might suit his more introverted style. It would also depersonalize the feedback and perhaps encourage more honest answers. The feedback from this questionnaire was again very positive, and once again the coach found herself questioning his honesty. It was at this stage that her supervisor suggested using FIRO Element B to explore her interpersonal needs further. The questionnaire results are shown in Table 16.3.

The scores are on a 0–9 scale. For the purposes of this interpretation, scores of 0–2 will be considered low, 3–6 average and 7–9 high.

Table 16.3 Questionnaire results

The coach's FIRO Element B scores					
Inclusion		Control		Openness	
See	Want	See	Want	See	Want
Do I include people	I want to include people	I control people	I want to control people	I am open with people	I want to be open with people
6	8	8	7	2	3
Get People include me	I want people to include me	People control me	I want people to control me	People are open with me	I want people to be open with me
2	9	6	1	3	8

Inclusion

The results show that the coach has a higher need to be included than the level of inclusion she feels she is currently getting (I want people to include me is 9, people do include me is 2). In fact, one reason for leaving her previous job was that she felt it was a 'quite lonely and technical role'. Her desire to work as a coach was, in part, to do with her need for contact with others. The story that emerged was that she had gone to a comprehensive school where there was not a strong work ethos, and she had been seen as 'too clever' to be accepted as one of the gang. At home she felt that her sister was always the one her parents talked about and of whom they were most proud. At school she had 'never felt part of the group', and FIRO Element B helped her to recognize just how much it still affected her. She recognized how the fact that her coachee was not accepting her offers for more contact was part of a much longer-term pattern – and that she was particularly sensitive when people did not respond to her. More generally this often prevented her from approaching others.

Control

The insights from FIRO Element B went much further than this since her control scores revealed a long-term pattern of high structure and independence (I control people is 8, I want to control people is 7 but I want people to control me is 1). While she believed that this pattern had served her well, she recognized that she was driven by a high need to be competent. She always feared that she would 'never be good enough'. Clearly this fear had helped her to achieve things of which she was proud, but it was not helping the relationships she wanted to develop – she had a reputation for being a bit bossy and she disliked her tendency to feel unnecessarily competitive.

In her previous job in IT this style had been accepted and even respected – but not won her many friends. Now in her new career she could see that she would need to beware of switching into being over-controlling. It was affecting her career transition because her 'high standards' meant she needed to be 'a fantastic coach' even though she was new and still learning. By reviewing some of her recorded coaching sessions, her supervisor had helped her recognize that she sometimes failed to listen and had a tendency to become a little directive. In fact, her methods were quite subtle and skilful – such as asking apparently open questions but returning several times when she was not getting the answers she hoped. This showed her strong need to control the process rather than follow the client's agenda.

Openness

The coach's openness scores also revealed a strong interpersonal need which was affecting the way in which she coached. She was basically low on being open herself but had a very high need for others to be open with her. She linked this to the confusion she felt about the label Extrovert and Introvert. Her reported type from completing the Type Dynamics Indicator (TDI) was ESTJ, but the TDI also measures what people feel is their ideal type whereby she reported INFJ.[5] The insight she gained from FIRO Element B was that she was a very social person but was not always comfortable in that role, and that her extroversion was loud and social rather than open and intimate. In fact she recognized how private a person she was – and yet FIRO revealed her strong desire for people to open up with her, to share more and become more intimate. In her personal life she approached new relationships with great caution. She found it hard to be open about her needs, her emotions and her weaknesses – especially with men to whom she was attracted. She admitted having lots of social mechanisms for appearing to get close but actually never really revealing much about herself.

The relevance of this for her as a coach was that her strongly stated belief that she was helping others was confused with a strong personal desire to get closer to people. Awareness of this was an important warning for her – and she was letting her professional life spill over into her private life and vice versa. Her experience with her coachee was already showing how her needs could blur the boundaries unless she was very careful. Additionally it is worth noting that she was surprisingly open during the coaching sessions. This was quite unusual, given her scores, and she admitted that she found it hard but was desperate to get the most out of our sessions – another part of her recurring pattern (ie, she needed to be fantastic under supervision!). She revealed that the low risk and low judgement she experienced in the coaching environment was the first time she had felt able to express some of her thoughts even to herself and that she was surprised and 'cautiously excited' – but did not yet feel ready to try it in her 'real life'.

The coach's experience of FIRO was profound. She discovered a lot about her needs, which she recognized could significantly affect her ability to coach. She acknowledged the value of continuing with supervision, which she had previously considered to be over-indulgent and unnecessarily dependent. She recognized that she had been striving to become a good technical coach and needed to learn to let go of models and structure and to separate personal needs from the career she had chosen. However, the FIRO insights also had a significant impact on how she understood many of her other relationships – especially close relationships that had failed and caused her a lot of pain. The benefit to her was therefore both professional and personal.

USING FIRO ELEMENT B WITH COACHEES

Why do people engage in a coaching process when the time and financial investment can be considerable? Most will have a 'presenting' issue or need. Some people come with very specific performance improvement needs (such as 'presenting a particular case with impact' or 'developing a tougher stance in negotiations'). Others have more general development issues (such as 'becoming more sensitive when dealing with staff performance issues' or 'deciding whether to change jobs and finding the kind of job that would be motivating over the long term'). However, in reality, a coachee's needs are interrelated and multi-faceted. Sometimes, simply dealing with the presenting issue misses the opportunity for effecting long-term and worthwhile change. A good coach has to work flexibly to help the coachee uncover what really matters. FIRO makes a special contribution because it can get to the core of an individual's most important issues very quickly and in a way that is both subtle and surprising.

The reasons it seems to work so well can be summarized as follows:

▐ It does not ask job or context-specific questions. The power of FIRO is the way it can transcend situations and focus on a core sense of identity rather than the roles we play.
▐ It asks straightforward questions that are easy for people to identify with and so does not require them to search their souls.

▌ The apparent simplicity represents the tip of an iceberg. It provides access to a much richer model that links behaviours to long-term patterns and needs, thus acting as an accelerator for discovering the coachee's core issues and needs.

To show how inclusion, control and openness can help a coachee, three important elements will be addressed – clarifying of direction (for the coaching session and the eventual outcome), understanding the coachee's personal style in both normal and pressure situations, and exploring relationships at work or elsewhere. For simplicity, the examples are based on people with 'all round' low and high scores. Clearly people's FIRO profiles can be far more complicated and more profound insights can be obtained than can be discussed here.

Inclusion

As previously described, this involves the amount of interaction a person engages in or seeks to achieve. It is driven by a desire to connect, belong and feel significant. How this affects work on direction, style and relationships is explored below.

Direction

Sometimes people are doing jobs that do not suit them. If coachees need a good deal of inclusion, then they should not seek work as traffic wardens – unless they are very clear that they satisfy their inclusion needs outside of work and are sufficiently robust to take the kind of contact that traffic wardens have to endure. One coachee had a FIRO profile showing very high inclusion scores. The surprise was the largely administrative and isolated nature of his job, where he was responsible for all the records in a large law firm. On the face of it, this would not seem to be a satisfying environment for him. However, there were no complaints about his work and he said that he was quite content doing what he did. As the story unfolded, it was clear that he enjoyed the peace and quiet of the day job because his evenings and weekends were full of interaction; he was in a rock band 'about to make the big time'. He sought coaching because of his moods before a gig; his band had demanded that he sort himself out.

One clear lesson in this is how not to use FIRO: simply because someone expresses a high desire for inclusion does not mean they need a high inclusion job. This coachee used the day job to provide balance in his hectic life, not to fulfil his life's purpose and direction. Working with the FIRO helped him to recognize how desperate he was for recognition, fame and visibility. Having felt ignored and insignificant as a child his whole purpose was to seek visibility – he gave plenty of examples of where he had done stupid things but had felt that any attention was better than none. One of his recurring dreams was the end of a gig where no one clapped, at which point he normally woke up in a cold sweat. FIRO helped transform the coaching goal from dealing with short-term issues to dealing with a long-term pattern of behaviours designed to avoid feeling insignificant and being ignored.

Style

A common danger is to assume that other people want the same level of interaction as ourselves. Consider a person with all-round low inclusion scores who makes this assumption. This can lead to rearranging activities, perhaps by subdividing them, in order to reduce contact and minimize situations requiring interaction, when the reality could be that more contact and closer collaboration would work better. Some of my coachees have been quite blind to their distortion in this area and believe sincerely that they are approaching the matter in the best way and helping to 'reduce unnecessary interaction and time wasting'. Clearly there may be times when they are right. However, FIRO can provide the signal for examining such situations with greater self-awareness.

One quite extreme example of distortion was a chief executive with very low inclusion scores. Even after two years in post he had still not met more than 50 per cent of his 250-strong workforce. He was completely unaware of what this signalled to staff (ie 'you are not important'). Such a signal is unlikely to create the strongest loyalty or the highest productivity, and so the initial purpose for the coaching sessions changed from learning to 'manage by walking about' to a much more fundamental process of how to help people feel included and significant.

Now consider a person with all-round high inclusion scores. Some of their traps and blind spots involve engaging in unnecessary interaction – something they may not realize since it fulfils their own unconscious desires. I worked with one consultant who found it really hard to write up her reports. Various behavioural and structural strategies (such as locking herself away, scheduling writing time) had failed to make a difference, and she was in danger of losing her job. Her own view of the situation was that she was too nice and not able to say 'no'. FIRO allowed us to explore this high inclusion and why she got so involved in everything. By reviewing every activity and meeting from the previous week we identified the ones she could have missed and hence had more time for the reports. When she imagined herself saying 'no' in these situations she quickly recognized a powerful feeling of being left out – a feeling she remembered from being the last to be chosen for teams at school. This fear of being left out meant that she took any opportunity to be 'in', but this was a strategy that was not very useful. We therefore worked on ways for her to feel included without having to attend everything. She came up with a strategy whereby her peers would keep her regularly informed and update her on meetings she missed. By also arranging 'interaction times', rather than 'writing times', she managed to become more effective. At this point she has still got her job and is enjoying it more.

Relationships

Consider a manager who was seeking coaching to develop her people management skills. During the coaching process one of her direct reports tendered his resignation after only six months in the job. His reasons were that there was not enough going on and people were too reserved. The manager was exasperated and surprised, saying, 'Well he wasn't the most outgoing himself!' We discussed whether he should attend the team build (planned previously) since he would still be working his notice. We agreed that it could be useful for both of them.

The FIRO Element B scores for the manager and the direct report, shown in Table 16.4, highlighted an incompatibility at a relational level. The manager has a low desire to initiate contact (I include people – 2) whereas the direct report has a very high desire to be included (I want people to include me – 9). The manager's style did not match the report's needs. She saw him as someone who was too reserved and 'always hovering'. Discussing their scores together they realized that he always expected her to approach and engage him more, while her approach was, 'If you don't ask, you don't want.' Although the discussion cleared the air, it was too late to affect this particular work relationship. However, her staff now report that she has become more attentive and that her espoused 'open door policy' now has more authenticity to it.

Table 16.4 FIRO Element B scores

	Manager's inclusion scores See	Want	Direct report's inclusion scores See	Want
Do	I include people	I want to include people	I include people	I want to include people
	3	3	3	8
Get	People include me	I want people to include me	People include me	I want people to include me
	2	3	5	9

Control

As previously described, this involves the amount of control and influence a person desires in their interactions with others. It is driven by a need to feel in control, self-determining and competent. How this affects work on direction, style and relationships is explored below.

Direction

People with a high desire for control like to reduce uncertainty and generally exert control in order to make things happen in the way they have planned. People with a low desire for control dislike too much predictability and what they perceive as too much structure. A career as an air traffic controller or working in a military may be more suited to the former than the latter.

Style

Consider a coachee with the FIRO profile shown in Table 16.5. This person started as a coachee because he was finding the work environment stressful (the noise, the bustle, the interruptions and the like). However, a visit to the workplace revealed a relaxed and pleasant environment. The coachee was disciplined, organized, purposeful, focused, pleasant and relatively accommodating. Colleagues would drop in, chat, ask him to do things and so on. In these interactions and interruptions, his smile appeared a little forced and afterwards he would appear pensive and tense. In later coaching sessions he admitted that he was constantly experiencing a dilemma: wanting to be attentive and nice, while desperately wanting to get on with his work.

Exploring his lack of openness about this exposed a tremendous fear of confrontation. The gap between 'I control people – 5' and 'I want to control people – 8' led to discussion about how his father had been extremely authoritarian. His survival strategy had been 'not to not challenge' and his need to feel in control had developed into a passive-aggressive style. FIRO helped him become aware of how his reactions in the workplace were an old

Table 16.5 Coachee's FIRO profile

	Coachee's control scores See	Want
Do	I control people 5	I want to control people 8
Get	People control me 9	I want people to control me 8

and familiar pattern of saying 'yes' even when he really meant 'no'. This insight refocused the coaching process on how to better manage his fear of confrontation.

Relationships

Consider a manager with the FIRO scores shown in Table 16.6. The scores shed light on his management style, which was to take almost any opportunity for getting people together and involving them in decisions. He was proud of his highly participative management style and was very critical of the higher echelons 'who are rarely seen outside of their office'. He saw himself as the voice of the people, the one 'in touch', one of the lads.

He was unaware of how inappropriate this was at times. People were frustrated by how long he took discussing issues without making decisions. The complexity of this manager's approach emerged through the use of FIRO. His highly inclusive behaviour was, in fact, a smokescreen. The discussion focused initially on the gap between 'I include people – 8' and 'I want to include people – 4'. However, the insight came through discussing his low control scores. He had a great fear of getting things wrong, and so would avoid taking responsibility. When he became a manager the pressure had increased, and his strategy had been to include more people to share the responsibility. Further coaching focused on allowing him the possibility of making mistakes and resulted in him becoming more decisive – and less tense.

Openness

As previously described, this involves the amount of disclosure and depth people seek in their interactions with others. It is driven by a desire for personal contact, intimacy and acceptance of who we truly are. How this affects work on direction, style and relationships is explored below.

Table 16.6 Manager's FIRO scores

| | Manager's inclusion scores | | Manager's control scores | |
	See	Want	See	Want
Do	I include people	I want to include people	I control people	I want to control people
	8	4	2	2
Get	People include me	I want people to include me	People control me	I want people to control me
	3	9	5	3

Direction

People with a high desire for openness like to feel they can connect at a personal level with the people around them. They like to share thoughts and feelings that go beyond the requirements of the immediate task or activity that may have brought them together. People with a low desire for openness dislike too much closeness and intimacy with too many people. A career as a spy or a customs officer would suit the latter more than the former.

Style and relationships

A successful board director for a large company was experiencing a crisis of motivation and had sought coaching in the hope of 're-energizing'. It was difficult to find a focus for the coaching until he completed FIRO Element B where he reported the scores shown in Table 16.7.

His reaction to the scores was focused on 'People are open with me (7)' and 'I want people to be open with me (3)' – initially saying that the scores were the wrong way round. His view of himself was as a very self-sufficient and independent person who was very discreet and private. He had three children; the eldest two had already left home and his youngest was shortly going off to university. One of his regrets was that his children only talked to him about immediate and practical things – hence his reaction to the scores since he would have liked his children to be more open with him than they were.

However, further exploration revealed that the scores strongly reflected his work environment, where people seemed to want to talk to him about lots of things he did not consider to be relevant. The feedback from work was that he had a reputation for being highly competent but rather distant, slow to make contact and highly driven. In fact the scores did more than reflect his approach at work because he realized that this is how he had been with his children while they were growing up. In effect, he had sold himself to success, and the cost in terms of open, trusting and rewarding relationships was high. His general lack of openness was coming to a head because, as his

Table 16.7 Board director's scores

	Director's openness scores See	Want
Do	I am open with people 1	I want to be open with people 4
Get	People are open with me 7	I want people to be open with me 3

youngest child was about to leave home, the lack of communication between him and his wife was becoming painfully obvious. In his words, he feared an empty and hollow home.

The biggest revelation for him came in discussing his score 'I want to be more open with people (4)' from a position of 'I am open with people (1)'. He had not consciously acknowledged this, and now realized that it was something he had been trying for a while, but found extremely hard, and he easily abandoned any attempt. At the core of this pattern, he admitted, was the fact that he did not think he was a very likeable person and so had defended himself by playing his cards very close to his chest. He had relied on success to build his self-esteem but agreed that this no longer seemed to be working for him. FIRO gave the coaching an important focus, and he is making small but significant progress. He has begun to take small risks in practising more openness and is finding that he likes himself better.

SUMMARY

FIRO Element B is the latest version of the FIRO questionnaires and represents the culmination of Will Schutz's thinking. It builds on his earlier work with FIRO-B and has proved to be one of the most useful tools for raising self-awareness in the coaching process for both coach and coachee. The combination of its great simplicity with its significant depth allows the skilled coach to move easily from specific and straightforward issues to long-term behaviour patterns that are sometimes deeply entrenched.

The power of FIRO Element B lies in its apparent transparency and straightforwardness. It is unthreatening and easy to administer – and yet, somehow, it gets at the parts that are often missed and can highlight issues that are barely conscious. FIRO theory provides a model for how behaviours act as signals for underlying feelings and issues of self-esteem. Bringing these into consciousness enables them to be unblocked, thus allowing change and development. As such, FIRO Element B uses behaviour as the tip of an iceberg, which helps identify little known issues that can then be addressed. The result is that the change process is accelerated.

Using FIRO has the great benefit that it not only enhances the process for the coachee but also has been found to greatly enhance the experience and skill of the coach – a win-win for all concerned.

Further reading

Childs, R and McDonald, AS (2007) *Manual for the Type Dynamics Indicator*, Team Focus Limited, Maidenhead

Guttman, L (1950) The basis for scalogram analysis, in *Measurement and Prediction: The American soldier*, Vol 4, ed SA Stouffer, L Guttman and EA Suchman, John Wiley, New York

Schutz, W (1958) *FIRO: A Three-Dimensional Theory of Interpersonal Behavior*, Rinehart, New York

Schutz, W (1967/1989) *Joy*, Ten Speed Press, Berkeley, Calif

Schutz, W (1979, 1982, 1988) *Profound Simplicity*, 3rd edn, WSA, Ventura, Calif

Schutz, W (1984) *The Truth Option: A practical technology for human affairs*, Ten Speed Press, Berkeley, Calif

Schutz, W (1987/1990/1998) *FIRO Element B: Behaviour guide*, Will Schutz Associates, California

Schutz, W (1992) Beyond FIRO-B: three new theory derived measures, *Psychological Reports*, 70, pp 915–37

Schutz, W (1998) *The Human Element: Self-esteem and the bottom line*, 2nd edn, McGraw Hill, New York

NOTES

1. From Bayesian Statistical theory.
2. Will Schutz emphasizes how the word 'needs' should not be taken to mean unchangeable.
3. The 1957 original version of the questionnaire (FIRO-B) used the term affection instead of openness. The similarity and difference between these constructs and why the term was changed will be explained later.
4. A note to FIRO-B users: FIRO-B users are used to the term affection instead of openness. Both terms cover a similar area – the underlying issue of likeability (ie, how much I like myself), but Will Schutz found that 'expressing and wanting affection' was too loose and that 'feeling affection' and 'behaving affectionately' were too easily confused. Openness was the clearest and cleanest way to add clarity to this area, a belief that is supported by the reduced correlations between openness and inclusion in FIRO Element B compared to Affection and Inclusion in FIRO-B.
5. The TDI is a questionnaire which identifies a person's preferences in terms of Jung's psychological types – see references.

17

Coaching with LSI

Quentin Jones

INTRODUCTION

Becoming aware of our behaviour, identifying and modifying thinking and behavioural styles that either support or sabotage our true potential, is at the heart of coaching with the Life Styles Inventory™(LSI) (Lafferty, 1987). Used at the beginning of coaching interventions, the LSI provides a clear – and at times challenging – starting measure of our thinking and behaviour. During the coaching intervention, the LSI provides an easy language to describe constructive and defensive behaviours, clearly prescribing what styles need development to achieve personal and professional goals. At the end of the coaching intervention, a retest can provide a valid measure of how the coachee has developed.

The LSI's strong cognitive and behavioural emphasis, visual presentation, and focus on generic 'life styles', makes it accessible to, and popular with, a wide range of clients and organizations. In business, the LSI has become a key tool in exposing how leader behaviour affect's organizational culture and subsequent business performance. Our research and consulting experience shows that LSI feedback, and subsequent coaching of the leader, is a critical driver of culture change.

This chapter will overview the LSI, its history, research basis, and how to enhance both the coach's and the coachee's effectiveness. While the following discussion primarily focuses on the LSI's use within business, its focus on generic Life Styles allows its use in a very broad range of settings.

THEORETICAL MODEL

The LSI was originally developed in the early 1970s by Dr J Clayton Lafferty, a clinical psychologist and founder of Human Synergistics. Lafferty asserted that people's self-images are shaped by their patterns of thinking – including their thoughts about how others see them (Sullivan, 1953), their perceptions of what they are versus what they think they should be (Rogers, 1961; Horney, 1945), and their beliefs about themselves (Ellis and Harper, 1961). Those who have healthy relationships with others and realistic views of themselves generally have positive self-images that enable them to strive toward self-actualization and become all that they can be. In contrast, those who have unhealthy inter-personal relationships, unrealistic standards of what they should be, or irra-tional and self-defeating beliefs about themselves have negative self-images that, in turn, prevent them from realizing their true potential. This is because they don't have a realistic understanding of what their true potential is.

Thus, monitoring and modifying personal thinking styles is an important strategy for the growth, development and realization of one's true potential – and the LSI provides the means for making this process more tangible.

Lafferty's research identified 12 styles or patterns of thinking and behaviour. Heavily influence by Louis Guttman's (1954) 'radix' approach to measurement, and Leary's (1957) application of this approach, he arranged 12 styles in a circle 'circumplex' so that the styles located next to one another are more similar and positively correlated than the styles that are placed further apart (the Human Synergistics Life Styles Inventory circumplex and style descriptions can be viewed at http://www.human-synergistics.com. au/content/products/circumplex/).

On the circumplex, the 12 life styles orientate around a concern for either task or people, and towards either higher-order needs for growth and satis-faction or lower-order needs for security and safety. This two-dimension framework was most influenced by the work of Horney (1945) and McClelland (1967) on needs, Leary (1957) on personality, and Maier (1952) on leadership styles.

More specifically, running horizontally across the circumplex is the people–task orientation derived from Stogdill's (1963) distinction between consideration and initiating structure, Blake and Mouton's (1964) concern for people versus production, and a distinction between employee-centred and production-centred management behaviour. The satisfaction–security orientation runs vertically down the circumplex and reflects Maslow's (1954) concept of lower and higher order needs.

Lafferty's original conceptual of four style 'clusters' was further refined by Dr Robert A Cooke's research in 1983 (Cooke, Rousseau and Lafferty, 1987) down to three: constructive styles (achievement, self-actualizing, humanistic-encouraging and affiliative), passive/defensive styles (approval, conventional, dependent, and avoidance), and aggressive/defensive styles (oppositional, power, competitive and perfectionistic).

THE LSI'S PSYCHOMETRIC PROPERTIES

Reliability

LSI reliability studies use internal consistency and interrater tests only. Test–retest measures are not suitable because the LSI measures personal styles that can change over time as the individual develops.

Internal consistency reliability

Studies have provided strong support for the internal consistency of the LSI scales. In one study, based on 1,000 respondents, alpha coefficients for the 12 LSI scales range from 0.80 to 0.88 (Cooke and Lafferty, 1981). In another study, based on 500 professional educators, alpha coefficients ranged from 0.79 to 0.87 with a mean of 0.85 (Nediger and Chelladurai, 1989).

Coefficient alphas of above 0.60 are generally viewed as acceptable; thus, these findings provide strong support for the internal consistency of the LSI scales.

Interrater reliability

In an analysis of variance completed on 556 managers (all levels) described by 2,922 'others', the F-statistic for this study was significant at 0.0001 level for all 12 styles, 'indicating that the variance in responses with the groups of others reporting on specific focal managers is smaller than the variance between these groups of respondents' (Cooke, Rousseau, and Lafferty, 1987, p: 5).

Validity

LSI validity studies focus on construct and criterion-related validity measures.

Construct validity

Simple construct validity was established using correlational analysis between the styles. The findings showed that styles close together on the circumplex had high positive correlations. As the distance between the styles increased, the correlation decreased to the point that those styles opposite each other had strong negative correlations (Cooke and Lafferty, 1981).

Further assessment of construct validity involves using factor analysis with loadings of above and below 0.4. Cooke *et al* (1987) demonstrated that the 12 LSI scales provide measures of three, more general, thinking and behavioural clusters: passive/defensive, constructive and aggressive/defensive. Other researchers (Ware, Leak and Perry, 1985; Nediger and Chelladurai, 1989) confirm these findings.

Criterion-related validity

Correlation or regression coefficients were found to be significant at $p<.05$ in a positive or negative direction consistent with the theoretical framework. For example, constructive styles have been found to be positively associated with manager effectiveness and negatively associated with managers' symptoms of strain, whereas passive/defensive and aggressive/defensive styles are negatively associated with manager effectiveness and positively associated with strain (Cooke and Rousseau, 1983; Gratzinger, Warren and Cooke, 1990).

Norming group

The LSI norm group reflects the characteristics of a management/senior professional group – the general target for most LSI based-based interventions. The LSI 1 (Self-Description) is normed on 9,207 adults, mostly from North America, but including people from Europe, Australia and New Zealand. The LSI 2 (Description by Others) percentile scores are based on 35,000 'others' who completed the LSI 2 by describing the style of these people.

THE LSI QUESTIONNAIRE

Inventory structure

The LSI includes two separate but complementary questionnaires. LSI 1 (Self-Description) is a self-report inventory designed to measure an individual's thinking styles and self-concept. LSI 2 (Description by Others) measures others' perceptions of the focal individual's behaviours.

Both the LSI 1 and LSI 2 inventories contain the same 240 items. Items are either single adjectives (eg 'thoughtful' or 'realistic') or phrases (eg 'easily influenced by friends' or 'overestimates ability'). Included with the 240 thinking and behavioural items are three other additional sections:

▮ *Outcome scales* (summary perceptions). These are 12 additional scales that report the focal individual's and others' perceptions, including effectiveness in current role, quality of relationship, stress and promotability.
▮ *Demographics*. Both inventories collect a range of key demographics, including gender, age, occupation and organizational level.
▮ *Satisfaction scales*. The LSI 1 contains an additional 10 satisfaction questions exploring the focal individual's satisfaction across a number of domains, including work, development opportunities, family, recreation and health.

Response scales

Respondents rate each item using a three-point modified Guttman (1954) scale, according to how accurately it describes the person. The LSI response options are:

2 – Like me/this person most of the time
1 – Like me/this person quite often
0 – Essentially unlike me/this person

where the 'like me' version relates to the LSI 1 Self-Description inventory and the 'like this person' version relates to the LSI 2 Description by Others inventory.

Summary perception and satisfaction scales use bi-polar Likert scales with seven and five points respectively.

Administration

LSI 1and LSI 2 can be administered either separately or together; either using paper inventories or hosting over the internet. Inventories take approximately 20–30 minutes to complete. General practice involves both inventories: LSI 1 to the focal individual, and five LSI 2 inventories to 'other' respondents.

Profiling styles

Once captured, the LSI item raw scores are normalized by plotting them onto the circumplex, creating 12 extensions from the centre. Each extension represents the style's strength as reported by the focal individual or as observed by others – presented as percentile scores on the circumplex.

Reports and support materials

Reports are generated, once all inventories are collected. Two basic report formats exist: hand or computer-drawn, supplied with a 100+ page self-development guide; and the STYLUS™ report, a 60-page computer-generated narrative.

LSI AND COACHES

The key to successful change is to understand the ultimate instrument of change – ourselves. Undertaking the LSI as a coach is not only critical to experiencing what coachees will experience but an essential step in the coach's own development. Without a deep sense of what we bring into the coaching conversation, our intra-psychic conflicts, our unresolved projections and transferences, our fears and defences, we limit our ability to support profound change in others.

Even with 20 years of working with the LSI, I am constantly aware of how my own defences play out in coaching conversations, and my need to remain constructive and present for the coachee. Recognizing that we are the ultimate change tool, we insist that new LSI coaches start with their own LSI. Incorporated into a 'reflective practice' accreditation module, we have seen extraordinary realizations and indeed transformations on the part of those undertaking their training to become LSI coaches.

In a recent sample of 107 coaches attending these reflective practice modules, we analysed their thinking and behaviour – what motivates them – and how this impacts their effectiveness.

Coaches' thinking and behaviour

In general, and perhaps not surprisingly, LSI 2 coach profiles are strongly people-orientated. Humanistic-encouraging and affiliative styles dominate, with weaker extensions on self-actualizing and achievement. With this people focus, the approval and avoidance styles dominate the passive/defensive styles. From a cluster perspective, coaches have above average constructive styles, with average to above average passive/defensive styles, and below average aggressive/defensive styles. By contrast, the average Australian/New Zealand manager/professional requiring coaching is more aggressive/defensive and passive/defensive and than constructive, with avoidance and oppositional being the primary and secondary styles.

Effective and ineffective coaches

Further analysis reveals that the most effective coaches display distinctive patterns of thinking and behaving. Coach effectiveness was measured using the LSI 2's (Description by Others) summary perception A: 'How effective is this person in their job or work assignment?' The top 25 per cent of coaches (n=26), with the highest scores on this effectiveness scale, had their LSI 2 results aggregated and plotted onto the circumplex. Similarly, the bottom 25 per cent of coaches – the least effective coaches – were combined and plotted.

These circumplexes clearly show that coach effectiveness arises from constructive thinking and behaviour, in particular, humanistic-encouraging and affiliative, while the passive/defensive styles of approval and avoidance reduce coach effectiveness. The following section explores each of the LSI styles in turn, reflecting on how each style supports or sabotages coach effectiveness when dealing with the average manager/professional coachee.

How the life styles support or sabotage coaching outcomes

Humanistic-encouraging (1 o'clock)

This is the coaching style that characterizes effective coaches. Based on the Rogerian attitude of 'unconditional positive regard for others' (Rogers, 1961), humanistic-encouraging coaches are empathetic, compassionate, willing to challenge and fiercely committed to the coachees' growth. A key tool is 'Socratic questioning', asking rich questions that cause the coachee to really analyse, speculate and think through his or her responses. The objective is to develop 'thinking competence' especially problem solving and decision making, the foundation of achievement, and the most effective management style (McCarthy, 2006).

Affiliative (2 o'clock)

Affiliative is the second strongest style in effective coaches. Highly affiliative coaches will enjoy the interpersonal relationship with their coachees; they like people and enjoy the social interaction. A small danger exists if the two parties in the coaching relationship become friends, potentially blurring coaching boundaries.

Approval (3 o'clock)

Approval can seriously limit the coaches' efficacy by their need for the coachees' approval. Fear of rejection will limit the coaches' willingness to confront and challenge the coachees' assumptions, thinking and actions. This is particularly challenging for high approval coaches dealing with aggressive/defensive coachees.

Conventional (4 o'clock)

Highly conventional coaches will limit their coaching interventions by sticking to 'tried and true' techniques, lacking flexibility in responding to coachees' changing needs, and lack creativity when assisting coachees' to develop solutions to their problems.

Dependent (5 o'clock)

Dependence will limit the coaches' willingness to appropriately take 'charge' of the coaching conversation. It is driven by an underlying belief that their effort can't make a difference for the coachees. In extreme cases, the coach will inappropriately allow the coachee to take 'charge' of the coaching session.

Avoidance (6 o'clock)

Avoidance leads to an unwillingness to confront or upset the coachee. A lack of true emotional and psychological engagement – being 'present' – will limit the coaches' efficacy. In coaches, approval will often be the underlying drive behind avoidance – the threat of disapproval limiting authentic engagement.

Oppositional (7 o'clock)

Oppositional behaviour rapidly erodes relationships and trust. While challenge is an important part of a coaching conversation, the oppositional style is experienced as critical, judgemental and cynical. Oppositional's 'opposite' on the circumplex is humanistic-encouraging, so coaches with this style will have a devastating impact on coachees' and their confidence to change.

Power (8 o'clock)

Power emerges when the coach feels insecure, taking over the coaching engagement to reduce their anxiety and maintain their status. This creates dependence, reducing the coachees' sense that their effort can make a difference.

Competitive (9 o'clock)

At the extreme, competitive coaching relationships degenerate into 'win–lose' posturing and arguments between two protagonists. Coaches need to manage their need to win the point, have the last word or intellectually 'trump' the coachee.

Perfectionistic (10 o'clock)

Driven to prove their perfection, coaches with this style tend to over-prepare and micro-manage every aspect of the coaching assignment. This leaves little room for flexibility and responsiveness in the coaching relationship.

Achievement (11 o'clock)

Developing the achievement style is critical for realizing goals and problem solving – a key outcome from solution-focused coaching approaches (de Shazer, 2005). Interestingly, while highly humanistic-encouraging coaches are effective at encouraging goal setting and problem solving in their coachees, coaches generally show a need to develop the achievement motivation in themselves.

Self-actualizing (12 o'clock)

Self-actualizing is a critical style for coaches, manifesting itself in an accepting, non-judgemental attitude, high personal integrity, and a sense of 'presence' with the coachee. At its heart, self-actualizing is how much the coaches invest in their own growth and development, ultimately what they want for their coachees.

So, the starting place for effective coaching is to be self-aware of our own thinking and behaviour, and to have the ability and skill to manage our own defensive reactions. Our data shows that the average coach will need to manage his or her need to seek approval and avoid conflict, especially in the face of aggressive/defensive management behaviour. The key development challenge for coaches is to maintain their strong humanistic-encouraging attitude and development of the achievement and self-actualizing styles. Achievement is the 'antidote' for approval; as we become clearer about what we want and develop the task skills to achieve it, pleasing others will become less important. Similarly, self-actualizing is avoidance's opposite, and as we express more of who we truly are, and seek to grow ourselves, withdrawing from others will diminish.

The ultimate challenge for coaches is to practise what we preach about change. As Quade and Brown (2001) describes, we need to recognize ourselves as the instruments of change and understand that 'until we practice change by changing our self, we will not truly be a leader for our coachees' change. This is what mastering change from the inside is all about.' The challenge for us as LSI coaches is to realize that every LSI coaching session is an opportunity to develop our own thinking and behaviour, and ultimately our own effectiveness as coaches and human beings.

USING LSI WITH COACHEES

The LSI is a powerful self-development tool capable of creating real individual transformation. In this section, we explore the differing levels coaches can work with the LSI, how to structure a coaching intervention, and the basics of debriefing and interpreting an LSI circumplex.

Beyond knowing and doing

So, what gives LSI its power to change individuals, indeed, to transform? How does a coachee with an LSI report not only get insights about how to be a better manager but gain deep insights about his or her very being in the world? The answer lies in the LSI's capacity to address three learning domains: knowing, doing and being.

Knowing

The knowing domain of learning deals with the 'what', that is, we 'know' more about a particular subject. Knowing is the primary focus of most educational and training activities. Ultimately, learning confined to the knowing domain produces limited change. Plenty of people know a lot about a subject, leadership for example, but it does not follow that they know how to lead. This knowing–doing gap describes well the human condition of knowing what we should do, but failing to do it (Pfeffer and Sutton, 2000).

Doing

Knowing is not enough; we need to translate knowing into doing. Development activities that include skills development, experiential and action learning methodologies go some way to enhancing doing. However, significant resources are expended on developing managers' skills with little transfer to the workplace. So, what is the key to unlocking behaviour change, if knowledge and skills training isn't enough?

Being

Being domain-learning goes beyond knowing and doing to the deeper examination of consciously and unconsciously held beliefs, assumptions and worldviews (Mezirow, 1991). This deep – and sometimes difficult – learning often only occurs when precipitated by significant life events: loss of a job, a sense of failure in not realizing our dreams in mid-life, organizational change and the like (Kets de Vries, 2006). If the LSI is administered at the time of this coalescing discontent, its impact can be dramatic and life changing. With expert coaching the LSI can provide a safe structure for coachees to understand themselves, their thinking and behaviour, their unconscious assumptions and beliefs. Importantly, the LSI can provide a language and road map to navigate through these challenging times.

Additionally, being-domain 'aha' moments are the essential triggers for personal transformation, and when they happen in leaders, are the essential foundations for cultural transformation in organizations (Jones *et al*, 2006).

STRUCTURING AN LSI COACHING INTERVENTION

In this section, we look at how to structure an LSI coaching intervention using the test–action–retest framework. For the purposes of this discussion, we make a distinction between 'debriefing' and 'coaching' LSI results. Debriefing occurs during the test phase, and is the process of introducing the LSI, discussing results and gaining initial awareness by the coachee. Coaching is the ongoing process of actioning the debriefed results, culminating in retesting.

Test (LSI debriefing)

At the beginning of a coaching assignment, establish context, boundaries and confidentiality, thereby clarifying the coachee's needs, challenges and goals. The first LSI measure (test) establishes current thinking and behaviour, and contributes to understanding 'reality' (R) in coaching models, such as, GROW (Whitmore, 2002). For LSI 'debriefing', we recommend two sessions separated by at least a week.

A useful model at this stage is the 3A's of change: awareness, acceptance and action. Debriefing covers the first two stages: awareness and acceptance. Debriefing must first create awareness. Generally, taking one to two hours, the coach needs to establish a basic awareness of the LSI model, and its cognitive/behaviour assumptions (Stimulus + Thinking = Response), and have the coachees establish an initial understanding of their feedback. See the next section for a more detailed overview for debriefing the LSI.

Acceptance is both a psychological and an emotional process. Upon receiving their feedback, coachees may experience confusion, dissonance and emotional upset. A framework to better understand this process is Kubler-Ross's (1969) grief stages: shock, denial, anger, bargaining, depression and acceptance.

The passing of time is essential for meaning making, and emotional resolution. Acceptance can take only minutes or sometimes years, and can happen in the most unlikely times and places.

Action (coaching)

Once some level of acceptance has occurred, coaching can start. Revisit goals and outcomes, and establish action plans. The LSI's self-development guide provides structure, direction and improvement ideas.

The structure of post-debriefing coaching sessions varies, but experience shows from six to eight one-hour sessions, fortnightly or monthly is optimal. This is where coaching techniques and models, such as solution-focused ones (de Shazer, 2005), come into play, supporting behaviour change and goal achievement.

Retest

LSI retesting is recommended 12–18 months after initial testing. At this time, go back and review agreed goals set at the beginning of the intervention, that is, in the test phase. Retesting provides tangible feedback about changes in thinking and behaviour. It also holds the coachee accountable for change, and provides an opportunity to celebrate, when progress is made.

DEBRIEFING THE LSI

This section describes a structure to follow when debriefing the LSI. As discussed, the LSI debrief focuses on achieving a basic level of awareness and acceptance in the test phase, before proceeding to coaching in the action phase.

Orientations

The orientations are the starting place for reviewing a coachee's LSI. First, with the LSI 1, illustrate the orientations by splitting the coachee's circumplex with a pen placed vertically down the middle from the 12 o'clock to the 6 o'clock positions. This split indicates the strength of either a people (right-half), or a task (left-half) orientation. Generally, managers show a stronger task orientation, pointing to development needs in the people orientation. Highly effective people display a balance of task and people styles in the constructive cluster.

The LSI's second orientation is the horizontal split running from 9 o'clock to 3 o'clock. This split indicates to what extent the individual's thinking and behaviour is focused on meeting either their satisfaction needs (top half), or security needs (bottom half). Coachees with a strong security orientation are focusing most of their emotional and psychological energy to protect themselves from a threatening external environment.

Clusters

The three coloured style-clusters are the most visually impactful aspect of the LSI. The constructive styles (coloured blue) are located at the top of the circumplex, passive/defensive styles (coloured green) are located on the lower right side of the circumplex, and aggressive/defensive styles (coloured red) are located on the lower left side of the circumplex.

Cluster colours provide a simple language to discuss thinking and behaviour, and their impact on performance. Effective individuals rate highly on the constructive 'blue' styles (well above the 50th percentile), have lesser amounts of aggressive/defensive 'red' behaviour (under the 50th percentile) and very little passive/defensive 'green' behaviour (around the 25th percentile or less) (McCarthy, 2006). Hence, development activities focus on increasing the 'blue' styles while reducing the 'green' and 'red' styles.

Primary and secondary styles

Next, focus on the individual styles. Identify the most extended styles: the furthest style from the centre is the 'primary' style, the next longest the 'secondary' style. Describe these styles and any others that are either similarly high, or very low, by way of contrast. It is important for acceptance building to question and discuss whether the coachee is aware of these thinking and behavioural styles, and can recall specific examples. During any interactions, coaches should be very sensitive to interactions with the coachees, listening and watching for patterns of speech, behaviour and stories that illustrate their dominant styles. Sensitive presentation back of the coach's observation can significantly increase coachee awareness and acceptance. For example, coachees whose primary style is oppositional are quick to criticize most things, including the lack of easy parking, the LSI diagnostic, and even the coach doing the debrief!

Mutually reinforcing styles, bow ties and opposites

Depending on the relative location of the primary and secondary styles, important patterns can be identified, including 'mutually reinforcing', 'bow tie', and 'opposite' styles.

Mutually reinforcing styles are driven by the same needs and orientation. For example, a combination of the constructive styles would be mutually reinforcing (eg, achievement and self-actualizing). Mutually reinforcing styles are an advantage when they are constructive (because they similarly promote healthy and effective thinking and behavioural patterns), but are a disadvantage when they are defensive (because they further reinforce passive or aggressive thinking and behavioural patterns).

Bow ties are characterized by primary and secondary styles driven by the same needs for security, but different orientations (task versus people). These combinations have a cumulative effect in promoting self-defeating thinking and behavioural patterns. For example, the perfectionistic (10 o'clock) and conventional (4 o'clock) 'compliance' bow tie reflects a strong fear of failure and strengthens highly risk-averse thinking and behavioural patterns. Similarly, the competitive (9 o'clock) and approval (3 o'clock) 'salesman' bow tie reflects a strong need to win the approval of others by aggressively striving for recognition, acceptance and attention. While useful for describing a distinctive psychological pattern, bow ties are driven by needs for security, and are neither desirable nor effective.

Opposite styles are driven by different needs (satisfaction versus security) and different orientations (task versus people). Thus, opposite style combinations are:

▌ achievement and dependence;
▌ self-actualizing and avoidance;
▌ humanistic-encouraging and oppositional;
▌ affiliative and power.

Development paths to effectiveness

The opposites are very useful for identifying development paths. Where there are long extensions in the defensive end of an opposite, a development path is clear. For example, if dependent is the primary style, and achievement is low, then the coachee should focus on developing personal goals, problem-solving skills and an attitude of 'my effort makes a difference'.

As a rule of thumb, always start developing plans with at least one constructive style. This will produce a pull effect on the defensive styles. Where coachees have exclusively focused on reducing defensive behaviours, they report some reduction in the 'red' and 'green' styles, but little improvement in the 'blue' styles, and little progress towards their broader goals.

Opposites are also useful for identifying patterns of cognitive conflict and stress. For example, equally large extensions on both achievement and dependence indicate strong inner conflicts about one's belief that our effort makes a difference. Such conflicts are generally driven by aggressive management styles that produce unsupportive defensive organizational cultures (McCarthy, 2006). This tension has three potential paths for resolution. The first option is to go 'green', and choose to succumb to the boss's aggression and the culture's passivity. The second is to become 'red', and aggressively argue and oppose their impositions. However, this is a short-term strategy, if the boss chooses to exercise positional power and remove the direct report. The third 'blue' option is to choose to remain constructive and 'manage up'. In the long term, if this doesn't produce results, highly constructive individuals will choose to find alternative environments that support constructive behaviour.

Development paths will vary greatly depending on the highly individual circumplex patterns. It is important to see the circumplex as an ever-changing 'system' with complex and dynamic style relationships. More complex development paths occur with the bow-ties styles. For example, the conventional style doesn't have an opposite. In this case, examine the constructive 'blue' styles and find the least extended style – commonly this is self-actualizing. In such cases, the coachee needs to develop and express a greater sense of self, their own preferences, values and behaviours, and not those of their societal, familial or organizational conditioning.

Developing constructive thinking

The LSI is premised on the idea that thinking drives behaviour, and behaviour creates the results we experience in our lives. To change the results, we need to change our habitual patterns of thinking and behaviour; and there lies the challenge – changing habits.

Clay Lafferty posited that the human mind habitually processes 5,000 to 8,000 thought 'strings' daily. However, like all habits that have been 'learnt', our thinking habits can be 'unlearnt' – with effort and determination. Coachees should be reminded that the LSI is only a 'snapshot in time' of these thinking habits. A powerful question to ask is whether their thinking was different in the past. Most people will answer in the affirmative, and with this acknowledge the 'plasticity' of their minds, and their ability to choose new ways of thinking and behaving.

The goal of coaching with the LSI is to help the coachee identify old defensive patterns and replaced them with new constructive patterns. Defensive thinking will have an 'irrational' theme to it. For example, the perfectionistic style is associated with extremes about performing tasks to impossibly high standards. This often sets up a 'self-fulfilling prophecy' leading the individuals to fail in their pursuit of their own impossible standards (Ellis and Harper, 1961). Defensive thinking needs to be replaced by more 'rational' achievement thinking, with goals and standards that are realistic but challenging. Useful tools include cognitive behavioural approaches, for example, challenging irrational beliefs, use of verbal affirmations and the like.

Summary perception and satisfaction questions

Depending on the flow of the LSI debrief, reference to the summary perception (measures of outcomes) and satisfaction questions can contribute significantly in building awareness and gaining acceptance of the results. Poignant relationships to point out are the ways that the achievement style correlates highly with effectiveness and promotability, and that oppositional styles sabotage quality of relationships, and the negative impact of the defensive styles on professional and personal satisfaction and happiness.

REFLEXIVITY: THE KEY TO INDIVIDUAL TRANSFORMATION

As we have discussed, general or specific 'dis-ease' about one's life is an essential catalyst for action. As human beings we need to reach a 'tipping point' where we realize that the cost of staying the same has become greater than the cost of changing and experimenting with new behaviours (Kets de Vries, 2006).

This emerging realization that all is not well, occurs as we come to realize that things are not as we thought. This capability to 'become aware of self in relation to others and to the organization' is reflexivity. The LSI is a critical tool in developing this capability, especially in leaders. Dunphy, in Jones *et al* (2006), reports that the development of reflexivity is a key capability to achieving organizational cultural transformation and performance improvement.

The LSI develops reflexivity by bringing into awareness the mismatch between self-concept and the observation of others. Comparisons between LSI 1 and LSI 2 show only a third of people report a good match between self and other descriptions (McCarthy, 2002). The LSI's ability to delve beyond the intellectual into the 'being' domain to expose profound value and attitudinal contradictions often creates enough cognitive dissonance and emotional turmoil to precipitate action for resolution and change.

The Coaches role in supporting reflexivity

To be effective, coachees need coaching support in all three learning domains:

- *knowing*: through introducing new facts, information and relevant stories;
- *doing*: through skill development via role playing new skills or with 'homework' activities;
- *being*: by helping the coachee navigate the 'cognitive dissonance' created by the LSI feedback, for which reflexivity is a key capability.

Coaches develop reflexivity in their coachees by constantly encouraging self-awareness of thinking and behaviour, and its impact on self and others. Feedback is critical to this process.

SUMMARY

The coaching phenomenon is a relatively new one, especially in business. Equally new is the idea that human thinking and behaviour can be measured and changed. The combination of these two emerging practices offers significant benefits to individuals seeking developmental coaching.

Most importantly, the LSI provides both coach and coachee with a valid and reliable measure of thinking and behaviour, a baseline from which to start a coaching intervention. During the subsequent coaching sessions, the LSI provides a powerful visual roadmap to improve effectiveness, and an enriched language to describe and work with thinking and behaviour. At the end of the coaching assignment it provides a true measure of what has been achieved or what requires further attention.

The LSI's flexible structure allows it to be used in differing learning domains: knowing, doing and being. Especially powerful is the LSI's ability to operate at the being domain. It does this by bringing into consciousness, and with masterful coaching, unblocking dysfunctional beliefs, assumptions and worldviews that so often limit knowing and doing domain learning.

References

Blake, R and Mouton, J (1964) *The Managerial Grid*, Gulf Publishing Company, Inc. Houston, TX

Cooke, RA and Lafferty, JC (1981) *Level I: Life Styles Inventory: An instrument for assessing and changing the self-concept of organizational members*, Human Synergistics Plymouth, MI

Cooke, RA and Rousseau, DM (1983) Relationship of life events and personal orientations to symptoms of strain, *Journal of Applied Psychology*, **68**(3), 446–58

Cooke, RA, Rousseau, DM and Lafferty, JC (1987) Thinking and behavioral styles: consistency between self-descriptions and descriptions by others, *Educational and Psychological Measurement*, **47**, 815–23 de Shazer, S (2005) *More than Miracles: The state of the art of solution-focused therapy*, Haworth Press, Binghampton, New York

Ellis, A and Harper, R (1961) *A Guide to Rational Living*, Prentice-Hall, Englewood Cliffs, NJ

Gratzinger, PA, Warren, RA and Cooke, RA (1990) Psychological orientations and leadership: thinking styles that differentiate between effective and ineffective managers, in *Measures of Leadership*, ed KB Clark and MB Clark, pp 239–48, Leadership Library of America, West Orange, NJ

Guttman, L (1954) A new approach to factor analysis: the radix, in Paul Katz *et al* (1959)

Horney, K (1945) *Our Inner Conflicts*, W W Norton & Company, New York

Jones, Q, Dunphy, D, Fishman, R, Larne, M and Canter, C (2006) *In Great Company: Unlocking the secrets of cultural transformation*, Human Synergistics International, Sydney

Kets de Vries, M (2006) *The Leader on the Couch, : A clinical approach to changing people and organizations*, John Wiley & Sons, West Sussex

Kubler-Ross, E (1969) *On Death and Dying*, Simon and Schuster, New York

Lafferty, JC (1987) *Life Styles Inventory*, Human Synergistics International, Plymouth, MI

Leary, TF (1957) *Interpersonal Diagnosis of Personality: a functional theory and methodology for personality evaluation*, Ronald, New York

Maier, NRF (1952) *Principles of Human Relations*, John Wiley, New York

Maslow, A (1954) *Motivation and Personality*, Harper & Row, New York

McCarthy, S (2002) *Leading High Performance Cultures: Measuring leadership style through the Life Styles Inventory Human Synergistics*, Australia / New Zealand Publication, Wellington

McCarthy, S (2006) *The Culture–Performance Connection: The research results book 2003–2006*, Australia and New Zealand Human Synergistics, Australia / New Zealand Publication, Wellington

McClelland, D (1967) *The Achieving Society*, Free Press, New York

Mezirow, J (1991) *The Transformational Dimensions of Adult Learning*, Jossey-Bass, San Francisco

Nediger, WG and Chelladurai, P (1989) Life Styles Inventory: its applicability in the Canadian context, *Educational and Psychological Measurement*, **49**, 901–09

Pfeffer, J and Sutton, RI (2000) *The Knowing–Doing Gap: How smart companies turn knowledge into action*, Harvard Business School Publishing, Boston

Quade, K and Brown, RM (2001) *The Conscious Consultant*, Jossey Bass, San Francisco

Rogers, Carl (1961) *On Becoming a Person*, Houghton-Mifflin, Boston

Stogdill, Ralph M (1963) *Manual for the Leader Behavior Description Questionnaire: Form XII*, Ohio State University, Bureau of Business Research, Columbus, Ohio

Sullivan, HS (1953) *Interpersonal Theory of Psychiatry*, W W Norton, New York

Ware, ME, Leak, GK and Perry, NW (1985) *Life Styles Inventory: Evidence for its factorial validity*, Creighton University, Omaha, NE

Whitmore, J (2002) *Coaching for Performance: Growing people, performance and purpose*, Nicholas Brealey Publishing, London

18

An overview of psychometric questionnaires

Jonathan Passmore

This book contains a small sample of the tools and questionnaires that can be productively used in the coaching relationship to aid the coachee. The items we have included are not recommended or endorsed by their inclusion. The Association for Coaching, the contributors and the editor do not recommend one product over another, and suggest that coaches review all suitable items on the market before identifying the product which best meets their coachees' needs. Our exclusion of items was a reflection of the limited space available in the book, and a wealth of questionnaires, competency frameworks and psychometrics that are available in the English language.

In this section we have attempted to identify the main products which coaches may wish to find out more about, but which there was not space to include within a chapter. Table 18.1 provides a short summary of other instruments, with the main theory identified alongside the primary scales used in the questionnaire. We have also attempted to list the publishers with contact details for each. The list is restricted to personality and competency questionnaires. However, it should be noted that there are a wealth of ability based questionnaires available. These cover areas such as verbal reasoning, numerical reasoning and inductive reasoning. While these are less frequently used in coaching, they may be of value to coachees, for example, in helping a coachee prepare for an assessment centre or gather data on their competence, compared with others, in a specific area, such as verbal reasoning.

However, no list of this kind is perfect and we apologize for errors and omissions, in the original list or as contact details change.

The nature of this book is such that the reader is likely to dip in and out rather than read it cover to cover. This table follows this approach. As in reviewing the instruments included in the book, we would encourage the reader in reviewing the instruments in the table to consider: how will this instrument or questionnaire help my coachee to move towards their goals?

Table 18.1

Name of tool	Name of publishers	Website	Brief description
16PF	OPP	www.opp.co.uk	The 16PF questionnaire was developed by Raymond Cattell in 1949 and is widely available across the globe. The instrument assesses 16 factors of personality. These are: Warmth, Reasoning, Emotional Stability, Dominance, Liveliness, Rule-consciousness, Social Boldness, Sensitivity, Vigilance, Abstractedness, Privateness, Open to change, Perfectionism, Abstractness, Apprehension, Tension and Self Reliance.
California Psychological Inventory	OPP	www.opp.co.uk	The CPI aims to give 'a description of personality which is relevant to the prediction and understanding of interpersonal behaviour in any setting, culture or circumstance'. It produces a description in terms of 'folk concepts' that people tend to use as part of daily life to describe personality and explain behaviour.
cdaq	CDA	www.cda.org.uk	cdaq is based on the neurolinguistic programming (NLP) concept of a 'metaprogramme' which is an approach to understanding the world and responding to it.
Cognitive Thinking Styles	Cognitive Fitness Consultancy	www.cognitivefitness.co.uk	Thinking Styles is a self-reported occupational psychometric instrument designed to measure individuals' preferences for the ways in which they prefer to think and to develop understanding. The questionnaire is based on three clusters; Sensory, People and Task. The questionnaire has four Sensory dimensions: Visual, Auditory, Kinaesthetic and Digital. It has eight People focused dimensions: Internally referenced, Externally referenced, Self referenced, Altruistic, Conforming, Challenging, Collaborative and Competitive. It has 14 Task dimensions: Detailed, Creative, Strategic, Logical, Options, procedures, Towards, Troubleshooting, proactive, Reactive, Simplicity, Complexity, Sameness and Difference.

Name of tool	Name of publishers	Website	Brief description
EQi	MHS	http://eqi.org/mhs.htm	Eqi is an emotional intelligence test developed by Bar-On and is a self-report questionnaire. Based on more than 20 years of research worldwide, the BarOn EQ-i® inventory examines an individual's emotional and social strengths and weaknesses. It has five main components – intrapersonal and interpersonal, stress management, adaptability, general mood, positive impression – and an inconsistency index. The instrument is useful for developing EQ in coachees, helping them reflect on their emotional strengths and identify areas for development.
LQF	NHS	http://www.nhsleadership qualities.nhs.uk/	The NHS Leadership Qualities Framework was developed specifically for the NHS and sets the standard for outstanding leadership in the service. The original qualities were developed from research with existing NHS chief executives. The LQF describes the qualities expected of existing and aspiring leaders both now and in the future. The framework consists of 15 qualities in three main scales: setting direction, delivering the service and personal qualities. The sub-scales are leading change, holding others to account, empowering others, effective and strategic influencing and collaborative working, which are part of delivering the service; self-belief, self-management, self-awareness, drive for improvement and personal integrity which are part of personal qualities; and broad scanning, intellectual flexibility, seizing the future, political astuteness and driving for results, which are part of setting direction.
McCann Window	TMS Development	www.tmsdi.co.uk	The Window on Work Values Profile has been created specifically for the workplace. Based on the research of Dr D McCann, it is a 64 item

	Publisher	URL	Description
on Work Values Profile	International Ltd		self-report questionnaire designed to elicit a hierarchy of value types for an individual. A total of eight different value types are assessed by the measure; these are compliance, conformity, collectivism, equality, empowerment, independence, individualism and authority.
MLQ	MLQ Pty Ltd	http://www.mlq.com.au/	The Multi-Factor Leadership Questionnaire (MLQ) is based on the Leadership Model developed by Bernard Bass and Bruce Avolio. It is a short and comprehensive survey of 45 items that measures a full range of leadership styles. The questionnaire can be completed by the manager and raters from which the report is generated. The questionnaire focuses on four dimensions: transformational leadership, transactional leadership, non-transactional leadership, outcomes of leadership, such as effort, effectiveness and satisfaction. With these four main dimensions the questionnaire reviews a set of sub-scales. For the transformational leadership scale these are: idealized (attributes), idealized (behaviours), inspirational motivation, intellectual stimulation and individualized consideration. For transactional leadership these are: contingent rewards, management-by-exception (active) and management-by-exception (passive). For non-transactional leadership there is one sub-scale laissez-faire. For outcomes of leadership there are three sub-scales: extra effort, effectiveness and satisfaction.
NEO	Hogrefe (UK) Ltd	www.hogrefe.co.uk	Neo is an international five-factor personality questionnaire has been adapted and standardized for the UK business market from the USA. Itexplores six facet scores for each of the five factors. The five broad domains measured are Extraversion; Negative Emotion; Openness to Experience; Agreeableness and Conscientiousness.

Name of tool	Name of publishers	Website	Brief description
Occupational Relationships Profile	Selby & Mills Ltd	www.selbymills.co.uk	The Occupational Relationships Profile is a personality trait measure with normative rating. The ORP was designed to measure a person's social interaction within the workplace.
Occupational Personality Profile	Psytech International Ltd	www.psytech.co.uk/	The OPP is a personality measure for use in occupational settings. It measures nine personality dimensions and has a distortion scale to help detect socially desirable responding.
Orpheus	Harcourt Assessment	www.harcourtassessment.co.uk	Orpheus is a big five measure of personality in the workplace. It also contains seven integrity subscales and an impression management scale.
Personal Profile Analysis	Thomas International Ltd	www.thomas international.net	The Personal Profile Analysis (PPA) is a 24-item, self-completion, and multi-scale instrument, designed for the assessment of work-related dispositions. American in origin, the PPA is an integral part of a system for use by line managers in work interviews.
Psygna	Business Minds UK	www.businessminds.co.uk	Psygna is a multi-trait, normative, self-report personality questionnaire with 10 bipolar scales. The underlying constructs, based on those measured by existing personality questionnaires, including the 16PF, were confirmed by factor analysis.
The Quest Profiler	ERAS Limited	w.erasltd.co.uk	The Quest Profiler is designed to be a new personality test – one that is 'determinedly modern' in that it includes scales like 'empowerment' that concur with current management thinking and which generates a report output that is comprehensible to non-expert readers.
Quintax	Stuart Robinson & Associates	www.sr-associates.com	Quintax is a self-report personality assessment intended to tap the Big-Five structure of personality, with a social desirability scale.

Rapid Personality Questionnaire	Psychometric Services Ltd	www.psl.co.uk	The RPQs are designed to give a reliable, valid, quick and simple-to-use general purpose profile of a subjects operational personality within a work setting. The RPQ1 and RPQ2 includes the same 80 adjectives, but for the RPQ1 half the items are answered in terms of 'How you feel you really are at work' while the other half are answered in terms of 'How you think others at work see you'. RPQ1 is therefore intended for use in employee development and selection whereas RPQ2 is intended just for selection.
RQ	OCG	http://www.ocg.co.uk	Relationship Q$\mathring{A}$ (RQ) is a relationship management questionnaire which is designed to improve the ability of managers and people at work in managing relationships. It is different from many of the tools featured in this list in that its focus is relationships rather than personalities. The results from using RQ provide a means of understanding why some relationships work well and some do not, the underlying approach to managing relationships, and thus can provide a basis for a discussion with the coachee about how they can go about improving them.
Strengths Deployment Inventory	Personal Strengths Publishing	http://www.personal strengths.co.uk	SDI identifies for individuals their personal strengths and motivations and how these relate to those of their colleagues – whether things are going well or badly. It demonstrates how to use these strengths effectively to improve working or personal relationships with others. The SDI provides insights into how to recognize the first signs of conflict in others and shows how to respond appropriately to resolve the dispute before it gets out of hand or unwittingly causes further antagonism. These elements can be usefully explored either in one-to-one coaching sessions or as part of group coaching.

Name of tool	Name of publishers	Website	Brief description
Team Performance Profile	TMS Development International Ltd	www.tmsdi.co.uk	The Team Performance Profile is based on the Dr C M Margerison and Dr DJ McCann Team Management Profile. It is a multi-rater instrument designed to be used to give 360-degree feedback on a team's performance.

Those interested in psychometrics can also visit the website managed by the British Psychological Society, www.psychtesting.org.uk which lists tests available in the United Kingdom.

Psychometrics glossary

360-degree feedback Process where one individual (employee or coachee) receives *feedback* from various sources, such as managers, co-workers and customers.

Ability test Psychological test that measures a person's mental capacity. Examples of these include verbal reasoning, numerical reasoning and spatial awareness.

APA Abbreviation for American Psychological Association. This is the professional and regulatory body for psychologists in the United States. The APA can be contacted at www.apa.org.

Appraisal Organizational activity where employees are assessed by at least one other person on past performance on agreed indicators and targets; this usually results in a training or development plan.

Appraisee Individual who is appraised by a manager.

APS Abbreviation for Australian Psychological Society. This is the professional and regulatory body for psychologists in Australia. The APS can be contacted at www.psychology.org.au.

Archetype In psychology, an archetype is a model of a person, personality, or behaviour; this was advanced by the psychologist Carl Jung, whose types have become knows as 'Jungian archetypes'.

Big Five Common abbreviation used for the five-factor model of personality. This takes a psychometric approach, where behaviours that define human behaviour are summarized statistically into five factors. This model underlies popular psychometric instruments such as the Hogan or 16PF®.

BPS Abbreviation for British Psychological Society. This is the professional and regulatory body for psychologists in the United Kingdom. It can be contacted at www.bps.org.uk.

CIPD The Chartered Institute of Personnel and Development is the professional body for human resource professionals in the United Kingdom. The CIPD can be contacted at www.cipd.co.uk.

Clinical need Behaviour or trait that deviates from normal behaviour and requires specialist care or intervention.

Competency Set of observable work behaviours that can be described with a label; an example is 'communication skills'.

Emotional intelligence Concept initiated by Salovey and Mayer, but popularized by Daniel Goleman. This suggests that there is a separate strand of intelligence that is concerned with how we understand our own and each other's emotions, and that is separate from general intelligence.

Fab Four This is the personality model underlying the Wave Personal Styles Questionnaire.

Face validity Particular form of *validity* that refers to whether something is judged as acceptable by users.

Feedback Communication process where a message is transmitted from one party to another.

Feedback message Information that is conveyed from one party to another during feedback.

Feedback recipient The individual that receives any feedback; in the context of this book, usually an employee or the coachee.

Feedback sender The individual or individuals that are giving feedback to someone else.

Freedom from bias The fourth of the *psychometric principles*, which refers to whether a measurement produces the same results for all people.

Great Eight *Competency* model as conceived by Rainer Kurz and Dave Bartram, holding that generic competencies hold true across different jobs and organizations.

Individual difference Personal characteristic that is related to sets of behaviour, such as someone's level of self-esteem or self-belief.

Intelligence This is a particular concept of *ability*, popularized by organizations such as Mensa, and researched by many psychologists. It is sometimes described as G, which stands for General Intelligence. Some believe that intelligence is only one factor, while other theorists, such as those of the *emotional intelligence* school, believe that there are many sides to this concept.

Level A Certificate of competence issued by the *BPS* that qualifies practitioners to use ability tests in the workplace.

Level B Certificate of competence issued by the *BPS* that qualifies practitioners to use a personality questionnaire that pertains to a particular model in the workplace.

Personal development plan (PDP) Document that is agreed by coach or manager and employee or coachee, containing a formalized set of activities to be undertaken by the coachee/employee to address development needs.

Personality questionnaire Questionnaire that measures people's underlying stable characteristics or preferences in an explicit, observable way.

Psychometrics The science of measuring behaviour and ability adhering to the four *psychometric principles*.

Psychometric model (of personality) This holds that a model of personality can be derived statistically by summarizing information (such as typical human behaviours or attributes).

Psychometric principles These are *reliability, validity, standardization* and *freedom from bias*.

Reliability First of the *psychometric principles*, which refers to whether a measurement is consistent in itself, across time and across people.

Standardization The third *psychometric principle*, which refers to whether a measurement has been set up in an objective and consistent manner.

Stress State experienced by an individual where demands exceed the resources that the individual has to deal with them. Associated with a range of mental and physical symptoms.

Trait instrument A *personality questionnaire* that measures to what degree people behave on different scales, such as 'extroversion' (how outgoing someone is).

Type instrument A *personality questionnaire* which classifies people into different types; this assumes that such types remain stable over time.

Validity Second of the *psychometric principles*, which refers to whether something measures what it says it does.

The Association for Coaching

AC MEMBERSHIP BENEFITS

The Association for Coaching (AC) is one of the leading independent and non-profit-making professional bodies aimed at promoting best practice and raising the awareness and standards of coaching, while providing support for its members. Since its inception, the AC has experienced rapid growth, and has become known for its leadership within the market and responsiveness to both market and members' needs. Becoming a member gives the opportunity to be involved in an established, yet dynamic, membership organization dedicated to excellence and coaching best practice.

The AC is a membership organization for professional coaches, coach training/service providers, and organizations involved in building coaching capability. The areas covered include *Executive, Business, Personal, Speciality* and *Team Coaching*.

Below are just some of the many benefits coaches and companies can access by joining the Association for Coaching:

- *Gain new customers and referrals:* through a dedicated web page profile on the AC online membership directory.*
- *Regular seminars and events:* monthly workshops and forums across the United Kingdom on current relevant topics. This allows an opportunity to network, compare notes and gain knowledge from industry experts and colleagues. Members are entitled to discounts on attendance fees.

- *Accreditation:*** eligible to *apply* for AC individual coach accreditation after being approved as a full AC Member for at least six months.
- *International AC conference*: attend the AC's annual conference (at discounted rates) with international speakers drawn from top coaching experts, which provides an opportunity to network, compare best practice and share knowledge with other HR and coaching professionals.
- *Press/VIP contacts:* raise the profile of coaching through PR activities, through the influential honorary board and contacts across the AC.
- *Member newsletters*: increase knowledge through sharing best practice and keeping abreast of the latest thinking and learning in the *Quarterly AC Bulletin* and *AC Update.*
- *Co-coaching*: increase coaching skills through attendance at our in-house co-coaching skills development programmes.
- *AC forums:* an opportunity to participate, build coaching skills and receive confidential support from other AC members via the online or co-coaching forums.
- *Industry/market research:* gain first-hand knowledge of latest industry trends via the AC's market research reports.
- *Dedicated AC website*: gain access to up-to-date AC activities, members' events, reference materials and members-only section.
- *AC logo/letters:** add value to your service offering and build credibility through use of AC logo / letters in marketing materials.
- *Ongoing professional development: acquire CPD certificates through attendance at development forums, workshops and events, and gain access to organizational development guidelines.*
- Improve coaching skills: through special invitations to professional coaching courses and participation in workshops.
- *Networking opportunities*: enjoy networking opportunities to draw on the advice and experience of leading-edge organizations that are also passionate about ethics, best practice and standards in the coaching profession.
- *Strategic partnerships*: receive member discounts, discounted training offers, and product and service deals through strategic partnerships.

*   Associate level and above only.
** Member level only.

Each approved individual member will receive a member's certificate with embossed seal.

For further information on the AC or joining, please visit the membership section of the website or e-mail members@associationforcoaching.com.

'promoting excellence and ethics in coaching'

www.associationforcoaching.com.

Index